EX LIBRIS

Also by Kate Williams

NON-FICTION

England's Mistress: The Infamous Life of Emma Hamilton
Becoming Queen
Young Elizabeth: The Making of our Monarch
Josephine: Desire, Ambition, Napoleon
The Ring and the Crown (co-authored)

FICTION

The Pleasures of Men
The Storms of War
The Edge of the Fall
The House of Shadows

RIVAL QUEENS

The Betrayal of Mary, Queen of Scots

KATE WILLIAMS

HUTCHINSON
LONDON

Hutchinson is part of the Penguin Random House group of companies whose addresses can be found at global.penguinrandomhouse.com.

Penguin
Random House
UK

Copyright © Kate Williams 2018

First published in Great Britain by Hutchinson in 2018

www.penguin.co.uk

A CIP catalogue record for this book is available from the British Library.

ISBN 9780091936709

Typeset in 11.5/13.69 pt Bembo
by Integra Software Services Pvt. Ltd, Pondicherry

Printed and bound in Great Britain by Clays Ltd, Elcograf S.p.A.

Penguin Random House is committed to a sustainable future for our business, our readers and our planet. This book is made from Forest Stewardship Council® certified paper.

MIX
Paper from
responsible sources
FSC® C018179

Contents

List of Illustrations

1. James V and Mary of Guise. Public domain.
2. Mary of Guise. GL Archive/Alamy Stock Photo.
3. Mary, Queen of Scot's family tree. Public domain.
4. Henry VIII with his children. Art Collection 3/Alamy Stock Photo.
5. Elizabeth I as a young woman. Getty Fine Art/Contributor.
6. Mary, Queen of Scots in her teenage years. Public domain.
7. Francis, the Dauphin. Getty Heritage Images/Contributor.
8. Rosary and prayer book belonging to Mary, Queen of Scots. His Grace The Duke of Norfolk, Arundel Castle/Bridgeman Images.
9. Elizabeth I in her coronation robes. Pictorial Press Ltd/Alamy Stock Photo.
10. Locket ring. Heritage Image Partnership Ltd/Alamy Stock Photo.
11. Mary, Queen of Scots by François Clouet. Getty Fine Art/Contributor.
12. Commemorative medal. Science Museum, London.
13. Holyroodhouse. The Picture Art Collection/Alamy Stock Photo.
14. James Stewart, Earl of Moray. Public domain.
15. Robert Dudley, Earl of Leicester. Getty/Dea Picture Library/Contributor.
16. Henry Stuart, Lord Darnley. ART Collection/Alamy Stock Photo.
17. Lennox Jewel. Royal Collection Trust/© Her Majesty Queen Elizabeth II, 2018.
18. David Rizzio. Royal Collection Trust/© Her Majesty Queen Elizabeth II, 2018.

19. Mary's chambers. Royal Collection Trust/© Her Majesty Queen Elizabeth II, 2018; photographer: Peter Smith.
20. 'The Murder of David Rizzio'. National Galleries/Presented by the 3rd Baron Strathcona and Mount Royal, 1927.
21. Mary, Queen of Scots with her son, James VI. Granger, NYC/ TopFoto.
22. James Hepburn, Earl of Bothwell. Getty/Dea Picture Library/ Contributor.
23. Kirk o'Field after the murder of Darnley. The National Archives.
24. 'The Mermaid and the Hare'. The National Archives.
25. Elizabeth I, aged around forty-two. Getty/Dea Picture Library/ Contributor.
26. Letter from Elizabeth to Mary, February 1567. British Library, London, UK/© British Library Board. All Rights Reserved/ Bridgeman Image.
27. Dunbar Castle. Getty/Universal History Archive/Contributor.
28. Letter from Elizabeth to Mary, December 1568. British Library, London, UK/© British Library Board. All Rights Reserved/ Bridgeman Image.
29. Letter from Mary to Elizabeth, October 1571. Heritage-Images/ TopFoto.
30. Thomas Howard, Duke of Norfolk. Public domain.
31. Mary's ciphers and codes. The National Archives.
32. Babington postscript and cipher, July 1586. The National Archives.
33. Tutbury Castle. NorthScape/Alamy Stock Photo.
34. Trial at Fotheringhay Castle. Granger, NYC/TopFoto.
35. Execution warrant for Mary, Queen of Scots, 1587. Lambeth Palace Library, London, UK/Bridgeman Images.
36. 'Armada Portrait' by George Gower. Getty/ Universal History Archive/Contributor.

Rival Queens

Prologue

The axe lay in a wooden box, cushioned, locked up in Mr Bull's modest home. He had been long expecting to use it for this, the biggest job of his life – for he kept up with the news and the pamphlets and he knew what was afoot, as anyone would, no matter what the queen and Cecil said officially. He had polished the axe, tended it, ensured the blade was shining. Finally, Walsingham's messenger came on his fine horse and Mr Bull saddled up his own, packed up his mask and cape, and tied the box containing the axe to his saddle. He sent a messenger to call for his assistants to accompany him. The three men rode quickly north. They stopped at taverns on the way but spoke to nobody, keeping away from the crowds and stowing the box in their rooms. Bull and his men had not been told for whom they and their axe were destined, but they could guess. They were nervous. They knew they would be expected to perform the job with speed and skill. No one forgot tales of executions that had taken ten or more blows. Nearly fifty years before, a fellow executioner had missed the neck of Margaret Pole when she knelt over the block and caught only her shoulder – it took eleven blows to kill her, during which she attempted to escape and was hauled back, screaming, to the block. Mr Bull knew he must kill in one blow. Particularly as it was a woman.

There was no room at the castle where the captive was held, too full of dignitaries who had come to observe. Bull and his men had been due to stay at the nearby home of Sir Walter Mildmay, but on arrival, they had been turned away, the man in charge of the household declaring it impossible. Mr Bull presumed Sir Walter had changed his mind about hosting an executioner and his axe; this was not uncommon. They took up at a local inn under extreme secrecy. No word could get out as to why they were there – in case she tried to escape or, worse, the queen heard of the matter and tried to put a stop to it. Already, it was risky that they had had to ride first to Sir Walter's and then on to the inn – the place was crawling with spies and they had made themselves conspicuous. They tried to hide, keep close. Mr Bull and his assistants dined together and received a message from the castle that all was ready to proceed. The innkeeper had become used to strange people coming to stay, foreigners who looked like spies, wild-eyed young men, priests in disguise, men whispering in corners. The captive at the castle was good business for him and he did not ask questions.

The scaffold was erected overnight. On the early morning of 8 February 1587, Mr Bull and his assistants picked up the axe and put it upon his horse. Before the inhabitants of the town were even awake, they rode out to the castle, leaving the inn and the lives of ordinary Englishmen behind.

In her rooms, at the castle, Mary, Queen of Scots had been awake all night. Waiting.

Introduction

'I am no longer who I once was', wrote Mary, Queen of Scots towards the end of her life. Elizabeth and Mary were two queens, ruling one island. One has always been seen as a success, the other often as a failure, at best a tragic queen. But Mary's very act of fighting for her rule should be looked at anew. She tried to rule as a king and she died for her decisions.

Mary set out on life with every possible glory and ended with nothing, her heart taken from her body and secretly buried. And in signing the final act which condemned her cousin to execution, Elizabeth I lost some of herself. Mary's end meant the death of a small part of all monarchs. For if a queen can be executed, what makes her royal at all?

The life of Mary, Queen of Scots throws up vital questions about how we think of women and their right to rule. Kings can be autocratic, usually are. But queens give up some power to survive. They must work more closely with ministers, accept the views of others. They are hailed as skilled in compromise and bringing people together, whereas kings are congratulated for deciding, commanding. I have dedicated much study to queens and it is clear that the progress of the state, the machinery of government and the power of parliament moves forward in the reigns of women.

Elizabeth could not have had more devoted ministers than William Cecil or Francis Walsingham, but they went behind her back. Victoria is seen as the first post-Reform Act Queen, castigated for showing favour to her prime ministers when her predecessors had done worse. And Elizabeth II is hailed as the ultimate constitutional monarch. Perhaps women are uniquely suited for the constitutional role. Or perhaps they are simply not given the same latitude as a king.

Mary is seen as misguided. But if we view her in terms of queenship, we can judge her anew based on her attempt to create a successful model for female rule, tolerant, open to incorporating the views of her counsellors while staking her own claim to ultimate authority. Unfortunately, Mary's lords and ministers tried to turn her into a figurehead, stage coups against her, and her attempts at tolerance collapsed into score settling and murder. But in England, Elizabeth pushed toleration and made it clear she would listen to advisors, and achieved great success. Perhaps Mary could have survived the tempests that troubled her reign but unlike Elizabeth, who played the dance of courtship, Mary married. And she chose the two worst consorts in royal history, men whose failings would inflict lasting damage on her rule.

For Mary, Elizabeth was a blood relative, a cousin, a fellow queen with whom she dreamed of a lasting friendship, swapping intimacies about a life surrounded by men who wanted to take their power. For Elizabeth, Mary was the woman who had tried to seize her throne, and would always be a danger.

Elizabeth's reign has been promoted to us as one of great glory, the wonder of the Virgin Queen. But at its heart there was a long struggle between queen and parliament for dominance. And although she won the battles over marriage, religion and foreign policy, she did not win the fight over Mary.

It is incredible now to read Mary's letters, bundled up into archives, the paper she touched almost as pristine as it was five hundred years ago, her neat script begging for mercy, power, recognition. It seems surprising that there is still material by her to be rediscovered – but there is, because she wrote so much, to everyone, endlessly.

'I am their queen and so they call me, but they use me not so,' said Mary. She was betrayed over the murder of her first husband – a new analysis of which is part of this book. But she was also betrayed by the body of a queen, a body which, to those around her, made her vulnerable to being exploited, seized. If she was a woman and they could take her body, then they could, it followed, take her power. She attempted to push back, control her own life and realm. She tried to rule – and hers was one of the hardest fights in royal history.

Chapter One
'Conducted by the Winds'

'All I can tell you is that I account myself one of the happiest women in the world.'[1] For Mary, Queen of Scots, the year 1558 was to be when she finally came into her own as a great and glorious queen-in-waiting, the wife of the heir to an empire. After nearly ten years of living at the French court, she was at last married to Francis, the Dauphin of France – and therefore beginning her new life as queen of both France and Scotland. She hoped and believed she would soon add Queen of England and Ireland to her titles.

This was the year that changed everything for Mary and her rival queen-in-waiting, Elizabeth, for it was in 1558 that the fight for England began.

Mary had become Queen of Scotland at only six days old when her father James V collapsed after defeat by the English at the Battle of Solway Moss. He died on 14 December 1542, reputed to have said in his final hours that 'It came wi' a lass, it'll gang [end] wi' a lass' – a dual reference to the story that the Scots were descended from the great Egyptian Princess Scota, and to the Stuart dynasty gaining the throne through Marjorie Bruce, the daughter of Robert the Bruce. His doom-laden view of female leadership – that the Stuarts would 'gang' with Mary – was shared by his people. Mary was never allowed to forget her father's words and the implication that her birth had hastened his death. But in 1558, all that seemed behind her. Mary, a queen in her own right, was the greatest prize on the marriage market. When she became Queen of France, she could esteem herself the most powerful woman in the world.

The wedding between fifteen-year-old Mary and the fourteen-year-old dauphin was a dazzling spectacle. King Henry II had turned the great Parisian cathedral of Notre-Dame into a fantasia of regal glory, with a stage outside the church and a walkway to the palace that was twelve feet high, hung over with a canopy of azure silk embroidered with golden fleurs-de-lys. The members of the wedding party assembled at the palace and then walked through in their finery, showing off their glitter to the gathering crowds. The entire city had devoted itself to celebrating the wedding, the buildings decorated with flowers and banners strewn with fleurs-de-lys and the marigold, Mary's symbol. Temporary theatres were put up to entertain; food sellers wove between the people, selling cakes, wine, meat.

The crowds longed to see the bride, the Scottish queen. They had some time to wait. Just before eleven o'clock came the Swiss Guards, resplendent in their uniforms, playing tambourines and fifes. Then Mary's uncle, Francis, Duke of Guise, the official master of ceremonies – and then a marvellous throng: musicians dressed in red and yellow playing every instrument from the trumpet and oboe to the violin; a hundred gentlemen of the king; the princes of the blood; abbots and bishops, archbishops, cardinals and the papal legate. Then came Francis the bridegroom with his brother Charles, and Anthony, the Duke of Vendôme. Catherine de' Medici, escorted by Anthony's brother and a dozen princesses, duchesses and ladies, including the young princesses (and the king's mistress, Diane de Poitiers), formed the final part of the procession, all sumptuously attired. Right at the end came Mary, escorted by her cousin, the Duke of Lorraine, and the King of France himself.

The Queen of Scots was a vision. 'A hundred times more beautiful than a goddess of heaven,' declared a courtier, Pierre de Brantôme, 'her person alone was as valuable as a kingdom.'[2] Tall even at fifteen and stately, she had chosen her own gown and asked that she be allowed to wear white, for she knew it would set off her pale skin and auburn hair – which she planned to wear loose down her back. Her request had initially been refused, for white was the official colour of mourning of the French royal family, but she had insisted – and she dazzled the crowds in white and gold. She was, as one said, 'dressed in clothing as white as lilies, made so gloriously and richly, it would be impossible to describe'.[3] Her sweeping gown was heavy with embellished embroidery and she wore a huge jewelled pendant around her neck. She stood perfectly erect and on her head was a superb crown of gold, diamonds, rubies, sapphires, emeralds and pearls. Two young girls bore her train of velvet and silk, which was twelve yards long and decorated with gems. Mary had received more jewels than she thought possible, including a giant diamond from her father-in-law, called 'the great H', big like the king.

Mary was a vision of beauty, of regal dignity and she was the symbol of a new and powerful alliance between Scotland and France. The aim was to capture England – a country riven with division and insecurities, ruled by a mere woman.

As the royal party moved towards the church for the nuptial Mass, the heralds threw gold and silver coins into the crowds. There was a terrible crush and some fainted – others shouting up to the heralds not to throw any more because of the panic.

Mary was married to the dauphin with a ring taken from the king's finger. She was now the queen-dauphine – and her husband the king-dauphin. As the tribute poets declared at the wedding, Mary's marriage would see England subjugated and France in power, the beginning of a brilliant dynastic line that would rule Europe. 'So shall one house the world's vast empire share,' vaunted one. 'Through you, France and England will change the ancient war into a lengthy peace that will be handed down from father to son.'[4] Mary acknowledged her husband as the King of Scotland.

Mary was a queen, but now, as the poets made clear, she was the conduit for male power; 'through her' peace transmitted from father to son. Mary was the pledge of alliance, her womb the source of the future, the consort and mother of the future king.

At the banquet and ball following the wedding, Mary danced with her father-in-law, admired by all the guests at the archbishop's palace. At about five, the party set off in procession to the Palais du Louvre for a second banquet, this time a grand state affair, cheered by the waiting crowds. The princes rode horses decked in gold and silver, the princesses sat in litters festooned with gold. Mary sat beside Catherine de' Medici, her new mother-in-law, only thirty-nine and not her greatest admirer. Her new husband followed her, accompanied by the Duke of Lorraine and various attendants, all on beautiful horses covered in crimson velvet and gold. The crowds were so great that the party moved slowly.

The palace had been so beautifully and elaborately decorated that a guest described it as more beautiful than the 'Elysian Fields'. After the meal, there was a panoply of glittering entertainments, including twelve pretend horses, 'conducted and led artificially', ridden by Francis' brothers and other small royals – and leading coaches full of musicians. Then came the *pièce de résistance*, an incredible *mise en scène* comprising six great mechanical ships with silver masts and gauze sails, blown by the wind from hidden bellows, sailing around the blue-painted floor of the hall. They appeared magnificently real, tossed by 'such force and abruptness and the top sails were so well-stretched that one would have said they were conducted by the winds artificially'. The king captained one, the dauphin another, and the rest were sailed by senior male royals. A narrator told the audience that the king in his boat was Jason, leading the Argonauts in their search for the Golden Fleece. When the king had his boat sail to Mary and she was lifted in and joined him sailing around the room, the meaning was clear – through her he would win an empire. It was almost as if the king himself had married this young girl, rather than his son the dauphin.

In all the glitter and the wondrous gold, the song and the lights – 'those who were in the hall could not say whether the flambeaux and lanterns, or the jewelled rings, precious stones, gold and silver were brightest' – the French saw their great triumph.[5] The party continued over the next few days, with further feasts and even more marriages.

The French king had gained the Golden Fleece. And the Scots had assented to it all, their future queen regnant turned into a consort, bound by fabulous cuffs of gold. So great had been the desire of the Scots to see England defeated that they had given up everything.

Nine days before the marriage, at Fontainebleau, Mary had publicly signed an official document that gained the happy approval of her Parliament in Edinburgh. She vowed to keep 'the freedoms, liberties and privileges of this realm and laws of the same, and in the same manner as has been observed in all kings' times of Scotland before'.[6] While she was out of the country, it would be governed by Mary of Guise as regent and the king and dauphin undertook to protect the realm.

The dauphin, it was agreed, would be named King of Scotland, and when he became King of France, he would govern both kingdoms.

Due to the Salic law, the ancient Frankish law written by King Clovis that formed the basis of the legal system and barred female monarchs, Mary could only be Queen Consort of France – she could not reign over it as a joint monarch. It was agreed that Mary and Francis' eldest son would inherit the joint kingdoms of France and Scotland. If the royal couple produced only daughters, the eldest would be Queen of Scotland, but France would pass to the nearest male relative. For the Scots, they felt they had gained an excellent bargain. As they saw it, matters would continue as they were, with various regents governing, and the French king would send troops whenever the English threatened to attack. It was, they believed, the best they could possibly achieve with such a useless thing as a female monarch.

But, despite his fine words, Henry was determined to make Scotland a province of France and one day do the same to England, through Mary's claim to the English throne. The dauphin would be King of France, Scotland and England because he was the husband of Mary. Eleven days before the marriage, the king had given Mary three secret documents to sign. They were utterly shocking. In the first, she agreed that should she die without heirs, the King of France would inherit Scotland – and every right and title she had held as queen. The ostensible reason for this was due to the 'singular and perfect affection that the kings of France had always had as to the protection and maintenance of the kingdom of Scotland against the English'.[7] If this wasn't enough, she also agreed that if she died without heirs, the King of France should gain all the revenues of Scotland up to the value of one million pieces of gold to reimburse him for his efforts in defending Scotland and funding Mary's education. This too was outrageous for he had done very little to defend Scotland, and educating Mary had hardly cost very much, let alone a part of a million pieces of gold. Mary and Francis then signed the third document in which she assented that she understood the undertakings she had made and everything that she had promised was valid and effective in law and would not be affected by any assurances she had given or might give in the future. She could not overturn the agreements or later change her mind.

In signing the documents, Mary had given up everything. She may have done so because she had little choice – pressured as she was by the king, her Guise relations and perhaps her fiancé. And, like most fifteen-year-olds, she naturally thought she was not going to die any time soon and certainly not without having given birth to a child. She trusted her Guise uncles and thought that what they advised was in her best interests, though in fact they cared only for ensuring their ascendancy in the French court. And, as they saw it, if Scotland became subservient to France, they could finally control it, taking revenge on those uppity lords who had caused Mary of Guise, Mary's mother, so many problems.

The young Queen of Scots had no choice but to sign. The king wanted to seize England and Scotland, and Mary was his tool.

At base, under all of it, the dazzle of the wedding, the words of the marriage contract, was a fundamental belief that women could not and should not rule. Empress Matilda in the twelfth century was widely seen as a disaster, whose attempt to gain the English throne had plunged the country into civil war. Although Mary I was on the English throne, she was not seen as a role model. Rather, to the King of France, she was a weak female monarch who could be swept away by the force of his son's new position: King of Scotland, one day to be King of France. As the French (and most of Europe) saw it, Scotland should feel fortunate to be absorbed into the great nation of France – to be 'fed on the breast of the great King of France', in the words of one poet.[8]

The Scots had sent over an envoy of lords to attend the wedding and watch the pageant in dazzled excitement. Four died on the way home (some said they were poisoned but it was more likely a plague that had taken hold at the ports). Those who managed to stagger back gave an enthusiastic report. The Scots Parliament, ignorant of the secret documents, even considered offering Francis the right to retain the throne of Scotland if Mary died, but they were energetically resisted by the Protestant sect and by the Hamiltons, the noble family who were next in line to the throne after Mary. And once the excitement had died down about creating an alliance that should surely terrify England, many Scots began to question the fact that they had an absentee queen. At fifteen, she was old enough to begin the work of ruling her own people, yet her mother Mary of Guise was still doing all as regent, and their monarch was the consort-in-waiting of France.

Mary knew little of Scotland and barely remembered it. She saw herself as the future Queen of France and the future Queen of England, Wales and Ireland, the glorious warrior of the Catholic religion and unity. Ireland had been a lordship, ruled by the Kildare family, effectively independent, but Henry VIII had re-invaded the country, largely because he feared the Kildares. There was a series of bloody rebellions and fights against oppression – including the Desmond uprising in 1569, when Lord Desmond resisted the imposition of an English governor – and one rebellion was put down with a terrible forced famine. Europe saw Ireland as England's possession, part of its burgeoning empire. Wales, too, had been repeatedly conquered – and largely pulled in by threats to the crown. In 1536, Henry VIII passed The Act of Union, in which the law of England was to be the law of Wales with twenty-six Members of Parliament from Wales to represent the country. When Mary said England, she meant Ireland and Wales too.

To King Henry and to Mary, England was the prize. Even though it was cold, isolated from the rest of Europe, and it had committed the anathema of breaking from Rome, it was a desirable acquisition. Its Queen, although hardly healthy, had brought back Catholicism; a true Counter-Reformation monarch. When she died, surely, no one would want the heretic Elizabeth on the throne. Henry VII and Henry VIII had been the ultimate propagandists, proclaiming the glory and power of the Tudors across Europe, the son throwing gold dust in everybody's eyes with his extravagant displays at the Anglo-French summit of the Field of the Cloth of Gold. England's agricultural land was excellent, its merchants energetic and its navy efficient, a greater player in the world order than Scotland seemed ever likely to be.

And Mary I – daughter of Henry VIII and now Queen of England – was reportedly very sick. In March, the whole court had assembled at Hampton Court for the birth of her child with Philip of Spain. The queen was swollen, ill and her menses had stopped. The court had gathered, but no child arrived, leaving the queen broken and despairing.

For the new queen-dauphine, it was worth throwing everything at the chance to be the heir. She had made her husband King of Scotland. Now, if she became Queen of England, he would gain that title too. The Tudor dynasty would be crushed.

Chapter Two
'It Will End with a Lass'

Mary of Guise arrived in Scotland in 1538 as a young widow aged twenty-two. It was a long journey, and, like most foreign brides, she thought she would never see her country again. Her son, three-year-old Duke François, had been left at Joinville with her mother and father, who benefited from his considerable lands. He wrote to his mother that every night he prayed for her, and once sent her a piece of string to show how tall he was.

Mary was quickly wedded to her new husband, James V of Scotland. His reign had been violent and troubled, his coffers bankrupted before him by his mother and her second husband. He had first married Madeleine of Valois, the sixteen-year-old daughter of the French King Francis I, in 1537. Her father had initially refused the match, fearful that the poor climate of Scotland would exacerbate the princess's fragile health. But James saw her, fell in love and insisted. Yet the French king had been right and poor Madeleine became ill after the journey and never recovered. She died a few months after the wedding. James was not discouraged. He was keen to marry a foreign princess, to ally with France and also to escape the jockeying for position among the noble Scots families, all desirous that he would make one of their daughters into a queen. He alighted on the somewhat less royal Mary of Guise, tall and strong where her predecessor had been frail. Mary had been friendly at court with Madeleine of Valois and may have met James during the initial marriage negotiations for the princess's hand.

The Guise family was rapidly gaining power in France and Mary's father, Claude, Duke of Guise, and her mother, Antoinette of Bourbon, were ruling the roost. She had enjoyed a pleasant, undemanding marriage to her first husband, Louis of Orléans, busy playing cards with her ladies in all his various castles. But Louis had died in June 1537, leaving her with a small son and heavily pregnant. The second child died not far into infancy and Mary was back on the marriage market.

Henry VIII had heard she was a girl of good constitution, and asked for her hand, after the death of Jane Seymour. The King of France was against the match for he dreaded the power of the Guises if one was married to Henry VIII. And even the power-mad Guises might have second thoughts of sending Mary off to a man who had already divorced one wife and executed another, essentially for failing to have a son. The would-be bride herself was heard to joke that she might be large, but her neck was very small. The Henry VIII marriage was never likely to happen; he was being encouraged towards a Protestant union. Still, although the French thought Henry VIII was king of a sinful, heretic country and hard on his wives, at least England was in some part civilised. Scotland, in the opinion of the French who had only heard the worst of it, was a cold and brutal land with an unhealthy climate which had killed off Madeleine.

Nevertheless, James and Mary were married by proxy at Notre-Dame and 2,000 Scottish nobles and their attendants and retainers came over to France to accompany her to her new bridegroom. She arrived in Scotland on 16 June 1538 with celebrations at St Andrews, married once more at St Andrews Cathedral and was taken on a tour of the churches and colleges of the town.

The marriage was not a happy one, for James was not greatly considerate of her and had a mistress he preferred. Mary wrote frequent letters to her mother, yearning for home and her son. After a year, the young queen was still not pregnant. She started to attempt to make her palaces feel more like home, bringing in French food and plants, and her own doctors and apothecaries. And when she was crowned Queen of Scotland in February 1540, with a brand-new crown, at Holyrood Abbey, Mary was carrying a child. Finally, in May 1540, two years after the wedding, Mary gave birth to a son, the new Prince of Scotland. The king was delighted, the public even more so. The queen quickly became pregnant again and, in April of the following year, gave birth to another son, Robert, Duke of Albany, at Falkland. Two days later, the baby was dead – and in further terrible news, his brother, afflicted by a childhood illness, died on the same day. The queen bravely tried to withstand her losses, telling the king that they were both young and would soon have more children.

Whispers began that the king was being smited by God for his sins. The queen's mother blamed the baby's death on overfeeding – a letter her daughter must have hated to read. But the king was growing paranoid and fearful. Two sons dying in quick succession seemed like fate and not cruel bad luck. The court gossiped that he was being punished for his treatment of Sir James Hamilton of Finnart, his second cousin, whom the king had become convinced was plotting against him and had executed for treason in 1540, despite there being no evidence. They said Sir James had appeared in a dream and told the king he would lose both his arms and then his head for what he had done.

Henry VIII of England, the Scots king's uncle, sensed weakness. He pushed James to assist him in sacking the monasteries and to break from Rome – but James refused. Henry issued a command to meet at York, which James also declined. Henry was furious at what he saw as Scotland's disobedience and talked of war, judging he might achieve easy victory and increase his popularity at home. By the summer of 1542, troops were in the north of England, ready to invade Scotland.

Yet James was hopeful. Mary was pregnant once more and thriving. They both wished fervently for a son. The king decided to fight Henry rather than give in to his demands. He was right to do so, for once Henry saw vulnerability, he would never let go. But there had not been sufficient time to plan and the Scottish army was disorganised. Lord Maxwell, the Scottish Warden at West March, raised over 15,000 men, but then confusion set in. Word spread that the commander was not Maxwell, who was universally respected, but Oliver Sinclair, one of the king's favourites and no military man. Some refused to fight under him. In contrast to the ruthlessly efficient English army, there was great confusion in the Scots ranks about the chain of command, whether it was Sinclair or another. The Scots, simply, were not ready to fight and the king had failed to lead them or even inspire them into battle.

On 24 November, the Scots encountered 3,000 English soldiers under Lord Wharton near the River Esk and Solway Moss – a large peat bog. The battle was catastrophic, and the Scots found themselves trapped around the bog itself. They surrendered their guns and the soldiers ran for dear life, many falling and drowning in the river in the panic. The English advanced without mercy and took 1,200 men, including many of the nobles and Sinclair himself. They chased down the remaining men hurrying away – not that they put up much resistance. Some of the Scots soldiers were so defeated that they surrendered to the camp's women.

James had been humiliated – and he thought his end was nigh. He went to Edinburgh and made an inventory of his treasure. He told one of his servants, who had asked him where he would spend Christmas, 'On Yule day, you will be masterless and the realm without a king.'[1] He visited the queen and then travelled finally to Falkland, where his son had died, and all the bad luck had begun. It had been his favourite palace, a handsome building he had extended in beautiful Renaissance style. He had enhanced the gardens and even built a real tennis court the previous year, now the oldest surviving court in Britain. There he took to his bed in shock, crying out in despair at the horror of life.

At Linlithgow Palace, in West Lothian, just under twenty-five miles from Edinburgh, Mary of Guise was in the final stages of labour. Her husband had been born there too in 1512 and in his reign he had renovated the palace, adding an outer gateway and a striking fountain in the courtyard. The ill-fated James Hamilton of Finnart had been keeper and added once more to the structure – before his execution two years earlier. Mary of Guise was particularly fond of it, judging it equal to a castle in the Loire. There, on 8 December, she gave birth to a daughter in a room overlooking the loch, her fifth child and one she desperately needed to live. The infant was judged very frail. 'The queen was delivered before her time of a daughter, a very weak child and not likely to live as is thought,' said one report.[2]

The king was still in a state of hysterical grief and it was in this shocking state that he received the news that his wife had given birth to a little girl who was still alive. The messengers were hopeful that the news might cheer him and prompt him to leave his bed. Instead, James sank into a terrible gloom. Scotland had been ruled by men called James since 1406, and she was a break in that line. The last female deemed Queen of Scotland (although never crowned) was a child, Margaret. King Alexander III's children had all died before him – and his daughter Margaret had left a daughter through her marriage to the King of Norway, also called Margaret, often called the Maid of Norway. In 1286, at three, she was declared queen, with the nobles governing for her. Her mother had died, there were no other children, and plans were made to marry her to Edward of Carnarvon, the future Edward II of England. She set off from Norway by boat to Scotland to start her new life in 1286 but died near the isles of Orkney of seasickness (probably extreme dehydration). Without her there was no clear heir and a battle began for the succession. It was hardly the most illustrious history for female rule.

James V fell into an even blacker mood. The birth of Mary was the end of everything and James lost his grip on hope. He died on 14 December, when the baby was only six days old. Many fathers in royal history have been disappointed with a daughter – Henry VIII included. But Mary was the only one whose birth plunged her father into a despair that seemingly speeded his death. It was a terrible burden for a child to bear, one that no one shielded her from and would often be thrown at her.

Mary was now queen. When her father had said that a princess would be the 'end' of his royal line or perhaps even the country, he meant that the realm would be absorbed into another when the young queen married a fellow monarch – as Philip of Spain always hoped to do with England. Or, at worst, another monarch would see weakness and invade. As James saw it, lost and grieving, his uncle Henry VIII would likely send in the troops and seize the baby queen and claim command of the throne. After Henry's cataclysmic victory at Solway Moss, who would prevent him taking over the whole country?

Mary was not the youngest monarch in history. That dubious honour goes to John I of France, who ascended the throne at birth in 1316, as his father had died a few months before his birth. His reign lasted a mere five days before he died, perhaps poisoned by his uncle who then took the throne. The youngest English monarch was Henry VI, who gained the throne at nine months in 1422 and then two months later became King of France. But France was later lost, the king suffered a bout of debilitating mental illness and then the Wars of the Roses exploded – which his side lost. Ivan VI became Tsar of Russia in 1741 at the age of two months, but his regents were deposed the following year. Ivan was put in solitary confinement and murdered at the age of twenty-three.

Child monarchs, particularly babies, tend to be failures: their position is weaker, nobles feel empowered to make a grab for power, babies are physically vulnerable and often die, so nobles constantly group around the next king-to-be. And Mary had an additional problem: she was female. Even though there was no Salic law in Scotland barring women from the throne as in France, by the standards of the sixteenth century, Scotland was particularly inhospitable to women.

Female learning within the elite was possible in England, even congratulated. Margaret Roper, daughter of Henry VIII's advisor Sir Thomas More, was a brilliant scholar, completing a translation of Erasmus' soliloquy on the Lord's Prayer, and the first book published by a woman was Julian of Norwich's *Revelations of Divine Love* in 1395. Anne Boleyn had a famously impressive turn for scholarship and spoke seriously to men of religion. Katherine Parr was the first woman to publish under her own name, translating John Fisher's psalms from the Latin, creating her own set of prayers and psalms, editing an English translation of the Gospels and publishing her work *The Lamentations of a Sinner* in 1547. It was not until the seventeenth century that women began to publish in Scotland, with the first being Elizabeth Melville's poem *Ane Godlie Dreame* in 1603.

Even by the standards of the sixteenth century, Scotland was a fighting, masculine culture. In both England and Scotland, plenty of women worked in the middling and lower classes, keeping taverns, brewing beer, working as seamstresses, cooks and servants, but the greater trade in and out of England meant more opportunities for women, assisting in the family business, keeping shops and ale houses – roles that gave a certain amount of independence and power and demanded a higher standard of education. In some parts of Scotland, women did more agricultural work as it was thought to be beneath men.

It was not easy to be an infant queen anywhere in the sixteenth century, but Scotland was particularly difficult for female power. Mary of Guise was a foreign queen, had few allies in the country – and although all countries and courts in Europe were dominated by factionalism, Scotland was especially riven by rivalries between competing clans and lords. Power and privilege were controlled by families who stretched back years, and to survive you needed to ally yourself with one of them. A clever Putney commoner like Thomas Cromwell could rise fast in England but his success would have been far less likely in Scotland.

The competing families all had claims to the throne. Whereas most of those at court in England were mere nobility, and some were from families that owed everything to the king, the Scots clans had a direct interest in fighting or undermining the monarch. There were rival groups of Stuarts, descended from younger children of former monarchs – the Lennox Stuarts foremost but the Atholl Stuarts, the Stuarts of Traquair and Blantyre and Ochiltree also wanted to have a say. Other families who played a great part in the drama of Mary were in lesser ways related to her: the family of Hamilton, headed by the Earl of Arran, who were next in line to the throne after Mary; the family of Gordon, headed by the Earl of Huntly; and the family of Campbell, headed by the Earl of Argyll. These families and earls would move in and out as Mary's supporters, crafting her life. She could never manage them, but then they were impossible to manage. The shifts of loyalty, hatreds, plots and aspirations were complex, ever-changing and shaped by age-old grudges, ambitions and slights.

The baby Mary and her mother stayed on at Linlithgow – now in deep mourning. Despite claims that Mary was too weak to live and some reports that she was already dead, the princess was stronger than those who had come before, and the news was that the baby queen was growing well. As one report sent back to England stated, she was 'as goodly a child as I have seen of her age and as like to live with the Grace of God'.[3] The Spanish ambassador in London, however, sent reports that both the baby and her mother were extremely ill and despaired of by the doctors, but perhaps it was the wishful or confused thinking of the English that he was communicating.

James, when deep in his misery, had no doubt expected his uncle Henry to storm the country, now there was nothing but a girl to stay his hand. But, although Henry had been planning greater and further incursions, he and his commanders suspended operations at news of the king's death. Forcing into the kingdom of a dead man, with only a baby as queen, was too much, even for Henry. His eye was always on public opinion at home and his people would have seen it as too easy and cruel a victory. His ostensible reason for inva-sion had been the king's reluctantance to join his Reformation, and that if the new men of power in Scotland decided to move towards the Protestant religion, the moral basis for his crusade would be gone. And he didn't want the French to retaliate, protecting Mary of Guise. Moreover, invading Scotland would be more trouble than it was worth – it was one thing fighting in England at Solway Moss, but the Scots would fight to the death to protect Edinburgh. And Mary's sex was actually a saving grace – Henry was pondering whether he might marry his son Edward to her, bending the Scots to his will through marriage.

The cause of Protestantism and the Protestant Reformation had support in Scotland. The Catholic Church there was wealthy and the rents and taxes it collected were viewed by many as extortionate. Local churches were underfunded and some churches had no priest at all. Many monks and nuns were accused of being absorbed in themselves, and not helping the poor. And there were close links between the nobility and the Church. James V had made illegitimate sons members of the clergy. Plenty of clergy were married – and the man who seemed to embody some of the worst abuses was David Beaton, Cardinal of Scotland. He was both the head of the Church and a political administrator. He had been Lord Privy Seal in 1528 and then ambassador to France, securing the marriages with first Madeleine and then Mary of Guise. Beaton had a long-term mistress, Marion Ogilvy, daughter of the 1st Lord Ogilvy of Airlie, who was his wife, to all intents and purposes – they shared a castle and had eight children. One would be master of the household to James VI, and one married into the aristocratic Gordon family and was an ancestress of Lord Byron. Beaton might have behaved in a secular manner, in one sense, but he was determined to be a loyal son of Rome – and to keep Scotland Catholic. As such, he had access to much wealth. The Church was a significant landowner and had an income of £30,000 a year, while the king received less than £20,000.

Nonetheless, although there was criticism of the Church, a wholesale break from Rome was worrying – people wanted reform from within. And they certainly did not wish to do anything because Henry VIII told them to do so.

And Henry had other, pressing issues. Catherine Howard had been executed in February 1542 and he was looking for a new wife. An invasion of Scotland wasn't top of his agenda.

James V was buried at Holyrood Abbey in Edinburgh, alongside his first wife, Queen Madeleine, and the bodies of his two sons with Mary, in a funeral of gloomy pomp and splendour. In the immediate aftermath of his death, no one in Scotland yet knew that Henry VIII had decided to stay his hand. The major nobles were fighting to be regent, all promising that they could protect and save Scotland as James V had not. And it was a great title to gain. Unlike in England, where the powers of the regent were limited, the regent in Scotland was practically a king – and Mary's young age meant that the chosen one would be the stand-in ruler for a long time. The regent could assume control of the royal palaces and, more importantly, access the jewels and treasure as well as administering the Crown lands. To become regent meant gaining the opportunity to shower one's self and one's family with gold.

James Hamilton, second Earl of Arran, head of the House of Hamilton and barely thirty, was the next in line to the throne after Mary, as his grandmother was Mary Stewart, Princess of Scotland, daughter of James II and sister of James III. But then Cardinal Beaton also threw his hat into the ring. Beaton was a keen supporter of the French and the Guise family and was determined to keep Scotland Catholic.

Beaton declared that the king had made a will on the actual day of his death at Falkland, decreeing that he wished there to be four governors (Arran, Argyll, Moray and Huntly), with him, Beaton, in overall charge of the new queen and the council. Although it was not unlikely that James had tried to provide for the regency, and dividing it between various men was a good idea, it was decided that the will had been forged, even though it was witnessed by more than ten individuals, including the Master of the Household, William Kircaldy of Grange, the king's treasurer, and the king's doctor. The fault lay in the choice of clerk; the man used was not a registered notary. As so often in the sixteenth century, a tiny legal fault was enough to collapse everything – and now the king was dead, the cardinal was unpopular and failing to sway opinion. Many at court and in the noble families laid the blame on him for the Battle of Solway Moss, seeing him as responsible for persuading the king to fight against Henry rather than negotiating with him. To add to the tangled web, James Hamilton of Finnart, executed by James V for treason when there was scant evidence, was Arran's illegitimate half-brother. Arran had been fond of him and gaining the position of regent would send a powerful message about the wrong the king had done.

What finally decided the matter was the arrival back in Scotland of the nobles captured at the Battle of Solway Moss. Henry had imprisoned them in England and demanded that they sign documents promising to support a marriage between little Mary and Prince Edward, in return for money and freedom. Some had even offered to help Henry gain Scotland, in the event of the infant queen's death. When these men arrived back at court in January, the die was cast. The government would have to be pro-English and pro-Protestant. Arran was declared regent and quickly had Beaton arrested. The cardinal was imprisoned at Dalkeith Palace, from the most feared man in the kingdom to a lowly prisoner. Rome, scandalised by the arrest of the cardinal, issued an interdict demanding all churches be closed and all communions ended. Henry VIII had ensured the best man for England had got the job.

At Linlithgow, Mary of Guise watched these events in horror. Cardinal Beaton had been a friend and support to her (so much so that there had been scurrilous, untrue accusations that they were lovers) and the movement away from allying with France to allying with England threw her into anguish. She wanted her daughter to rule a Catholic country, a friend of France; for the Guise family to control matters, not Henry VIII.

Arran ignored Mary of Guise. He was declared regent and tutor to the baby queen, and appointed governor and protector. Yet while Arran might have been all-powerful, he could hardly rest on his laurels. Beaton was in prison — but he had another enemy.

Matthew Stewart, Fourth Earl of Lennox, was young, bent on power and had a strong claim to the throne. He was a great-grandson of Princess Mary and thus in the line of succession he stood behind James Hamilton and his children, already numerous by 1542 — and Lennox's line also came from the daughter of Princess Mary, rather than her son, thus pushing him further down the succession. But he declared that Arran's father had not been properly divorced when he married his second wife, Arran's mother. It was a little murky. The 1st Earl of Arran had been granted a divorce in 1504 when he'd found that the husband of his wife, Elizabeth Home, had still been alive in 1490, the date of his marriage to her. But then the divorce was repeated in 1510 — so it was said that he had continued to live with Elizabeth after 1504, which complicated the validity of the divorce. He married Janet Bethune in 1516 and she had given birth to Arran and other children — but to the Lennox Stewarts, this marriage was not legitimate; and nor were any of the children. Unlike Arran, the Earl of Lennox came from a line of perfectly legal marriages. But Arran had luck: Lennox was in England and the new regent hoped to encourage Henry VIII to keep him there.

Henry VIII was a supporter of Arran, who he believed would push forward the treaty for a marriage between the baby princess and Prince Edward, aged just five, in return for Henry's support. Arran had hoped to see Mary married to his own son and Henry attempted to mollify him by offering up Princess Elizabeth instead. For there seemed to be little other choice of future spouse – in France, Catherine de' Medici, wife of the king, had no children after ten years of marriage and was assumed barren, at the age of twenty-four. By now, Mary of Guise was considering the English match, for she both feared Henry VIII and the anger of the clans if she were to marry her daughter to Arran's son. She invited the English ambassador to her in early spring and showed him Mary unclothed, to prove there was no deformity.

The marriage plans were moving ahead and on 1 July 1543, treaties were signed at Greenwich providing that Mary would be sent to England when she was ten to be married to Edward. Yet the wider alliance between the two countries was beginning to crumble. Arran could see popular opinion turning against the English and towards the French – for the scars of Solway Moss still ran deep. The news of the signing of the treaty was greeted with distrust and anger. Earls and commoners alike naturally thought that Henry wished to subsume Scotland into England through the marriage, Scotland as subservient as a wife. And, on a more personal note, Arran's friends reminded him, throwing his lot in with Henry angered Rome – and the last thing he wanted was the Pope to cast doubt on his father's marriage. The Earl of Lennox was circling. In March 1543, with Mary not even six months old, he had arrived from exile in England to stake his claim to be regent over Arran. Arran needed to hang on to legitimacy, Henry suspected that he was losing his hold on Scotland, and there were rumours that French ships were near.

Beaton escaped from his captivity and decided that he needed to save baby Mary from abduction by the English and from Arran's influence. Mary of Guise agreed. Beaton and 7,000 men, along with Earls Huntly, Lennox, Argyll and Bothwell, marched to Linlithgow, demanding she be moved to Stirling, a stronger fortress. The infant Mary was whisked to Stirling Castle. Henry VIII attempted to put a brave face on it, declaring that the English ambassador should be her guardian and saying that he refused Mary of Guise permission to stay with her daughter – not that anyone listened. He even tried to win over Cardinal Beaton, an impossible attempt. Unfortunately for Henry's new friendly act, some Scottish ships were impounded by his own on the way to France, and goods taken, and anti-English sentiment surged again. The Scots and those around Mary were now doubly determined to resist.

In September, Arran panicked. He realised – not without reason – that he could not get the better of Henry VIII and that public opinion was against him. He travelled to meet Beaton and took the Catholic sacrament on the 8th of that month. The next day, Mary was crowned at her new home of Stirling Castle. The ceremony for the nine-month-old queen was rushed and peremptory, with scant pomp and glamour – it was, as the English ambassador put it, 'not very costlie'.[4] Nor was it the most auspicious day, for it was the anniversary of the crushing failure of the Scots at the Battle of Flodden. The pro-English nobles were not there. The Earl of Arran carried the crown and the Earl of Lennox held the sceptre. Mary was queen.

Chapter Three
'Rough Wooing'

The marriage alliance with Prince Edward had well and truly collapsed. Arran had got above himself and was now hoping to marry his own son to the baby queen – much to the distress of Mary of Guise, who felt it would be awarding him too much influence. At the end of the year, on 15 December, the Scots Parliament refused to ratify the Treaty of Greenwich. It was a slap in the face for Henry. Five days later, Henry declared war by sending a messenger to Scotland. His campaign would later be called the 'rough wooing' – a phrase coined by the writer Sir Walter Scott, probably based on a report of the Earl of Huntly which said, 'We like not the manner of the wooing, and we could not stoop to being bullied into love.' Indeed, it was more war than wooing, more total attack than bullying. Henry's men were sure of themselves, convinced that what they saw as the broken promise permitted the cruellest punishment.

No one backed down. Mary of Guise refused to change her mind and betroth her daughter to the English Crown. Conflict was inevitable – although there would be a break until the weather turned sufficiently fine for Henry to send troops into Scotland. The Guise party was also strengthened by the news in January that Catherine de' Medici, long thought barren, had produced a son who would be the future King of France. He was surely a much better option as a husband for the young Mary.

In March 1544, Henry VIII demanded the nobles he had released from the Battle of Solway Moss be sent back to him. In May, under the command of the Earl of Hertford, the English landed at Granton on the coast, occupied Leith and headed to Edinburgh, entering at Canongate. The provost offered to give up the keys of the city in return for mercy – but Hertford said he had no mandate to bargain and the troops continued. Scottish soldiers fired the cannons to defend Edinburgh Castle and in response the English set the city alight, sacking and burning the royal palace and chapel. Edinburgh was almost destroyed, apart from the castle. What remained was looted and the ships at Leith loaded up – and Leith razed as the boats left. The army set off back to England, ransacking, attacking and burning down the Scottish towns and villages they passed, including Craigmillar Castle, Newbattle Abbey, Haddington and its friary and nunnery, and Dunbar. Other raids took place back over the border – Sir William Eure, the governor of Berwick-upon-Tweed and his sons led men to burn down houses and farms – with the aim of crushing those living there to obedience. In one particularly horrific incident Eure and his men set fire to Brumehous Tower, with the lady of the house, servants and children trapped inside. All this devastation over the hand of a tiny girl who might not even live to adulthood.

Henry VIII's spies were everywhere in the country, some spreading sedition, some promoting Protestantism. There were already many pro-Reformation and anti-Catholic pamphlets coming from England – and plenty being produced in Edinburgh itself. Henry ensured that many more were printed and disseminated. He set his spies to encourage unrest, putting it about that Cardinal Beaton was to blame for the invasion, with the aim of collapsing the pro-French alliance.

In 1544, Mary was moved to Dunkeld Castle, thought to be even more secure than Stirling. The nobles were worn down by English attacks – and everyone thought Arran was weak. The papal envoy said Scotland was a 'poor Kingdom', so 'divided and disturbed that if God does not show his hand and inspire those nobles to unite together, public and private ruin is clearly to be foreseen'.[1] The court was on fire with plots and Mary of Guise was stuck in a labyrinth of conflicting loyalties. She dreaded betrothing her daughter to Arran's son. The French royal family – and her own Guise relations – had been making overtures, and it seemed to her the best option. Although Mary of Guise knew that the Scottish nobles and people would prefer their little queen to be independent, she hoped they would accept the necessity. The only country that could scare off Henry VIII was his great rival, France. And so Mary of Guise plumped for encouraging an allegiance.

In 1545, the Scots fought back against the English aggression. The crushing attacks of Henry VIII were having the opposite effect to that intended, and nobles previously at loggerheads were coming together to oppose him. The earls of Angus and Arran had once fought in the street in Edinburgh, but Henry's attacks meant their old divisions were forgotten and they joined together for what would become known as the Battle of Ancrum Moor. A small group attacked the English force while they camped – and when they pursued in retaliation, they found a large Scots army hidden over the hill. The Scots pikemen charged and the English fell, disorientated by the wind that sent the gunpowder smoke their way. The English army was compelled to flee, many men dying as they ran, or later killed by the locals who caught them. Eight hundred of Henry's men were killed, including Sir Ralph Eure, son of Sir William. The devastating victory had its desired effect: Henry withdrew and paused the war.

Although the English had been pushed back, Henry's whispering campaign against Cardinal Beaton had been successful. He was more hated than ever. Anti-clerical feeling was growing among both nobles and commoners, fuelled by the ideas in reforming pamphlets that pointed out clerical abuses and the huge wealth of the Church. Itinerant preachers and speakers toured the country, promoting Calvinist and Lutheran ideas and talking of abuses. In 1544, George Wishart, a young priest of around thirty, was travelling and speaking forcefully of what needed to change. Beaton ordered his arrest and Bothwell seized him and sent him to Edinburgh Castle, where he was put on trial. He was hanged and burned at St Andrews in early 1546, with Beaton and his friends watching as he died. Wishart was immediately judged a Protestant martyr. Three months later, on 29 May, a band of Protestant lords broke into St Andrews, where the cardinal had been spending the night with his mistress, and murdered him. They strung his mutilated, naked body in front of the castle.

Beaton's killers had been hoping Henry VIII would send an army to begin a coup, but he sent nothing. The king had other things on his mind than Scotland: he was dying. The once hale and handsome king was terribly obese and increasingly infirm, manoeuvred about by mechanical contraptions, roaring in pain, tormented by boils, gout and infection. He died on 28 January 1547, aged only fifty-five, and was buried at St George's Chapel, Windsor, next to his beloved Jane Seymour. Unfortunately, Jane's brother, Lord Hertford, who had attacked Edinburgh with such savagery, then became Lord Protector for the nine-year-old Edward VI and the uneasy peace that had followed the Battle of Ancrum Moor was at an end. For Hertford, Scotland was unfinished business. Scottish men began moving towards Edinburgh, keen to defend their capital and castle.

But events in France changed everything. Francis I had died in France on the day of his son Henry's twenty-eighth birthday, 31 March 1547. Henry was not – as his father had been – bombastic, confident. He had too long been the second son, second best to his brother and the heir, Francis, who had died after a tennis game, seven years previously. When Henry had been a small boy, his father had been taken prisoner after the Battle of Pavia, and in March 1526, the king's two young sons were taken to the Bidassoa River, rowed from the French side to the Spanish and formally exchanged for their father. The children were to be held hostage until Francis gave the Holy Roman Emperor everything he demanded – including large swathes of Burgundy, as well as relinquishing his rights to Milan, Genoa and Naples, and providing the emperor with a naval fleet for his coronation. The minute Francis I was free, he refused to keep any of the terms. The boys were locked up, initially with reasonable treatment, but as Francis would not relent, their conditions became more miserable, and they were surrounded by guards, given poor food, reminded every day that their father had deserted them and was doing nothing to hasten their return. They had one tiny, dark and airless room, with iron bars across the windows, and nothing but two stools and a hard pallet as furniture. There were no toys or books and they were not given any education. They had no French attendants and had to learn Spanish to speak to the guards, forgetting their own native language in the meantime.

Finally, thanks to the diplomatic manoeuvres of their grandmother, Louise of Savoy, who had been negotiating with the emperor's aunt, Margaret of Austria, a new treaty was negotiated, with less onerous terms for Francis. But the emperor wanted money for his captives – over one million gold crowns. Louise of Savoy raised the money by asking the whole country to contribute and finally, in the spring of 1530, the boys and Eleanor of Austria, sister of the emperor, and their future stepmother, set out for France, accompanied by noble ladies as attendants. One of them was Diane de Poitiers, then thirty. The children had suffered greatly in captivity, without affection, education or even hope. Of course, it touched their characters: Francis' sombre attitude and habit of wearing black was blamed on the experience. Henry was strongly affected by Diane de Poitiers, pretty much the first woman he saw out of captivity, and relied on her on the journey – and he began an affair with her when he was around sixteen and she was thirty-five. His marriage to Catherine de' Medici had little impact on his adoration of Diane. And with this new king now in place, who was younger and more susceptible to Guise influence, the family began demanding he help their kinswoman in Scotland. They worked hard to win Diane to their cause, knowing the influence she held.

In September 1547, the forces of England and Scotland met at the Battle of Pinkie Cleugh. Somerset entered at the head of an army, demanding Mary. Arran was a poor commander and told his troops to charge when they would have fared better holding their position. The English army, practised, savage, routed them and the Scots fled; the fields filled with dead bodies. The English set up a garrison at Haddington, not too far from Edinburgh, from where they threatened further violence. Young Mary was sent to the greater security of the Priory on the nearby island of Inchmahome. She was moved back to Stirling for winter and then on to Dumbarton in early spring. If Hertford's forces had managed to seize the infant queen, it would have been a horrific blow – and probably the end of Scottish independence – and so the constant movement continued. Mary must have known, sensed some of the constant panic and fear over her safety.[2]

Scotland was a war zone and little Mary was the cause. Her mother's relations were encouraging her to send the child to France for marriage to the dauphin, only a few months her junior. Yet Henry II, influenced by Diane de Poitiers, had his own ambitions. Mary would be yet another child, royal or otherwise, made to suffer for their family's lust for power. Arran's failings, the frequent inability of the lords to come to a consensus, Henry VIII's and Hertford's brutal attitude to Scotland, the Guise family's desire for power in France, Mary of Guise's wish for French assistance, and Henry II's ambition to crush England – all these led to negotiations that would see Mary treated more like a toy than a queen. On 8 February 1548, the Scottish lords met at Stirling and agreed that Mary should be sent to France. Arran and Mary of Guise were enthusiastic about the plan. The English had not won themselves any support with their cruel looting and burning, and the lords themselves were weary of fighting, unwilling to lose yet more sons. Plenty of them thought that with the queen gone, Mary of Guise's position would be weakened, and they might better pursue their ambitions. Arran was richly rewarded for his enthusiasm for the marriage – the King of France created him Duke of Chatelherault on the same day.

There were risks. Little Mary could be lost at sea or catch a disease and die (like the unfortunate Maid of Norway). English ships might try to kidnap her, a prize to be paraded back to London and kept at the English court. But the greatest danger was to Mary's future standing as queen. By sending Mary out of the country to be married to a future King of France, they gave her up to the subservience this entailed, both as woman and as representative of her country. In her absence, the country would be governed by regents and ministers. She would lose all her power. The deal was that she would always live in France, never to return – an impossible queen. A woman needed a man to rule, and who better than the King of France to do it for her?

A prince would not be sent away thus. Putting Mary on a ship to France so young kept her safe and, it was hoped, would secure the French alliance and frighten off England. But, unlike Elizabeth I and her standing in the country she would rule, it meant that Mary would never be seen as truly of her nation and, just as importantly, she would not have direct experience of the warring groups that controlled her country. Elizabeth I, like Mary I her sister (and Victoria, much later), grew up watching and listening, largely excluded from court but understanding it through reports. All of them were treated as outsiders, all three learned in childhood how the public's affection could wax and wane. As such, all three were acutely aware of the factions controlling power and of how the public had to be courted. Mary was regarded as a great queen from the beginning in France – but it would make her an alien when she returned.

The most calculating of the lot was the King of France. He had plans for the tiny queen. A good marriage alliance was part of it, but the bigger prize Henry II had in mind was a claim for the throne of England, then occupied by a sickly boy.

Mary was a pawn. The adults around her did not protect her, others were using her to win what they most desired. Already, at five, she was being failed.

Chapter Four
'A Princess on This Earth'

In March, the great plan for Mary was held in the balance. She was seriously ill with a sickness that appears to have been measles. It looked as though all the dynastic dreams were at an end and that, with Mary dead, the Earl of Hertford would invade Scotland and demand that Edward VI, rather than Arran, should be king. After all of Arran's failings, and given the division between the lords, he would have found it difficult, near impossible, to hold on to his position. Yet with careful nursing Mary recovered and, having moved to Dumbarton, preparations began for travelling to the continent. In June, the King of France sent an early wedding present – five thousand soldiers who besieged Haddington, rattling their sabres at English aggression. The message to England was clear: attack Scotland again and the full force of the French military would respond.

In July, the Scots Parliament agreed the marriage, with the proviso that Henry II should protect Scotland as he protected France and that he would guarantee Scots independence. There was little suggestion of what could be done if the King of France failed in his promise to defend Scotland. It appears that few of the lords saw Henry's true ambition: to gain England through Mary, or at least infuriate and harry England by using her to make a claim to the throne.

Mary's servants began readying her for her journey, packing piles of dresses of silk and velvet, adorned with gold and silver thread, furniture, tapestries, books, toys. The French courtiers arrived to discuss matters. One declared her a perfect little being. 'It is not possible to hope for more from a Princess on this earth,'[1] he said. They would wait for fine summer weather for good sailing and then send her off. Families jostled to send attendants and female companions with Mary. Not only was she the future Queen of France, but she would have a great position in the French court in the meantime: the king had agreed that she would rank before both of his daughters.

As a mark of respect, Henry sent his own royal ship to collect the little queen. The Scots hoped it would dissuade the English from intercepting and boarding the ship, kidnapping Mary for their own – France would see taking the king's ship as an act of war. It was also decided that Mary would embark at Dumbarton, and then take the longer route from the west as a way of dodging the English navy.

Little Mary's train of attendants was assembled. With her was her long-term guardian, Lord Erskine, who was responsible for Stirling Castle and thus knew the child well, and Lord Livingston, another guardian. At their side were a governess, the widow Janet Stewart, Lady Fleming, natural daughter of James IV, forty-six and the mother of eight children (seven of whom remained behind); the Countess of Bothwell; various nurses, including one Jean Sinclair; religious advisors, including the prior of Inchmahome who had become devoted to her; and a collection of aristocratic children as honourable companions. Among them was James Stewart, the future Earl of Moray, then seventeen and twelve years Mary's senior – who would have a great effect on her life. James was also the grandson of Lord Erskine, through his mother, Margaret Erskine, favourite mistress of James V – so he already had a position of some dominance in the group. Also in the train were Mary's half-brothers, Robert Stewart, fifteen, son of James V and Euphemia Elphinstone, and John Stewart, also fifteen, son of James V and Elizabeth Carmichael. Mary of Guise had become fond of her husband's early illegitimate children – James, Robert and John had been fathered long before she arrived. She was already beginning to wonder if James Stewart, once a few more years had passed, might be a better regent than Arran. In this, she demonstrated her essential Guise nature: the idea that family and family loyalty would always trump that of the individual.

Mary was also accompanied by four small girls, all called Mary – Mary Fleming, Mary Livingston, Mary Beaton and Mary Seton. Mary

Fleming was the daughter of Janet Stewart, Mary's governess, and Lord Fleming, who had died at Pinkie Cleugh. Mary Livingston was the daughter of the guardian who was travelling with them, and Mary Beaton was part of the family of the still-feared Cardinal David Beaton. The Marys Beaton and Seton were the daughters of French ladies-in-waiting to Mary of Guise who had come over with her for her marriage, and thus had learned some French from their mothers.

Mary of Guise was heartbroken to see her daughter go. There was no way she could go with her, as it would leave a power vacuum and royal brides, however young, travelled without their parents. They had their court and that should be sufficient. The Scots waved her off, hoping that this meant security from England's aggression. Little Mary set off for France on 7 August 1548, after waiting on board for some time for the correct wind. The journey was rough, and the rudder was smashed passing Cornwall. Everyone was seasick, apart from the young queen.

The ship landed on 13 August, at Brest in northern France. Mary and her party set off, first to Morlaix, where they lodged in a convent, and then to the Seine, where they boarded another ship. The journey was ill-starred: the drawbridge broke on their way into Morlaix and the Scots suspected treachery, Lords Livingston and Erskine were very ill and one of Mary Seton's relatives died.

On the way to the palace of Saint-Germain-en-Laye, twelve miles to the west of Paris, Mary was given over to her grandmother, Antoinette of Guise, for the final stages of the journey. Antoinette was deputised to ready the girl for the elegance of the French court. She did so – but she also ensured that the Guise influence was strong over the child. The king had already decided that Mary should be separated from her Scots attendants and given companions and maids from the French aristocracy – and Antoinette was quite in accord. She wanted the child surrounded with her relations, not James V's illegitimate sons and men such as Erskine and Livingston, who would always put Scotland first.

It was not uncommon for foreign princesses to lose all their attendants from home, but it was hard. Mary was not even six and set to be separated from the only friends she knew. Antoinette also judged Mary's clothes, lovingly and carefully assembled to show off the best Scots craftsmanship, to be poor quality. New French clothes were needed.

Everything about the little queen was to be French now, from her clothes to her friends, even her speech. Scotland, her old home, was quickly being rubbed out.

Antoinette thought the Scots rough, dirty and unwashed. She could only tolerate Janet Stewart, Lady Fleming, whom she thought clean at least, which was fortunate, for Mary of Guise sent word that she wished her daughter to retain her governess.

There was no such mercy for the four Marys. Their parents had hoped they would be received at the French court, make alliances and possible marriages there. Instead they were sent off to the Dominican Royal Priory at Saint-Louis at Poissy, even Mary Fleming, whose mother remained with the child queen. This was a highly regarded priory and the four Marys would receive an excellent education, but their mistress would grow up dancing at the French court and they were summarily excluded.

The Duchess of Guise approved of her little granddaughter, whom she judged pretty, intelligent and set to be a great beauty in adulthood. Mary also met her half-brother, Duke François, Mary of Guise's first child, left behind with her parents, and he declared her an excellent sister.

On the final journey, Mary's grandmother was firm with her: she was told to speak French and given the rudiments of the language. Finally, they arrived at Saint-Germain, the beautiful palace in the fresh country air that was the usual home of the royal children. The palace had been so assiduously cleaned and prepared in expectation of her coming that the royal children were not in residence. Henry II was determined that his daughters would be friends with Mary – a difficult demand given that she had deposed them from their positions. She, whom the king called 'ma fille, la Royne d'Ecosse', would walk ahead of the French princesses because she was already a queen and would be the dauphine. For many courtiers, this was a shocking act – a blood princess of France was, in their estimation, much greater than a queen of a backwater such as Scotland. But the king was convinced otherwise, and he was backed up in this by his mistress, Diane de Poitiers.

Catherine de' Medici had little power over the king, but what she did have inhered in her children. Diane had encouraged the king to procreate, for such was his duty, and she was kind to his offspring.

Nevertheless, to see Catherine lose a little power because Mary was advanced was good for Diane's position.

The young queen was given a new friend, Princess Elisabeth, two years younger at three, a good-natured and playful child, who was welcoming to Mary. Also in the nursery was Claude, only eight months old. Mary was introduced to the dauphin, who was nearly five. Though rather small and weak, he was an intelligent and kind-hearted little boy and the two seemed to take to each other well. The king, who met Mary that November, decided she was the most perfect child and spent hours talking to her. Lady Fleming, keen to hold on to her position in the French court, noticed that the king had also been paying her some attention. Diane de Poitiers had been ill and Lady Fleming, at forty-six, was just the type of mature lady he liked.

Unfortunately for Mary, the power over her life was not in the hands of Lady Fleming or those who accompanied her, but the endlessly machinating family of her mother, the Guises. Mary was in court as the feted, powerful queen – but under all the gold and dazzle, she was a sacrifice to Guise ambition.

By the end of the year, Mary appeared to have learned enough French to get by and it would be the language she wrote in and spoke for many years. She was everybody's pet at court. She was given the finest clothes of all the children, with gowns of gold damask and bonnets of silver, fur edging, velvet and taffeta and so many jewels that she needed three bronze chests to hold them all. She and the dauphin were close friends and danced together beautifully at a court wedding, much to the displeasure of the English ambassador. Mary and Francis were dutiful children who recognised that playing together and talking together was a certain way to please the adults around them. But they were also genuinely fond of each other. For Mary, who had been moved about so early in her childhood, her new life was one of safety and pleasure. The royal children had their own establishment and shifted between the great royal castles with all their nurses, servants, tutors, assistants, furniture, toys and dozens of pets. Henry II, in captivity, had sometimes only had the company of a little dog and he never wished his children to be so deprived, so they were provided with countless dogs, pet birds and other small animals, along with horses for exercise and even a pair of bears.

Mary was taught Latin, Italian, Spanish, as well as practising French composition, dancing, needlework, singing and the lute. She would never possess the genius of Elizabeth I, but she was hard-working and quick-witted and pleased her tutors. In religion, she was purely Catholic: Mary of Guise had instructed that her daughter hear daily Mass and she had both her faithful prior of Inchmahome and her own French chaplain. In France, she was given her beautiful Book of Hours, now in the National Library of Russia, probably one of many, but this she kept for her whole life. She wrote upon it when she was twelve, 'Ce livre est à moi, Marie Reyne'.[2] The Book of Hours, unused before, gives us Mary's voice throughout her life – and her desire to survive.

Aged seven, Mary wrote to her grandmother that she had 'joyful news', the 'Queen my mother' had written to say that she would be coming to visit and 'she will be here very soon to see you and me'. It was 'greatest happiness which I could wish for in this world, and indeed I am so overjoyed about it, that all I am to be thinking about now is to do my whole duty in all things and to study to be very good'.[3]

Mary of Guise wished to see her family, hopeful that a personal visit would press them into helping her seize the regency from Arran. If she was going to launch such a complicated campaign, she would need money to gift to supporters, as well as for herself, so she could give the correct image of riches. Arran, of course, was the man in charge of the treasury as regent, and, quite simply, she was poor. She brought with her a collection of Scottish gentlemen whom she needed favours for, including the Earls of Huntly and Cassilis. She landed at Dieppe and met the court, then at Rouen for a festival, on 25 September 1550. Mother and daughter were delightedly reunited and spent every possible moment together. They rode with a court procession, which held banners of Scottish castles, making clear the alliance to all. Mary and her daughter visited the Guises, spent time with Mary's son, fifteen-year-old François, and travelled with the king and his huge retinue – to Tours, Angers and Nantes. The little Queen of Scots was perfectly happy.

Mary of Guise's presence was less pleasing to the king, however, for she constantly importuned him for money and he soon grew weary of her and tried to encourage her to return to Scotland. In the same year, Mary Fleming declared she was pregnant by the king – and was quickly packed off home. For Diane, a pregnancy was a step too far. The Scots were becoming, to the king, one giant headache. He began to negotiate the marriage of his eldest daughter, Elisabeth, Mary's great friend, to Edward VI, despite the complaints of the Pope that he would excommunicate Elisabeth if she married the English king. Henry paid no heed. He would push his way into England on two fronts, with both daughter and daughter-in-law.

In the autumn of 1551, after a year in France, Mary of Guise finally embarked on her return. Her son accompanied her to Dieppe, but on the journey sickened and died. She was devastated – as was young Mary, who had lost a kindly older brother and friend.

Mary of Guise still had to leave – the weather would be too rough for travel in winter and she was expected at the English court. Her daughter was heartbroken to see her go and clung to her. It had been the happiest year of her childhood.

In England, Mary of Guise visited Edward VI and was well received – another point in her favour for gaining the regency. On her return to Scotland, she found the question of religion was ever more divided. Archbishop Hamilton, brother of Regent Arran, led those who wished for Catholicism, while the Earl of Argyll headed up those who wanted reform. James Stewart, Mary's half-brother, was behind him. Mary of Guise gathered her supporters, and at the end of 1553, Henry II agreed to ask Arran to give up his regency. Luckily for Mary of Guise, he had managed to annoy and alienate a large swathe of nobles with his tedious arrogance – and they were only too happy to depose him from his role.

Mary, by now aged just twelve, also signed an order sent to her in France requiring him to give up his position. Seeing he had lost much of his support, Arran resigned and Mary of Guise became regent. But, afraid both of England – now ruled by Mary I after Edward VI's death – and the resurging power of the Hamilton family, she patronised Protestants in an attempt to counterweight the influence of Arran's brother, Archbishop Hamilton. The reformed religion in Scotland proceeded fast – and by 1556, John Knox, fiery reformer and preacher, had been welcomed into the country. He had fled to England in 1549 and in 1551 was appointed chaplain to Edward VI. When he returned in 1556, he found much more interest in Protestant ideas, notably from James Stewart, Mary's half-brother. He wrote to Mary of Guise suggesting she start the Protestant Reformation, but she ignored the letter and he promptly went back to Geneva.

The Queen Regent Mary gave France more power in Scotland. She appointed Frenchmen to oversee the treasury and the Great Seal and as comptroller, as well as allowing the French ambassador, Henri Cleutin, excessive say in court and even an occasional voice on the Privy Council. These were the men she trusted, and she relied on them and her Guise relations for advice. But these roles were highly prized by Scots aristocrats (the position in the treasury was a particularly lucrative one) and there was much discontent. In 1557, a group of Protestant lords, including the Earl of Argyll and the Earl of Morton, had signed an agreement opposing young Mary's marriage to the dauphin and banded together in the ambition of making Scotland a Protestant country. The French dismissed the reports as the comings and goings of minor lords.

The Guises were satisfied. Mary had gained power in Scotland and their little future dauphine was performing her duties to perfection. As reported by the Cardinal of Lorraine, her uncle, she 'increases daily in dignity, goodness, beauty, wisdom and virtue, that she is the most perfect and accomplished in all things honourable and virtuous as is possible'. Mary also charmed her future father-in-law. 'The King takes such pleasure in her, that he spends his time well in talking with her for an hour and she is as able to amuse him with pleasant and rational conversation as a woman of five and twenty.'[4] Catherine de' Medici was more dubious about Mary but she admired her efficacy at embroidery. Catherine, often excluded from affairs by her husband, who gave all his attention to Diane de Poitiers, focused her razor-sharp intelligence on her children, in the hope of gaining influence through them. Being kind to Mary, she realised, could please both her son and the king. For, even though Mary of Guise was a problem and the Scots lords hanging around the court loud, rough and undesirable, the king was gleeful about his bargain.

Mary, acutely intelligent and with a child's eagerness to help, never tired of trying to please the king and befriend the little dauphin. She and Francis diligently practised dancing, in expectation of the grand balls that would follow their wedding. In the evenings, they would play cards together and she often won. The dauphin was pale, thin and constantly prey to coughs, colds and respiratory infections but he was a young man of great affections and he was genuinely devoted to Mary and very loving to his siblings and parents. He cast her as his romantic prize in masques or little plays. Mary was very attentive to the dauphin and seemed to bring him out of himself. She was proud of her good effect on him. Childhood friends, fond of her fiancé's family and siblings – Mary had the best possible start for royal marriage.

Mary, Elisabeth, Claude and the dauphin were joined by more children in the nursery. The French king had invaded the Lorraine and taken Charles III, its nine-year-old ruler, to be brought up at the French court. A little prince, Louis, was born in 1549 but died in the following year. Catherine de' Medici was almost constantly pregnant. Charles was born in 1550; Henry in the following year, just before Mary of Guise returned to France; Marguerite, born in 1553; then yet another Francis, two years later. Mary loved children and enjoyed moving between palaces with her little royal relations. But in 1554, when Mary was twelve, Catherine de' Medici decreed her rather pleasant childhood was at an end. Now they were approaching adulthood, it was determined that Mary and the dauphin should spend more time at court, to learn proper statecraft and be correctly supervised. Mary was given her own establishment (after some tedious arguments over it between the Guises and the king). There, she became more prone to Guise influence – on her first night, she invited the Cardinal of Lorraine for supper.

Mary's expenses were much greater, for she had to be properly clothed for court functions, and there were many arguments about money between her governess, Mme de Parois, the replacement for Lady Fleming, and the king's comptrollers, as well as the Guises. Everything finally blew up over gowns: Mary wished to give her old gowns to her Guise relations, her servants and to a nearby nunnery – but Mme de Parois said they were hers. The resulting fallout made Mary ill – she even wrote to her mother saying it had nearly killed her because 'I was afraid of hearing through these disputes so many false reports and cruel things said of me'.[5] She suffered from fainting, dizzy spells, headaches and stomach problems, all probably brought on by nervous exhaustion and anxiety. Her uncle Guise blamed her fainting and stomach aches on overeating and childish greed – but there was more to it than that. Her feelings of mental stress were not just thanks to the dreaded Mme de Parois. Lady Fleming, now attending Mary of Guise in Scotland, had been trying to come back, to see her beloved king, and introduce him to his son – but Diane de Poitiers and Catherine de' Medici refused her permission. Still, the king sent tokens of favour to Lady Fleming and later gave favour to her son, who was legitimised and given positions of honour.

Now she was growing into adulthood and living at the court, Mary saw how she was surrounded by jockeying for power, factions and plots. Her Guise relations pushed her to gain concessions or positions that she could not. She even signed a set of blank sheets of paper at their behest – an unwise move, for any possible treaty or declaration could be written in above, but she had no choice. Mary missed her mother, and no one was coming to help her. She had to make her way on her own.

At about this time, Mary shot up to her incredible height of somewhere around five feet eleven, an impressive height for a man at the time, let alone a woman. It was more compelling evidence that she was born to rule.

The Guise relations sent enthusiastic letters back to Mary in Scotland. 'I give you every assurance, madam, that there is nothing more beautiful or more modest than the Queen your daughter, and also very devout,' enthused the cardinal. 'She rules the King and the Queen.'[6] He was not being entirely truthful. Although the king was truly pleased by his little dynastic claim, Catherine de' Medici was wary of Mary and had no particular affection for her. The cardinal lied to his sister because he knew that everything depended on her daughter marrying Francis and becoming the dauphine. If Mary fell out of favour and Henry decided to marry his son to a Spanish heiress instead, it would be a shameful loss for Scotland – and if the great protection was no more, England would surely attack without mercy.

In 1556, Catherine de' Medici was brought to confinement with twins, but one, Joan, died in the womb, and Victoria died a month later. Doctors told the king there should be no more children and he left the queen's bed entirely for that of Diane de Poitiers. Catherine lost what little influence remained. In the same year, Mary turned fourteen – and the king started to use her as a pawn. When he heard that there was talk of a marriage between Princess Elizabeth of England and

Archduke Ferdinand, son of the Holy Roman Emperor, Henry declared he would marry Mary off to Lord Courtenay, an aristocrat with a claim to the English throne. Mary, again, was not seen as a queen in her own right, but a possession of the King of France, to be disposed of as he wished.

The possibility that Mary would not be married to the dauphin was terrible to Mary of Guise and the Guise relations. Fortunately, the idea of a union between Ferdinand and Elizabeth faded away and Lord Courtenay died – but the chance was there that Henry II could double-cross them all at the last minute. The cardinal and the Duke of Guise began pushing hard to have Mary married to the dauphin as soon as possible. Mary of Guise appointed her mother, Antoinette, to act as proxy.

The new year, 1558, began auspiciously as the French seized Calais, after a secret attack in the dead of winter – the town had been taken from them by the English in the Hundred Years War. Overwhelmed, the deputy of Calais, Thomas Wentworth, relinquished the keys to the city to Mary's uncle, the Duke of Guise, on 7 January. Henry II arrived in Calais to secure his claim sixteen days later. Lord Wentworth was taken as a prisoner of war. Queen Mary I was devastated at the loss of Calais; to Henry II, it was the beginning of his new relationship with the English: one of dominance.

On 19 April 1558, Henry II finally announced the date of the marriage between his son and Mary at a public ceremony at the Louvre. The Cardinal of Lorraine joined their hands as the couple exchanged a ring. The dauphin declared that of his own free will he would marry Mary on Sunday 24 April, five days hence. A grand ball followed after the announcement and Mary danced with the king. Behind the scenes, embroiderers, cooks, builders and pageant masters were working day and night to bring the king's great vision of unity and French strength to fruition.

With her pale skin, red-gold hair and incredible height, graceful carriage and sweet voice, Mary was much admired – the Venetian ambassador called her 'the most beautiful princess in Europe'.[7] Her height and stature always made her look healthier than she was.

Plans for the marriage proceeded apace. The king wanted to dazzle and throw gold to distract the populace. But even more important were the secret treaties that Mary signed – providing that, if Mary died with no heirs, Scotland would become a vassal of France. Henry congratulated himself on his brilliance and pushed his daughter-in-law to claim the kingdom of England for herself. On the eve of her wedding, Mary had everything. Glory, accolades, beauty, Queen of Scotland, one day Queen Consort of France – and soon to be Queen of England. It was an intoxicating vision.

Chapter Five
'Marvellous in Our Eyes'

Six months after Mary's grand ceremony in 1558, young Princess Elizabeth thought she had a great prize within her grasp. It was November, the dreary winter of a bleak year, and at the palace of St James', her elder sister, Queen Mary I, was dying.

Just five years earlier, on 3 August 1553, Queen Mary had ridden into London in a blaze of triumph to take her throne against all the odds. Her father, Henry VIII, was long dead, and her younger brother, Edward VI, had ruled for fewer than six years. Edward had attempted to ensure that his cousin, Lady Jane Grey, would be his successor so that she continued his Protestant reformations. But Mary had the greater claim and Jane had only reigned for nine hopeless days before the firstborn daughter of Henry VIII seized the advantage. Resplendent in purple and gold, she had 800 nobles in her train – and, most importantly of all, her half-sister Elizabeth by her side, waving out to the people and showing the assembled crowd the possessors of the true Tudor blood.

The nineteen-year-old Elizabeth, handsomely dressed in the Tudor colours of green and white (she was certainly not mourning Lady Jane), had processed through London accompanied by 2,000 soldiers to meet her sister at Wanstead, just outside the capital. Mary gave her sister a wonderful necklace of coral beads set in gold and a ruby and diamond brooch, and the two embraced in a thrilling display of familial unity. The government had been protecting Lady Jane Grey, with gunships in the Thames and troops across the country. But Mary, determined the crown would be hers, stormed into London with a huge entourage. Her following had begun in East Anglia with a small troop of local men and now she was surrounded by guards and attendants and carried by the weight of popular adoration. For the people of England, she was the true queen. Elizabeth by her side only added to the glory.

Elizabeth always meant to dazzle, both with her spectacular wit and her dress. She was not judged a perfect beauty, but she had the grace of her mother, Anne Boleyn, and her father's sense of ceremony. She was very tall and slim with a slender waist and small, high bosom. She had dark, expressive, dancing eyes, like her mother, but a somewhat long face and pointed chin with the Tudor rather hooked nose. She had her father's thick red-gold hair but an olive skin, which she covered in a toxic paste of borax, alum, poppy seeds and powdered eggshell to lighten it. Her voice was attractive, and she was most vain of her delicate hands, which she was fond of showing off at every opportunity. Elizabeth was young and energetic and much more beautiful than her older sister – but she knew her place. Her role was to ride behind the new queen, imply she had no ambition of her own, be the supporting actress in the Tudor comeback drama.

The country threw itself into celebration, and Mary and Elizabeth appeared together at every public event. The people cheered their ruler, believing that the conflicts and violence of the past years were over. Not since Matilda, in 1141, had a woman claimed the throne in her own right – and she had been judged an unequivocal disaster, blamed for a terrible civil war as her cousin, Stephen, fought for the right to rule. But Mary was the true heir of Henry VIII, and under her the country would see glory once more.

Mary I was committed and determined, politically careful and intelligent. Her attempt to prompt England to Catholic loyalty, to turn it into the epitome of a counter-reformation country, had much support – but ground had been lost, particularly due to Edward VI's imposition of a more ascetic Protestant religion. And the queen's most unpopular act was her effort to secure the throne and protect herself by marrying Philip of Spain. The people were convinced they were being subordinated to foreign interests – and plots to dethrone the queen grew. Elizabeth was implicated in one and was thrown into the Tower, occupying the same rooms her mother had lived in before her execution twenty years before. Only by her cleverest wiles (and the refusal of the accused to implicate her, despite terrible torture) did she manage to escape blame and regain her freedom. She then lived quietly at Hatfield, attempting to keep away both from plots and attending court, where she was forced to take Mass.

Mary I was painfully obsessed with Philip of Spain and convinced herself she was pregnant. But – as everybody but she came to understand – she was not. Instead she probably had a tumour in her stomach – and it was killing her. By early 1558, she was dying and refusing to name Elizabeth as her heir. She declared furiously that Elizabeth was 'neither her sister nor the daughter of the queen's father, King Henry, nor would she hear of favouring her, as she was born of an infamous woman, who had so greatly outraged the queen her mother and herself'.[1] But already the great men of the country were moving to her sister. Elizabeth was kept constantly abreast of the happenings at court – as one parliamentarian later recalled, 'Few things could be spoken either in the Privy Council or the Privy Chamber of the queen her sister but they were revealed unto her Majesty.'[2]

Almost everyone wished for Elizabeth to be queen, including many Catholic supporters of Mary – for the heretic daughter of Anne Boleyn was a better option than being thrown into uncertainty, or even, knowing the eagerness of Philip II to declare his claim and 'assist' in ruling, becoming subject to Spain. Mary had to give in and on 8 November a messenger arrived to tell Elizabeth at Hatfield House that the queen had declared her the heir. Elizabeth had known what was afoot – for Mary's trusted lady had already arrived with a selection of the queen's jewels, an indication of what Elizabeth would soon receive. Philip of Spain had made it known that he would not protest Elizabeth's accession. Elizabeth was ready. Ever-loyal William Cecil busied himself drafting the letters that were to be sent out when the new queen took the throne. On 17 November, in the early hours of the morning, the queen died – declaring anyone who cut her open would find 'Philip and Calais inscribed on my heart' after the humiliating defeat by French troops that lost England their last land in France. A messenger was sent to Hatfield and Elizabeth fell to her knees, overcome with emotion. She quoted in Latin, 'This is the doing of the Lord; and it is marvellous in our eyes.'[3] It was a beautiful scene but Elizabeth was putting on a show to be reported back to court. She had already been informed by her own spy, who had ridden faster than the messenger, that Mary was dead.

As Elizabeth later told the Spanish ambassador, her first act as queen was to thank God for her peaceful accession and ask that 'He would give her grace to govern with clemency and without bloodshed'. Between eleven o'clock and midday on 17 November, Elizabeth was formally announced as queen outside the Palace of Westminster and other positions in London. England's first queen regnant had been defeated by illness, but she had set an effective model for the female role, and had been a warning of the problems Elizabeth would face.

On 20 November, the Privy Council and key members of the peerage came to the great hall at Hatfield to hear Elizabeth make her first public address and see who had been chosen as her advisors and councillors. Under a canopy and on a rather makeshift throne, she pronounced, 'The burdaine that is fallen upon me maketh me amazed and yet considering that I am God's creature, ordained to obey His appointment, I will yield thereto.'[4] She was being disingenuous – the brand-new twenty-five-year-old monarch had been carefully planning her triumph for years. And her aim, above all, was to create unity. As she continued in her speech, 'And as I am but one body, so I shall require you all, my lords, to be assistant with me.'

Among them was one of her very favourites, the young and handsome Lord Robert Dudley, her friend since childhood, whose father had been the second Protector to Edward VI and who had been under threat of execution when she was in the Tower, whom she immediately made Master of the Horse and put in charge of the coronation. Although she had packed her closest circle with her supporters, such as her trusted William Cecil, and Sir Francis Knollys, Sir Nicholas Throckmorton and Katherine Parr's brother, William, as well as keen Protestant lords – she retained ten of Mary's councillors. Elizabeth had long been acting as a monarch. Now finally she was Queen.

Elizabeth planned the theatre of her victory. On 28 November, she adorned herself in purple velvet and jewels and formally entered the City as queen, parading with 1,000 men to the royal apartments in the Tower of London. The procession was led by the Lord Mayor of London and Garter King of Arms. Pembroke bore the sword of state and Dudley rode behind the queen on a black stallion. The streets were packed with waving crowds, all the church bells rang, and trumpets along the way announced her arrival. Her subjects were not disappointed. As one ambassador wrote later, 'Such an air of dignified majesty pervades all her actions that no one can fail to suppose she is a queen.' But for Elizabeth – unlike her fellow monarchs, who were terrified of letting the royal mask slip – dignity did not mean ignoring the people who cheered for her. As one observer recalled, she excelled in engaging with the crowd. 'Her spirit seemed to be everywhere', he judged, declaring that 'her eye was set upon one, her ear listened to another, her judgement ran upon a third, to a fourth she addressed her speech . . . distributing her smiles, looks and graces so artfully that thereupon the people again redoubled the testimony of their joys, and afterwards, raising everything to the highest strain, filled the ears of all men with immoderate extolling of their prince'.[5] As he put it, 'If any person had either the gift or the style to win the hearts of the people, it was this queen.'

For, as Elizabeth told the Spanish ambassador – when he declared she owed the crown to the influence of his king – she was on the throne thanks to the people of England and her only gratitude was to them. She never forgot it.

When Elizabeth neared the Tower there was a 'great shooting of guns, the like was never heard before'. She looked up at the great and terrifying building where she had once been imprisoned – and where her mother had died – and brought her horse to a stop. 'I am raised from being a prisoner in this place to be a prince of this land. That dejection was a work of God's justice; this advancement is a work of His mercy.'[6]

The queen entered the Tower and promptly told the lieutenant – who had been her jailer – that she would appoint another in his place. She gave her judgement kindly, but she would never forget those who had been loyal to her. And she expected her word to be obeyed. As the Spanish ambassador wrote gloomily to his master, Philip of Spain, 'Her Majesty seems to me incomparably more feared than her sister and gives her orders and has her way as absolutely as her father did. We have lost a kingdom, body and soul.'

To the French king and the Guises, however, Elizabeth's arrival on the throne only strengthened their case that it should truly be Mary, Queen of Scots who ruled. The new queen was a heretic, born of an adulteress. In their plan to gain the English throne, they now had God on their side.

What did Mary think of Elizabeth, growing up in the French court? They were cousins, relations – and Mary was, of course, by her very actions attempting to disinherit her cousin. She was influenced by the perception of England in France. She knew England as the enemy, even if she had only the very vaguest memories of the attacks and the invasions of Hertford's men. And everyone knew and judged Elizabeth's mother, Anne Boleyn, once a lady-in-waiting to King Henry's mother, Queen Claude. The French and the Guise family were watching England: every false step, every failed pregnancy.

Nearly ten years before Mary was even born, Anne Boleyn had been at her triumphant coronation on 1 June 1533. Finally, after six years of chasing, Henry had won her, in the process divorcing his wife, Catherine of Aragon, alienating Catholic Europe and breaking from the Church of Rome. The people had lived through schism and disruption – but on the day of coronation, the symbolism was all unity. London was transformed into a vision of celestial Jerusalem with Anne as the Virgin Mary. Her hair was loose around her shoulders and she was gowned in white – and visibly pregnant, rounder than one might expect given that she had been married for only four months. Along the way was a great tableau of a castle against a hill. As Anne passed by, a tree stump on the hill streamed forth a tumble of red and white roses, an outpouring of Tudor symbolism, and then a (well-trained) white falcon emerged from a painted cloud and flew to the flowers. An angel appeared out of the cloud and put an imperial crown on the head of the white falcon. The crest of the white falcon alighting on roses was Anne's own – and the import of the tableau could not be mistaken. Anne was bringing new life to the Tudor dynasty.

No one was buying it. Londoners lined the route, but they were dull and unenthusiastic. As the ever-critical Spanish ambassador Eustace Chapuys said, the coronation was a 'meagre and uncomfortable thing, to the great dissatisfaction, not only of the common people, but also of the rest'.[7] Instead of cheering for the royal couple, the crowds saw the initials of Henry and Anne and turned them into a joke, shouting 'Ha, Ha,' as the queen passed. They still loved the old queen, Catherine of Aragon, now living in exile at The More Palace in Hertfordshire, barred from seeing her teenaged daughter, Mary, and kept in privation. She called herself the queen, rather than the Dowager Princess of Wales, the title Henry wished her to assume as the widow of his brother Arthur. Catherine, praying and pious in Hertfordshire, was a constant thorn in Henry's side.

Every day the new Queen Anne grew larger with her child, which she was convinced was a boy. In August, as Anne prepared to go into confinement, the royal couple removed to Windsor and then Greenwich, where Anne would give birth. Henry's daughter with Catherine, Mary, now no longer a princess but simply Lady Mary, was ordered to join the ladies and attend the queen, to witness the victory of her mother's nemesis, as she gave birth to a prince and proved that everything the king had done to marry her had been ordained and rewarded by God. He had broken from Rome, exposed his subjects to excommunication and opened years of religious strife, but a boy would prove that it had been a virtuous battle.

Anne needed to hold the king's affections. He had been her devoted swain when he fell in love with her eight years earlier in 1525. She had played the cruel mistress, charmed him, kept him wound around her finger. The court had marvelled over how obsessive his love had been. But, now she was pregnant and married, she heard gossip that he had been chasing other women and challenged him on it, expecting him to play the subservient lover, as he always had. But instead, the king had told her she must 'shut her eyes and endure' as her betters had done. Anne was furious, and everybody whispered that she was losing her hold over Henry. As they said, she was 'very jealous of the king and not without legitimate cause'.[8]

A queen was supposed to go into confinement four to six weeks before the child was born. But Anne's due date had almost certainly been fudged – for she and the king had begun sexual relations before they married, and Anne was probably pregnant when they did finally wed. Anne took her seclusion on 26 August, after hosting a great court banquet. Her rooms were hung with tapestries, and rich velvet covers adorned the bed. The aim was to reduce infection by shutting out natural light and air, but the place was unbearably suffocating and not conducive to a healthy birth. But Anne was young and strong and on 7 September, not even a fortnight after going into confinement, she went into labour. The king planned jousts and celebrations to commemorate the birth of his sacred prince. The courtiers and ambassadors waited eagerly for news and the ladies of the chamber rushed to and fro. Not long after three o'clock in the afternoon, Anne gave birth to a fine, healthy child with a rush of Tudor red-gold hair. The baby was lusty and strong – and a girl. Outwardly, the king was calm and engaged in the jousts and celebrations he had planned. He told Anne that they could expect to have more children and announced that the baby would be Elizabeth, named after both his mother and Anne's. Anne was immediately devoted to her daughter, delighted that she had been born on the eve of the birthday of the Virgin Mary and wanted her daughter always by her side.

Chapuys said that the king felt 'great regret' and he was correct. Although he was pleased with a healthy baby, the king had turned the world upside down for a son. Even though he was confident that he would have more sons, he was growing less convinced that Anne should be their mother.

Anne's enemies scented weakness – and began to circle. Now she had failed to bear a son, perhaps another mistress should take her place. 'There is little love for the one who is queen now or for any of her race,' reported one French observer ('her race' meaning the ambitious Boleyn family).[9]

The baby Princess Elizabeth was christened on 10 September at the Chapel of the Observant Friars at Greenwich. Neither parent was present, as was customary. She was carried to the font by the Duchess of Norfolk, wrapped in a purple and ermine mantle, her train borne by the Countess of Kent. Five hundred torches accompanied her back to her mother – who was still in confinement. Anne had demanded that she be named Mary as well as Elizabeth. She wished, she told the king, to commemorate how the princess had been born on the nativity of the Virgin. But she also wanted a second Mary, to replace Henry's first daughter. The king refused, much to her fury. Elizabeth was pronounced the king's first legitimate child. Elizabeth, not Mary, was his heir.

Anne wanted the baby always with her. When the queen returned to court after her confinement, the courtiers were shocked to see the baby princess next to the queen, on a velvet cushion, under the canopy of estate. Infants were never seen at court. Anne begged Henry to allow her to breastfeed the child, but the king refused such a scandalous request. Anyone of rank hired a wet nurse – breastfeeding was simply not done by aristocratic women, let alone a queen. Anne poured her heart into caring for her daughter, playing with her openly in public and giving her dozens of gifts. But the baby was also a form of protection – she proved Anne could have children and give birth to a son. And once Anne had the longed-for prince in her arms, her enemies would never be able to unseat her, no matter how much they hated her or called her 'the Great Whore'.

As was customary for the heir to the throne, Elizabeth was to have her own establishment. Royal children should live in the countryside, away from the poor air of London. Henry had chosen the beautiful palace of Hatfield in Hertfordshire. At the end of the year, Elizabeth, aged just three months, was sent there, along with a host of female attendants – nurses, governesses, stewards and servants. Anne had ensured that her own relations were at Hatfield, including her aunts Lady Shelton and Anne Clere, and Lady Bryan, Anne's mother's half-sister, was Elizabeth's 'Lady Mistress'. Still, Anne was deeply pained to lose her daughter just before Christmas. The baby was taken off in a velvet litter by the dukes of Norfolk and Suffolk and a large train of ladies and gentlemen and paraded around London for the cheering crowds on her way to Hatfield. Anne was bereft, but she knew that her place was smiling at the king's side. She must fall pregnant again and the child had to be a boy.

Chapter Six
'A Thousand Deaths'

Little Princess Elizabeth flourished in the countryside, full of physical energy and 'as goodly a child as hath been seen'.[1] She was taken out for airings and lived a regular life overseen by Lady Bryan and surrounded by her attendants, twenty senior staff posts given to members of the gentility, and a hundred servants. Henry accommodated Elizabeth with excellence and grandeur, as a princess should be kept. Elizabeth clearly did not know her mother well and most likely did not remember her. Her first memories would have been of Lady Bryan and the rest. As she later said, 'we are more indebted to them that bringeth us up well than to our parents'.

Elizabeth and her retinue moved frequently between palaces, as was customary, both for changes of air and to allow the palaces to be cleaned, travelling from Hatfield to Eltham, Hunsdon, Langley, the More and Richmond. Anne could see her only infrequently and had to rely on the letters of Lady Bryan. She continued to lavish presents on the baby girl and sent the most ornate gowns of velvet, which she rarely saw her wear. But even the smallest question was important. In the autumn of 1535, it was reported to the king that the two-year-old princess could now drink from a cup and was ready to be weaned. The king and council considered and agreed she should be weaned with 'all due diligence'. Anne sent her own private letter to Lady Bryan with details on how it should be done. Tudor children moved to purée and then were supposed to eat plain food. Lady Bryan was adamant that Elizabeth should not sit up to eat at the table, as she might get overexcited.

Elizabeth's life was that of her nurses and household. But the king did occasionally come to see her, and to her nurse's relief, she won him over. 'Her grace is much in the king's favour', reported one courtier after he visited. Elizabeth was clever, charming and looked just like Henry – so how could he not be delighted?[2]

When Elizabeth was just a month old, Henry told his daughter Mary that she was to lose her household and must go to attend on the baby princess. Foreign ambassadors were shocked, declaring Mary was being treated as little more than a lady's maid. She was sent there in a litter of leather rather than velvet, attended by a small selection of attendants rather than the grand train of golden-clad gentlemen she had been used to. At Hatfield, she refused to submit to her new role. When told to pay her respects to the princess, she declared she 'knew of no other princess except herself'.[3] Henry gave her barely any allowance and she was without attendants or even enough clothes. When Mary was spotted by some locals walking in the gallery at Hatfield, they saluted her. Henry was angry and from then on Mary was kept as a virtual prisoner, her windows barred so that no one could see her.

Henry visited Hatfield but refused to see Mary and sent Thomas Cromwell to speak to her. Mary bided her time and, when the king was about to depart, she clambered to the top of the house and appeared at a terrace, kneeling to him. The king was charmed and, always keen to accept reverence, bowed to her. But if she had hoped he might improve her position, she was wrong. He may have still loved his first daughter, but all his hopes were focused on the next Tudor. If he gave too much favour to Mary, it would work to the power of his enemies and his former wife. And Anne was pushing him to treat Mary with disdain – for she saw Mary's every gain as Elizabeth's loss. 'She is my death and I am hers', she said of her eighteen-year-old stepdaughter.[4]

When, in 1535, Mary refused to accompany her sister to Eltham Palace, she was put in her litter by force and her jewels were confiscated. Mary protested vociferously, declaring she feared being poisoned by the mistress of the king. She frequently fell ill, tormented by low spirits, the miserable situation of her mother and the cruel treatment she received from her sister's household. Lady Shelton had shaken her, threatened to have her dismissed from the house and when Mary was seriously ill, told her she hoped Mary would die. We might say that her captors were in an impossible position, expected to 'persuade' Mary to respect her father's new alliance and afraid of showing her too much favour. And Mary never had her sister's emotional charm or winning ways. She was vulnerable and surrounded by enemies, and the unkindness of those around her only drove her into herself more, and confirmed her view that her God was the true God. Although Mary hated the way she was treated and the drop in her status, she found solace in the childish innocence of her half-sister, the only purity in a court that seemed to her all vicious corruption.

Catherine was growing more ill in exile, but Henry was intransigent. Unless Mary accepted that her mother was princess dowager (as the widow of Arthur) and that she herself was illegitimate, she could not see Catherine. She would also have to accept that her father was Supreme Head of the Church of England. For Mary, to do so would be an act of sin and she would never relent. Henry was genuinely fond of his first daughter and if she had given in, he would have treated her with respect. But she could not, and so the battle lines were drawn.

Meanwhile, Anne tried to bolster her own position by attempting to gain an alliance for Elizabeth. She wanted Catholic Europe to see Elizabeth as the true daughter of the king, not Mary – and if a foreign power engaged in a betrothal with Elizabeth, it would be a tacit acceptance of Henry's and Anne's marriage. Indeed, a French ambassadorial party went to see the princess at Eltham and she was presented to them entirely naked – as was not uncommon, they wished to be satisfied that her fine clothes hid no physical flaws. Henry negotiated with King Francis I of France for a marriage between Elizabeth and Francis' third son, Charles. A junior son was hardly the most glittering alliance, but it would give Anne and Elizabeth much-needed legitimacy. Unfortunately the talks collapsed, largely because the French disliked the demand that Charles be sent to England for his education.

Anne had been too imperious to engender much love at court and she was becoming increasingly isolated. But she was confident that she could solve all her troubles at a stroke by giving her husband a prince. Then, in July 1534, she was delivered of a stillborn child. This time, Henry was less hopeful. His thoughts turned to wondering if God was punishing him for marrying Anne – and so he began to turn on his wife. Childlessness was always the woman's fault – and a man such as Henry, who believed God had a direct and daily hand in his life, felt any failure to be a form of judgement. He even began to wonder if she had been a virgin before they took up together – for she had been excessively experienced, he thought. And he allowed himself to fall into a suspicion that she had entranced him with witchcraft. Anne grew frantic, took to following the king around, trying to regain his affection. But the shock of the stillbirth and the insecurity was taking its toll on her looks. In 1533, she had been the most glamorous woman at court. Now, she looked tired and her skin was sallow and sunken. The Venetian ambassador called her 'that thin old woman'.[5] Henry had long since moved his affections to the ladies at court – but in late 1534, Anne's greatest fear happened. The ever-susceptible king fell in love.

Mistress Jane Seymour was a quiet and virtuous lady-in-waiting to the queen and had once served Catherine of Aragon. Jane was respectable and reliable, but she was judged no great beauty and she was still unmarried at twenty-seven, even though families sent their daughters to court in the hope that they would gain husbands. She was excessively pale and had a rather plump face, small eyes, thin lips and something of a double chin. Unlike Anne, she had little wit and was not greatly interested by books. But even Chapuys, who hated Anne for he blamed her for the break from Rome, struggled to see what the king found so appealing in her lady-in-waiting, deciding that she must have a fine '*enigme*', or 'secret', a reference to the female genitalia. But in that he was wrong – Jane was holding the king off. She had learned from Anne that it was possible to resist the king and retain his respect (and one's head).

The king fell in love with Jane because she was the absolute opposite of Anne. She appeared meek and submissive, spoke little and was always calm. For the king, weary of his queen's tempests and jealousy, Jane was an oasis of tranquillity. She deferred to him in everything – except relinquishing her chastity. In this, and only this, she borrowed from her mistress's early strategy, coyly refusing the king and protesting her modesty. When he sent her a purse of money with a love letter, Jane kissed the letter but sent it back unopened, saying there was 'no treasure in the world that she valued as much as her honour, and on no account would she lose it, even if she were to die a thousand deaths'.[6] Jane's aim was to add to the downfall of the queen. She had been devoted to her first mistress, Catherine of Aragon, and then saw how Anne had treated the queen when she was in her ascendancy over the king. Jane was a follower of the Catholic religion and Princess Mary – and when the king began to pay her serious attention, Jane sent messages to Mary promising her that her troubles would soon be at an end.

Jane hoped to push forth the king's disaffection and see Anne put aside. The king was being played with exactly the same tools that Anne had used – but he seemed delighted by the game and keen to act out the role of chasing lover all over again. Jane's family and supporters wondered if he might go all the way to marriage. In 1535, the king made a summer progress with Anne Boleyn and paid a visit to the Seymours at Wolf Hall that cast Anne into paroxysms of jealousy, thanks to the attention he paid Jane.

On that same summer progress, Anne played her trump card. She fell pregnant again. Henry was delighted by the news and began to show her more respect in public. But in private, he had little interest in her. All his attention was bound up in Jane. Sick and exhausted, Anne was more jealous than ever and prone to dark moods. Forced to see Jane every day, for she was her lady-in-waiting, Anne grew wild and slapped and insulted her rival. Jane calmly accepted the attacks, which infuriated Anne even more.

In late 1535, Catherine of Aragon was dying. There were whispers that she had been poisoned, but she probably had a cancer of the heart. The king would not relent and had declared that Mary could only attend her dying mother if she accepted that she was illegitimate and that he was the Supreme Head of the Church. He cruelly ignored his daughter's pleas for mercy. The former queen died at the age of fifty on 7 January 1536. Mary was told of her death abruptly by Lady Shelton, who had no patience with her heartbreak.

Anne and Henry were delighted that Catherine was dead. The king ordered great celebrations and he and Anne dressed themselves in festive yellow for a grand banquet. Elizabeth was already at court and, after being taken to church to the sound of trumpets, Henry took her to the banquet and then to the chamber where the court was celebrating with a dance. He carried little Elizabeth in his arms and lifted her high for everyone to see, 'like one transported with joy'.[7]

Anne felt as if all her prayers had been answered. She was pregnant, and her great enemy was dead. What she didn't realise was that Catherine had been a form of protection for her. If Henry had divorced Anne or tried to set her aside, Catholic Europe would have attempted to push him to reconcile with Catherine. It was a conflict he could ill afford. But with Catherine gone, he could, if he wished, put Anne aside and take another wife. He could choose Jane.

On 29 January, Catherine was buried at Peterborough Abbey. Poor Mary was refused permission to attend. Anne hoped to celebrate with her husband. But when she went to find him, he was hidden away, enjoying the private attentions of Jane Seymour. The queen was possessed by a rage greater than any her attendants had ever seen. She attacked the king and Jane and her attendants feared for her unborn child. They were right to do so. A few hours later, overcome by distress, Anne miscarried after fifteen weeks of pregnancy. Those with her thought it might have been a boy. She had lost everything. 'I see that God will not give me male children', said the king.[8] As Chapuys wrote, 'the king shows great distress'. He was not just mourning the baby – it was also the end of his love for Anne. Although he appeared next to her at court and made a good face of it in public, he no longer had any feeling for her and was regretting he had ever married her. That evening, Thomas Cromwell had a secret meeting with Chapuys in which the ambassador suggested that, now Catherine was dead, the king might consider an imperial alliance. Although, the ambassador said, the world would never accept Anne, the same would not be true for a bride taken after the death of Catherine. Anne was assailed on all sides. Chapuys put it with a terrible clarity in a letter to the emperor: 'she has miscarried of her saviour'.[9]

Anne took solace from her misery in ordering beautiful clothes for Elizabeth. In April, the king allowed the princess to visit the queen at Greenwich. Anne was transported with happiness and played with her little girl, now a delightful two-and-a-half-year-old with a grasp of language and a sunny personality. She hoped that the little girl might win over Henry too. But he was fully occupied in chasing Jane Seymour. He had rooms for Jane installed next to his own in Greenwich, for he had to see her constantly. As Chapuys carped, 'for more than three months, the king has not spoken ten times to the Concubine [Anne] . . . when formerly he could not leave her for an hour'.[10] Now it was Jane whom Henry could not leave. Thomas Cromwell was gathering evidence to rid Henry of Anne for ever.

Anne played with her daughter unawares. She knew that she was losing the king's favour – she had even written a friendly letter to

Mary, although Mary, of course, was having none of it. But the queen thought only that she would have to suffer a parade of mistresses. She did not see the truth. Cromwell occupied himself in creating a solid case against her. For Henry had a problem. He could have simply annulled the marriage, on the basis of his prior relations with Anne's sister, Mary Boleyn. But Catherine of Aragon had refused to go quietly, and she had been a constant thorn in his side. Catherine had dealt in quiet resistance, but Anne was outspoken. She was younger, more energetic and could be a focus of Protestant plots. He needed to set Anne aside with a vengeance, with charges she could never protest. And in doing so, he would have to expose her to the possibility of execution.

Cromwell interviewed, pressed and sent his spies for evidence that the queen had been committing adultery. Anne had always been fond of receiving handsome young courtiers – and had been particularly enamoured of the musician Mark Smeaton and Sir Henry Norris, Groom of the Stool to the king. Anne had captured Henry with her skill at the verbal barbs of flirtation, exchanging pretty verses and engaging in mockery of others. She was a genius at the art – and when the king no longer wished to play the game with her, she unwisely played it with others.

Anne was no Catherine of Aragon, embroidering virtuously in her rooms. A queen should receive men in order to introduce her maids to possible suitors – but she had certainly received more than necessary. And she had been guilty of flirting and of making some indiscreet and risqué comments. But that was all. It would have been impossible for her to be unfaithful to Henry without the information getting out before, surrounded as she was by enemies and spies. Moreover, despite her ambition, she did truly love the king and prized his love for her. And there was certainly nothing untoward in her relationship with her brother, George Boleyn. He was something of a lothario at court, but Anne was no incestuous lover. Unfortunately, Anne was friendless at court and had no reputation for virtue – and even some of her family had turned against her, including her uncle, the Duke of Norfolk. She had long since alienated Cromwell, after clashing over how the revenues from the dissolution of the monasteries should be spent.

Even her arch enemy, Chapuys, reported no gossip of affairs back to his imperial master. If he had heard even the vaguest imputation of faithlessness, he would have passed it on with glee. Still, the rumours about flirtatious chatter played into Cromwell's hands. Her handsome musician, Mark Smeaton, was arrested on 30 April, tortured and confessed to hiding in the queen's cupboard until she pulled him into her bed after hours. At some point, Anne heard that there were plots against her and she threw herself on Henry's mercy. She seized Elizabeth in her arms and dashed to the king, begging him through his open window to see her and have mercy upon her. Surely, she thought, he could not abandon the mother of his most beloved child. But even little Elizabeth could not move him. The king was angry with Anne and refused her pleas. It was the last time Elizabeth would ever see her mother.

The implication that Anne had enjoyed adulterous relationships with so many was beyond scandalous – and Anne could not come back from it. If Anne had truly conducted such affairs, she would have needed the assistance of her female attendants – as in the case of the ladies sent to the Tower for later abetting Henry's fifth wife, Catherine Howard, in concealing her adultery. But no woman was arrested. Cromwell was aiming for scandal and a quick solution.

On 1 May, the king and queen attended a May Day tournament at Greenwich, but the king left abruptly, without saying a word to Anne, and rode back to Westminster. He had greater matters in hand. The next day, Anne's brother, George, and Henry Norris were arrested, and then four further men: Sir Francis Weston, William Brereton, Richard Page and the poet Thomas Wyatt.

On the morning of 2 May, Anne was watching a game of tennis when she was called to the Privy Council and told of the charges against her. She promised she was the king's true wife and faithful, but it did no good. She was taken back to her apartments to eat with her ladies under guard. At 2pm, the Duke of Norfolk came to take her to her barge for the voyage to the Tower. She was not given time to change or say goodbye to Elizabeth. She hoped that she would be found not guilty or at least simply cast aside, and then she would be able to see her daughter once more. For who would ever execute a queen?

Chapter Seven
'Excluded and Banned'

Elizabeth was at Greenwich Palace, with her household, when everything changed. For in a moment, Anne went from queen to prisoner. In the Tower, she occupied the same beautiful apartments that she had on the night before her coronation – but now she was hysterical with fear and grief. On 17 May, the Archbishop of Canterbury annulled her marriage with the king. Elizabeth was now illegitimate. She was, as the Act of July 1536 put it, 'utterly foreclosed, excluded and banned to claim, challenge or demand any inheritance as lawful heir'.

At the trial, at which her uncle was one of those sitting in judgement, Anne defended herself with spirit, 'giving so wise and discreet aunswers to all thinges layde against her'. Henry shrugged it off. 'She hath a stout heart but she shall pay for it', he declared when he heard the details of the trial.[1] It was a show trial – a foregone conclusion. Henry had already ordered a skilled swordsman from France so that Anne's head could be cut off cleanly – his only act of mercy to his former wife.

She was convicted of treason and sentenced to death. Anne was hysterical after the trial, making awful jokes about her fate – but what else could she do? The king had forsaken her, her daughter had been decreed illegitimate and she was about to die. Henry had little interest in her and spent the period of the trial dallying with Jane Seymour. On 19 May, Anne gave her final speech to the crowds at the Tower. Brave until the end, she praised the king as one of 'the best princes on the face of the earth'. Perhaps she thought that he'd been pushed into it. But more likely she hoped to ensure some sort of protection for Elizabeth. For, as she knew, her daughter would be as reduced and friendless as Mary had been. Henry was busy with Jane Seymour and had not even thought to arrange a coffin for his queen of three years, and she was buried in an old arrow chest. On the day after the execution, Henry announced his engagement to Jane, delighted to be rid of his Boleyn queen. As Chapuys put it with horrible glee, the king had 'the joy and pleasure a man feels in getting rid of a thin, old and vicious hack in the hope of soon getting a fine horse to ride'.[2] He would not wait – the wedding was due to take place in less than two weeks.

No one told Elizabeth, then aged two years and eight months. Her father had ordered that she be kept to her rooms at Greenwich in the immediate aftermath. Henry did not wish to see his daughter – and doing so would have suggested affection for Anne when all his hopes were now caught up in Jane. As with her sister Mary before, the little girl was now Lady Elizabeth, not a princess. She was moved to Hunsdon in the next few days – and her household appeared to be reduced. It seems as if Lady Bryan at first kept the details from her. But Elizabeth was an intelligent child – and she could see that things had changed. As she asked Sir John Shelton, 'how happs it yesterday Lady Princess and today but Lady Elisabeth?' He barely knew how to answer her. It was impossible for her to understand what had happened – children at such a young age who experience the death of a parent tend to ask when he or she is coming back. As she had seen Anne only infrequently, she probably imagined she would arrive to play with her soon enough. Once the news was broken, it was the task of those around her to patiently and repeatedly tell her that this would not be the case.

'Now, as my Lady Elizabeth is put from that degree she was in, and what degree she is at now, I know not but hearsay', wrote Lady Bryan to Cromwell in desperation.[3] In the aftermath of the execution, there were few instructions to Lady Bryan on how to run the transformed household. Moreover, the servants were in confusion and the question of how much money would be received was unresolved. As Lady Bryan continued, she had no idea of the precedence that should be kept. 'I know not how to order her, nor myself nor none of hers I have the rule of – that is her women and grooms.' Mealtimes were chaos with no one knowing what the status of the child was – Sir John Shelton wanted her to dine in state daily but Lady Bryan fretted that if the child did so, 'she will see divers meats, fruits and wine, that it will be hard for me to refrain her from'. Elizabeth was in great distress from teething and everyone was in disarray. Lady Bryan was worried that Elizabeth's income would now plummet and she made the acute judgement that she should try to extract money while she could. She wrote that Elizabeth had no gowns or petticoats, nor smocks or shoes or even nightgowns. Although Anne Boleyn had showered her with clothes, it seems as though they were more majestic than practical. Lady Bryan wanted money as fast as possible – before she was expected to keep an entire household on the pittance due to a bastard.

Elizabeth no longer had the company of Mary. Jane Seymour had been a supporter of the first princess, and the king was now prepared to be magnanimous – although not, as Jane suggested, to go so far as to restore Mary to the succession (the king told her she should focus her thoughts on her own future children). The king invited his troublesome eldest child to court after the execution and gave her presents of Anne's jewels. He gave her back her household, and although it was a joint one with Elizabeth, Mary would be senior as she was the elder. She would be able to remove her own staff from the household if she went to court – and suddenly those who had tormented and beaten her had to curtsey and obey. Jane Seymour had been correct in promising Mary that her troubles would soon be at an end. But it was clear to Mary that if she wished to remain at court, she must bow to Henry's will and accept that his marriage to her mother had been invalid. Initially, she resisted, infuriating those sent to persuade her – two dukes declared that if she were their daughter they would beat her head against the wall 'so violently that they would make it soft as baked apples'. However, perhaps thanks to the influence of Jane, she eventually realised that there was no hope in restoring her mother's position. She agreed to do as Henry wished and also said she accepted Elizabeth – 'I shall never call her by other name than sister'. She was naturally hoping that she might be restored to the succession, with her sister next along from her.

Henry and Jane were married at the end of May 1536, just eleven days after Anne's execution. It was an unseemly marriage, too hasty, but Henry didn't care. He was the king and he was desperate to be married to his Jane.

In October 1537, Jane gave birth. And finally, Henry had all his desires. Jane had given him a healthy son. But she was sick and death followed twelve days later. Henry was saddened, but not stricken with grief. For him, Jane had died in pursuance of the greatest goal of all – giving England a prince and an heir. The country celebrated with fireworks and the king threw lavish banquets. At the grand christening of Edward, Elizabeth was invited to bear his train, although the heavily embroidered material was far too heavy and the Earl of Hertford, the brother of Jane, carried her up in his arms to help her.

The country was thrilled by the child and the king was overcome with delight. Everything he had done had been worth it. God had given him a son. But Elizabeth's status was even more unclear. If she had been Edward's sister, her future would have been simple: marriage to a foreign royal power. But the proposed engagement to the third son of the French king had failed even when Anne had been alive, and now there was even less enthusiasm overseas for the king's illegitimate daughter. When the possibility was raised that she might marry a nephew of Charles V, the emperor 'noted the life and death of her mother'.[4] No one wanted a bastard daughter. Henry's council believed that it would be difficult to marry either sister abroad unless their status was raised to that of 'some estimation at home', a solution Henry would not entertain. It is possible that Henry might have managed to bribe a marriage to a minor royal with a huge purse of gold – but he wasn't willing to do so. All his money was for him, who had been confirmed as the great king by God.

Princesses were expected to be betrothed and, without potential husbands, Mary and Elizabeth were even more reduced in the eyes of the court. Nevertheless, although the king may have been little motivated to address Elizabeth's marriage prospects, he was keen that she should be properly educated. As she herself wrote later, 'the face I grant, I might well blush to offer, but the mind I shall never be ashamed to present'. Much is often made of Elizabeth's unique education by historians – forgetting that the Tudor court was a place of educated women. Henry might have preferred blondes who giggled and said little as mistresses, but he preferred educated women for his wives.

Sixteenth-century women were often told to hide any learning they had from their husbands, and scanty female education was often justified on the basis that learning might scare off potential husbands. But Catherine of Aragon had been educated by her brilliant mother, Isabella of Castile, a woman so powerful and intelligent that she impacted even on the rules of chess – before her reign, the queen could only move one square at a time, but then came her successes. Chess manuals were published enthusing about the power of a queen and new rules created in which the queen piece could range freely across the board. And Mary too had been given much learning. Elizabeth was taught French, Italian, Spanish and Flemish, history and geography, became skilful at mathematics and astronomy, graceful at dancing and riding, and reasonable at music. Embroidery, however, was not a strong point (a failing she shared with Queen Victoria), unlike Mary who excelled at it and would send Elizabeth hand-sewn presents in the hope of charming her. Unlike other girls of her age, Elizabeth also learned Latin and was apparently expert in it by the age of three, although it has to be said that her tutoring was not always systematic in her early years, because her governesses changed – Kat Ashley had joined the household and Lady Bryan was sent to care for the young Prince Edward. However, Elizabeth was delighted by Kat, the daughter of West Country gentry. Elizabeth later said Kat 'took great labour and pain in bringing me up in learning and honesty'.[5] Young and fun, she was very different to the strict Lady Bryan.

Kat became a friend to Elizabeth, when there was otherwise a bewildering procession of ladies at court and stepmothers. First was Anne of Cleves, who arrived from the Netherlands in December 1539 to marry Henry the following month. She was the daughter of the Duke of Cleves and Cromwell had hoped that the match would form an alliance against Catholic Europe. She was twenty-four, sweet-natured and rather tall, but heavyset. Unfortunately, waiting for her as an attendant was the young and beautiful Catherine Howard – and when Henry saw her, he fell headlong in love, aided by how terribly unappealing he found his new wife. The king declared he would have the marriage annulled on the grounds of non-consummation, and his rejected bride should live as his sister. Anne of Cleves had learned from the lives of the previous wives and she knew that resistance was futile – so she gamely accepted the decision, and, in reward, Henry gave her estates, including those that had once belonged to the Boleyns. As time passed, she was invited more to court and given a good position – Henry liked to reward loyalty – and so she came to know Elizabeth and form a strong bond with her and Mary. But for the six-year-old Elizabeth, Anne was just another in a dizzying train of ladies to whom she was told to pay her respects.

Henry, forty-nine, fat and suffering from leg wounds, decided he had to have Catherine Howard for himself, even though she was probably only seventeen or so (we do not have an exact record of her birthdate), younger than Henry's eldest child. Catherine had been a young and exploited girl, and while living with her father's stepmother, the Dowager Duchess of Norfolk, she was groomed and assaulted by her music tutor. Now she found herself catapulted into a marriage she did not want, solely to please her ambitious family. She was fond of Elizabeth – the two might have been sisters, with only a few years between them – and she gave her small presents of beads and jewellery. But then in 1541 Henry declared Catherine had been having an affair and she was sent to the Tower, in the way of her predecessor Anne Boleyn, and executed – although Henry did not give her the grace of a French swordsman and instead she was beheaded with an axe.

Finally, in July 1543, Henry married Katherine Parr. She was well educated, twice widowed, and, as she was in her early thirties, positively mature for Henry's tastes. He was sick and often in pain and made little attempt to produce more children. Katherine took her duties as stepmother seriously. In 1544 the princess Elizabeth gained her own tutor, William Grindal, who was a great scholar of Latin and the classics and had learned under Roger Ascham, and her Latin and Greek was much improved. Elizabeth was also in great favour with her stepmother and knew how to please her with mature discussion of religion and displays of learning. In 1544, she wrote to Katherine that 'Inimical Fortune' had 'deprived me for a whole year of your most illustrious presence'.[6] Katherine was acting as regent for Henry, since he was off on (a failing) campaign in France. She signed declarations, dealt with budgets and was in discussion with the lieutenant in the Northern Marches, the Earl of Shrewsbury, about the relationship with Scotland. Her effective and efficient ruling was a brilliant advertisement for a female monarch – and one that Elizabeth noticed. In 1546, when Elizabeth was nearly thirteen, Katherine had her brought to court to be with her as lady-in-waiting, the first in her household after Princess Mary. Elizabeth was delighted to be at court, surrounded by what she had discovered she loved best: glamour, money, celebration, plotting and power.

Most monarchs hoped to have an heir and a spare, two boys to ensure the throne was secure in the days when terrible plagues could sweep the country and children were the most vulnerable of all. But Henry had done his duty. All hopes for the succession were invested in the little prince – but in 1543, the king decreed that should Edward die without heirs, the throne should pass to Mary and then Elizabeth. It would be impossible, in his view, that Edward should die childless, but his advisors persuaded him to pass an Act, the Third Succession Act, just in case. For in Scotland, a child had just been born with a greater claim to the throne than anyone bar Edward, Mary and Elizabeth.

In the years immediately after the birth of Mary, Queen of Scots, Henry VIII was obese, fractious, sick and suffering from boils on his body and a constantly suppurating leg wound. He found it increasingly difficult to walk and was pushed about in various mechanical contraptions, a sad reduction for such a proud man. He was so at the mercy of his advisors that he nearly sent Katherine Parr to the Tower for suspected evangelical Protestant sympathies – and she had to use her quick wit to escape. Anne Askew, a twenty-five-year-old Lincolnshire noble-woman, was not so fortunate. She had been arrested for heresy and was so tormented on the rack that she had to be carried to her execution at Smithfield because her elbows and knees had been dislocated and walking caused her horrific pain. The interrogators had hoped for Katherine's name or at least those of her ladies, but Anne had refused to implicate anyone, and was slowly burned alive.

Henry's advisors pushed him to make further provision for the succession, after his son Prince Edward. Although his daughters (heirs, but he had not made them legitimate – 'lawfully begotten' was added next to their names in his will, but later crossed out) were the next to inherit after the little boy, the possibility must be considered that all three children might die childless. To Henry, this was pure legalese and he had no expectation of such a ridiculous occurrence – even though he had not bothered himself to arrange marriages for his daughters.

In strict generational terms, the heir after Edward, Mary and Elizabeth was the granddaughter of his elder sister, Margaret, who had married James IV of Scotland – Mary, Queen of Scots. Instead, Henry decided his own heirs, overturning common laws of succession and primogeniture. Mary, Queen of Scots was pushed out of the running. Henry favoured the children of his younger sister, Mary, who had married Charles Brandon, ensuring that the crown stayed English. The will was 'dry-stamped', which has led Mary's supporters throughout history to declare it was problematic and invalid. But as historian Suzannah Lipscombe has shown, Henry assented to the will and it was legal. For him, the idea of Mary, the infant Queen of Scots and future Queen of France, also becoming Queen of England would be a disaster. The country would become no more than a province of France. Little Mary was dangerous and should never be allowed to come near Henry's throne.

Chapter Eight
'A Calm Mind'

On 29 January 1547, thirteen-year-old Elizabeth was at Enfield when she was told her father had died. Her brother Edward had been brought to see her and they received the news together. She was struck with grief, but soon revived herself. Her nine-year-old brother was now her king. He later wrote to her, still kindly, not yet assuming the position of demanding awe. 'There is very little need of my consoling you, most dear sister, because from your learning, you know what you ought to do, and from your prudence and piety you perform what your learning causes you to know.' As he put it, 'I perceive you think of our father's death with a calm mind.'[1] Henry had left provisions that the country should be ruled by the Privy Council until Edward came of age – but he should have known that he was leaving a vacuum, and within three days, Edward, Earl of Hertford, persuaded the Privy Council to appoint him Lord Protector and the habit was so directed towards a one-man rule that there was little resistance.

Henry had hardly left his daughters rich. Both had a meagre £3,000 a year and then, on marriage, each would receive a one-off payment of £10,000 in 'money, plate, jewels and household stuff'.[2] This was a hopeless dowry and it would be impossible to sway any foreign prince to marry either of them for so little – moreover, the council had to approve any husband. And the annual stipend was not enough to set up a household. There were lands and properties that were rightfully Elizabeth's, but she was not given them. Neither was Edward enthusiastic about gifting his sisters more money, and so they had to make do.

Elizabeth went to live with her stepmother, Katherine Parr, in Chelsea. Now, without her father, she was entirely unprotected and prey to those who wanted to use her for their own gains. Mary had invited Elizabeth to live with her – no doubt out of affection for her fellow orphaned half-sister, but perhaps also fearing that Katherine's influence would sway Elizabeth to the reformed religion. Elizabeth preferred Katherine – but she might have been safer with Mary. For the rest of her life, she would have to live watchful, always nervous of who meant to exploit her. Her life at the outskirts of court was an excellent preparation for her future.

The young king was kept under strict restrictions, often feeling as if his pet spaniel was his only friend. Those around him, including his Lord Protector the Earl of Hertford, who had created himself the Duke of Somerset, used him to gain power. But he had strong religious ambitions and he and his council embarked on a set of Protestant reforms. Two years after his accession, the Book of Common Prayer was introduced, a complete form of services in English for daily and Sunday worship and Holy Communion, as well as services for baptism, confirmation, marriage and funerals. Many parts of the country resented its abrupt imposition, and the Act of Uniformity of 1549 made it unlawful to use the Latin forms of service. A group of Devon parishioners decided to march to Exeter to protest against the new book and it was soon a wholesale rebellion. Fuelled by discontent at poverty, widespread enclosure (as the gentry closed off previously common lands for their own use) and spiralling prices for wheat, men shouted for a return to the service as it was in 'King Henry's time' and talked of bringing down 'all the gentlemen'.

The nobles took refuge in castles. The king and Protector sent Lord John Russell with his army to fight in support of the king. After a fierce battle at Clyst St Mary, Russell's forces won the upper hand, leaving around 2,000 rebels dead and hundreds as prisoner. It was said that all these were killed, another 900 in total. More of the rebel fighters were killed at the further Battle of Sampford Courtney. The final death toll was around 5,500 Devon and Cornish men. It is a reminder that history is truly written by the victors that we remember Mary for burning 300 Protestants, but not Edward for punishing his subjects so severely. Such was the risk of fighting against the state of Tudor England – and the Devon and Cornwall men had been ready to fight to the death.

The king's stepmother was still only thirty-five, attractive and the dowager queen. She did not wish to live out the rest of her days in widowhood, especially after a marriage to a man she did not love. After the death in 1543 of her second husband, Baron Latimer, she had fallen in love with the handsome Thomas Seymour, brother of Henry's third wife, Jane Seymour, and Admiral of the Fleet. She hoped to marry him. But unfortunately for her, as she put it, 'God withstood my will therein most vehemently', and instead Henry had fallen for her and chosen her to be his wife.[3] Seymour had been sent to Brussels to get him out of the way. Although she had come to care for Henry and feel affection for him, she was always in love with Seymour and hoped that he might return to her arms now she was free.

Thomas Seymour was a man of frustrated and miserable hopes. Appointed to the Privy Council five days before the death of Henry, he had hoped – like many others – to gain power over the new young king. As one of Jane's brothers, he had pushed the quiet, rather colourless girl into the king's presence, trained her on what to say, and he expected his reward. His blood was in the future king and surely that counted for much. Unfortunately, his elder brother the Earl of Hertford was faster, and gained all the influence. He gave Thomas the position of Lord High Admiral, but that would be all. And Seymour was the type of man to dazzle women but to be rather dismissed as a pretty face by other men. As Nicholas Throckmorton – the future diplomat, who served in Katherine's household alongside Seymour – acidly put it, he was 'fierce in courage, courtly in fashion, in personate stately, in voice magnificent but somewhat empty of matter'.[4]

Seymour, annoyed and resentful, decided to gain influence another way – and that was through Elizabeth. He renewed his suit to Katherine, who was delighted and abandoned her mourning to pursue a full-blown affair. The Regency Council would never agree to Katherine remarrying so soon – indeed, as the dowager queen, she was expected to remain in dignified mourning for Henry VIII for some time to come. But Katherine was utterly infatuated with Seymour, stealing clandestine nights with him.[5] They married secretly, probably in May 1547, less than six months after the death of Henry. Seymour moved into Katherine's handsome house in Chelsea. Kat Ashley, Elizabeth's nurse, was equally fascinated and thrilled by him – and together they threw Elizabeth into the lion's den.

Elizabeth, now fourteen, was vulnerable and lonely and had few friends of her own age. She had been pushed from pillar to post and she was very unsure of her position now her brother was king. She had a small crush on Seymour and blushed when she heard him praised. A better man would have ignored it and behaved as a father to her. But instead Seymour engaged in a cruel and exploitative effort to win influence over a girl who had recently lost her father and was essentially friendless in the world. It started as horseplay and compliments and soon escalated. Kat Ashley entirely lost her reason and began to encourage his attention to Elizabeth, and he began coming into her bedchamber early in the morning and made as if to enter her bed, spanked her and even came into her room barelegged in his nightshirt – which even for Kat Ashley was going too far. Katherine could have stopped it. But in the early stages of pregnancy and perhaps fearing a loss of influence, she turned to aiding him, attempting to tickle Elizabeth alongside him and even holding Elizabeth's arms while Seymour cut her gown to pieces – presumably telling herself all the while that it was nothing but harmless fun.

Although grooming is a modern word, the Tudor world was aware of the concept of men attempting to inveigle themselves into the affections of girls too innocent to understand until it was too late, and society was obsessed with the fact that girls should be untouched before marriage. Catherine Howard had been executed partly because of what had happened to her at the hands of her tutor when she was a young girl, who had testified at her trial that she was not pure. Katherine and Seymour were exposing both Elizabeth and themselves to great danger. Elizabeth was an heir to the throne, and her marriage – and thus her body – was at the behest of her brother and her criminally irresponsible, even criminal, step-parents were committing an act that veered too close to treason. Katherine and Seymour had been given one job: to keep Elizabeth safe. They were doing the exact opposite: risking her reputation and her peace of mind for their own exploitative ends.

Finally, in spring 1548, Katherine discovered Elizabeth alone in Seymour's arms and she flew into a rage. Presumably, she was content enough to sanction dubious horseplay when she was part of it all, but seeing it continue when she was absent inspired her jealousy. Five months pregnant, she wanted to be surrounded by calm and so she interrogated Elizabeth, who used a strategy she would always use in difficult times – saying as little as possible. Katherine ordered Elizabeth out, and sent her to live with Sir Anthony Denny in Hertfordshire, whose wife was Kat Ashley's sister. It was very painful for Elizabeth to be sent away, for it was yet another loss. Her beloved tutor, William Grindal, had suddenly died and it seemed to the young princess that her life was a constant play of cruel and unwelcome change.

Yet Elizabeth being removed from the house, whether Katherine was prompted by consideration for her ward or jealousy of her husband, was a blessing. Away from Seymour's powerful sexuality, Elizabeth began to reconsider her affections, and when Seymour sent her a flirtatious letter, she sent a sharp reply. Kat Ashley still promoted Seymour, and Elizabeth admonished her angrily for the mention of him. As she dwelt on the horror that might have occurred, how incensed her brother and the Regency Council would have been at the goings-on, she grew unhappy and sick and by summer she was in bed with headaches, severe fever and faintness. Like Mary, stress manifested itself on her body. Elizabeth begged her tutor, Roger Ascham, who had recently replaced Grindal, to remain with her all summer and not take the holiday to Cambridge that he had planned. She clung to those who were still with her, afraid of losing yet another friend.

On 30 August, Katherine gave birth to a baby girl at Sudeley Castle in Gloucestershire, the property of her husband. It does not appear that Elizabeth was invited to attend the birth, although various family members were there. The baby was healthy and Katherine looked to be recovering well. Elizabeth received the news when she was too ill to leave her bed and her spirits were so low that even tidings of a healthy baby did not cheer her up. A few days later, Katherine fell ill with the dreaded puerperal fever and died on Elizabeth's birthday, 7 September. Elizabeth was devastated, and her illness intensified.

Katherine's body was barely cold when Seymour started making plans for marriage to Elizabeth. He was fortunate that his wife had died of a childbirth complication that none could deny – because otherwise, people might whisper he had poisoned her for his own ends. Seymour kept his wife's set of ladies intact, for he had plans to replace her with a new royal wife and he was already trying to gather supporters for a coup against his brother, to replace him as Lord Protector. The Lord Privy Seal, John Russell, tried to warn him that a marriage to either sister of the king would be 'his utter undoing', for he did not have permission for it and it would not be granted to him, but Seymour was too bent on power to care.

Kat Ashley was pushing her mistress to bring Seymour back into their lives and she pressed Elizabeth to write to him. She even told Seymour, scandalously, that 'she would her Grace were your wife of any man's living'.[6] He may have promised Kat great riches if she could sway her mistress and he had almost certainly bribed Elizabeth's cofferer or household manager, Thomas Parry, to discuss Elizabeth's accounts and lands. Elizabeth was cautious now, reminding Kat that the king, her brother, and his council would have to agree any marriage. But still, Kat talked about their love as if it was a sure thing – and word began to leak out. Seymour got desperate and, in January, burst into the young king's room to try to sway him to his cause. Edward's pet spaniel barked in panic and Seymour shot it dead. Seymour was promptly arrested and sent to the Tower. The Protector was in no mood to be merciful, and when he heard that his brother had been attempting to marry Elizabeth, as well as trying to seize his own position, all hell broke loose. Kat Ashley and Parry were promptly arrested and likewise sent to the Tower, and Elizabeth was sent to the guardianship of Sir Robert Tyrwhitt, who was instructed to interrogate her. He was confident, he said, that he would make her 'cough out the whole'.[7]

Elizabeth was terrified and very exposed. The gossips said she had been having an affair – and as she well knew, any conspiracy to marry her without the king's permission was treason, and she was in danger of being accused of encouraging it. She did not know the absolute worst of the gossip – that her time in bed after she arrived at Anthony Denny's house was because she was pregnant by Seymour and had either miscarried, or even secretly delivered a child that was whisked away by a midwife. There was no evidence but this did not stop the stories from multiplying, billowing in scandal and bile. When Sir Robert came for her, Elizabeth, still only fifteen at the time, was strong. She agreed that she had spoken to Seymour, but only about business. The relationship had been perfectly decorous and there was no proof to the rumours. If Kat and Parry had had discussions about marriage, she had not been privy to them. She said that she had told him that she could never marry without the consent of the king and that Kat 'would never have me marry, neither in England nor out of England, without the consent of the King's Majesty'.[8] Sir Robert tried to draw blood but Elizabeth was graciously intransigent. She would not give in. She declared that she wished a proclamation would be issued to refute the rumours.

Sir Robert interrogated and demanded but could not find a chink. She was secure in her own virtue. Kat panicked and told everything – even the details of the shocking episodes in Chelsea, much to Elizabeth's distress. But still, the young princess remained strong and said she would never have married or discussed it. Elizabeth had saved herself – but Seymour was lost. He was executed on 20 March 1549 and, despite everything, Elizabeth was deeply pained at the news. Elizabeth begged that Parry and Kat Ashley should be released – and her wish was granted. Indeed, as she had been found essentially innocent, so had they. But they had revealed themselves as being misguided and not good custodians of a princess and so all royal favour for them was at an end. The council decreed that Elizabeth should be overseen by Lady Tyrwhitt, and Kat Ashley was not permitted to return. Elizabeth was to be watched strictly – much to her chagrin. She comforted herself with learning and scholarship with the ever-devoted Ascham and spent her mornings bent over her Greek New Testament and further Latin and Greek literature.

However, fortunately, Edward's favour was still hers – for he was much more preoccupied by their sister's loyalty to the old faith. The king was furious with Mary's insistence on hearing Mass and he told her it was a 'scandalous thing' that she 'should deny our sovereignty'.[9] Mary refused to listen. And so when Mary of Guise, mother of Mary, Queen of Scots, came to court six months after Seymour had been executed, it was Elizabeth who was invited to attend. Aware that the rumours were still circulating about her, she took care to appear in the most modest dress. However, the Seymour disaster had one good effect. The Lincolnshire lawyer and civil servant William Cecil was appointed to look after Elizabeth's lands – a man who would be of crucial importance to Elizabeth's reign as queen.

The perfidy of his brother had driven the Protector Edward Seymour into paranoia and panic. Such was his lust for control that he essentially seized the king and took him to the Tower. It was simply too much for the country and he was pushed out of favour – and John Dudley, Duke of Northumberland, father of the boy who would one day become Elizabeth's great favourite, was the new Protector. Although power-hungry himself, he was a better Protector than Seymour. He both treated the king with kindness and ruled through council, rather than imposing his will.

The advent of the Dudleys was of great advantage to Elizabeth. Edward Seymour would have always feared and resented her, after her association with his brother Thomas. She was invited to court for Christmas and Dudley also granted her the lands and properties that had been due to her on her father's death, including lands in north-west London, and Durham House, to be her town residence – where Anne Boleyn had once stayed while Henry courted her. The new Protector married his son to Amy Robsart, daughter and heiress of a wealthy Norfolk landowner, and the wedding in 1550 was marked by festivities and fun (including the unappealing game of tying a live goose to a pole and cutting off its head).

In spring 1552, the young king caught measles and smallpox in quick succession. After a lengthy and difficult summer tour, he fell ill again with tuberculosis. As Edward lay in bed in the sweltering summer, the prospect of his rebellious sister Mary succeeding him and undoing all his reforms became a present horror. Dudley was equally keen to organise the succession – for he would be thrust out of influence if Mary gained the throne. Edward and Dudley plotted to disinherit both his half-sisters, completely against the wishes of his father, and move the crown to the line of Henry VIII's younger sister, Mary. Henry VIII had ruled that her line should take the throne if all of his children died childless. But the two sisters were still in robust health and Edward and Dudley wanted them expelled from influence.

There was an argument that Elizabeth and Mary were illegitimate, but if so, strictly speaking, the new queen should be Mary, Queen of Scots, granddaughter of Margaret Tudor, Henry VIII's elder sister, the second out of Henry VII's four children. But just as Henry had removed Mary, Queen of Scots from the succession before he died, so Edward now embarked on an even more reckless act and eventually gifted the throne to Lady Jane Grey, elder daughter of Frances Brandon, herself the daughter of Princess Mary, Henry VIII's younger sister. Jane was a Protestant who would, the king expected, continue his religious legacy. Edward threw out both his sisters from the succession – and Dudley rubbed his hands with glee, for as the king sickened, the Protector ensured that Lady Jane was married to his son, Guildford Dudley.

By early 1553, the fifteen-year-old king had grown seriously ill and was in constant distress. Dudley understood that Edward would not last until Lady Jane Grey bore a son and so the document was altered to assent that Jane should inherit the throne. Dudley forced Elizabeth to exchange Durham House for Somerset House, perhaps so he could keep a better eye on her. He fed the king with arsenic potions to lengthen his life, which made the poor boy vomit yet more.

Dudley invited Mary to attend her brother's deathbed – but she heard suggestions that there was a plan to kidnap her and so wisely stayed away. A set of guards was sent to 'secure' her at her home near Hertford, but she got wind of the plot and rode to Norfolk. On 6 July, the young king died and Jane was moved first to Syon and then to the Tower. On 10 July, she was proclaimed as queen to the country. Mary wrote to the council to argue her right, but Dudley continued on his course. What followed was a true David and Goliath battle. Dudley and the council had the wishes of the king in their hands and they controlled the army. Gunboats were moved to the Thames.

Elizabeth was in an impossible position and she did what she would always do in moments of great difficulty. Of course, she hoped Mary would be queen – for this would restore her own position in the succession, and she also naturally resented the council and Edward Seymour for their acts. But Mary could be risking the Tower and execution – and after what had happened over Thomas Seymour, Elizabeth had no wish to be imprisoned again. And so she hedged her bets, neither supporting the council and Dudley nor offering Mary troops. Instead she waited to see which way the wind would blow.

On 14 July, Dudley and his army rode east to force Mary to submit – taking his sons, including Robert, with him. But without his presence, the council's resolve began to crumble. Almost as soon as he left, they began to fear their choice – they were, after all, going against Henry VIII's wish. They were also denying the general rules of succession – and for some, that meant denying God's will. Moreover, the popular will – both in London and across the country – was for Mary. Perhaps if Jane had not been married to Dudley's son, she might have had more of a chance. But to many, Dudley was thinking of himself, would have his son rule through Jane and was bolstering his own power – rather than that of the country.

In East Anglia, the troops began to desert and by 19 July, the council had completely changed its mind. They ordered Dudley to disarm and decreed that Mary should be queen, sending two aristocrats to apologise to her – and she was proclaimed at nine o'clock that night.

Meanwhile, another Mary – Queen of Scots – though aged only ten, was old enough to understand the news from England. Everyone – including her own father – had thrown doubt on the possibility that she could be queen, on a weak female coming to rule. And yet, here was a woman, restored by the people to her rightful place.

The first ever uncontested queen regnant was on the English throne.

Chapter Nine
'Not of Ladies' Capacity'

Elizabeth moved to her London property, Somerset House, and waited for the arrival of her sister Mary. On 31 July 1553, she rode out to meet Mary at Wanstead, dressed in the Tudor colours of white and green, attended by a huge retinue – some said 2,000 horsemen. The queen and the princess returned to London to adoring crowds on 3 August and Elizabeth rode beside her sister in the coronation procession. To the people, the new order was clear: the Tudor queens were back.

But Elizabeth's position was shaky. She had no husband to protect her and she refused to countenance Mary's religious reforms. Mary promptly repealed all the religious acts of the previous reign – and refuted the annulment of her mother's marriage. She was the lawful queen, and hers was the lawful religion. She was crowned in a blaze of glory – and put on the coronation ring, which married her to the nation.

Mary was gratified by her sister's support but she wished even more proof of sisterly affection. She demanded Elizabeth attend Mass. Elizabeth did finally agree, but said she had a stomach ache and did the whole thing with a 'suffering air'. Mary then declared the marriage between Henry and Catherine of Aragon valid once more, reiterating her sister's reduced status. Elizabeth knew she was better off out of Mary's sight – and left in December to live in the country. There was some discussion of Elizabeth's marriage prospects. Edward Courtenay, Earl of Devon, a Catholic descended from Edward IV, had been released from the Tower when Mary came to the throne. Perhaps, the councillors thought, he might marry Elizabeth? But for Mary, the risk that Elizabeth might bear a son who would be a focus of plots attempting to dethrone her for him – even a baby boy was worth more, in royal terms, than a woman – was too great.

Mary was determined to secure the succession. Parliament wished her to marry an Englishman for they feared giving too much influence to a foreign country. Mary was convinced God had ordained her to marry Philip of Spain – and indeed his father, the Holy Roman Emperor, had pressed the suit almost immediately after Mary's accession. He happily informed Mary that she needed a husband 'to be supported in the labour of governing . . . and assisted in matters that are not of ladies' capacity'.[1] Mary believed him and thought in similar fashion – as would her much younger cousin, Mary, Queen of Scots, many years later. The new queen desired nothing more than a Catholic union that would bolster her project of returning the country to Catholicism. But the marriage question threw into relief the unique problems of a female monarch. If a woman was always subject to her husband, then a queen would be subordinate to her husband – and so would her country. Even marrying an Englishman would have plunged Mary into difficulties, for she would seem to be favouring one family over another. Moreover, royals traditionally married each other rather than break the line with ordinary blood, even that of an aristocrat. Mary had resented her father's own marriage to a commoner and was hardly likely to do the same. She wanted Philip. The news was received badly, and when the imperial ambassadors arrived in London, schoolboys threw snowballs at them.

By the first weeks of 1554, there were plans for what became known as the Wyatt Rebellion, prompted by various reasons but notably anger against the match between Mary and Philip: four uprisings – Kent, Devon, Leicestershire and the Welsh Marches – which would then join together and head to London, throw Mary from the throne and crown Elizabeth, with the Earl of Devon installed as a consort. Mary got wind of the plot – and moved to quash it. She summoned Elizabeth to court but the order was refused, with Elizabeth saying she was unwell. Mary rallied her troops in the City, telling them she loved them 'as the mother doth the child'.[2]

But, unaware, Thomas Wyatt set off from Kent and took his men to London to unseat Mary. He was swiftly captured and sent to the

Tower – and was there interrogated about Elizabeth's part in the matter. Thomas Wyatt did admit that he'd written to Elizabeth, but only advising her to get away for the sake of safety – and she had replied via a servant that she would proceed as she thought best. That was almost enough for the investigators – Elizabeth had been seen in conversation with some conspirators, she had refused an invitation to court when the rebellion was imminent, and her name was simply recurring too often. Mary ordered her to court – and this time, Elizabeth knew better than to resist. Unwell with swellings and pain, she entered London on 23 February, declaring that the curtains of her litter should be open so that all saw how ill she was.

After the Wyatt Rebellion, Mary toughened her stance on all the rebels in the Tower. Jane Grey was executed on the day Elizabeth set out for London, and Robert Dudley was put on trial and sentenced to death. It was clear to the investigators that the rebels had dropped hints to the princess and that her household had been in contact with the rebels. But if she had known specifically about the rebellion and assented to it, the evidence was proving hard to find. The conspirators would not condemn her, and Wyatt denied he had told her about the conspiracy. Elizabeth was essentially put under house arrest – and then on 17 March, she was told she was being charged with conspiracy and would be sent to the Tower. The Earl of Sussex and Marquis of Winchester arrived to escort her, and she begged them for the time to write to her sister. She was persuasive and desperate – and they allowed it. But she wrote slowly, and they missed the tide that would carry them by boat – gaining herself another night. She shaded in the rest of the paper, so that no one could add any extra words on what became known as the 'Tide Letter'. She begged her innocence, but Mary would not change her mind. Elizabeth was to be taken to the Tower.

Had Elizabeth wished for her sister to be deposed? She does seem to have known about the rebellion, but not assented to it. She probably heard what was said and did nothing with the information. Life in Tudor England was full of people whispering in corners and plots that came to nothing – and why should this be any different? But the very fact that she might have known something and did nothing was evidence enough, for a truly loyal sister would have gone to Mary with all that she knew.

Elizabeth arrived in the old royal palace of the Tower on Palm Sunday. Mary gave her the royal apartments – those that Anne Boleyn had occupied on the eve of her coronation and then before her execution.

Elizabeth had to save herself from the same fate and she had nothing but her wit. It might well be the case that Mary would have not executed her, at the final stage, for it would have created much anger: it was one thing chopping off the heads of insubordinate nobles, for that was all about power, but Elizabeth was royal, her own sister, and very popular. Moreover, she was a woman – and thus could be excused as not having a true understanding of what was going on. For a woman to execute another of her gender was viewed with disapproval, as Elizabeth later found. After the execution of Lady Jane Grey, Mary might have felt that one woman was enough, and in that case she had obvious proof of an attempt to take the crown. But even if the queen had not had Elizabeth executed, she could have condemned her to a perpetual prison in the Tower or miserable house arrest for the rest of her life.

On Good Friday, Elizabeth's interrogation began. The questioners were insistent on the point that the French ambassador had recorded that the castle at Donnington was being fortified, and Elizabeth was being sent there to await victory. They argued that she had been told to go to Donnington and so she must have known about the plot – and used the evidence that Elizabeth's property there had been loaded with arms and provisions. Elizabeth resisted and although she admitted she had been told to go, and that she had a house in Donnington, she was adamant that she had never slept there. Wyatt went to the scaffold on 11 April declaring that Elizabeth had had no knowledge of the uprising 'before I began',[3] and the interrogators couldn't gain hard evidence. Mary and her council knew that they could not execute Elizabeth without proper proof. And her own feelings were also turning against the deed. To execute a young fellow princess, the other daughter of Henry VIII, was going too far. Moreover, Mary was preparing for her marriage to Philip of Spain. It would look better for her to have her sister by her side, smiling and cheering at the happy news.

In early May, Sir Henry Bedingfield arrived with a hundred guards for Elizabeth. In shock, she asked about the scaffold that had been used for Lady Jane Grey, fearing she too was due to be executed. Instead she was free – but she would have to live in the custody of Sir Henry at Woodstock. On the journey to her new home, she was surrounded by enthusiastic crowds who threw cakes and presents into her litter. Her two months in the Tower had been terrifying and the crowds cheering her freedom were almost overwhelming.

At Woodstock, Elizabeth was constantly watched and not allowed to correspond with the outside world. She chafed under her restraint, complaining to Sir Henry about the lack of everything from an English Bible to a pen. But she felt it was only a matter of time. As she scored onto a window in the house, 'Much suspected by me / Nothing proved can be'. And her servants were still allowed to move as they pleased. Thomas Parry set up offices at the nearby Bull Inn.

In July, Philip and Mary married, and by the end of the month, the Lords and Commons had agreed to return England to Catholicism. Philip was a reluctant husband, unenthusiastic about Mary and angry that Parliament had refused to grant him the crown matrimonial. By autumn, the queen was convinced she was pregnant – and she was utterly thrilled. God was smiling upon her; a Catholic succession would be secured and Elizabeth would be a minor and irrelevant royal for ever.

The queen wanted heretics arrested and executed by burning. John Rogers, vicar of St Sepulchre's and prebendary of St Paul's, was arrested and sent to Newgate, and on 4 February 1555 he was taken to Smithfield to be burned. On the way, he was allowed to briefly see his wife and ten children, one a baby at the breast. On the stage, he was offered a pardon if he would recant. He refused and was executed 'washing his hands in the flame as he was burning'.[4] Thomas Cranmer, who had been Archbishop of Canterbury under Henry VIII, Edward VI and briefly under Mary, was arrested and recanted from Protestantism, brokenly and desperately expressing his eagerness to be a Catholic once more. But even though heretics who recanted should, by canon law, have been pardoned, Mary denied him that grace and he was burned at the stake in Oxford in 1556. She was as hard on those she saw as traitors as her father and brother had been.

The queen's pregnancy continued apace. With her reforms underway and a child in her womb – the ultimate proof that she had been correct – she could afford to be magnanimous, and she wished Elizabeth to be at court when the baby was born. Philip also encouraged her to be lenient on the princess, for if Mary was to die in childbirth and lose the child too, then Elizabeth would be queen and he needed to be on good terms with her. And if Mary died childless and Elizabeth had been executed then the new monarch would be Mary, Queen of Scots, with all of France behind her, and Philip would do anything to resist the growth of French power.

Elizabeth set off for court diplomatically carrying a present of baby linen, embroidered to commemorate the next Tudor heir. She was called to the queen at night and Mary told her off for her refusal to confess. Elizabeth was resolute and said only that she would not say she had been wrongfully punished. She was willing to tell Mary she was her true subject, but no more.

Mary withdrew to her birthing chamber at Hampton Court as was customary, surrounded by her ladies in a shut-up room, hung with the most ornate tapestries and furnished lavishly for the birth of a royal baby. The court waited with bated breath at the end of April – but no child was born. Swollen and in pain, shut up with her ladies, Mary waited for her baby through May, June and July. No baby came and finally, in August, Mary quit the birthing chamber in dreadful humiliation, accepting that no child would come. She found that Philip was not there to give her solace, for he had long since left for Spain, and her misery was compounded. The charitable among her subjects and overseas courts said she had miscarried. Others, as the French ambassador reported, said that it had never been a pregnancy, merely a 'woeful malady' of swelling and sickness.[5] Elizabeth attempted to keep a low profile at court, afraid that Mary would lash out at her. She knew her sister still suspected her of collusion with the Wyatt Rebellion and she dreaded her every move being watched, any common greeting with a courtier or diplomat fodder for misinterpretation.

Finally, in October, Elizabeth was permitted to leave court and return to her own estates at Hatfield, where she could live freely. There, she made the wise resolve to give the impression of passing her days as quietly as possible. She took back Kat Ashley and Thomas Parry, and Roger Ascham arrived to engage in her scholarly studies. Behind it all, however, she was gathering her political allies and considering what she would do if her sister died childless. For she had an unlikely ally in Philip of Spain. He was less interested in religion than politics and he had plans of marrying Elizabeth after her sister's death. As he was a keen Catholic, one might think that he would prefer the throne to go to Mary, Queen of Scots, to ensure religious unity. But, for Philip, Mary was utterly allied with France and if France controlled England, then Spanish ships would not be able to pass through the Channel to the territories of the Spanish Netherlands. Mary of Guise had sent her daughter abroad to marry to ensure her safety, to create a French alliance and ensure French support for her own efforts to keep the Scottish nobles in check. But by doing so, she had ensured that Mary was forever allied with France – and so Philip plumped for Elizabeth, as the lesser evil.

Elizabeth was keeping up a good pretence of living quietly but in 1556 another plot began, with her at the nub. Once more, powerful men with overseas assistance aimed to overthrow the queen and put Elizabeth in her place. When the plotters were rounded up, Elizabeth wrote to the queen protesting her innocence – but her London home, Somerset House, was searched and libellous pamphlets and drawings of Mary and Philip were found. At Hatfield, Kat Ashley, Elizabeth's Italian tutor and two of her servants were arrested. It seemed as if there was some truth in the allegations – the pamphlets did not appear to be have been planted. And, as the Venetian ambassador reported, it looked as though her friends were involved in all the plots. But once more, Elizabeth escaped interrogation. Philip had intervened on her behalf. Indeed, although Mary was confident that she would one day have her own child, the mere possibility that Mary, Queen of Scots would rule the country was almost as awful to her as it was to Philip. Elizabeth might be difficult, rebellious and open in her refusal to bow to the Catholic faith – but at least she was English.

By 1558, poor Mary was growing very ill. Her health had never been strong and two supposed pregnancies that never came to be anything but ghosts had naturally plunged her into distress. A failed campaign against the French, in an attempt to support Philip, had the dreadful outcome of losing Calais, the last continental port that England possessed. Mary never forgave herself and she knew that her people were incensed that she had lost an English possession in an attempt to support a Spanish war. Philip was dismissive and cruel, refusing to spend time with her, even though she wrote to him begging and offering him his favourite cakes. He had long since given up on an heir from his wife and he was turning his attentions to Elizabeth. Mary had believed she was pregnant once more in the spring of 1558, but no one except her had thought it possible.

The young princess, meanwhile, was beginning to sustain and create her networks – with her trusted William Cecil at the helm. London's Somerset House had become the place where she assembled her loyal men and her court-in-waiting – and possibly saw those pamphlets against the queen. The Venetian ambassador had noted that gentlemen in the kingdom were seeking employment in her train and that all eyes were turned to her as successor. She was ready.[6]

On 17 November, Elizabeth received the news. Mary had died, and she was queen. She did not legitimise the marriage of her parents and thus herself. The country had loved the former queen, Catherine of Aragon. But they did not feel the same about Anne Boleyn and so for now, Elizabeth refrained from restoring her mother's status. Being a queen was surely enough, and yet retaining her illegitimacy opened her up to challenge. Particularly from the next in line to the throne – Mary, Queen of Scots.

Chapter Ten
Queen of All Realms

On the death of Mary I, King Henry II of France moved quickly. He formally declared his daughter-in-law Queen of England and Ireland, as well as France and Scotland. Mary was put into mourning for the late English monarch and the courtiers around her told everybody that she was now the Queen. King Henry, however, did not attempt to enforce his claim with military action or even diplomatic moves. Instead, he made constant reference to his daughter-in-law's new position, much to the annoyance of the English ambassador. A great seal was struck for Mary and Francis, referring to them as King and Queen of France, Scotland, Ireland and England. Mary rode under flags bearing the arms of England and had them engraved on her plate, the Queen of England, Wales and Ireland, as well as Scotland.

The King of France was banking on the Pope decreeing Elizabeth illegitimate. As a female heir, she would get little support, a male monarch would be required, and deposition would be simple. But Henry knew that to the Pope he must be the restorer of all Catholic glory, any invasion allowed because it would be bringing back the correct religion. Henry was rattling sabres, threatening England to ensure that France would get what it wanted in any negotiations, whether political or trade. But if Henry was to take the English throne, he needed it to be a two-pronged invasion – and thus Mary of Guise needed to secure Scotland as a Catholic and pro-French country. And unfortunately for him, Mary of Guise had already given a degree of power to the Protestant lords, as a way of crushing the influence of Arran and his family.

Mary was claiming herself as Queen of England and Ireland to please her husband and father-in-law, bringing glory to France as she thought she always must. But she also had long believed the Guise promises that Elizabeth was the illegitimate heretic and she was the true queen. For her, nothing could be more glorious than Scotland, England, Ireland and France, united under one crown. She was not even sixteen, with all the rashness, innocence and wild enthusiasm of youth. What to Elizabeth was a hostile act of war was to Mary a dream of glory.

In the aftermath of her wedding, Mary had been feted and admired. She also had another jewel in mind: in the summer she had been faint and pale, travelled to Saint-Germain for better air and worn the loose tunic that was sixteenth-century maternity wear. She probably was simply suffering from dizzy spells and pain as she often did, but Mary, conscious of the desire to have an heir, turned everyday illness into pregnancy. Plenty of women did the same and it reflects how seriously Mary took her role. Scholars have argued that Francis was too weak to consummate the marriage, but Mary's behaviour shows that at some point he was capable. The Guises would have made sure that Mary's position was as strong as possible, and Antoinette told her about how to conduct the wedding night. And if Francis was sufficiently strong to go hunting, he could have managed the duties of the marriage bed. Unlike most kings, he had a wife he genuinely esteemed and admired. The dream of pregnancy had not succeeded that time, but the couple were young and had time to try again.

The lords who had attended the wedding arrived back and everybody seemed keen to gloss over the fact that men of their number had died on the way home. The mood was one of all praise for the wedding and the great union of peace with Scotland. James Stewart, Mary's half-brother, had made it back safely, luckily, as he was a favourite of Mary of Guise. Supporters were already massing behind him in case Mary of Guise died and he became the next regent.

After the wedding, the French king had considered movements towards peace with the Holy Roman Emperor, after nine years of war. Both sides were heavily in debt. The Guises wished to remain at war, for they had gained much success from it, while Diane de Poitiers and the powerful Montmorency family were supporters of a peace. Discussions dragged on between the countries until a peace between Henry and

Philip II of Spain was signed at Le Cateau-Cambrésis, in northern France on 3 April. Henry was no longer facing a war on multiple fronts, but he had failed to break the power of the Holy Roman Emperor, as he had hoped, and Spain affirmed its control of much of Italy.

Diane de Poitiers and the Montmorencys had won. Diane married off one of her granddaughters to one of the Montmorencys. It was the beginning of the end of Guise influence.

The first year after her wedding was one of the happiest periods of Mary's life. She had been married in a blaze of glory and now she was participating in the greatest and grandest banquets for other court marriages, holding precedence over everybody, save the king and queen and her husband. By the terms of the treaty, Mary's old playmate, Princess Elisabeth, fourteen, would be married to Philip of Spain, eighteen years her senior, as his third wife. No one at the court had great confidence about Philip as a husband, since he was famously unfaithful and had treated poor Mary I with little kindness. But the king was pleased with the magnificent marriage, glistening with power and alliance, and the court threw banquets, jousts and receptions and revelled in the union. Elisabeth was married by proxy at Notre-Dame and the court threw celebrations to commemorate her before her planned departure for Spain in November 1559. Eleven-year-old Princess Claude had already been married to the sixteen-year-old Charles III, the Duke of Lorraine, who had been held at the French court since he was nine, at Notre-Dame in a great wedding and the young couple expected to leave just before Elisabeth. Mary was sad about losing two childhood friends – but she meant to dance, eat and rejoice with them before they departed.

Henry turned his attentions to Scotland and to England. After Lorraine had been so easily taken and pacified through marriage, Scotland would surely be similar. Unfortunately for him, the Reformation was proceeding apace. John Knox had been living and preaching in Geneva with émigrés from England, busily writing his *First Blast of the Trumpet Against the Monstrous Regiment of Women*, about how unfit women were to rule. His target was Mary I but he also meant Mary of Guise and Mary, Queen of Scots. As he put it, 'woman in her greatest perfection was meant to serve and obey man, not to rule and command him'. Nothing, indeed, could be more 'against God' than the rule of a woman, since Genesis had commanded 'he shall bear dominion over thee'. It was 'repugnant to nature' and an insult against God and the 'subversion of all good order, all equity and justice'.[1] In the autumn after it was published, Elizabeth came to the throne, and the émigrés in Geneva began returning to their homes. Knox, too, decided to return to Scotland – although he had a lengthy journey because Elizabeth I was so angered by his *Trumpet* that she refused him a passport. On 2 May 1559, he arrived in Scotland and Mary of Guise immediately declared him an outlaw. She also attempted to demand that all persons should profess the Catholic faith and loyalty to the Pope – and this turned Protestant lords towards the cause of Knox.

Knox and his supporters fled to Perth, where he preached fire and brimstone and a mob rushed out and looted two local friaries. Perth was on the brink of uprising and the whole country could be dragged into civil war. Mary of Guise sent Argyll and James Stewart to negotiate and promised that she would not send French troops if Knox and the others agreed to leave Perth. They did so but Mary sent Scots soldiers who were being paid by France and this, for James Stewart and Argyll, was enough to make them defect. Argyll, certainly, had been looking for an excuse to join Knox, for he had signed the agreement and wished Scotland to be of the new religion. Through her earlier strategy of favouring the Protestant lords as a way of pushing Arran out of favour, Mary had strengthened them. Now, with the accession of Elizabeth in the neighbouring country and the return of Knox and other Protestant preachers, they had the weapons they needed to succeed in their plans.

In France, Mary and her father-in-law were sure that French troops would be able to stop the madness in Scotland. What they didn't understand was that the public mood had moved against the French. The vision of happy unity trumpeted by the poets at Mary's wedding, the idea of the crowns joined together and Scotland happy to be the junior partner – it had all crumbled. For those lords ranged against Mary of Guise, France wished to seize Scotland's independence, subsume it in an act of aggressive Catholicism – and they would be better off allying with Protestant England. When the French had landed troops at Leith, just before little Mary had embarked her ship, they had been met with great enthusiasm. Now, twelve years later, they were seen as occupying forces, the army of oppression.

Knox set off for St Andrews to preach sermons and gangs of people looted the nearby churches and monastic houses. Knox and his supporters moved towards Edinburgh. Many Protestant lords had joined him in a bid to seize power. They called themselves the Congregation.

In France, Mary read the letters and reports and saw that her mother's authority was crumbling. She and her father-in-law were convinced that French troops could force the rebels back. After all, he had just signed a peace treaty with Elizabeth I and Philip II – he had troops to spare. The king continued to celebrate the peace of Le Cateau-Cambrésis and the marriage of Princess Elisabeth with great jousts, banquets and parties. He and Philip II had also agreed a wedding between Margaret, Henry's sister, who had rather been thought on the shelf at thirty-six, and the Duke of Savoy, five years her junior.

In summer 1559, the queen, Catherine de' Medici, had odd premonitions. She saw the king in a joust, his eye pierced by a lance. The king laughed it off. The court was beginning on another round of celebrations for the weddings of Elisabeth, Claude and Margaret. The marriage contract between Margaret and the duke was agreed on 27 June.

On 30 June, at Place des Vosges, in a celebration of the marriage between Elisabeth and Philip, Henry II was jousting against Gabriel, Count of Montgomery. During the joust, Montgomery's lance hit Henry's helmet and in a freak accident, a splinter went through Henry's eye and lodged in his brain. The king collapsed and was carried off unconscious, 'as one amazed', as the English ambassador said, to the nearby Tournelles Palace.[2] The doctors were called. Henry begged for Diane de Poitiers but Catherine de' Medici refused to send for her. He absolved Montgomery from blame and ordered that his sister should be immediately married, in case the duke withdrew from the agreement after his death. Instead of the great wedding at Notre-Dame, there was a miserable midnight wedding near Tournelles on 9 July. Francis and Mary remained by the king but the queen oversaw Margaret's wedding, weeping throughout. The king called the dauphin to him, tried to speak. 'My son, I recommend you to the Church and my people'.[3] But he could not go on and kissed his son. In the early hours of 10 July, as the newly married couple were exiting the church, the king fell into a coma. He died at 1 a.m., hands and feet swollen in pain. The whole court sank into shocked mourning.

Mary was now the Queen of France, and Francis her king. Mary shut herself up in mourning, as she had to do, wearing white rather than black. She mourned with Catherine in their dark, closed rooms. Henry II was buried on 15 August, surrounded by Guise family members, with Cardinal Charles conducting the burial. They were now, as they saw it, the rulers behind the throne. Catherine de' Medici banished Diane de Poitiers to her estates (the mistress helped herself to a good portion of the crown jewels as she left) and the Montmorencys were also excluded. Catherine de' Medici was pushing to expand her influence but the Guise family had the power over the new king and his queen. The English ambassador declared that the Guise brothers were ruling the country, Guise loyalists were gentlemen of the bedchamber and Mary put her aunt and grandmother in charge of her household.

Mary was Queen of France but her mother was losing her grip on her other realm. In Scotland, the death of the all-powerful French king was good news for the Protestant lords. They believed the new king would not have the strength to hit against them and they moved towards Edinburgh and seized all but Edinburgh Castle. By all appearances, Knox was succeeding at thrusting a queen off her throne. Mary of Guise fled to Dunbar. Knox set off secretly to Lindisfarne to negotiate with English officers for troops to come to assist them. When French troops arrived to support Mary, English troops advanced. It was a stalemate. In the end the lords and Mary of Guise signed a treaty at the close of July in which she offered a degree of religious toleration.

The new Queen of France's suspected pregnancy over the summer had come to nothing. But now she had all eyes upon her and a pregnancy: for her child (if a boy) would be next in line to the throne.

In September 1559 Francis was crowned in a poor ceremony, all those attending dressed in black for the late king, except Mary, who was still wearing mourning white. All the other ladies wore black and court mourning resumed on the following day. As at her wedding, Mary cut a striking figure, the white-gowned queen, taller, more beautiful than anyone else. Mary was not to be crowned – it was thought that because she was Queen of Scotland, she need not be crowned as the wife of Francis. She had a brief meeting with her handsome fourteen-year-old cousin, Henry Stuart, Lord Darnley, whose father Matthew Lennox was constantly declaring he should be Mary's heir. Lennox had sent him to the Court, now Mary was queen, to beg for her help in regaining the family estates. Mary gave him 1,000 crowns instead.

In the winter, the family travelled towards Blois to send Elisabeth on her way. Catherine and Mary were heartbroken and Mary sent a letter to Philip as '*Votre bien bonne soeur, Marie*'. For Mary, it had been a year of great loss. Young and trusting, her reaction to the losses was to give too much power to her Guise relations and to trust them to save her mother in Scotland.

Meanwhile, from England, Elizabeth wrote to Mary offering to send a portrait and pledged her affection. Mary wrote back expressing her pleasure at receiving the portrait and told her cousin 'her affection is fully reciprocated'.[4] Mary told the English ambassador, 'The queen my good sister may be assured to have a better neighbour of me being her cousin, than of the rebels.'[5] It all seemed charming. In reality, Elizabeth was plotting to resume hostile military action against Scotland by backing up the Protestant lords. Attacking Scotland would be easier now the great king was dead.

The treaty signed between Mary of Guise and the lords at the end of July fragmented. In September, Arran joined with the Lords of the Congregation as their leader – and essentially declared themselves an alternative government. Mary of Guise fled to Leith, and her secretary, William Maitland, left her and moved to the Protestant side and was allowed to continue in position. Mary of Guise was losing her grip and she was shocked and heartbroken. She had done everything, tried everything.

As spring resumed, the Scots brought men to their cause by complaining about French domination. Mary of Guise's dream of unity was shattered. She had fought so hard for the French union and it had been welcomed with great excitement and congratulations. But now that the memory of English harrying was fading, the Scots saw the French troops at Leith, the French advisors to the court and even Mary's marriage to the dauphin as evidence of oppression. In January, Arran and the other Protestant lords wrote a letter complaining how they had been 'handed and suppressed by strangers and already invaded by fire and sword for the debating of the true ministry of god's word and liberty of this realm'. They proceeded to accuse the French of wishing for their 'wild slavery and bondage' and the 'utter extermination of us and our posterity'.[6] And thus, they had been driven to beg for English support. In February, Arran and the Protestant lords and the Duke of Norfolk, representing Elizabeth I, agreed the Treaty of Berwick, by which Elizabeth would send troops to support the lords in their effort to expel the French troops. English forces would be sent on sea and by land. Elizabeth issued a proclamation, declaring her determination to keep the peace.

The English and Scots laid siege to the French garrison at Leith. Once the symbol of freedom from English tyranny, it was now seen as a foreign occupation. Mary and Francis sent troops to Scotland, along with learned men keen to debate with Scottish Protestants.

But despite his affection for his wife, Francis had his own problems: a rebellion against the Guise control of government had sprung up in Nantes, and when the king retired to Amboise for security, they planned an attack in March 1560. Their coup was betrayed, the Cardinal of Guise demanded terrible reprisals and over a thousand men, most of them Huguenots, were hanged and quartered or drowned in the Loire. The Guises believed there would be more unrest and wanted all the troops at home. They saw Scotland as a lost cause and the Cardinal of Lorraine actually suggested France and Spain ally to crush Scotland, then England. Bewildered, afraid, Mary of Guise and her supporters fled to Edinburgh Castle. She was forty-five and ill with a form of dropsy, barely able to walk due to swelling of her legs, besieged on all sides, not knowing who to trust. The fighting continued throughout the spring. In France, Mary did not understand the severity of the situation: she thought the uprisings isolated rebellions. She wrote an enthusiastic letter to her mother, telling her she would support her, and her husband would do the same – and God would do so too.[7]

In May, the queen regent's forces beat the English at Leith – Knox claimed she admired the men laid out dead over the fields as the 'fairest tapestry'.[8] Still, the English began digging mines towards Leith to gain the town. Mary received the Protestant lords at Edinburgh Castle for a dinner but she was losing hope. The English were ruthlessly determined, working through spies and underground networks. She felt isolated from France, desperately ill and alone, without the resolve or health to fight any longer. On 8 June, she made her will. She called the Lords of the Congregation to her bedside and begged them to understand that she had been trying to protect Scotland in her actions. She soon fell into delirium. On 11 June, she died in her rooms at Edinburgh Castle, without family, as she had been for most of her life. Her ladies, including Lady Fleming, kept vigil over her body in the castle.

Mary of Guise had fought until the end. The English ambassador said she had 'the heart of a man of war'.[9] She had thrown her soul into attempting to keep the country pro-French and Catholic for her daughter and son-in-law. No one could have done more. But it had not been enough.

Chapter Eleven
'A Rash and Hazardous Young Man'

The news of Mary's death was kept from her daughter until the end of the month because the Guises feared she would be greatly distressed. On 28 June, the Cardinal told Mary that her mother was dead and Mary collapsed in grief and mourning for the woman she had not seen in nine years. Funeral rites were held on 12 August but it took some time to have the body sent to France.

After Mary of Guise's death, the Protestant lords moved in to govern and negotiate with the English and French for the withdrawal of all foreign troops from Scotland. This peace, the Treaty of Edinburgh, was punishing to the French and to Mary. Her country would be governed by the Protestant lords. She also had to agree to accept Elizabeth's title and claim to the English throne. Mary would not try to claim England and Ireland – they were Elizabeth's. She must no longer claim English arms and insignia. To add insult to injury, Francis and Mary were told that if they failed to abide by the terms of the treaty, England was once more empowered to threaten Scotland and intervene. By this point, Elizabeth could afford to be magnanimous and declared that Mary's 'injurious pretensions' to her throne could be laid at the door of the ambitions of the Guises, rather than Francis and Mary, who were 'very young'. Mary and Francis had been entirely excluded from any chance to expand their power into England.

The treaty decreed that the council of nobles would govern in Mary's place. And swift upon the heels of the treaty came more laws issued by an assembly of Parliament in August: the lords abolished the Pope's jurisdiction, banned the celebration of Mass (punishable by death) and began the Scottish Reformation. Parliament agreed to pursue the marriage of Arran's son, James, to Elizabeth I – an unlikely event – but it made their import clear: England was the ally now. Although there was still much Catholic feeling among the ordinary people, Mary was suddenly a less desirable queen. The mood of the country was changing and Mary had been left behind. The nobles who had supported her mother moved towards the monasteries, sacking them and taking their land.

Mary was still courageous – when she met with Elizabeth's ambassador, Throckmorton, she refused to express her assent to the Treaty of Edinburgh, instead saying it was up to the king. As she said, 'I pray her to judge me by herself for I am sure she could ill bear the usage and the disobedience of her subjects which she knows mine have shown unto me.' Mary emphasised how everything had been done against her will. 'My subjects in Scotland do their duty in nothing', she said. 'I am their Queen and so they call me but they use me not so.'[1] She would not ratify the Treaty of Edinburgh or agree with any of the acts of the Congregation Lords. The Reformation Parliament had been enthusiastically received, but not ratified. Elizabeth was on alert. William Cecil, now forty and the queen's ever-loyal advisor, detested Mary, was convinced she wished to overthrow Elizabeth, and thought of her as a danger to England.

At some point in the autumn of 1560, Mary received a visit in Paris from the Scottish noble James Hepburn, 4th Earl of Bothwell, twenty-six and spoiling for adventure. Gruff, not handsome and barely polite, but possessed of a forceful, magnetic personality to which it was hard to say no, the man who would change her life and tear it apart was the Lord High Admiral and had recently sailed around Europe. Already, he showed signs of cruelty. In Copenhagen, he had met a Norwegian noblewoman, Anna Tronds, and probably married her. If so, the marriage was not successful, and Bothwell demanded she sold her possessions because he was so short of cash. He set off to the French court and was kindly received by Mary and Francis, most likely because they knew he was a supporter in Scotland of the late Mary of Guise. As he recorded, 'The queen recompensed me liberally and more honourably than I had deserved.'[2] That might be a motto to fit his whole life and relationship with Mary. Throckmorton was deeply worried by Bothwell's visit and told London that spies should watch him for he was a 'rash and hazardous young man'.[3] He soon set off again but would be back for a visit in the spring. Mary was, as a fault, too loyal and laid too much emphasis on the relationships of her youth. It was fate that she met Bothwell in France, for those Scots she met early in her life remained indelibly important to her. When most of the lords had committed great treachery against her and driven her mother to illness and death, Bothwell seemed different: loyal and devoted.

Even though the rebellion at Amboise had been ruthlessly routed, Francis still feared he would be kidnapped and killed. There were complaints in the Grand Council that his guard was too numerous and was a division between him and his people. He, Mary and Catherine moved away from Paris in the hope he would be safer in the countryside at Orléans. There, the young king went hunting, encouraged by the Guises who wanted to govern without his interference. The weather was damp and freezing but still the king hunted, hoping to improve his strength. On Saturday 16 November 1560, Francis returned from hunting with a dreadful earache and fainted the next day in chapel. He collapsed in bed, sick and feverish. Mary and Catherine took up constant vigil at his side. The Guises lied to the court and the ambassadors, telling them it was a minor chill. The Spanish ambassador was refused entry to the king's chamber and the rumours that the king was dying began.

The king was racked with shocking fevers, swellings and pain. Holding his hand in his darkened sickroom, Mary tried to comfort her childhood friend and husband through the tyrannies of the disease. Her Guise uncles shouted at the doctors to do more, making everything more nervous and strained, pushing the doctors to do unnecessary treatments, bleeding him excessively and forcing him to purge and vomit. The king needed calm and to be made comfortable, but they did not even give him that.

By 27 November, Elizabeth's ambassador was writing to her that the king had ruined his constitution with hunting and he was unlikely to live. Mary could not leave his side and exhausted herself nursing, making herself ill but refusing to rest. Francis needed her and she knew he was in danger. The swelling on his face was particularly severe – and then it moved towards his brain. On 3 December, he was so ill that the doctors paused their bleedings. Two days later, he collapsed unconscious and Mary sat by his side, clutching the hand of a man who no longer knew she was there, wiping his brow, hoping against hope he would recover. By the evening of 5 December, the king was dead, not yet quite seventeen. His heart was taken in a lead vase to Saint-Denis, where it was placed on a pillar surrounded by flames carved out of stone.

Mary was devastated at losing her husband and childhood friend. 'Her unhappiness and incessant tears call forth general compassion', wrote the Venetian ambassador.[4] She wore white and fled to a darkened room lit only by torches as she mourned for her allotted forty days. She wrote a broken little poem:

Wherever I am out
Whether in forest or meadow
Whatever time it may be
Whether dawn or evening
Without end, my heart still feels
The pain of who is lost.
As I am at rest
Sleeping on my couch
I feel that he is near
I feel that he touches me
In work or repose
He is always near me.[5]

Francis had been her friend since she was four, and then her husband. They had been always together, enjoying a golden childhood in the royal nursery, surrounded by their pets, married in glory, the marvel of the world. In the space of little over a year, she had lost her mother, her father-in-law, both sisters-in-law to marriage overseas – and now her dearest husband. In her mourning chamber, wearing the white that had been so glorious at her wedding, she abandoned herself to paroxysms of grief.

The new king was now Charles IX, aged only ten, Mary's old playmate, the little boy who had once been mooted as a husband for Elizabeth. Catherine de' Medici, so long pushed out of influence by her husband's mistresses, finally gained power as regent for her son.

She immediately demanded the return of the crown jewels from her daughter-in-law.

Mary was no longer the queen.

All of Henry's work and plotting, the secret treaties and the late-night discussions, had been directed towards Francis outliving Mary, the possibility that she would die without heirs. Instead, Francis had died, almost without warning, and Mary's certain and glittering future as Queen of France was smashed to pieces.

For the first fifteen days, Mary was too heartbroken to receive anyone and guests were restricted only to those of great rank. Catherine de' Medici was also grieving but she was manoeuvring and working for position. She wished to thrust the Guise family out of power. Mary was in a precarious position, no longer wanted at court for she was a reminder of the old influence. As one court observer said, she was 'widowed, has lost France, and has little hope of Scotland'.[6]

By the terms of Mary's marriage contract, she was permitted to remain in France and keep a position at the French court after her husband's death. She had received estates in Touraine and Poitou as part of her marriage jointure, so she could have theoretically gone to live there, in rural exile like Diane de Poitiers. But Mary was fundamentally a court soul and her ambition was to live out a royal life. She needed a powerful husband (it was unfortunate that Philip of Spain had just married Elisabeth), a ruler who had an army to back her up in Scotland. For now that Mary of Guise was dead, the lords were ruling as they wished.

Mary wrote a careful letter to the Scottish Lords and Parliament suggesting she wished to return and asked for the royal accounts accrued since her mother's death. She told Throckmorton that she intended to return to the country of her birth, at the request of her subjects.

After Mary's first fortnight of grieving was over, she was expected to receive ambassadors – and all of them were keen to suggest suitors for her hand. As Throckmorton declared to the council, only three weeks after the king's death, as 'the Scottish queen is left a widow, one of the special things your lordships have to consider, and have an eye to, is the marriage of that queen'.[7] Various royal men were mooted, including the kings of Denmark and Sweden, and Philip II's heir – or even the new king, little Charles. Mary told Throckmorton at an interview on New Year's Eve that she would be guided by advisors. The ambassador thought her interest in wise advice excellent. 'I see her behaviour to be such and her wisdom and kingly modesty so great, in that she thinketh herself not too wise but is content to be ruled by good counsel and wise men (which is a great virtue in a Prince or Princess, and which argueth a great judgement and wisdom in her).'[8] The 'her' was important. Back in England, Elizabeth was showing herself anything but biddable.

After Mary had completed her forty days of mourning, locked up in her dark room, dressed in white and writing poetry, she attended a service for the king's death at a convent in Orléans and took occupation of a nearby palace with her grandmother, Antoinette. Henry Stuart, Lord Darnley, fifteen and already taller than Mary, arrived to express his sympathies. He was something of a wunderkind, said to be very clever, a superb horseman and skilled at hunting, good looking and charming. Moreover, he was a Catholic. His parents staked everything on his brilliance and golden good looks. He was Mary's cousin through his mother, Margaret Douglas, daughter of Margaret Tudor, daughter of Henry VII and former Queen Consort of James IV. He was in line to the throne after Mary and, arguably, as a man, was more desirable – in other words he was a direct threat to her ambitions to get the throne of England (and Wales and Ireland). Mary had already met him before Francis' coronation. Then, his parents had been hoping he might charm Mary into restoring the family estates. Now, they wanted her to see their (very) handsome son and think of marriage.

But the widowed queen was not to be swayed by anything but a great foreign power – as Throckmorton fretted, 'she more esteemeth the continuation of her honour and to marry one that may uphold her to be great'.[9] Catherine de' Medici would never allow her to marry the new King Charles. And so Mary set her sights on Don Carlos, Prince of Asturias, fifteen-year-old son and heir of Philip II with his first wife, Maria of Portugal, who had died in 1545. Carlos was barely healthier than Francis had been, but he marked the possibility of a great alliance, and her Guise uncles threw all into promoting it. The Spanish ambassador made lengthy visits to the young widow. Everything seemed to be progressing marvellously. But no one had reckoned on Catherine de' Medici. The Queen Regent wanted to get rid of Mary as quickly as possible – but she didn't want her marrying Philip's son. Her own daughter, Elisabeth, had not yet had a child and Don Carlos was Philip's only offspring at this point. Ideally, for Catherine, he might die off, and then Elisabeth's child would be heir. But if Don Carlos had a child with Mary, Elisabeth's position would be much reduced. Catherine wrote to Elisabeth asking her to push Philip towards marrying Don Carlos with her own sister little Marguerite instead, even though she was only seven. For Philip of Spain, Mary's marriage to his son had too high a price to pay: his young wife, of whom he was very fond, did not wish it and he expected it would mean he had to send troops to Scotland to restore Mary. Elizabeth I was against it (she didn't want Mary backed up by Spanish power) and Marguerite might be a better ally.

Elizabeth sent an official embassy of condolence to France in February and Mary received the Earl of Bedford politely and praised her cousin queen for 'showing the part of a good sister, whereof she has great need'. Unfortunately for Mary, in the following meetings Bedford demanded she ratify the Treaty of Edinburgh. Mary, grieving and isolated, was still courageous and she refused, stalling and saying she must speak to her council. She suggested also that she and Elizabeth should meet personally to talk and thus 'satisfy each other much better than they can do by messengers and ministers'.[10] She was not unwilling to ratify the treaty, but she wished for Elizabeth to give her a gift in return: to declare her heir to the English throne.

Mary was increasingly unwelcome at the French court. Catherine de' Medici was manoeuvring to exclude her at every possibility and so she set off to make some extended travels and visits to her Guise relations. She visited the convent of her aunt Renée at Rheims, where her mother's body finally arrived. Away from the French court, she was visited by John Leslie, Bishop of Ross, who told her she was needed by the Scottish Catholics and she should come to Scotland, where he would have 20,000 men waiting to restore her by force. Leslie struck a poetic argument, telling her she would be like a newly risen sun, dispelling the clouds that had come across Scotland. She was also visited by her illegitimate brother, James Stewart, son of her father and Margaret Erskine, who had been one of the men accompanying her to France when she had first left the country of her birth, and after his return to Scotland had become a key member of court and a leader of the Protestant Reformation. On the way to visit Mary, he had met Cecil in England and made various promises. Not long after his arrival, James Stewart told Mary to become a Protestant. She refused but did make a concession: she said that if she came back, she would celebrate Mass in private. On the way back, James visited Throckmorton and told him everything Mary had said, and was rewarded with gifts of money for himself, Arran and others of their supporters.

James Stewart thought he could control Mary and inch her towards Protestantism. Despite all Elizabeth and Cecil's fine words, the Scots lords were deeply distrustful of England and Mary's claim to the throne might act as an excellent ballast against further English aggression. And if Mary was content to celebrate Mass in private and support the Reformation in public, then who could complain?

Mary continued on her peregrinations and visited Claude, the twelve-year-old Duchess of Lorraine. The city gave her a beautiful reception but Claude was not friendly, presumably because she too had been told to work against any marriage between Mary and Don Carlos. The duchess had once been great friends with Mary, but now, as with all the remaining French royal siblings and their mother, the happy relationship of intimacy was over. Mary was no longer useful and could limit any future alliances that Catherine de' Medici and the new child king might want to make. For poor Mary, the end of her friendship with a little girl who had once looked up to her felt like a dreadful betrayal, the final straw. Nothing could make Mary's much-reduced position more obvious to her. She was not wanted, not liked, not respected. The Guises, particularly her uncles, were no longer so interested in her, the court was focused on the new king and Catherine, and now Claude, had little desire for her company either. Mary fell ill with nervous exhaustion. When she finally recovered, she returned to the French court with her mind made up. It was her duty to go back to Scotland. No one seemed to esteem her in France and no marriage alliance was forthcoming. And, for Mary, a woman of great religious faith, God had created her Queen of Scotland and so His will must be respected. James Stewart sent a letter on 10 June requesting her return and it was an irresistible invitation. She began to practise the Scots language, asking those around her who knew it for help. She told Throckmorton she believed Knox the most dangerous man in the kingdom – and she was half right.

On 18 June, Throckmorton asked again for Mary to ratify the Treaty of Edinburgh. She told him that she would deal with the matter when she returned to Scotland, which she soon expected to do. Still, Mary wanted Elizabeth to make two concessions: to withdraw the proviso that she could interfere in Scotland and make Mary officially her heir. If Elizabeth gave this concession, Mary would be in a position of great strength.

Mary had lost everything: no longer Queen Dauphine of France, out of favour and influence at the French court, and her country in the hands of Protestants. She was determined to return herself to power. And yet the lords had been used to governing themselves as they pleased. The Scottish Reformation had been set in train by Parliament. They wanted a figurehead, who would rubber-stamp their decision. Mary wanted to rule. The stage was set for a battle of wills.

Chapter Twelve
'I Will Never See You Again'

Mary was eighteen and about to embark on becoming a queen regnant, ruling in her home country for the first time. She had no understanding of Scotland and little memory of it. It was to her a foreign country. The nobles, vivified by complicated family loyalties and conflicts, were very unlike those she had known in France: they were driven above all by the fight for family power and unlike the French lords, they refused to pretend.

Mary planned her departure. Elizabeth denied her application for a safe-conduct pass until she ratified the treaty and Mary set off without it. She told Throckmorton politely that she had travelled safely between Scotland and France before and would do so again. As she said, 'I am determined to adventure the matter, whatsoever come of it; I trust the wind will be so favourable as I shall not need to come on the coast of England'. If she did, she was ready for the worst, and declared dramatically that if Elizabeth 'be so hard-hearted as to desire my end, she may then do her pleasure and make sacrifice of me'.[1] She told a rather stunned Throckmorton that she was leaving the matter up to God.

Mary's Guise uncles did not try to dissuade her from going. Instead, the Cardinal suggested Mary might leave her jewels with him for safe keeping. Mary refused but did give her beloved grandmother a handsome necklace of diamonds, rubies and emeralds – as the only Guise member who had been truly kind to her.

On 8 August, Mary sent another request for a passport. Arrangements were made for her ships. Unfortunately for Mary, James

Bothwell, still Lord High Admiral, had come to assist with arrangements, along with the Bishop of Orkney and Lord Eglington.

On 14 August 1561, Mary's transport was assembled for the journey that might take a week or so. She would be accompanied on her boat by the four Marys, retrieved from the Priory, a second boat carrying her other staff. Ten more ships were packed up with her things; tapestries, gold, plate, gowns, jewels, paintings and animals and forty-five dismantled beds. As they left, a ship sank in front of them, killing all the sailors, and the party was devastated. Still in mourning for her husband, Mary burst into tears as she sailed away to her new life and cried over and over, 'Adieu France. I think I will never see you again.'

Mary spent the journey back in very low spirits. Her incredible courage, so strong as she had prepared for her journey, deserted her. The fear of the unknown, the new land ahead of her, and what she had left behind struck deep at her heart. Elizabeth had actually sent a message that she could have safe conduct, but it had arrived too late for Mary to see it.

Mary progressed swiftly, so fast that they arrived at Leith on Tuesday 19 August, in advance of expectations and Holyrood Palace was not yet ready for her. The port of Leith, so long fought over while Mary had been in France, was intended to be the first stopping point in a reign of peace and unity. She dined at a house there and then a party of lords, including Argyll and her half-brother, James Stewart, came to escort her to Edinburgh. Everything that Mary said, James would report back to Cecil's men. James had failed to persuade Mary to become a Protestant but he and Cecil both hoped that she would be malleable, and allow James to push forward the Protestant Reformation.

James Stewart, thirty to Mary's eighteen, had always been in the inner circle of power. Mary of Guise had even considered making him regent in place of Arran. He was clever, well spoken, a skilled fighter and entirely unscrupulous. He had an excessively solemn manner and a face that always looked dour at rest, though this worked to his advantage. Foreign ambassadors thought him a man of great gravitas and intellectual capacity, more driven by law, reason and religious faith than passion and ambition − when the reverse was entirely the case. Unlike Mary, he knew the way to work with the lords: divide and rule, do not tell the truth and always think of your own advantage. He did not always tell her what he knew or suspected – but at this point, he was by her side, her great supporter. Still, he meant to manipulate her, a mere woman who knew nothing of Scotland.

The people of the country were delighted to see her. They sang and lit hundreds of bonfires as she made her way to the royal apartments at Holyroodhouse – the palace had been laboriously rebuilt and repaired after it had been burned down by the English in 1544. Mary's new home had originally been an Augustinian abbey and the abbey guest house was probably first used as a royal residence in the fourteenth century, and over the following century dedicated royal apartments were added. When James IV came to the throne, he built a new palace next to the abbey in order to house him and his new bride, Margaret Tudor, sister of Henry VIII, around a quadrangle, with a chapel, new royal rooms and a great hall. He even added a lion house to display his incredible menagerie. James V rebuilt the palace in symmetrical Renaissance style, renovated the north-west tower to add brand-new royal apartments and converted the chapel into the council chamber. He transformed Holyroodhouse into a full, working royal residence, with an armoury, the mint, a forge and huge kitchens meant for entertaining.

Holyrood was hardly Fontainebleau or even Saint-Germain, but the palace was large and well appointed – and it was all Mary's. She took the apartments that her father had rebuilt in the north-west corner: a large presence chamber, a sizeable bedroom and two small rooms, a dressing room and a supper room. Her ladies tried to make them homely and in the morning, six hundred amateur musicians lined up under her windows to play music to welcome her.

The four Marys were greatly pleased to be out of the convent and finally preside at a court. Mary Fleming was always the senior, for she was Mary's actual kinswoman, as a half-cousin, and she was pleased to be reunited with her mother, although only briefly for Lady Fleming departed to France within a few days, hopeful of advancement for her son, now Diane de Poitiers was firmly out of favour. Mary Fleming, only a few months older than her queen, was sweet-natured and a generous friend – Mary later took her as her bedfellow after the shocking Chastelard affair. Mary Beaton was the prettiest of the Marys, a fair-haired and merry girl, who captivated the men at court, and she and Mary enjoyed playing cards and games together. Her handwriting was oddly similar to Mary's – and Mary may have used her to write letters at times. Mary Livingston was gay and fond of dancing. Mary Seton, who remained with Mary for the longest, because she never married, was the closest of the four to a lady's maid, she helped Mary dress and she was skilled at arranging and styling Mary's magnificent hair.

Mary began decorating her apartments. All her life, she loved beautiful surroundings and fine dress. When an inventory was taken of her clothes in 1562, there were sixty gowns (fewer than Elizabeth's thousands, but still plenty), many of gold and silver or expensive velvet. Mary liked white or black – she preferred simpler designs to Elizabeth – but she also had gowns of crimson, orange, yellow and blue, many of them beautifully and intricately embroidered. Mary knew that she was expected to be the most well-dressed and magnificent woman at court and she had grown up in one of the most fashionable courts in history. But, like many queen regnants, Mary liked to sometimes dress as a man and dressed at least once in this way to lead her army.

She kept an intricate record of her marvellous clothes and incredible collection of jewels. Many of them had been given to her, but she also bought her own from Edinburgh jewellers, including beautiful Scottish pearls, of which she was particularly fond. She most often wore rubies – a striking contrast against her white gowns. In her collection, she had necklaces, rings, bracelets, belts, earrings and golden caps on her furs. One of her pendants – rubies, diamonds and emeralds set in gold and enamel – was engraved with a serpent coiled around the tree of life and the words '*vie et mort*'. She held tight to her jewels from her mother and those given to her in France by the king and the dauphin, reminders of the childhood that had been lost for ever.

Mary brought in a court that had entertainments and masques focused on women and queens – her Marys would sometimes dress as historic queens for the enjoyment of the court. But under all the beauty, grace and festivity, the court was a place where masculine power was fighting to be resurgent. Mary was surrounded by men. And they were all jostling for control, using her to get power in whichever way they could. She trusted James Stewart and made him her chief advisor. The advice he gave her was usually in his own interests and he always reported back to the English, who were as keen as ever to see him push forward the Protestant Reformation, and might have given him further financial reward – as we know they did for his efforts to persuade Mary towards supporting the Reformation in early 1561.

After James Stewart, Bothwell and the elder Arran, the nobles who had the most influence over Mary's life and who recur most in her story were Huntly, Argyll, her secretary Maitland and James Douglas, Earl of Morton. Argyll, at twenty-eight, had only just succeeded to the earldom after his father's death in 1558. He had married Mary's half-sister, Jean Stewart, daughter of James V and Elizabeth Bethune, in 1553 – and this was a powerful alliance, for Jean had been brought up at the court of Mary of Guise and would be a companion to the Queen of Scots. Argyll was a keen Protestant and he was an admirer of John Knox and a strong ally of James Stewart. But he also had loyalty to Bothwell, who had attempted to help his father claim his position on baby Mary's council, provided for by James V in his will but denied by Arran. George Gordon, 4th Earl of Huntly, was a member of the Regency council and had accompanied Mary of Guise to France. He fell out with Mary, Queen of Scots when she gave his historic title of Moray to her half-brother, James. He died in 1562, and so it was his successor, his second son, also called George Gordon, who would have the impact on Mary's life: he was a great ally with Bothwell, and married his sister to him, and would be one of the men to sign the fatal Craigmillar bond.

The Earl Morton was around forty-four when Mary arrived in Scotland, part of the large and territorial Douglas family, a man of great family loyalty and a lot of energy and intelligence. Tall, with gingerish hair and beard, he had a pale complexion and wasn't much of a fighter – he was the type better suited to writing a strategy behind the scenes. He had been no supporter of Mary of Guise, had strong Protestant sympathies, and signed the Treaty of Berwick to expel the French troops and fatally undermine her. Now, if he were given the choice between James Stewart and Mary, Queen of Scots he would choose James Stewart. William Maitland, whom Mary appointed her Secretary of State, was intelligent, hard-working and probably the nearest the queen had to a loyalist. All of them would shape her future – James Stewart most of all.

On Mary's first Sunday in Edinburgh, she heard private Mass with her servants and attendants. The priest attending trembled as he conducted the service.

Mary pronounced that she would keep religious matters as they were – and issued a declaration that there should be no change to the state of religion that she had found when she arrived in Scotland and that her French servants and attendants should be allowed to keep their religion. This seemed an excellent idea and the kind of reasonable announcement that Elizabeth I has been congratulated for – it was very close to Elizabeth's own pronouncement that she would not look into men's hearts. But the fact that she heard private Mass was too much for many of the nobles. The ever-furious Knox declared that one Mass was more awful than ten thousand foreign soldiers landing in the country. Most of the lords had been disposed to give Mary a chance – but to Knox, forty-seven to her eighteen, she was the enemy, another one of the 'Monstrous Regiment'.

For Mary, there was too much history, division and hatred close at hand. She had seen her arrival in Scotland as a new start. But to the Scots, they could not see her rule free of the horrors of the past years, with the battles at Edinburgh and Leith, the deaths and wars over religion. The lords laid these miseries at the door of Mary of Guise and her daughter was blamed as a matter of course. Yet Mary proved herself once more a measured and excellent queen and invited Knox to a meeting. Initially, there was a rapprochement and when Mary challenged him about his tract on the Monstrous Regiment, Knox said he would not condemn Mary on the grounds of her sex alone. Certainly, some aspects of his pamphlet were coming to seem rather rash – Elizabeth was so offended by it that she had refused to allow him to be part of the negotiations over the Treaty of Edinburgh and it was very unlikely she would offer him sanctuary in England or even safe passage if he returned to Geneva. But if Knox had softened his position on female rulers now he was surrounded by them, he was still resolute on religion. If Mary retained the Catholic faith, it was against the true word of God and her subjects could be allowed to rise up against her.

Mary was infuriated by Knox but not unduly upset. Her people were still delighted by her and greeting her at every opportunity. She was convinced of the rectitude of her principle that the current religious status should continue and she should worship privately as she wished. And many key leaders of the reformation, clerical and noble, strongly disliked Knox's message of uprising. Scotland had suffered enough bloodshed.

At the beginning of September, Mary sent a diamond shaped like a heart to Elizabeth and staged a full triumphal entry into Edinburgh, with pageants and an angel descending from a mechanical cloud with the keys of the city for the new queen. It was a vision of pure harmony, but the lords were already fighting behind the scenes. She had appointed her sixteen-member Privy Council and although it included both Protestants and Catholics and representatives of noble families, it wasn't enough. For the noble families, James Stewart, Maitland and Bothwell had too much power.

It was arguably impossible to govern between the factions of lords and Mary did her best. Her great mistake in these early days was not sending back her French attendants. She was fond of them and relied on their counsel, but as far as the Scottish lords were concerned, she was actively excluding them and their relations from court positions. Naturally, at only eighteen, she wanted a gay, beautiful court of French elegance like the one she had grown up in.

Mary's other problem was that her crown, unlike Elizabeth's, was impoverished. James V's coffers had been much reduced and some lords had helped themselves to what was left after Mary of Guise's regency. The income was a paltry £18,000 in Scots money. If she wanted to go to war, she would have to convene Parliament and ask for rises in taxation – never a popular request. She simply could not afford war. Another mistake was listening too intently to James Stewart. He was her half-brother, he was familiar with Scotland, feared, respected, powerful. He was naturally fond of a half-sister. But she was also a block to all the things he wanted: a Protestant reformation and power over the country.

The queen set off to visit her birthplace and her mother's old home at Stirling – and tried to attend high Mass in the Chapel Royal where she had been crowned. James Stewart stopped it – she was allowed to hear Mass only at her chapel in Holyroodhouse.

Mary still refused to ratify the treaty. James Stewart begged Elizabeth's pardon that Mary had ever made designs on her throne – and she was persuaded to be merciful. She agreed that both sides could appoint commissioners to review the treaty and consider the future.

Mary thought she had won over Scotland – and she wanted England. She hoped to pay a visit to Elizabeth. Unfortunately, Elizabeth had changed her mind and decided Mary should ratify the treaty as it was. She did not wish to declare Mary her heir in case this led dispossessed

English Catholics to gather around the Scottish queen. According to the Catholic Church, Elizabeth was a heretic and, as the daughter of the shocking Anne Boleyn, illegitimate. Mary, however, was truly royal, the bearer of real Tudor blood.[2] Elizabeth could not afford to give her anything. 'Princes cannot like their own children', she told Mary's envoy, the experienced administrator, William Maitland, bluntly. 'Think you that I could love my own winding-sheet? How then she shall I, think you, like my cousin being declared my Heir Apparent'. Moreover, as she said, she knew the 'inconstancy' of the English people, how 'they mislike the current government and have their eyes fixed on the person that is next to succeed.' She was right to say that people tend to prefer the 'rising than the setting sun'.[3] Mary was the rising sun in Scotland and the English found her popularity over those she ruled disturbing.

Mary had asked for her 'cousin's' portrait, but Elizabeth still hadn't sent it, prevaricating that the artist was ill. Nevertheless, Mary was still convinced that if she and Elizabeth met and spoke together, face to face, without advisors interfering, then they could reach a settlement.

And Elizabeth had to choose someone to be her heir for, no matter how much she proclaimed her health, the court fussed over who would come next. Someone had to be the 'winding sheet'. The sisters of the ill-fated Lady Jane Grey, Katherine and Mary, were still threats and would have been Elizabeth's heirs, had she died, since Henry had enfranchised the children of his sister, Mary. They were also seen as the ideal Protestant solution. Elizabeth disliked Katherine, the eldest, in particular and 'could not abide the sight of her'.[4] Queen Mary had been fond of the girls and given them positions (and Katherine had nearly married the scheming Earl of Hertford), but Elizabeth had them dismissed as ladies-in-waiting and installed them as lower maids of honour, who would get little time with the queen.

Elizabeth stated early that she did not wish Katherine to succeed her – and Katherine was furious and openly dissented against her queen. However, when Mary had declared herself Queen of England back in France, Elizabeth had suddenly became kinder to the Grey sisters, bringing Katherine back to the bedchamber and calling her 'her daughter'. As one observer put it, 'the queen has thought it best to put her in the chamber and makes much of her in order to keep her quiet. She even talks of formally adopting her.'[5] Unfortunately, Katherine gave the outward mien of being a dutiful daughter to the queen, but she was still in love with the Earl of Hertford, son of the Protector of the late Edward VI and nephew of Jane Seymour. Elizabeth would never have agreed to their marriage, for they had a joint claim on her throne and if they produced a son, then his own claim would have been so strong that people might wish her deposed for him. But Katherine was in love and wouldn't listen and secretly married Hertford. By marrying in secret, as both the queen's cousin and her Lady of the Bedchamber, Katherine was taking an impossible risk – for the act was treason. She fell pregnant but then Hertford decided he was going to France, probably because he had begun to panic about what he had done. He had always been the less enthusiastic of the pair; he had charmed Katherine with seductive words because he dreamed of how powerful the marriage might make him. He rather forgot in the haze of power-hungry passion that the queen would see his acts of love as terrible, even treasonous, works of disobedience. Katherine begged him to return but he did not, for he valued his head. By the time she was seven months pregnant, she was desperate, unable to hide her condition for much longer. She pleaded with Robert Dudley to intercede for her – he went to the queen, and she was furious. Katherine was sent to the Tower and Hertford was summoned back and also arrested. Katherine's only hope was to give birth to a girl, who would be no threat. But on 24 September, Katherine gave birth to a boy. Elizabeth had the Archbishop of Canterbury annul the marriage, so barring the child from succession.

Elizabeth's fury with Katherine Grey made her more sympathetic to Mary, Queen of Scots – but not much. Mary was a true queen, and Elizabeth was always a great respecter of royal blood. Really, as the queen had told Maitland, she didn't want to hear any talk about her successor at all. This was somewhat difficult, given she was choosing to play the role of the Virgin Queen. Mary, however, remained convinced she could win over her cousin by speaking to her, and she humorously said she would have no husband but Elizabeth. Mary sent her a friendly letter in which she said that she valued Elizabeth's advice above that of any other prince. She asked once again for the meeting, saying, 'If God will grant a good occasion that we may meet together . . . we trust you shall more clearly perceive the sincerity of our good meaning than we can express by writing'.[6] She also sent some charming and flattering poetry dedicated to the queen. In January 1562, Elizabeth wrote to say she did not object to a meeting and in May, Mary gained the council's agreement, brushing aside their concerns for her safety if she was to enter England. But the English council declared such a meeting would be too expensive. After all, two queens could not simply meet up for a chat over embroidery. It must be a great festival and celebration, planned meticulously, with banquets and receptions – rather like the meeting between Francis I and Henry VIII at the Field of the Cloth of Gold in 1520. Despite these objections, York was proposed and Elizabeth sent Mary a letter that she liked so much that she put it in her dress, next to her heart.

Matters were looking optimistic and a meeting was mooted for high summer, when travelling would be easiest. Cecil had even decided that his mistress might be able to persuade Mary to adopt the reformed religion and certainly thought it would end the historic alliance between France and Scotland. But terrible events in France changed everything. The Duke of Guise ordered his men to fire on a Huguenot meeting in Wassy and over sixty worshippers were killed. Hostilities between the two sides mounted, but on 25 June a peace treaty was signed in France and courtiers in England resumed planning the great banquets that would mark the meeting of two queens. Cecil organised the safe passage to England for the Scot queen. But then fighting in France began once more in early July and it seemed impossible that Elizabeth should go travelling into the north of England, when she might be needed at any time to discuss sending troops to France to support the Huguenots there.

Mary was told that the meeting would be postponed for at least a year. Mary was heartbroken, took to her bed and wept in misery. For she was right in her hunch that she would have been able to press on Elizabeth's heart if they met. But the queen's advisors were dubious and she too worried about giving too much favour to a Catholic queen. In the end, the power balance was writ too large.

For Mary, the meeting with Elizabeth was of vital importance, a strong demonstration of both her own position in the succession and her statesmanship. But for Elizabeth, it was a minor matter – with Scotland largely considered neutralised, her attentions were on her own court, Spain and the French wars of religion.

In the autumn of 1562, Elizabeth had a bout of terrible smallpox. She recovered, with scars that could be covered with make-up, but her faithful lady, Mary Sidney, who had nursed her throughout, was left shockingly, as her husband said, 'as fowle a lady as any smale pox could make her'.[7] Mary hoped that the illness of the queen would bring the question of succession to the forefront but although the Privy Council wished to see a successor named, they did not wish the lucky soul to be Mary. Cecil was as mistrustful as ever and declared that the risk was that the Guises would 'build their castles so high' and make themselves so great that they would push Elizabeth off the throne for Mary.

The Guises gave Mary more trouble than anything else. Her grand-mother Antoinette had supported her and her mother had tried her best, but her Guise uncles remained power-obsessed – and now, by fuelling the wars of religion, they were throwing their niece into insecurity. With Protestants being killed in France, Elizabeth was under pressure to be tougher on Catholics in England and showing favour to a Catholic queen was suddenly highly unpopular. Cecil, too, was focused on the Guises. And on the question of Mary, Cecil was vividly preoccupied. On 11 January 1562, he attempted to remove her from the succession with the Act of Exclusion, seemingly with his mistress's assent. When she heard the news, Mary was close to nervous collapse and confined herself to bed for nearly a week. At every move, she was being outplayed by Elizabeth and Cecil. Mary had had enough. She had become obsessed with being declared Elizabeth's heir, believing it would prove her royal blood and quell Knox and the others who spoke against her. But ever since she had arrived in Scotland, Elizabeth and her advisors had prevaricated, escaped her grip. Mary was begin-ning to fear that she could no longer rely on the bonds of blood with her 'sister'. It was time to seize her position in the succession – and she would find a husband to help her do it.

In early February, James Stewart married Lady Agnes Keith, a bright and determined young woman of twenty-two he was lucky to have: she had royal blood for she was a descendant of James I and although attractive rather than beautiful she had great wit, spirit and political nous. The wedding took place at Holyrood and the queen threw three days of fine banquets and parties, dancing, eating, drinking and laughing to celebrate the marriage, much to the chagrin of John Knox. She also gave her half-brother the title of Earl of Mar and Earl of Moray. George Gordon, Earl of Huntly and previous holder of the title of Moray, retired to his Highland estates in protest.

The lords pretended unity but there had already been fighting. At the end of the previous year, a drunken Bothwell had tried to enter into the house of James Hamilton's mistress, Alison Craik, broke the door and a fight ensued with the Hamilton party the next day. It was hardly the polite formality of court that Mary had been used to in France. Fortunately, James Stewart and Argyll managed to put down the disruption and Mary sent Bothwell to his castle for two weeks. But she refused to have Bothwell and the others tried for their crimes – and there were complaints that Bothwell was a favourite and gaining unfair preference.

James Hamilton and Bothwell agreed to bury the hatchet but Hamilton had been distressed by the affair and seemed to be losing his grip on reality. As Elizabeth's ambassador, Thomas Randolph, put it, he was 'drowned in dreams'.[8] He said to the queen that he and Bothwell had been plotting to carry her off to Dumbarton Castle, where they would treat her however they wished until, as he said Bothwell planned, she agreed to whatever they demanded and would submit to them and then the two of them would take over government. Arran, his father, rushed to say it was all invented by Bothwell to discredit the Hamilton family and shut up his son in a spare castle to stop him from talking further. Lord James Stewart demanded them both arrested and Bothwell accused him of feeding lies to the maddened James Hamilton to repeat. Both men were locked up at Edinburgh Castle, James Hamilton in mental distress, Bothwell imprisoned without trial. Arran wept and begged Mary to ignore the ravings of his son. Mary was shocked that a noble whom she considered a friend would treat her so but she was unsure of who to believe. It was easier to tell herself that Bothwell had been set up.

Had Bothwell truly been plotting such a thing? Probably. Late at night, fuelled by alcohol and bravado, lords did speculate about kidnapping Mary and seizing the government. In the summer of 1562, Mary took a tour to the north-east of Scotland and was received graciously by the Earl of Huntly's wife at Aberdeen. But Huntly was still angry over the loss of the Moray title and as the queen left Aberdeen, Huntly's son, Sir John, started following her and threatening violence. Mary heard that if she stayed at the family stronghold of Strathbogie, there was a plot to kill her escorts, the new Earl of Moray and Maitland, and seize her until she agreed to marry Sir John. When she arrived at Inverness Castle, it was blocked against her, on the orders of Huntly, and she and her supporters had to fight for access. The queen declared him an outlaw and he was captured in October 1562 and his possessions taken by the crown and given to Moray. He died not long after his capture and Sir John was executed – his second son, George, took the title and was, despite this history, loyal to Mary and Bothwell in future.

It was not just the Scots nobles who thought that capturing and assaulting Mary was the way to glory. On Saint Valentine's Day 1563, one of Mary's French courtiers, the twenty-two-year-old poet, Pierre de Bocosel de Chastelard, was found hiding under her bed by two grooms. She had him sent from court but when she travelled to St Andrews, he burst into her bedroom and attempted to attack her, when she only had a few women as protection. She cried out and Moray rushed in to find a man in his sister's chamber. He captured him and Chastelard was promptly executed, wishing adieu to the 'most beautiful and most cruel princess' as he died. Mary took Mary Fleming to her bedchamber as protection.

Such was the great difference between Elizabeth and Mary. No matter how much Elizabeth's nobles detested her or reviled her plans, they would never indulge in late-night chat about sexually assaulting the queen into submission and seizing the government. It would be a horrific crime, reviled by the public at large, and would never gain them the assent of the people. If the English nobles were to attempt to overthrow Elizabeth at all, they would do it by military force or legal action, seen as the proper way. But Mary was vulnerable and, as in the case of so many women at the time, a woman without a husband was fair game. Even though she was a queen.

Bothwell escaped captivity in August, fled towards France and was forced to abandon ship in Northumberland, where he was captured. After he was released from imprisonment, he remained in Northumberland, working for Mary in secret, much to the distress of her close advisors. James Hamilton did later collapse into insanity, not helped by four years of chained, solitary confinement. Unfortunately, this meant Bothwell's threat to kidnap the queen was believed to have been entirely fabricated – a great mistake.

Surrounded by kidnap threats, the nobles at war, keen to have an heir, Mary wished to marry. But who was sufficiently strong to intimidate Elizabeth? The Guises suggested Mary take Archduke Charles of Austria, third son of the Holy Roman Emperor, Ferdinand I. Her uncle started negotiating with him in secret. Mary rejected him for being too close to Elizabeth and having already asked for the English queen's hand. She still wanted Don Carlos and the powerful support of Philip of Spain, even though she knew Catherine de' Medici would do all she could to stop such a marriage. John Knox was flung into fury and gave an emotive speech to the Scottish Parliament about the dangers of marrying a Catholic, announcing that Mary was betraying her reign and it would end in sorrow.

When Mary called Knox to her and demanded he justify his behaviour, he repeated his accusations and she was so shocked by his rudeness that she burst into tears. He shrugged that he had no choice, speak or 'betray my Commonwealth through my silence'.[9] Knox had initially given Mary the benefit of the doubt, seeing her popularity with the people and aware that he could hardly flee to England, since Elizabeth was angry about his writings. While the uneasy concord between Protestants and Catholics lasted, he held back from putting on his passionate anti-queen one-man shows. But the question over Mary's suitor plunged the Protestant side into a whirl of action and Knox was leading the way. It seemed that the biggest problem for a queen was whom to marry. And she had to marry. Scotland would never have accepted Mary setting herself up as the Virgin Queen.

Chapter Thirteen
'A Stone of Marble'

'Everything depends on the husband this woman may take',[1] wrote the Spanish ambassador, not long after Elizabeth had ascended to the throne.

The Archbishop of Canterbury, Cardinal Pole, had died twelve hours after Mary I. For many, it seemed like a sign that the old Church was in its death throes.

Elizabeth had done everything she could to disassociate herself from her sister's disasters. Although she ordered a splendid funeral and a procession with a life-size effigy of Mary on the coffin parading through the city, she wanted to make clear to her people that her reign would be different to that of Mary. As Elizabeth had added to the epitaph about her sister: 'Marie now dead, Elizabeth lives, our just and lawful queen / In whom her sister's virtues rare, abundantly are seen.'

And in every way, Elizabeth was gaining revenge for her own humiliation during the reign of her father and for the horrific treatment of her mother. She exploited the legacy of Henry VIII, identifying herself as sharing his strength and magnificence at every opportunity. But whenever she could, she showed herself as the inheritor of her mother. Anne's emblem had been the white falcon and Elizabeth brought it front and centre to the pageantry of her glittering coronation. Her palaces became ornamental aviaries, tributes to the white falcon, which appeared on everything from furniture to swords.

Robert Dudley, on behalf of the new queen, consulted the philosopher Dr John Dee about the best date for her coronation. He reported that his astrological charts suggested 15 January 1559 would ensure a reign of glory and success. It did not give them very much time. The queen desired the most splendid and lavish coronation possible as a reward for her supporters and a warning to her enemies. Despite all the hot air and outrage expended on Spain, the real threat came from France. There lived Mary, Queen of Scots and her claim to the throne. French diplomats had been trying to push the Pope to declare Elizabeth a bastard – which would leave the way open for the Queen of Scots to claim the throne. Philip of Spain was blocking this attempt for he hated France and still hoped to gain ascendancy over England. But Elizabeth could not rely on Philip's fear of France lasting for ever and, after the actions of her father, the Pope could still choose to declare her illegitimate. She needed to get herself anointed and onto the throne as quickly as possible. John Dee was simply telling his queen what she wished to hear. As one of her subjects stated, 'in pompous ceremonies a secret of government doth much consist, for the people are both naturally taken and held with exterior shows'.[2]

Robert Dudley, overseeing the coronation, devoted himself to turning the city into a pageant of colour and devotion for the new, twenty-five-year-old queen. As one visitor noted, somewhat astonished, 'They are preparing here for the coronation, and work both day and night, on holidays and weekdays.'[3] Customs officers had even prevented all sale of crimson cloth that entered the ports – until the queen had acquired what she wanted, everyone else would have to wait. The royal coffers were ransacked to buy gold, silver, velvets and satin, decorations, costumes, horses and to plan pageants – and it all came to over £17,000, a staggering amount. The city was made anew – tapestries were hung on buildings, triumphal arches were erected, the streets swept and covered in new gravel. Seven hundred yards of blue cloth was used to make a carpet all the way from the abbey to Westminster Hall. Mary's coronation robes were altered to fit her more slender sister, and Elizabeth planned her other elaborate coronation outfits.

On 12 January, Elizabeth was taken from Whitehall to the Tower by boat. She was accompanied by the mayor and aldermen in barges glittering with decorations, thousands watching as she made her way. Two days later, her ladies dressed her in a dazzling robe of twenty-three yards of gold and silver cloth, overlaid with gold lace and adorned with ermine, and put a gold cap and princess's crown on her head. With 1,000 mounted dignitaries, Elizabeth climbed into a great chariot

Right: Originally married to Louis of Orléans, Duke of Longueville, Mary of Guise was a desirable prize for a European monarch after his early death – both Henry VIII and James V asked for her hand.

Below: 'It will end with a lass'. Mary of Guise was James's second wife and she bore him three children during their marriage, although their two sons died young on the same day. Mary, Queen of Scots was their surviving child.

Left: Daughter of the Scottish king and the powerful Guise family of France, great-granddaughter of Henry VII and great-niece of Henry VIII, Mary was of the highest possible birth.

Below: Henry VIII was determined to have an heir, and in the end had three children, all of whom went on to reign after his death: Edward VI, Mary I and Elizabeth I.

Left: Although Elizabeth's father was initially fond of her, she spent a large part of her childhood living on a knife-edge, removed from the succession, constantly at risk.

Below: Dauphin Francis had weak health, but he was kind and affectionate and his marriage to Mary was happy.

Left: A portrait of Mary, aged around thirteen. 'It is not possible to hope for more from a Princess on this earth.'

Left: Mary's Book of Hours and rosary. Mary infuriated her keepers by refusing to give up her rosary and crucifix while imprisoned – and she held tight to her crucifix when she was sent to her death.

Below: Elizabeth knew she had to make her mark as queen, and her coronation in 1559 was an expensive public display of her royal lineage.

Below: Elizabeth's mother-of-pearl locket ring, dating to around 1575. When closed, the ring shows 'ER' in diamonds. Underneath them, secretly, are paired portraits of Elizabeth and Anne Boleyn, the mother she could never acknowledge.

Left: Mary at about eighteen. Six feet tall, red-haired and beautifully dressed, Mary was striking and regal. But her robust looks belied a delicate health; she was often tormented by sickness, stomach problems and muscle pains.

Above: Smallpox was frequently a deadly disease, and Elizabeth's recovery from it in 1562 was seen as a blessing to be celebrated. Various medals were struck to commemorate her survival.

Above: Mary turned Holyroodhouse into a graceful and beautiful court – and yet it became the location of some of the most horrific scenes of her life.

Above: James Stewart, Earl of Moray was Mary's half-brother, her trusted confidant and friend. She trusted him too much.

Above: Robert Dudley, Earl of Leicester was brilliant, witty, handsome and always by Elizabeth's side. Mary was outraged by the offer of him as a husband.

Above: Lord Darnley aged seventeen or eighteen – handsome, charming and entirely corrupt.

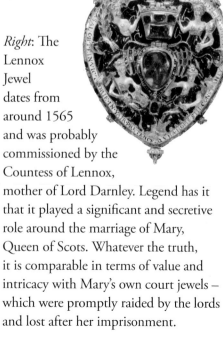

Right: The Lennox Jewel dates from around 1565 and was probably commissioned by the Countess of Lennox, mother of Lord Darnley. Legend has it that it played a significant and secretive role around the marriage of Mary, Queen of Scots. Whatever the truth, it is comparable in terms of value and intricacy with Mary's own court jewels – which were promptly raided by the lords and lost after her imprisonment.

Left: Mary promoted her musician, David Rizzio, to the post of secretary, much to the fury of the court. He was suspected by everybody and the consequence was a murderous plot.

Below: In a complicated and violent world, Mary hoped her bedchamber and adjoining rooms could be a place of peace.

Above: Rizzio screamed and held onto Mary's skirts but the conspirators dragged him away. One held a gun to the queen's womb.

Left: Despite the trauma of Rizzio's murder, Mary gave birth to a young boy, James, in 1566 and her messenger rode post haste to give Elizabeth the news.

furnished in white satin and gold damask and sat back on the enormous satin cushions. The queen thanked God for giving her the throne, and for dealing 'as wonderfully and as mercifully with me as thou didst with Daniel, whom Thou delivered out of the den from the cruelty of the raging lions'. The litter set off through London, accompanied by her guards in crimson damask, ladies in crimson and gold, musicians in red uniforms, privy councillors in satin – and footmen in red velvet jerkins bearing the initials ER and the Tudor rose.

There was a light dusting of snow across the city – but the streets were crammed. All along the route the city staged allegorical tableaux. In each, a narrator stepped forward as the queen approached and recited in rhyme what the actors represented – each scene was meant to show the queen vanquishing the old world of division and strife under Queen Mary. The first speaker was a child attempting to utter welcoming verses – but they struggled to be heard over the crowd. The queen asked for silence and listened to the child attentively 'as if the child's words touched her person'.

There was no subtlety in the pageants. The first was on a platform showing the Tudor dynasty – supported by actors representing Unity and Concord, Elizabeth herself at the top. At the bottom were Henry VIII and Anne Boleyn. The new queen left it in no doubt – Anne Boleyn was no longer 'the Great Whore' but the rightful consort of Henry the king. At Cornhill, a child played Elizabeth on the Seat of Worthy Governance while other children acted as the virtues; one, Good Religion, defeated the vices of Ignorance and Superstition. The city had done everything possible to please the new queen. At every stop, Elizabeth watched with fascination and declared her delight in the show. At one tableau, a child offered her a Bible, reciting verses about how to change a ruined state into a great empire. Elizabeth kissed it and thanked the city warmly for it, 'promising to be a diligent reader thereof'.[4]

Elizabeth was keen to show her appreciation of all those who cheered for her. Unlike her sister, who had been painfully stiff and shy in crowds, she waved and often stopped the chariot (somewhat to the despair of those accompanying her, who had hoped for a quicker progress through the chill) to speak to ordinary people along the way or accept small gifts of flowers – she kept one sprig of rosemary, a present from a poor woman, beside her for the entire journey to the Palace of Westminster where she retired, content with a task brilliantly executed.

Despite the show of unity, there had been division behind the scenes – over religion. It had been customary for the queen to celebrate Mass in her private chapel on Christmas morning, at a service given by the Archbishop of Canterbury. But Pole had not been replaced since his death in November and the Archbishop of York, who suspected Elizabeth was a Protestant, refused to fill in. The Bishop of Carlisle reluctantly agreed to conduct the service. Elizabeth wrote to him demanding he did not include the part of the service known as the elevation of the Host. This went to the heart of the wars over religion. The moment when the bread and wine became the body and blood of Christ was for Catholics the most sacred part of the service, the great miracle of transubstantiation, which Protestants denied.

The bishop ignored the request and conducted his service as usual. As he started to raise the bread and wine, the queen told him to stop – much to the shock of the onlookers. The bishop carried on – and the queen was incensed. She marched from the chapel, making her feelings clear. In the following weeks, the bishop was not invited back and instead clergymen willing to follow Elizabeth's strictures conducted the royal service. Three days after the Christmas fiasco, the queen issued a proclamation that the Epistles, the Ten Commandments and some prayers were to be read out in English, although the rest of the service would be in Latin – as had essentially been the case in the reign of Henry VIII. This situation would remain until after the queen and Parliament had decided on measures 'for the better conciliation and accord of such causes as at this present are moved in matters and ceremonies of religion'.[5] But it was clear which way the wind was blowing – the queen, in the eyes of the bishops, was a Protestant sinner. The Archbishop of York refused to crown her and other bishops agreed. Carlisle was again pushed into doing it – but he had one condition: the coronation service should be conducted in medieval Latin. Elizabeth agreed but she would not give in entirely – the Epistle and the Gospel would be read in English. For English Catholics, this was enough provocation to cause them to gather behind any other claimant to the throne who might uphold the true faith – and that was Mary, Queen of Scots.

On 15 January, her coronation day, the queen emerged from Westminster Hall to the sound of all the bells in London and the pipes and drums of her musicians. She was more resplendent than ever in her coronation robes and a silk mantle, a crimson velvet cap adorned with pearls and gold on her beautiful red-gold hair. She processed along the blue carpet to Westminster Abbey – and as soon as she passed, the crowd fell on the material, tearing at it to get a souvenir of the coronation. All the peerage of note and councillors had been waiting in the abbey for hours, under the flickering lights of hundreds of torches and candles.

The queen pointedly retired when the bishop began raising the Host – much to the delight of the Protestants in the audience. She took the Coronation Oath from an English Bible held up by William Cecil – but did promise that she would be 'Defender of the True, the Ancient, Catholic Faith'.

On the chair of state before the altar, she heard herself proclaimed queen four times. When she was presented for the acceptance of her subjects, there was an incredible clamour of shouts and applause, along with bells, trumpets and organ music. She retired to change into a gown of crimson velvet, over which she wore a mantle of gold. Then came the climax of the ceremony – the ring that married her to her people was placed on her fourth finger. She was then crowned, first with St Edward's Crown and then the Imperial Crown (all seven pounds of it!), which was then replaced with a smaller crown – possibly the one worn by Anne Boleyn at her coronation.

Elizabeth walked triumphant from the abbey to Westminster Hall, sceptre and orb in her hands, smiling and greeting those lining the route. She and her peers sat down to the huge coronation banquet from three in the afternoon until one in the morning. The queen's champion, Sir Edward Dymocke, rode in to the banquet and flung his gauntlet onto the floor, declaring he would fight any man who doubted the queen's right to the throne.

It was a delightful piece of theatre – engaging and a chance for those there to cheer. But although no one stood up, the queen was surrounded by enemies. Her coronation had been a triumph of pageantry, display and Tudor romanticism, yet the problems of religious division were already surfacing, and even though everybody in the hall clapped their queen, some were secretly plotting against her. One Mary – her sister – was dead. But another – her cousin – was watching the throne.

The queen had received the consecrated (indeed, transubstantiated) bread and wine, but in private, where no one could see. She had been anointed by the same oil as her sister, who had acquired it from the Bishop of Arras. Elizabeth thought it greasy and unpleasant. 'Likewise for their holy oil, it is great superstition to give credit to it, or to any such feigned things invented by Satan to blind the simple people.' As far as Elizabeth was concerned, the best use of the stuff was in cooking. 'Their oil is olive oil, which was brought out of Spain, very good for salads.'[6]

On the day after the coronation, the queen retired to bed – suffering from a cold. The pageants continued without her. She had done her duty.

'And in this end, this shall be for me sufficient, that a marble stone shall declare that a queen, having reigned such a time, lived and died a virgin.'[7] Such were Elizabeth's words to her first parliament in 1559. Her audience probably thought that she was simply aiming to increase her value on the marriage market. She may have been born on the eve of the Virgin's birth – but no woman remained a virgin out of choice, unless she was a nun. Women were meant to marry, for they were too weak and simple to govern themselves alone, let alone a realm.

One of Elizabeth's earliest visitors had been the Spanish ambassador, who breezily suggested she had gained the throne through Philip's influence. Not discouraged by the queen's reaction, he then conveyed a marriage offer from Philip, who, eternally arrogant, made the considerate offer of relieving her of 'those labours which are only fit for men'.[8] She turned him down, but clever as always, played the card of modesty and restraint, for she could not afford to lose his support. But even though her subjects had no desire to see her marry Philip, they expected her to marry *someone*. Elizabeth needed a husband to ally with her and fight for her. Edward Dymocke and his gauntlet could only go so far. If Elizabeth did not marry, she would be at the mercy of her enemies and the country would be lost.

Characteristically and cleverly, Elizabeth put off the decision and devoted herself to pomp and glory.

As in the coronation, Elizabeth put on the greatest show on earth. 'She lives a life of magnificence and festivity such as can hardly be imagined, and occupies a great portion of her time with balls, banquets, hunting and similar amusements with the utmost display', declared one rather overwhelmed envoy. The 'court of Queen Elizabeth was at once gay, decent and superb' said another.[9] But although the glitter and the sheen was there, it was meretricious – what was underneath was shaky and threatened. Elizabeth was surrounded by enemies. Many around her wished to push her aside and put a man in her place and her greatest threat was France. For there, King Henry II had only one desire – to bring England to heel as subservient state. And his daughter-in-law, Mary, although she was only sixteen, wanted the same. For, unlike Philip of Spain, she had a legitimate claim to the throne.

Elizabeth knew that most in Catholic Europe saw her as illegitimate, and not the rightful queen, and the royal supremacy had to be restored. Mary's religious legislation was repealed and the Act of Uniformity passed. The Book of Common Prayer was now the book that all should follow (it was similar to the 1552 Book brought in at the end of Edward's reign, with some changes) and Mass was now illegal. The Act of Supremacy declared Elizabeth Supreme Governor of the Church of England. She was Governor and not Head – for there were objections a woman could not be the latter. Elizabeth's opinion was that as long as her subjects obeyed her and attended the services of her church on Sundays, their private thoughts and feelings could be as they wished. As she famously said, she did not wish to 'open windows into men's souls'. Her ministers did not always agree with her, judging her naïve about the Catholic threat.

The queen had dodged the marriage offer of Philip of Spain with skill (and she was most relieved to see him married off to Elisabeth of Valois) – but she could not escape the issue of being wed so easily. Everybody, it seemed, was telling her to marry. As she herself later said, there seemed to be a 'strong idea' that 'a woman cannot live unless she is married'. Even her loyal William Cecil – who surely recognised that his influence would be reduced if his mistress took a husband – was proposing marriage as the 'only known and likely surety' for both the queen and the realm. In that first parliament of her reign, she was implored to marry to secure the succession, told that if she were to remain 'unmarried, and, as it were, a vestal virgin'[10], she would be deeply unpopular. Elizabeth was angered by their argument, retorting that she would be forever a virgin.

At that point, she was probably attempting to hold off Parliament – and dampen the ardour of her endlessly keen suitors. If she had announced that she planned soon to marry, then she would be overwhelmed with proposals and pressure to choose. Deferring the matter was a wise move.

Over the years, her youthful speech would become codified into a doctrine, a promise, a myth – and the most brilliant piece of royal propaganda in history. For if the most important role of a monarch is to produce heirs and continue the succession, Elizabeth signally failed. Unlike her sister, Mary, and her cousin, Mary, Queen of Scots, she didn't even *try* to marry. But her fervent refusal was reshaped into devotion to the country and a revelation of personal excellence and sacrifice.

There were enthusiastic efforts to change her mind. The Church of England clergyman John Aylmer said that if she married one of her subjects, 'she may not be the head, I grant that, so far as pertaining to the bands of marriage, and the office of a wife, she must be a subject; but as a Magistrate, she must be her husband's head'. A husband would lead in 'matters of wedlock' but she would be responsible for 'the guiding of the commonwealth'.[11] This set-up was rather akin to that of later queens, Victoria and Elizabeth II, who took on the rule of the country but styled their husbands as head of the household. But Victoria succeeded a collection of dreadful and debauched kings and their brothers who had made male rule look so bad that the country was wildly keen on an innocent girl. The alternative to her would have been the Duke of Cumberland, who was rude, untrustworthy and had probably murdered his valet. She also arrived on the throne after society had become more accustomed to arguments about female independence and women maintaining their identity after marriage, even if they promised to obey. Early feminists, such as Mary Wollstonecraft, and even some novels of the time, had begun to promote these new ideas, and the prospect of a woman on the throne was not the horror it might have been.

Elizabeth II ascended in a quite different era, when the Crown's power itself was much diminished and female rule was even more acceptable. But in the sixteenth century, a woman who failed to obey and bow to her husband in all things was not just defying society but also refusing to accept the authority of God. Of course, there were many determined and independent-minded wives and obedient husbands. But when push came to shove, if Elizabeth and her husband were to disagree, Parliament would be within its rights to follow the wishes of the husband. Marrying a Habsburg or a Valois from France meant choosing one side over another, and Philip of Spain was too powerful and too Catholic – and, even if he and his ideas did not overrun the country, he might try to haul England into the wars that he so keenly prosecuted and had proved so disastrous for her sister.

Elizabeth's initial attempt to stop Parliament from interfering became a vision she would never relinquish. Perhaps if all of her advisors had agreed on a man, then she would have taken him as a husband. Childbirth was risky and even if she had all success and bore a healthy son, this would have opened her up to the threat that she might be deposed for her child. But still, the succession would be secure, and Mary, Queen of Scots swept out of the way in an instant. As it was, Elizabeth was the Virgin Queen and the Queen of Scots was snapping at her heels.

Chapter Fourteen
'Malicious Talk'

Elizabeth was surrounded by admiring men. Twenty-five years old on her accession, graceful, vibrant and superbly intelligent, she was wonderful company and if she was never the most beautiful woman in the room, her charisma and glamour made up for a lot. And although she claimed she would never marry, she was openly spending much of her free time with her Master of the Horse and old friend, the handsome flatterer and courageous swordsman, Robert Dudley, who was devoted to the queen, even though he had been married to the heiress Amy Robsart since 1550.

The Spanish ambassador reported more than friendship. As he put it, 'Lord Robert has come so much into favour that he does whatever he likes with affairs. It is even said that Her Majesty visits him in his chamber day and night.' Elizabeth rode out with him every day and spent more time with him than any of her other advisors. The earls of Norfolk and Arundel later complained that he had excessive privilege. Her ministers were permitted to appear in her bedchamber, but not before she was dressed. Yet Robert was allowed to do exactly that, 'handing her the shift she would put on'.[1] They had also seen him kiss her without being invited.

If she had chosen anyone to end her state of being a virgin queen, it would have been Dudley. But did she? Some ambassadors fussed, but others saw nothing. The Swedish chancellor reported in 1560 that 'I did see many signs of chastity, virginity and true modesty so that I would stake my life that she is most chaste.'[2] After all, there was some distance between the flirtation of handing her a chemise and having full-blown sex. And sex, in the days before reliable contraception, was not a mere dalliance but could have great consequences. As pregnancy and fertility were very poorly understood, women really did think they could get pregnant at any point in the month. As it tends to be impossible for two people who are intensely attracted to each other to have sexual intercourse on a single occasion if they remain in close proximity, we might argue that if Elizabeth and Dudley had consummated their relationship once, they would have found repeated occasions to do so. But no lady talked of any gossip and Elizabeth did not fall pregnant. It has been argued by some recent scholars that Elizabeth was infertile, or even born with male chromosomes, but the princes who proposed marriage certainly received information from their spies that she had a correct feminine cycle and Cecil always believed she could marry and fall pregnant, until her age made it too late. When she was thirty, her doctor told a French diplomat that she was capable of bearing ten children.

It is most likely that Elizabeth and Dudley went no further than flirtation and some heavy petting. For Elizabeth, sex was fraught with dangers. Her early experience at Seymour's hands had been terrifying, and she realised how quickly sexual activities could change and rebound and lead to her being thrown into the Tower. She barely remembered her mother, but her story was etched into her mind, and she had seen Catherine Howard fall due to sexual congress – and Katherine Parr die in the aftermath of childbirth. Her father, her stepfather in the form of Seymour, the behaviour of Philip of Spain towards her sister Mary – various men along the way had shown her how faithless men could be.

The pair had much in common: playing together in childhood, staying in the Tower at the same time with the threat of execution hanging over them, and a preference for the reformed religion. Did he grow hopeful? He was the son of traitors, but still, Parliament had wanted to instruct Elizabeth in February that she should only marry an Englishman, although decided against issuing the command at the last minute. Perhaps Elizabeth thought him a safe option to spend time with – for as he was married already, no one would imagine that he was trying to marry her.

Plenty of other suitors offered their hand, including Prince Eric of Sweden; the son of Ferdinand, Holy Roman Emperor; and various

Englishmen, including the Earl of Arundel and the diplomat Sir William Pickering. In the past, when Elizabeth heard about Francis and Mary declaring they would lay claim to her throne, she cried, 'I shall take a husband who will give the King of France some trouble.'³ She meant James Hamilton, the younger Earl of Arran, whose father, the former regent, had suggested him as a husband for Elizabeth, and was in line for the Scottish throne. Had Elizabeth done so and claimed herself and Arran as some kind of joint monarchy over Scotland and England, she would have made it very difficult for Mary to gain the throne. Marrying Arran might have made the entire story completely different. But instead, Hamilton was left unmarried and went mad over the accusations he had made about Bothwell.

Elizabeth was a woman of words, but cautious in her actions, and she made loud threats of marriage and scattered kind words to envoys – but she continued to spend her time with Robert Dudley. The gossip swirled. Kat Ashley, her First Lady of the Bedchamber, told Elizabeth that she had gone too far and her 'behaviour towards the Master of the Horse occasioned much evil speaking'. Elizabeth said it was ridiculous to accuse her, since her ladies were always with her and would see any impropriety. Kat tried again, but Elizabeth summarily refused to give him up. She needed his friendship for she had lost so much, and 'in this world, she had so much sorrow and tribulation and so little joy'.⁴ As always with Elizabeth, when she was pushed to do something, she resisted and dug in her heels. There was similarity with Mary's relationship with Bothwell. In the future, Mary would struggle to give up Bothwell because he seemed to her to be the one person who had never turned against her or tried to exploit her. Elizabeth felt, too, that everyone had abandoned her when she had been suspected of treachery by her sister Mary. As the ambassador to the Duke of Saxony later reported, she 'was more attached to him than any of the others because when she was deserted by everybody in the reign of her sister not only did he never lessen in any degree his kindness and humble attention to her, but he even sold his possessions that he might assist her with money and therefore she thought it just that she should make some return for his good faith and constancy'. As the imperial ambassador put it, 'It is generally stated that it is his [Dudley's] fault that the queen does not marry',⁵ and the Holy Roman Emperor began to question whether he should even consider marrying his son to a woman who appeared to be engaged in an affair.

The ambassadors comforted themselves that any marriage would be so unpopular with the people that the queen would not go through with it. But still, they fretted that there was 'not a man in England who does not cry out upon him as the queens' ruin',[6] and passed on rumours that Dudley planned to divorce his wife. Certainly, Amy was never at court, but then few wives ever were. Elizabeth's own ladies were the main female presence – and the queen excused it by saying there simply was not room for wives. Then the news spread that Amy, only just twenty-seven, had a terrible malady of the breast, presumably some type of breast cancer. Speculation was rife that her eventual death would clear the way for Dudley and Elizabeth to marry.

Cecil was angered by the intimacy and wanted Robert gone. He turned to the Spanish ambassador and seemed to pour out his heart. As Álvaro de Quadra put it, he 'perceived the most manifest ruin impending over the queen through her intimacy with Lord Robert. The Lord Robert had made himself master of the business of the state and the person of the queen.' So far, nothing that de Quadra had not previously said himself in his reports. And then Cecil turned to scandal. 'He said that they were thinking of destroying Lord Robert's wife. They had given out that she was ill, but she was not ill at all, she was very well, and taking care not to be poisoned.'[7]

This was a shocking allegation against the queen and her closest confidant, and a scandalous and out-of-character display of loose lips from Cecil. De Quadra naturally thought things could get no more cloak and dagger than the suggestion that the queen was plotting to murder one of her subjects. He was wrong.

On Sunday 8 September 1560, the day after Elizabeth I's twenty-seventh birthday, Amy Robsart gave all her servants permission to leave the house for a day to visit a nearby fair. She was staying at the home of Sir Anthony Forster, a friend of Dudley, at Cumnor Place in Berkshire (now in Oxfordshire), which had been before the dissolution of the monasteries one of the granges owned by the very wealthy Abingdon Abbey. She wished to be alone in her part of the house. Her husband was not present but at court with Elizabeth, enjoying the aftermath of the birthday celebrations. Perhaps Amy was expecting a visit from a secret messenger whom she wished no one to see. Or, perhaps, if it was the case that she was sick from the abscess in her breast, she wished to be alone with her pain. She sent away her most devoted maid,

Picto, and was angry with some others who didn't want to go to the fair, and was equally discouraging to Mrs Odingsells, a widow who also lived in the house, when she said the fair was too crowded on Sundays and would rather remain at home.

Amy managed to send everyone away into the fine September day. To us, this may seem a normal occurrence. Now, we crave solitude when sad or overstrained. But people of the sixteenth century were never alone. Women were always attended and accompanied at every move – to be bereft of all servants was simply unfitting. Amy had to compel her servants to leave her, against all tradition and propriety.

When they returned, they found her dead at the bottom of the stairs.

Had Amy wanted everybody gone because she wished to commit suicide? And if she did, was this because she was in mortal pain, or because she suspected her husband was in love with another woman? Did someone push her to suicide by manipulating her? Or did she receive a messenger who demanded she see him alone – and who then killed her? Or had she simply had an unlucky fall?

When Robert heard the news, he sent his man, Thomas Blount, to investigate. He was panicking about the evil talk that might pin the murder of his wife on him. 'I do understand that my wife is dead, and, as he [the messenger] saith, by a fall from a pair of stairs. Little understanding can I have of him. The greatness and suddenness of the misfortune doth so perplex me until I do hear from you how the matter standeth, or how this evil should light on me, considering what the malicious world will bruit [say], as I can take no rest.'[8]

Robert left court in a hurry for a small palace at Kew that Elizabeth had given him. He was right to hide from the peering eyes of ambassadors and courtiers – but many questioned why he did not rush straight to Cumnor, to see his wife's final place of death and pay his respects to her. That would be the behaviour one might expect of a loving husband. But Robert was in shock and confusion and no doubt feared that he might be suspected or questioned if he arrived at Cumnor. He wanted Blount to tell him whether it was 'by evil chance, or by villainy'. Blount rode to Abingdon, lodged at an inn and asked the owner for information. It was this man who told him the astonishing piece of information that Amy had been alone when she died because she had commanded all her servants to go to the fair and 'would suffer none to tarry at home'. Blount interviewed the maid Picto, who swore that it must have been an accident and Amy would never have committed suicide, although she did agree Amy had been melancholic in recent months. Not only were suicides in the period cruelly dealt with and widely condemned, but if Amy had been so depressed as to kill herself, her maid might also be considered at fault for not comprehending her mistress's saddened state.

Amy was buried at the Church of Our Lady in Oxford on 23 September, with a full procession, although Robert did not attend. The 'malicious talk' that Robert feared had come to pass. Throckmorton fretted about the 'dishonourable and naughty reports . . . which every hair on my head stareth at and my ears glow to hear'. It was not so much about Robert – but the queen. 'Some let not to say, what religion is this that a subject can kill his wife, and the prince not only bear withal but marry him.'[9] Had Elizabeth and Robert plotted together to kill Amy so he could be free? An inquest concluded that Amy 'by misfortune came to her death'.

Dudley gave the Cumnor estate manager a huge sum of money, the equivalent of around £70,000 today. Perhaps it was a cover-up, or perhaps he had believed it was suicide and wanted to try to ensure no one knew. Or perhaps there were simply outstanding debts that he needed to pay. Robert's letters after Amy's death are very much those of a man in shock – and even if he wanted her dead, it was surely a better option to wait out the year or so of her illness. He would have known that her death would throw suspicion on him and also on his beloved queen.

A death by natural causes seems too much of a coincidence, although it is possible. It is also possible that it was a suicide and Dudley and the servants rushed to cover it up so that Amy would receive a fit burial. Although her servants reported her sadness, some scholars have noted that she had recently bought a handsome velvet gown, suggesting she had plans for the future, and while her breast cancer, if that is what it was, would have led to an excruciatingly painful death, she was at that point probably not suffering too badly. The inquest has recently been unearthed in the National Archives, in which there was a note of two 'dynts'[10] in Amy's head but no indication of much more, which does not seem enough to kill, even if they were received before the fall. Many at the time drew the conclusion that a third party was involved. And as there was no record of robbery or ransacking, they believed it must have been planned.

Cecil has been considered as a possible murderer. He hated Robert. The last thing he wanted was poor Amy dying of cancer, leaving Robert an innocent widower, free to marry Elizabeth. With Amy's public death, all suspicion would turn to Robert – and if he tried to marry the queen, he would open himself to more charges of guilt. Murdering Amy was the perfect crime, for it would push Dudley permanently out of the way.

Or perhaps the killer was a foreign spy who wanted Robert eliminated so that his master could be considered a suitor. Or one who believed Robert blocked his country's influence and also suspected that Robert's interest in reformed religion was persuading the queen to his side. It is part of the job of a foreign spy to assassinate or threaten, without being discovered, and Robsart's death, if it was planned, was certainly a brilliantly executed job – no one saw the death and if there were any visitors to Amy that day, they slipped in undetected. De Quadra's enthusiastic condemnation of the queen and Robert might have been a smokescreen to divert suspicion that the killer had been in the pay of the Spanish. The Holy Roman Emperor, Philip of Spain and plenty of others hated Robert and wanted him deposed from his position. They genuinely believed that he was the one stopping the queen making a dynastic marriage. Killing Robert himself would have been too obvious and brought the queen's vengeance onto whoever she thought responsible. But his wife was an easy target.

It is a baffling part of the whole mystery that de Quadra claimed Cecil had said the queen and Dudley wished for Amy's ruin and were 'thinking of destroying' her.[11] Why would Cecil say such a thing, especially to someone he knew would immediately report it? Cecil was a measured, strategic man, intelligent, and spoke carefully, according to his ends. He was discreet, careful and ambitious. But telling de Quadra that the queen and Dudley wanted Amy dead was wild and terrible. Had he simply been at the end of his patience with them, blurting something out that seemed impossible – and then, unfortunately and coincidentally, Amy committed suicide or fell? Still, speaking in anger to an ambassador, whatever the subject, was not a good tactic and de Quadra doesn't record any other such instances. Or had he been planning the murder and was attempting to divert suspicion away from himself? This is possible, but if he condemned the queen, he faced a great loss of influence if she came to hear of it. Or was de Quadra lying? Had his spies or those of networks he knew of been plotting Amy's murder, and he was at this point wanting to put himself beyond blame?

We cannot know the truth behind Amy's death. But the consequence was immediate and absolute: Elizabeth could not and would not ever marry Robert. He was not a sad widower, his wife dead so young of illness. The taint of murder was about him. Even suicide reflected badly on him, as people might think his love for the queen surely broke his wife's heart. Overnight he went from the position of being considered by many a favourite, most likely to be chosen if Elizabeth ever agreed to wed, to a suitor with less chance than Philip of Spain. Unlike Mary, Elizabeth could put her head over her heart. She truly believed him innocent. But the world did not think him free of guilt and so she had to cool her friendship with him. If she was to marry Robert, even after a decent period of a year or so had passed, people would accuse her of having been in on the plot to kill Amy. Elizabeth had seen Robert as her friend, her source of joy in a cruel world. Now she had to lose him as well. As she herself later said to the Spanish ambassador, 'They said of me that I would not marry because I was in love with the Earl of Leicester and that I could not marry him because he had a wife already, yet now he has no wife, and for all that I do not marry him.'[12] Still, after the dust settled, she kept him as her devoted companion, giving him rooms next to hers in the palace, rights to export clothes, and rights over the customs duties of sweets, wines, silks, velvet, oil and even currants. It may have been more than he had any right to expect, but Elizabeth remembered his loyalty during her difficult times.

The parliament of January 1563 was preoccupied by Elizabeth's marriage. The Virgin Queen had been a virgin for far too long. Elizabeth was petitioned to marry and thus produce 'an imp of your own' and she should wed 'where it shall please you, by whom it shall please you and as soon as it shall please you'.[13] Elizabeth fought back, prevaricating and offering different opinions. Parliament had to retreat, defeated, until another day.

In Scotland, Knox was waging war on Mary, feeding the rumours that she had been a lover of the poet Chastelard, and declaring she had been captured by the 'venom of idolatry' and that 'The queen's Mass shall provoke God's vengeance.'[14] It was becoming easier and easier for him to speak such dreadful words. The beautiful young queen was doubted and distrusted and the rumour that she was unchaste spread fast.

The answer was for Mary to marry and so protect herself against such insults. But Elizabeth was now determined that Mary should not wed without her say-so. Everyone around the young Scottish queen was trying to control her. Don Carlos of Spain had fallen down the stairs in 1562 and been submitted to head surgery to save his life. But the surgery had brought on attacks of mental illness and so he was off the list of possibles, at least until he recovered. Mary's uncle set off to Innsbruck and signed a secret treaty for her marriage with Archduke Ferdinand – and when Elizabeth's spies told her of it, she informed Mary that if she married Ferdinand or anyone from the imperial family, she would consider their good relationship to be at an end. The days when Mary said that the only husband she wished for was Elizabeth were resolutely over.

Chapter Fifteen

'To Use Me as Her Sister or Daughter'

After only a few years in Scotland, Mary was in an impossible position. Knox and the Protestant lords were stirring dissent against her, Catherine de' Medici refused to openly ally with her, and Elizabeth was refusing to play the tender cousin. In late 1563, Elizabeth laid down what she expected of Mary's marriage. Ideally, she would marry an Englishman, but the queen was prepared to consider a foreigner, although not Spanish, French or Austrian – which pretty much ruled out all the power players in Europe. If Mary obeyed, she would be rewarded and would in time be decreed as heir. As Elizabeth wrote, 'we will not be behind on our part to satisfy her as far forth as if she were our only natural sister or dear only daughter'.[1]

This was too much for Cecil. He got rid of 'dear only' before 'daughter' and then scratched out the entire section. Instead, if she 'show herself conformable', they would set up an 'inquisition of her right', to which she could submit evidence regarding her right of succession. A judgement would then be made on whether Mary should be deemed the queen's 'natural sister or daughter'. Afraid of the Guises and obsessively protective of the queen, he went too far. One might ask, if Elizabeth was determined to be the Virgin Queen, who would succeed if not Mary? The queen's instincts were right and she should have retained the first draft. Instead, Mary was now to be subject to an English court and her rights examined by judges – when surely blood should be enough? No one was saying that she was not legitimate, or that her family had not been. There was no possible reason to put her claim on trial – especially when Elizabeth had been deemed illegitimate and had not reinstated her parents' marriage. The idea that a queen's claim could be judged and made subordinate by lawyers was a typical Cecil move, but it contained within it the beginning of the end for absolute royal rule. If Mary's claim could be examined by the courts, then why not any monarch's? We can be sure Elizabeth had mixed feelings about the document, for ahead of its arrival, she sent Mary a handsome diamond ring.

Mary kissed the ring and expected a kindly letter from Elizabeth. When the document arrived, she was shocked but restrained her anger. There was no use fighting back. She needed to encourage Elizabeth to trust her – and Knox's insubordination and rudeness had grown so extreme that she dared not offend the queen. For, if it came to it, she felt sure Elizabeth would back her against the rebellious lords – and she had become convinced that if she only gained her dynastic rights, then they would respect her. She had Knox put on trial for suggesting that two imprisoned Calvinist priests should be freed by a 'convocation of brethren'. To Mary, that was treasonous and she felt sure she had caught Knox in his own web. But he defended himself nimbly, said that he was a minister and authorised by the Kirk to intervene, and he was acquitted. Mary was furious, and demanded that the verdict be re-examined. She was beginning to look powerless and she believed that Knox would never dare behave so if she were married. In this, she was perhaps right. But still, Elizabeth was proving reluctant to name a possible fiancé.

It simply wouldn't have been possible for Mary to create the brilliant propaganda vision of the Virgin Queen, as Elizabeth did. Elizabeth ruled a country where no noble would talk openly of assaulting and kidnapping her; she had grown up in England; no one could accuse her of split loyalties, and the qualities that underpinned the wider political governance were the rule of law and bureaucracy. Mary's lords had been used to doing as they pleased for too long – and Mary needed support.

There was not a large pool of suitors. Poor Don Carlos was still suffering from mental illness after his operation and showed little signs of recovery. Catherine de' Medici was suggesting the suffering and mentally distressed Earl of Arran, but Mary had no desire to give more power to his father – and she felt sorry for the young man, so could never love him. The Guises were enthusing a union with one of their own, the young Duke of Guise, but Mary wisely knew that if she married a Guise, she would be much condemned.

Mary pushed the English ambassador, Thomas Randolph, to gain an answer from the queen for a possible groom – and one came. The queen wished her dear cousin to marry Robert Dudley, who all Europe said was Elizabeth's lover.

As Randolph informed Mary at Holyrood that her cousin had named Dudley, she listened quietly, essentially in shock. Dudley was not royal and the matter of Amy Robsart's death had been seen as greatly scandalous in Europe. 'You have taken me at a disadvantage',[2] she said to him, in confusion. When she recovered her senses, she was outraged. She knew well that Robert had been Elizabeth's admirer, if not lover. He was also a committed Protestant and, as she knew, he would be Elizabeth's spy after any marriage – and possibly even continue as her lover. Elizabeth had proposed a husband for Mary who would always be loyal to Elizabeth. Even worse, he was the son of a traitor, the executed Earl of Northumberland, and had no land that Elizabeth had not given to him. He was entirely the English queen's man. 'Do you think it may stand with my honour to marry my sister's subject?' she demanded. Randolph tried to dig himself out of the hole by saying Dudley was a nobleman and would add to her claim to the throne. The idea that a minor aristocrat could assist her in her claim, when she was of royal blood, naturally infuriated Mary. She did not restrain her language and told poor Randolph that her family would never allow 'that I should abase my state as far as that!'[3] Her blood was truly special and would only be tainted if she married Dudley or someone of his ilk. Royals married royals – that was the whole point of the European marriage market. She was being offered someone who was so far below her that she couldn't even consider it.

Elizabeth had actually suggested Robert to William Maitland, Mary's envoy and secretary of state, some months earlier. He had been quite nonplussed, managing to recover himself to say that Mary would not wish to take 'joy and solace'[4] away from Elizabeth. An experienced diplomat, he thought on his feet and made the polite suggestion that Elizabeth should marry Dudley and Mary take him after Elizabeth's death. He had hoped that it was all a passing fancy and that Elizabeth would not wish to lose her companion. He had not reckoned on Cecil, who was keen to get rid of Robert Dudley.

Cecil pushed hard for the Scottish marriage plan and Elizabeth grew persuaded. Elizabeth cherished a romantic vision that Mary and Dudley would live together at the English court, and they would be a happy threesome together, but Cecil was keen for Dudley to go to Scotland and stay there. Dudley himself, of course, had no desire either to marry Mary or go to Scotland. He blamed Cecil for the plan, complaining to the Scottish ambassador about his 'secret enemy'.

Mary was infuriated. Still, she could not afford to offend Elizabeth and she spoke to the ambassador confidentially. If she married Dudley, would Elizabeth 'use me as her sister or daughter'?[5] For, if she would, then perhaps the price was worth paying. And she had a point: had she married Dudley and her groom, as one might expect, spent most of his time popping back to see Elizabeth and England, she might have had the advantage of a husband and pregnancy, without the disadvantage of a man trying to meddle. And even though Mary resented Dudley as Elizabeth's lover, she knew that some of the Scottish lords would be intimidated by his riches, power and connection to the English queen. She would have strengthened her alliance with England and also, to a degree, been able to control the messages fed back to her cousin. And Dudley was a loyal man, a good strategist, and his genius for spectacle might have created effective propaganda for Mary in Scotland. But Mary didn't want a husband simply to produce an heir. She wanted a strong shoulder to lean on, someone to help her with the business of governing. She had come to believe that a husband could quell the troublesome and power-hungry lords and force them to respect her.

But, as she soon found out, Elizabeth didn't want Dudley in Scotland and desired both Mary and Dudley at the English court, with Elizabeth paying the bills. This was impossible. Mary would be her cousin's subordinate in every way. And Elizabeth, at the heart of it, found the idea unsettling too. When she entertained Mary's new envoy, Sir James Melville, she showered him with questions about Mary's appearance and personality: who played the virginals better? Who was fairer? Melville tactfully replied that Elizabeth was 'whiter, but my queen was very lovely'.[6] If Elizabeth did send Dudley up to Scotland, she didn't want him falling in love.

Melville was a Fife man, who had gone to France aged thirteen – in the year after Mary had arrived there – to be a page in her train. She had become very fond of him and the King of France had trusted him to work for his government. Mary took him into her household on her return to Scotland and trusted him absolutely. As she saw it, if anyone could sort out the problematic web of the question of marriage, it was Melville.

The spies were reporting, everyone whispering in corners, bribes offered for information. Poor Thomas Randolph, the English ambassador, was caught between two queens. He had started operating in Scotland in 1559 and worked hard to encourage dissent with Mary of Guise. But the wars over the throne and regency were as nothing, compared to this. He began confiding in Mary Beaton, forty-five to her twenty-two, entranced (like most men at court) with her pretty face and gentle manner. He began courting her in earnest – which the queen did not mind, for she wanted Randolph on side. But he grew so desperate that he tried to compel Mary Beaton to spy on the queen – and that was too much. The love affair crumbled; the lady put the queen first. In September 1564, Elizabeth made Dudley Earl of Leicester, which surely, she hoped, would make him more acceptable to her troublesome Scottish cousin.

Moray and the lords closest to Mary, such as the pro-English Argyll, encouraged the English plan. It was not just in keeping with Moray's pro-English foreign policy. It would also be an ideal situation for Mary's half-brother if his troublesome younger sibling were to go to live in England with Dudley – for he would be the obvious candidate to be regent in her absence. Then, he could gain all the power he desired. He encouraged his half-sister to think of Dudley, but found she was proving annoyingly independent. She remained very upset at the suggestion she should marry.

The marriage proposal was a fatal error on Elizabeth's behalf. It turned Mary against her and convinced Mary that she should find her own husband. Undermined and thwarted by the Guises, her mother-in-law, her cousin and her lords, she had decided to rely on herself, no matter what happened.

Mary agreed to Elizabeth's request to allow the Earl of Lennox to return from his lengthy exile in England. Elizabeth was simply trying to be a thorn in Mary's side and annoy her by sending back a troublesome lord. But when Mary agreed, it opened up the possibility in Lennox's mind that she might marry his son, handsome, seventeen-year-old Henry, Lord Darnley.

With the paucity of choices, Darnley was certainly an interesting option. Three years younger than the queen and handsome, he had come twice to visit her in France. Later, Elizabeth had imprisoned him and his mother for fear of plots against her throne and then released him to be something of an enforced court prisoner and he was called on to play the lute for her. If Mary married him, her claim would be much strengthened for he had blood rights to the English throne – and like Dudley, he was English born and he would hopefully be similarly popular with the English. He was also Catholic. Married to an Englishman who had been at court with a claim to the throne, Mary felt she could not be set aside as Elizabeth's successor. The throne would have to go to her.

Too late, Elizabeth realised what she had set in motion and tried to stop Lennox's return. But Mary now had the idea in her mind and she was making the right noises about marrying Dudley, whilst asking questions about Darnley. He seemed to be the answer to all her problems. Suspicious, Elizabeth asked Melville what Mary thought of Darnley. He hurried to deny the possibility, declaring that a woman of spirit would never choose 'such a man that was more like a woman than a man'. As he pointed out, Darnley was 'lusty, beardless and lady-faced'.[7] Elizabeth was not much comforted. The courtiers thought him a lover of men as well as women, but she enjoyed his company and could see how Mary might feel the same. To add to the web, Dudley, who knew that refusing to marry Mary outright would displease Elizabeth and Cecil, was busily using his friends at court to push the Darnley marriage. Back in Scotland, Lennox, Darnley's father, showered Mary with gifts and gave hefty jewels to her advisors. The would-be lover gave her a 'marvellous fair and rich jewel' and all in all it was enough to make Mary fall in love with him.

Mary had made Holyrood beautiful and elegant, decorated with her tapestries and hangings. She created her own library, so large that she later left it to the University of St Andrews. It was filled with beautiful leatherbound volumes of Italian, French, Latin, Spanish and English poetry, histories and translations, even a few books in Greek. Among the translations she owned were Plutarch, Ovid, Cicero and there were copies of the *Decameron* and *Orlando Furioso*. She had hundreds of books in French, particularly history and poetry, including romantic tales such as the *Chanson de Roland*. She even had a book on astronomy and others on her beloved music. Mary herself played the lute and the virginals with some skill and loved to sing. Her real talent was for dancing. She was beautiful, skilled and graceful – but sometimes over-tired herself with her enthusiasm.

Mary's spirits were rather low around the winter of 1564 and she suffered from various ailments. She longed for the support of the Guises, which had been fragmented by the death of the Duke of Guise, her uncle. She badly needed a friend. Mary's trusted French secretary, Pierre Raullet, was discovered to have been accepting bribes from English agents. He was dismissed and Mary replaced him with one of her musicians, a charming but rather plain Italian, David Rizzio, who was fond of luxurious clothes and brilliant at flattery. In his early thirties, he had come to Scotland attending the Savoyard ambassador and the queen had been delighted by his lute playing and excellent bass voice. She pressed him to stay and be part of her musical quartet. Her circle was quite happy to let a foreign lute player carry on making sweet music but when she promoted him to secretary, there was great resentment. James Melville thought he couldn't even do the job, failing to write out the letters so that Mary had to do it herself. The rest dubbed him a manipulative, upstart spy and thought his lack of good looks denoted a cruel heart. Mary trusted him and saw him as her own man. She always believed that those she had raised would forever remain loyal to her – a mistake she would later make with Darnley. Mary had long been criticised for employing French servants and courtiers when she could have appointed Scots men and women to such position. Using an Italian minstrel as a secretary was a step too far and to the Protestant Lords it was more evidence that she was making secret Catholic plots.

Darnley headed up to Scotland and arrived to meet Mary at the castle of the Earl of Wemyss on Saturday 17 February 1565. Darnley, at over six foot, was one of the few men taller than Mary and he was incredibly handsome. He was generous, deferential and courtly – unlike most of the men she dealt with daily. She had met him before but this time she saw him anew and called him the 'properest and best proportioned long man that ever she had seen'.[8] She was delighted by his charming manner and good looks, as well as his suitability. Under the handsome sheen, however, Darnley was a vain, conceited and spoilt young man, obsessed with his own gratification, but Mary saw none of it. Some scholars have wondered at why Elizabeth sent Darnley up to Mary, such a handsome little bomb as he was. But Elizabeth didn't think that Mary would fall in love with him: what she wanted was to divide and rule, spread unrest, amass people behind him against Mary and the Hamiltons. Darnley was an heir to her throne, after Arran, and was keen to fight for his rights. But he didn't have to. Mary had chosen him.

In March, Mary Livingston married the younger son of Lord Sempill, to a predictable chorus of complaints from John Knox, who even claimed the bride was pregnant. Mary, who always loved a wedding, paid for the dress and the banquet in a grand celebration. She also gave the couple a fine bed of red and black velvet with embroidered curtains. Mary Fleming was still being enthusiastically courted by William Maitland, recently widowed and forty to her twenty-two. 'She has begun to marry off her Maries,' said the French ambassador, 'and says she wishes herself were of the band'.[9]

The teenaged Darnley was now the frontrunner for Mary's heart. Elizabeth complained but she didn't do what might have changed Mary's mind entirely and declare that Mary would be her heir if she married Dudley. If she had stated this – and said that Mary would not have to live in England as Mrs Dudley (after all, it would be irritating to have another, younger, better-looking queen always beside her, holding Dudley's hand) – Mary might have agreed and Dudley would have had no choice but to accept that marriage to a monarch, if not the one he'd wanted, was still a prize. But Cecil simply said that the question of Mary as heir would be discussed and that was not enough.

With Darnley as a possible husband, Mary was confident enough in her position to express her regret about Elizabeth's treatment of her. 'How much better were it that we being two queens so near of kin, neighbours and living in one Isle, should be friends and live together like sisters, than by strange means divide ourselves to the hurt of us both.'[10] Darnley was full of youthful bravado and was convinced he had charmed the queen. He attended court and danced with Mary but she was not showing any signs of particular favour in public. She was waiting to hear from Elizabeth.

Finally, Elizabeth replied. There would be no discussion of Mary's position as heir until Elizabeth either married or decreed that she would never marry. Mary was furious and did 'nothing but weep and write'.[11] The letter was the final straw – and it pushed Mary into Darnley's arms. She was gay and high spirited with love. On Easter Monday, in residence at Stirling, she and her ladies dressed themselves up like merchants' wives and wandered the streets, asking for money for their evening banquets, delighting in pulling the wool over people's eyes, a proto-Marie Antoinette desire to mingle and not be recognised (of course, the ordinary people pretended: everyone recognised the tall beautiful woman surrounded by ladies as their queen).

In April, the young swain fell ill with a cold and a rash, possibly measles or an early sign of the effects of syphilis. Mary accommodated him in the royal apartments, visited him at all hours and he played the complaisant, gentle, sickly lover. Mary was delighted by him. She made up her mind. There was clearly no use attempting to please Cecil and the Queen of England. She sent her messenger to Elizabeth to demand she be allowed to marry Darnley. Elizabeth and Cecil panicked and both wrote demanding she put him aside. But they had tarried for too long and they were too late. The Queen of Scots was determined. She created Darnley Earl of Ross and gave him land in Scotland. She was in love with him, she wanted to marry and he was a marvellous way of standing up to Elizabeth. Mary has been viewed as wild and rash for marrying Darnley, but what other choice did she have? And Darnley had come to the kingdom to cause trouble. By marrying him, she was attempting to neutralise his threat.

Randolph thought Mary was so overcome with love that she was barely the same person. Cecil was shocked and terrified. His policy had always been 'to hold the queen unmarried as long as he could' – a foolish one, since she was always determined to marry somebody.[12] He feared Mary and Darnley would create a new dynasty and it would unseat Elizabeth. He was right. Such was the importance of a man that a baby boy born of their union had the potential to throw Elizabeth from the throne. He whipped up the Privy Council into a frenzy, suggesting Darnley was set to raise an army, invade England

and create civil war. Elizabeth had Lennox and Darnley recalled to England and put Margaret Lennox, still in England, under house arrest. Father and son refused to obey the summons and Mary was furious. She told the ambassador that Elizabeth had 'went about to abuse me' and said that 'being as free as she is, I would stand to my own choice'. Elizabeth, she said, had wrecked everything and brought it on herself. Had she just been kind, she 'cannot have a daughter of her own that would have been more obedient to her than I would have been'. When it was suggested she might become a Protestant, Mary lost all patience and said 'it will be as well for her to lose my amity as hers will be to me'.[13]

As Elizabeth could offer Mary no one better than her discarded lover as a potential husband, she can hardly be criticised for taking matters into her own hands. She and Darnley continued in a passionate haze of admiration. Unfortunately, her subjects hated him. Maitland and the other administrators on their mission to the English court dreaded Elizabeth's anger. Darnley had punched Arran while on his sickbed. Knox disliked him, and even the four Marys expressed their concerns. Moray detested him and feared he would lose all influence over Mary once she was married. Darnley had been swaggering around, making it clear that he would be ruling the roost once he was married. He threatened that he could deprive Moray of his possessions, telling him that he thought his future brother-in-law had too much land. Moray, already nervous about Elizabeth's wrath, tried to dissuade his sister – but she would not listen. Until this point, Moray had tried hard to play the supportive advisor, despite his ambitions, even though he fed information to the English. The advent of Darnley changed everything. He feared Catholic resurgence under Darnley, knew that it would mean a diminution of his own power – and knew he had to act so as not to lose everything. A plot bubbled up to seize Darnley and his father, to send them back to Elizabeth and force Mary to submit – and there was even talk of a kidnap attempt in summer, one that Mary's spies helped her dodge.

Meanwhile, the husband-to-be was demanding the title King of Scotland and, despite Parliament's complaints and her own uncertainty, Mary persuaded the Privy Council to assent and it was announced that Darnley would indeed be dubbed King of Scotland. Mary, so long occupying a sensible route, ruling with strength and courage, had given all to love. She pushed forth the wedding, even though Elizabeth had refused her consent and the papal dispensation (because of their relation as step-first cousins) had not yet arrived. Three weeks before the wedding, Mary pulled her fiancé into one of her favourite games: dressing up. She and the future king donned a disguise and wandered the town, amused by the reactions of those walking past. The future king and queen were playing happy, basking in the delight of the ordinary people.

Chapter Sixteen

'The Scots Proclaim Much But Their Threats Are Not Carried Out'

On Sunday 29 July, Mary rose early and her ladies gowned her in a black dress and a white hood, to show that she came to her new marriage as a dowager queen. She was escorted by the Earl of Lennox, Darnley's father, and the Earl of Argyll to the chapel at Holyrood, where she waited for her future husband to arrive. The groom wore a suit embroidered with jewels, the peacock, glittering centrepiece of the ceremony. They made a beautiful couple, both tall, handsome and young. The nobles in their finery tried to seem cheerful, the Lennoxes and their supporters gloried in their triumph.

The pair exchanged rings and Mary received three, representing the Trinity. All the nobles were invited and, in a masterstroke of ceremony, Mary allowed each one to remove a pin holding her veil to her gown before she went to her ladies to change from her black clothes. Mary received the nuptial Mass alone, for Darnley hurried off to the royal apartments. He came out again for the endless balls, banquets and celebrations that followed. Mary showered him and his extensive entourage with gifts, even going so far as buying new blue bonnets for his fools. Elizabeth's ambassador suffered in silence.

Elizabeth was incandescent and confiscated the Lennox properties in England. She would not agree to the arguments of her Privy Council that she should declare war. Elizabeth was wise. Since many of her people still wished her to marry and could not understand why she did not, to attack another queen for doing so would have been an unpopular move. And Mary was feeling strong. Now she was a married queen, there was to be no more constant waiting and chasing of Elizabeth's favour, holding on for scraps of attention or regard. She told her dear sister and cousin that she and her husband would not enforce their claim to the throne, ally with English rebels or work with foreign powers who wished to depose the queen. In return, Elizabeth would not associate with Mary's rebels – and Mary's and Darnley's succession to her throne should be settled by an Act of Parliament.

Philip of Spain had sent his assent to the marriage. When he congratulated Darnley's mother, he suggested her son would be King of Scotland and 'King of England, if this marriage is carried through'.

Elizabeth's lute player had come a long way.

Any remaining goodwill for the marriage within the nobles dissipated when the proclamation was made that all documents would be signed jointly by 'Queen Marie and King Henry', 'in the names of both their majesties as King and Queen of Scotland jointly'. They were scandalised at the idea of a dual monarchy. Even though they thought a woman too weak to be queen, the nobles didn't want one of their rivals ruling over her and feared that he would turn his efforts to attempting to remove their power. They were sickened by the medals and coins that were created, bearing his name first.

The nobles began to openly dissent, refusing to wait on the new king. The Earl of Moray still hated Darnley and saw in the marriage the end of all his hopes. Within a month of the wedding, he was raising forces against the queen, backed up by Arran. Mary told Arran and Argyll that they would be outlawed if they assisted Moray and she moved to confiscate his property. Moray totted up the various grievances: Darnley; that Catholicism would resurge under Darnley and Mary together; foreigners at court, including Rizzio; improper selling of church lands, and divisions of the funds from the church. He had wider problems with his half-sister's reign than just her husband.

The rebels gathered in Ayrshire and on the last day of August, Moray led them into Edinburgh for what became known as the Chaseabout Raid. Mary's forces shot the cannons of Edinburgh Castle and the rebels retreated, sending Melville to beg Elizabeth for arms and men. There was no help forthcoming and so Moray and his men fled to England, where he had always been welcome. In October, he was called by Elizabeth to explain himself.

Moray endured a lengthy telling-off from Elizabeth, in front of the French ambassadors. Elizabeth was outwardly all respect to Mary, declaring that no prince could think well of what he had done and he should understand the 'duty which the subject ought to bear towards his monarch'. She was thinking of her position and putting on a show for the benefit of Catherine de' Medici and Charles IX: she feared that the newly powerful Mary would gain foreign support, particularly from France, who in turn would threaten her. Behind the scenes, Cecil and her ministers talked in friendly ways to Moray. He was Protestant, they could deal with him. He was allowed to remain in England for as long as he wished – which was significant. Elizabeth and Cecil shared his fear of Darnley and Catholic influence. They could not endorse open rebellion. But they could help him if he did something more back-handed. Elizabeth's ambassador, Randolph, was instructed not to recognise Darnley's authority and channel funds to Moray.

Mary had created a public triumph. And by autumn 1565, she was pregnant. When she started taking to her bed with sickness, the English ambassador flew into a panic and started bribing her maids for information about Mary's cycle. He dreaded having to tell Elizabeth the news.

Despite the outward appearances of happiness, there was trouble in the marriage. Darnley had expected to be the king, with Mary as little more than his consort. He was not particularly interested in government or administration – instead he pressed Mary to spend more money and expressed anger that her name was written first on documents, rather than his. He wished to be a great king in Europe and he was growing increasingly frustrated that his wife would not bow to him as he expected. He wanted all the lords to be subordinate to him and demanded of some to take Mass. They refused and he flew into a rage.

Darnley had little affection for the queen – preferring to spend his time in the taverns of Edinburgh with both men and women, behaving notoriously. The only person in the world the teenage king would listen to was his mother, Lady Lennox, and she was still in England, watched with a hawk eye by Cecil. Without his mother to upbraid him, he behaved wildly, unwisely, drinking and seducing. At the end of the night, he crawled back to Holyroodhouse, drunk and spoiling for a fight. He was high-handed and cruel and Mary stood up to him, resulting in terrible arguments. She had thought he would be grateful to her for raising him up. Instead, he expected her to submit to him and was furious when she would not. As he saw it, he had a greater claim to the throne than she, because he was a man.

Mary was incensed by his insubordination and decided he had gone too far and that he should be demoted to the position of 'the queen's husband'. She might be pregnant with his child, but she was still the monarch, not him. She refused him the right to bear royal arms. He would not have the crown matrimonial and would have no claim to the throne after her death. It was all good news for England. As Randolph remarked, 'this queen repenteth her marriage; that she hateth him and all his kin'.[1] She no longer visited Darnley at night. Instead, she spent time with her friends, including the gentle secretary, David Rizzio. Darnley seethed with hatred for the secretary, believing that he had stolen the influence that should have been his.

Mary's husband was a disappointment but her pregnancy made her powerful and the lords certainly seemed better behaved. Moreover, the aged Pope Pius IV, who had refused to support her dynastic claim, had died at the end of 1565. His successor, Pius V, was much more enthusiastic and he sent a personal letter to Mary not long after his election. If he threw his weight behind her as Queen of England, Wales and Ireland, then she could have all Catholic Europe at her fingertips.

In early February 1566, foreign ambassadors were invited to a banquet before Darnley's investiture. Mary hung a portrait of Elizabeth in the hall in advance. In the midst of the banquet, she stood and announced that 'there was no other Queen of England but herself'. She had thrown down the gauntlet. Elizabeth had treated her badly and prevaricated and failed to behave to her as a sister. Now, she would take her revenge. Mary sent Randolph, Elizabeth's ambassador, home, accusing him of having given money to Moray and his rebels.

In the same month, Bothwell married Huntly's sister, Lady Jean Gordon, and Mary supplied the silver cloth for the bride's dress – a sign of great favour. Lady Jean was in love with Alexander Ogilvie – and had an unfortunate habit of wearing black for her loss of love. Still, she brought a big dowry and was a sensible, intelligent woman, so Bothwell could hardly complain. Mary paid for the lavish reception.

Ogilvie married Mary Beaton two months later, the second Mary of the four to leave her mistress.

In the shifting allegiances of Scotland, no moment of power lasted long. The nobles were already plotting to stop Mary. A new parliament was due, and in it Mary planned that Moray and his fellow Chaseabout rebels would lose their land and titles under a bill of attainder. All the lords, Protestant and Catholic, were opposed to this, for to them their claim was ancient and no mere monarch could overthrow it. The Protestants also feared that there would be a strengthening of Catholicism. Darnley had come to hate his wife and he too began to plot. His father told the Earl of Argyll that if Darnley were appointed King of Scotland, he would pardon the exiles and the religious order would be returned to the way it was before Mary arrived. But someone had to be blamed for Darnley's previous suggestions that he was opposed to the Protestant lords and would seize their land — and everyone alighted on Rizzio. Powerless and Catholic, hated by the court for his influence and mistrusted as homosexual and a papal spy because he was foreign, he was the perfect candidate. The Chaseabout supporters blamed him for Moray's continued exile — he had too much influence over the queen. Darnley, as high-handed, suspicious and easily manipulated as ever, listened to men who told him that Rizzio had betrayed him and had poisoned Mary against him, and grew convinced that it was the secretary's influence that denied him the crown matrimonial. The gossip got so wild that there were whispers Rizzio was Mary's lover and even the father of Mary's child.

The friendless secretary was surrounded by sharks on all sides. A plot had been growing during the early months of the year, led by nobles including the Earl of Morton — who Mary had honoured with the title of Lord Chancellor — and the Douglases, the Earl of Ruthven, the Earl Lindsay, all emboldened by winning over Darnley. They were Protestants, loyal to Moray who was in communication about matters behind the scenes, and the first three were related to Darnley and saw his advancement as creating theirs. Rizzio was just a small obstacle — what they really desired was to push the queen into a subordinate position, with Darnley as the ruler, while they pulled his strings.

The post-Rizzio plan was simple: Mary would be taken to Stirling until the birth of her child and Darnley would be king, pardoning Moray and the others for the Chaseabout rebellion, recalling those in exile and then the lords would encourage him to pursue the Protestant Reformation on the basis that they had given him power. This would also head off the risk that when Mary reached twenty-five, the age of majority, she could rescind gifts of land – and many lords had helped themselves to choice spots of the Catholic church possessions. Cecil thought the plan was simply to despatch Rizzio, and he was not opposed to it. The wily statesman had been outfoxed by his old friend Moray, for had the council thought there was a possibility of Mary being pushed into subordination and Darnley brought forth as king, they would have refused to support it. Elizabeth would not countenance it, for it hardly reflected well on female sovereigns, and she thought Darnley unpredictable and wild. She had always refused to recognise Darnley as King of Scotland and she would have never accepted him as sole king.

Morton and Ruthven thought Rizzio should be either put on trial on invented charges and publicly hanged, or killed while walking in the garden or playing tennis, a swift and easy death. But Darnley wanted him murdered in front of Mary, to teach her a lesson and make her afraid. The other lords balked – what if the queen was so distressed that she miscarried? Or got caught in the melee and injured? But Darnley was insistent. His wife must see her servant killed.

The English ambassador wrote to Leicester that the plans were underway and Rizzio 'shall have his throat cut within these ten days'. And it got worse. 'Many things grievouser and worse are brought to my ears, yea, of things intended against her Majesty's own person.'

Heavily pregnant, Mary was too confident. When she was told that she should pardon Moray or the lords might take revenge, she shrugged it off. 'What can they do? What dare they do?' She said that her countrymen tended to 'proclaim much but their threats were not carried out'.[2] Parliament assembled on 7 March and Mary pressed for the bill to deprive Moray of his property. The date for the bill was set as 12 March.

Melville tried to warn Rizzio, but he refused to listen and 'disdained all danger'. A French astrologer told Rizzio to be careful and encouraged him to return home. But Rizzio was of one mind with his mistress. 'What can they do?'[3]

Chapter Seventeen

'I Would Have Taken My Husband's Dagger and Stabbed Him with It!'

O
n the night of Saturday 9 March 1566, three days before Moray was due to be deprived of everything, Mary was eating dinner at Holyroodhouse with a small group of friends, including her half-sister Jean, Countess of Argyll; the Countess's mother (and former mistress to James V), Elizabeth Bethune; her half-brother Robert Stewart; the Master of the Household and the Master of the Horse; her French apothecary, and Rizzio. She was in the small dining room that led off her bedroom, which, along with the dressing room and presence chamber, constituted her apartments. Now that she was five months pregnant, Mary preferred to dine quietly at home with friends. She presumed her husband was out, behaving badly in taverns. She was wrong. Downstairs, in Darnley's apartments, eighty conspirators were grouping together.

The party were enjoying their meal when Darnley arrived in the chamber from the stairs below. Mary and her companions had not been expecting him but still, he was her husband and did come and go between the apartments. He sat beside Mary and started chatting, as if everything was quite normal. But then, the Earl of Ruthven, dressed in full armour and looking shockingly ill, staggered in and demanded Rizzio be given to him 'for he has been overlong here'.[1] Mary demanded Darnley explain and he, all cowardice, said he knew nothing. Ruthven declared that Rizzio had caused great offence to Mary, the king, the country and the nobility. He had promoted the Catholic religion and Catholic countries and denied the lords their lands. Ruthven told her that she had 'ruled contrary to the advice of your nobility and counsel' and said Rizzio had 'offended your honour, which I dare not be so bold to speak of'. And he had denied Darnley the crown matrimonial and encouraged Mary to banish the nobility and lose their lands. The Italian servant was responsible for all of Scotland's problems, it seemed.

Mary defended him and said he should be tried in Parliament if he was guilty of any misdemeanours and told Ruthven to depart on pain of treason. But the earl lumbered forth in his armour, pale and sweating with the exertion and made to grasp at Rizzio. Screaming, the secretary backed against Mary and the queen's attendants tried to pull Ruthven off but he waved his dagger and shouted, 'Lay not hands on me'. At this, more conspirators burst into the room from the staircase, some bearing guns. Ruthven seized the queen and told her not to be afraid, pushing her towards Darnley. 'Take the queen your sovereign and wife to you.' In the ensuing fight, a candelabra smashed to the ground, near the tapestries and the Countess of Argyll had the presence of mind to pull it away – otherwise they all could have burned. Ruthven and another stabbed at Rizzio as he cowered behind Mary's back and the dagger came so close to her that she felt the wind as it passed her. She was terrified that she would be killed next. As she now understood, the palace was filled with enemies, her servants and the palace guard had been overpowered and her husband was leading the way.

The conspirators grabbed Rizzio. Mary again tried to protect him but Andrew Ker, a Douglas ally, threatened her with a gun to make her keep back. She said later that he pointed his gun at her womb and tried to shoot but failed, and another conspirator said that another man had offered to stab the queen. But even though she thought herself on the brink of death, Mary valiantly tried to save her secretary, as he screamed and held on to her skirts. The men prised his fingers away from her gown and dragged Rizzio through to the top of the stairs, where the other men were ready for them. There they fell upon him and stabbed him in a shocking scrum of bloodshed while the queen and her friends listened, powerless in frozen horror, to the secretary's terrible screams. Darnley hung back but the men wanted his mark on the killing. One seized Darnley's dagger and used it to give Rizzio the final blow of death – and then he left the dagger sticking out of the corpse. As Mary said later, the murderers 'most cruelly took him forth of our cabinet and at the entry of our chamber gave him fifty-six strokes with whiniards and swords'. In her bloodstained chamber, she and her other guests heard it all – and feared the men were coming next for them. The reality was better, but not much. Mary was told she was now imprisoned.

Darnley had shuffled back in after the murder and she turned to her husband and demanded why he would see her treated thus – after she had taken him from a 'low estate and made you my husband'. 'What offence have I made you that you should have done me such shame?' Darnley started complaining, moaning that she had not 'entertained' him ever since she took to Rizzio and never visited him anymore. Mary dismissed his words, still brave, despite the horror and said it was his responsibility to visit her. But Darnley, bursting with adrenalin and furious about being treated as merely the queen's husband, launched into a tirade, saying she had promised obedience, and even if he had been from a 'baser degree', marriage made him her husband and her 'head'. Mary was almost speechless. His behaviour, the murder, the blood, his jealousy, was all too much. She told him, 'I shall be your wife no longer nor sleep with you anymore' and would not rest until he too had a heart as sorrowful as hers. Ruthven trudged back into Mary's presence, demanding a cup of wine because he was exhausted after the frenzy of fighting and killing. Mary shook her head at him. 'If I or my child die, you will have the blame.'[2]

The people of Edinburgh had heard the commotion and had assembled under the queen's windows, asking to speak with her. Lord Lindsay marched into her chamber and told her that if she spoke to them, 'we will cut you into collops and cast you over the walls'. Darnley told the men that it had been a minor domestic disturbance and all was well now. In the blink of an eye, Mary had become a prisoner.

Ruthven and Darnley finally left. Darnley had the men drag the corpse out of the chamber, throw it down the stairs and drag it off to the porter's lodge, where it was stripped of its belongings, Rizzio's beloved fine clothes taken away and sold. Next day, Rizzio's body was bundled into a grave at Holyrood. Bothwell, who had been elsewhere in the palace and whom the gang had also hoped to murder, fled with Huntly.

Mary was under strict surveillance and was isolated in her rooms, allowed only a few female attendants, with threatening men standing guard outside her door and patrolling the palace gates. High on his own success, Ruthven declared that if she tried to escape, 'we will throw her to them piecemeal, from the top of the terrace'.[3] Mary was on her own, entirely at the mercy of the conspiring lords. She feared they might use her as a puppet queen, to front their rule – or they might imprison her, unseat her and kill her. They hoped, above all, that the child would be a girl – for then what legitimacy could the queen have? All the power would be theirs.

Darnley dissolved parliament so that Moray's goods were safe, but he was having second thoughts. He was unnerved that the conspirators had been so eager to see his dagger in Rizzio and, now that they had won, none of them seemed very enthusiastic about listening to his plans for kingship. He began to worry that they had only used him and would throw him aside.

Mary spent all night unable to sleep and next morning wrote to the thirty-four-year-old Earl of Argyll, begging for his help. Although he had been an ally of Moray and a keen Protestant, he was married to her half-sister, who had been forced to witness the murder as Mary's companion and he was a man who was traditional and supportive of the monarchy. She gambled correctly in writing to him. She decided that the only way to escape was by getting Darnley onside, even though he had killed a man in front of her and humiliated her. That afternoon, when Darnley visited, she berated him for his betrayal. 'You have done me so grievous an injury within the last twenty four hours that I shall never be able to forget it' – and she ignored his protestations that he had been dragged into the plot. She played on his paranoid nature, planting the seed of possibility that the lords might be double-crossing them both, that he too might be locked up with her. Darnley, beginning to panic that Moray and the others might exclude him or imprison him too, told her that the plan was to confine her at Stirling and govern without her and she realised she had to act fast. She understood that the whole plan had been about her, not Rizzio. Yes, he was unpopular and disliked, but killing him in front of the queen had been a way of bringing her to heel and an excuse for imprisoning her, forcing her under their control. Mary instructed her errant husband that he had to save her: 'you have placed us both on the brink of the precipice, you must now deliberate how we shall escape the peril'.[4]

That afternoon, she declared she was about to miscarry and needed her gentlewomen. Without an heir Darnley was nothing, so he forced Ruthven to allow the doctor and midwife to visit the captive. They said that the queen was delicate and should be attended by her ladies as normal. Ruthven agreed to send away some of the guards, convinced that Mary couldn't escape. Mary's ladies were immediately on her side, took letters to Bothwell and Huntly, who advised her to escape from Holyroodhouse however she could, leaping over the walls by ropes and chairs if she had to, and then flee. The enterprising Countess of Huntly even managed to smuggle a rope ladder to the queen, hidden between two dinner plates – but as Mary would have to clamber out of the window in full view of the guards, she decided it was impossible.

Moray was already widely suspected of being involved. The fact he'd been away wasn't fooling anyone. He popped up again, having returned fortuitously on the day after the murder, visited Mary and pressed for a pardon for all the lords. Mary made gestures to please him, accepting that he had not been involved but she refused to acquit all the lords. She said that she felt she had been too lenient in the past, and this had emboldened the nobles to misbehave. She saw herself, the queen, as the dispenser of justice and said she owed it 'to everybody' and so could not give them a 'full pardon the minute you ask'. She would, however, if they behaved well and loyally, 'endeavour to forget'. When Moray reported back, the lords were furious. She could still prosecute them for the murder in the future and they still felt she could take back the church lands. The lords refused the offer. Mary was stuck.

Mary believed that she had to escape. She might have done better to stay and attempt to rule the lords by dividing and conquering – being friendly to Moray and those who had backed his Chaseabout Raid while punishing Ruthven and the murderers. The news was slowly leaking out to the public that Rizzio had been brutally killed and their queen was being held and the uneasy alliance between conspirators was already crumbling.

She continued to persuade Darnley to help her flee. She offered to come to him as a wife and he was won over. Mary spoke to him cleverly, telling him that he couldn't trust the lords and they would never give him the crown. She told him that the best way to govern was to be above the various factions. He was entirely convinced and agreed to help her escape to Dunbar, the nearest royal fortress and the home of the sister of Bothwell.

Mary used her pregnancy again. She, Darnley and her ladies said she needed air otherwise she might miscarry. The lords had to assent. She said she would sign paperwork pardoning them and they duly prepared it. That night, she said – using her health just as Elizabeth so often did – that she did not feel well enough to sign documents but would do it in the morning. She had, of course, been feeling perfectly well and that night, at midnight, she left her rooms clandestinely, through the servants' quarters and out, over the land where poor Rizzio was buried, onto horses prepared by her servants. It was a long, dark journey of five hours to Dunbar – and Mary suffered through it. But she was free.

The lords had been outwitted. They guessed where she had gone and wrote to her asking for the pardons to be signed. Mary did not reply. Instead, she wrote at length to Elizabeth of the miseries of her treatment, drawing a parallel between them both as queens, the dreadful treatment that Mary had suffered and Elizabeth might yet experience.[5] As the days ticked on and Mary still did not sign the collective exoneration, some nobles lost their nerve and asked for individual pardons and made overtures to Argyll about discussing a settlement. The queen knew, then, that she had her power back. Bothwell and Huntly gathered an army for her and on the morning of 18 March, Mary returned to Edinburgh with nearly 8,000 men, as well as Darnley, Bothwell, Huntly and her older supporters – and was welcomed with enthusiasm by her people. She took a house in the High Street rather than Holyroodhouse, because for her it was still tainted, her old home a bloodstained prison.

Mary sent messages to Moray's Chaseabout rebels that they would be pardoned as long as they did not attempt to assist the murderers of Rizzio. All of the Rizzio conspirators were declared outlaws and Mary pronounced that everything they owned should be given to the Crown. Darnley declared that he had nothing to do with the plot and hadn't even known about it, thus undermining the rebels at a stroke. Morton, Ruthven and Andrew Ker – who had waved the gun at her – fled to England and begged Cecil for his protection, declaring they had only been following Darnley's orders. Elizabeth was less than pleased to have the plotters in her realm and sharply told Morton to go elsewhere; Ruthven, long sickly, died in Newcastle soon after being denounced as a rebel. Knox, who expected to be caught up in the recriminations, dashed to Ayrshire, where he wrote his history of the Reformation in Scotland. Mary, it seemed, had won, even if it meant Bothwell now thought he had power over her.

Poor Rizzio was forgotten in his makeshift grave, all his possessions forfeit. The lords had genuinely disliked him and thought he had too much influence with the queen. But Mary had a goodly number of French and Italian servants. And if it had simply been about him, they would have killed him and that would have been that. But they wanted to confine her, reduce her, rule instead of her. The attempt was upon her, the ultimate end to imprison her at Stirling as Darnley had confessed. The queen had used all her courage, ingenuity and strength to escape and it had been a brilliant coup.

Mary had Rizzio reburied in a Catholic ceremony and she even appointed his brother, Joseph, young and very inexperienced, as secretary in his place to show them she could not be cowed. But she saw her reign was weakened, that she did not have enough support to pursue a policy of Catholic reform and she would have to be careful of the lords thenceforth. And the lords had sent her evidence that Darnley had signed the document taking responsibility for the plot against Rizzio and promising pardons for all concerned. She could have had Darnley executed for treason, but it would be a terrible scandal, half the aristocracy would be implicated, and she needed him to assent to the legitimacy of their child. She had to tolerate him but she resolutely excluded him from court business, which only made him angrier, drunk every night, ruing how he had been tricked by everybody. But with the rest of the lords, Mary had reached an uneasy truce. Even though Moray had led one rebellion against her and failed to save her from imprisonment post-Rizzio, she was attempting to trust him again. He was her half-brother, she thought, her old friend and surely would be loyal to her from thenceforth.

Elizabeth's spies told her of the events of 9 March and the aftermath. She read the reports and Mary's letter in shock. She would never be treated so! 'Had I been in Queen Mary's place, I would have taken my husband's dagger and stabbed him with it!'[6] Perhaps Mary would have been better off if she had. Elizabeth was keen that no one thought she had any knowledge or involvement with the plot and was seen wearing a miniature of Mary at her waist. She hated what Darnley had done and was delighted by Mary's request to act as godmother to the forth-coming baby. It seemed that one benefit had been born of the horror: a rapprochement between the queens.

Chapter Eighteen
Looking Through Their Fingers

As Mary grew closer to childbed, Cecil worried. A male child would be a challenge to Elizabeth; her Catholic subjects might be keen to depose her for him, her Protestant subjects too, simply to have a man on the throne. He devised a cunning plan of sending a spy, Christopher Rokesby, who would pose as a Catholic and tell Mary that the nobles in England wished her to be queen – if only she would give him a token or signature to assent to the plot. Mary was suspicious and sent the man away. Rokesby returned to England to collect signatures of support and then arrived back in Scotland. Mary had him arrested and his papers confiscated – and a note from Cecil in code was found in his effects. It was deciphered and turned out to be offering a reward if Rokesby had success. It was a ham-fisted plot and now Mary had certain evidence that Cecil meant to pull her and Scotland down and she had no doubt that Elizabeth had not known and would not approve. She sent him a subtle letter, carefully suggesting that he should devote himself to the 'nourishing of peace and amity'.[1] If he didn't, she would tell Elizabeth – and Cecil would be in trouble.

Darnley, difficult as ever, demanded attention and caused arguments – and Mary tried to avoid him whenever she could. She was worried that conflict could explode during her confinement, as if the lords were a tinder box of rebellion that her absence would set on fire in a moment. Moray and Bothwell were in dispute again and Moray was trying to push his rival away from court. Mary moved to Edinburgh Castle for safety and took her new secretary, Joseph Rizzio, with her, an unwise move.

Mary called her lords to hear her will, in case she died in childbirth. A regency would be pursued through a committee and she left most of her goods to her child and the Scottish Crown. She decided on the distribution of her jewels, many to the Guises, but she also remembered Darnley's parents, Moray, Robert Stewart, the four Marys, and various lords including Argyll, Huntly and Bishop Leslie. Darnley would receive one of her wedding rings. 'It was with this that I married. I leave it to the King who gave it to me.'

In early June, the queen took to her confinement in Edinburgh Castle, her rooms hung with velvet and tapestries to block out the windows, all chosen because they bore calming images rather than visions of biblical vengeance, in order to soothe mother and child. One small window allowed light and air through – for it was thought that too much light could damage the woman's eyes and a chill for the baby was feared, even in June. On 18 June, her labour began and she transferred to her cabinet, a small room off the main bedroom. It was long and very painful. Her ladies panicked and begged the doctor to help her, but there was nothing that could be done but tell the queen to be strong and bear the excruciating pain of the contractions. Like most women, she would have begged God for assistance, clutched holy relics or called on St Margaret for help – she had been eaten by a dragon but then spat out because she was holding a crucifix; the ideal was that a baby should be born as swiftly as St Margaret had been sent out of the dragon's mouth. The Reformation had come into the delivery room: Protestant women could not hold crucifixes, relics, call out to the saints. And thus, perhaps it was some comfort for those, like Mary, who at this moment of great fear and pain were able to cling on to the physical objects of the old religion. The poor queen said she was 'so sore handled that she wished she had never been married'.[2]

Twenty hours later, after the hour of ten in the morning on 19 June, Mary gave birth to a perfect baby boy. 'I have borne him,' she wrote later, 'and God knoweth with what danger to him and me both.'[3] As she lay, weary and suffering, the city around her erupted into joy for the birth of a boy. The castle guns were fired and five hundred bonfires were lit across the city. Mary Beaton had rushed to Sir James Melville with the news and he set off immediately for London with tidings that the Scottish crown now had a 'fair sonne'. Elizabeth greeted him with some distress: the queen had a son and 'I am but of barren stock'.[4]

Mary was exhausted and could not recover her health. Even five days later, she could barely summon the energy to speak to the English envoy, Henry Killigrew, when he visited, but he was more interested in the baby, whom he judged very healthy. The little boy would be James, the great name of kings borne by her father, grandfather, great-grandfather, great-great grandfather in a straight line of men called James back to her great-great-great grandfather, James I, who came to the throne in 1406, after the death of his father, King Robert III.

Darnley visited her too and Mary had to swallow her pride so he would accept the child as his own. As she said, 'this is your son, and no other man's son'. She wished everyone there to bear witness and said 'he is so much your son that I fear it will be the worse for him hereafter'. She was still broken-hearted at Darnley's betrayal. 'I have forgiven all but will never forget', she said, begging him to remember that Andrew Ker had held his pistol to her belly.[5] Darnley was incensed and went out drinking in Edinburgh every night of Mary's lying-in, staggering back so late that he had to demand the castle doors were opened for him. His son was both a bolster and a threat to him – for the child pushed him further down the line of succession. And, if the child lived, Mary had no more real use for a husband.

Elizabeth was torn. Little Prince James was a threat to her: the king that England so desired. Catholic Europe might be emboldened to invade, on the basis of putting him on the throne. As politic as ever, she put on a good show of being pleased for Mary and made sympathetic noises about noting Mary as her successor in the next parliament. She agreed to be godmother but said she could not attend personally and would send lords and ladies as stand-ins. The baby's other godparents were Charles IX of France and the Duke of Savoy. Mary was making her son a European king, untouchable by her nobles.

Mary was both strengthened and weakened by the arrival of a son. She had performed her duty and continued the line, the great role of a monarch and a queen. But a boy, even one who couldn't yet lift his head, was worth more than a woman, and if the lords deposed her for her son, there would be significant support in the country for a regency from those lords who thought they would gain power and favour from Moray. And even though Darnley was generally disliked, if he was to throw himself behind a regency, the lords might take him up once more. But Darnley, at his moment of greatest power, behaved most irrationally – and said he was leaving Mary to live abroad. He was behaving so oddly that the Privy Council wrote to Catherine de' Medici to note that he was insane and to ask for her support in preventing him from setting up a royal court in exile. In the end, he remained in Scotland, hanging around, going out late, causing trouble.

The baby prince was sent off to Stirling, as was often the case for royal children, accompanied by four hundred soldiers, arriving at a nursery sumptuously furnished with tapestries and gold and silver accoutrements. Plans were made for a great christening and both commoners and nobles seemed united in their enthusiasm for the child.

Mary was still very ill after her difficult birth. In July, she travelled for some sea air and then on to Traquair, home of the captain of her guard. There, she began to suspect that she was pregnant again. Although it was very soon, Mary had the symptoms of early pregnancy for she was sick and dizzy. Darnley told her she had to accompany him hunting and she whispered in his ear that she thought she was once more with child. He shouted roughly, 'Never mind, if we lose this one, we can make another.'[6] The company was stunned. It was obvious to everyone that Darnley had not a shred of esteem left for his wife. In fact Mary was not pregnant but simply unwell. Darnley, though, clearly didn't care whether she was ill or pregnant. The French ambassador, Philibert du Croc, tried to talk to Darnley to moderate his behaviour but came away feeling it was a hopeless case. He could see no likelihood of 'good understanding between them' because 'the King will never humble himself as he ought' and the 'Queen can't perceive any one nobleman speaking with the King, but presently she suspects some contrivance between them'.[7]

In only five years, Mary had been constantly challenged – by Arran and Bothwell, by Moray and the rebels, and by Morton and the Douglases – as well as facing plenty of minor rebellions along the way. She was naturally concerned about plots to harm those about her, whether it was Joseph Rizzio, other confidants or even her son. In England, Elizabeth's ministers were likewise terrified that their own queen could be threatened and killed, hence their paranoid panic with spies and attempt to create sedition in neighbouring countries. Mary felt the same, but she bore all the fear herself for she could trust no one. As Darnley's friend Ker had waved a gun at her and another had offered to stab her, she naturally fretted that his associates still wanted to kill her. Now he had a son, his position was secure. If Mary died, he could be regent for the child – and he and his family would have all the power. It was obvious that life would be better for Darnley if his wife had died in childbirth. Mary saw plots all about her and this was because some of them were real.

Mary had come to lay particular trust in Bothwell. He was Lieutenant of the Borders and she relied on him to keep this most troublesome region under control. Bothwell had a superficial gloss of sophistication: he was well read, had travelled widely and could speak French. But he was a man who settled every dispute with his fists, an old-style feudal lord always looking for a fight. He had constant affairs with young servants and anyone he could persuade to be his mistress (and we have already heard of one of his abduction fantasies about the queen). Some way from Darnley's male-model looks, he was smaller than Mary at five-feet-six, called ugly by most of the courtiers, because he had un-appealing features and a large nose that had been broken a few times in scuffles. He was strong and fast, a skilled horseman and quite a good military commander. And his plain appearance actually worked to his advantage; in Mary's history, handsome men like Darnley and Moray had betrayed her, whereas the plain men like Rizzio were devoted. Most importantly of all, he had known Mary for years and she lay great store by friendship over time. Although she had made the gestures of forgiving those who had plotted against her, in her heart she was still afraid of them. Bothwell, who had been innocent of the Rizzio conspiracy and helped her escape, was now firmly lodged in her mind as a loyal man she could trust, come what may.

In early October, the queen had to travel to Jedbergh, near the border with England, to hold a court, accompanied by Moray and the rest of her circle. Bothwell was resting nearby at a castle, after fighting near the border had left him severely wounded. They all set off to pay him a brief visit in the day. When Mary returned, she fell severely ill. She was suffering convulsions and vomiting, in one spate sixty times, and, on one terrifying day, lay almost dead for half an hour. Within a week, she was lying stiff and cold, her limbs contorted. Her doctor bandaged her tightly and then poured wine into her mouth and forced her to swallow and Mary began to show signs of recovery – one of the few times when the practices of sixteenth-century doctors had a beneficial effect. The Privy Council blamed Darnley for her state and decided that his obsession with power and being crowned and his ill-treatment of the queen had caused all the problems. First Rizzio, now Darnley was the scapegoat. And Mary was losing her spirit. She told Moray that with Darnley, she could never have a happy day in her life.[8] 'I do believe the principal part of her disease to consist of a deep grief and sorrow,' reported the French ambassador. She often cried, 'I could wish to be dead.'[9]

She may have had a stomach ulcer or perhaps symptoms of porphyria, but her illness was definitely influenced by her low spirits. For Maitland, 'the root of it is the king' – she had raised him, but 'he has recompensed her with such ingratitude and misuses himself so far towards her that it is heartbreak for her to think he should be her husband'.[10] Bothwell came to her often to visit. He was a faithless lothario who saw the queen as a means to power, like they all did, and aimed to exploit her trust in him by playing the swain, attempting to make her fall in love with him. Darnley could still be executed – or the marriage annulled. And then she would need another husband. Bothwell thought himself the perfect candidate. He quite fancied himself as king.

Mary thought she might die and was directing her thoughts to her child. Anyone was better than Darnley as the baby's protector and so she turned to her cousin queen, vowing that after her death 'the special care of the protection of our own son' was to be given to Elizabeth, who should see James as her child. Elizabeth, she knew, respected monarchy and would protect his life. Elizabeth assented to the proposal and Mary wrote to thank her 'dearest sister' for doing so.[11] The offer of James entirely won Elizabeth's heart and a ready-made son in the wings was helpful for her efforts at fighting off potential husbands. The Queen of England was frustrated with her own advisors and their obsession with marriage – and Mary's letter was perfectly timed. Elizabeth suggested she might abandon the Treaty of Edinburgh and begin with another one, that was focused on 'amity'[12] and would declare Mary heir apparent, as long as Mary accepted she would lose any claim if Elizabeth had children. She would also have to promise not to attempt the English throne and each party would recognise the other as a lawful queen. What Mary had wanted for so long had finally been achieved.

By the close of the year, Mary's advisors had had enough of Darnley. He was highhanded and rude, threatened whatever action he pleased and his debauched behaviour gave a bad impression of Scotland to the overseas ambassadors – quite apart from being a blackmail risk. They shared the queen's suspicions that he was plotting with other men against her. The idea of Darnley as regent for James after Mary's death was hateful to them. The Lennoxes would have all the power. Moray and Arran would be much reduced – as would Morton, Maitland, Argyll and Huntly – as well as Bothwell, whom Darnley hated.

At Craigmillar Castle, on her way to her son's christening, Mary discussed divorce with her loyal lords. According to Huntly's later account, it was Moray and Maitland who first spoke of divorce to Argyll, and then to Huntly and Bothwell. The five of them went to Mary with the idea.[13] They wanted Mary and Darnley separated and him sent abroad. They would have to destroy the papal dispensation (issued because Darnley and Mary were related) to do so and the Pope would have to be consulted, and he might very well refuse the request. Mary was reluctant to start proceedings for she was afraid of her husband but, as they pointed out, he was only going to start plotting again, if he wasn't already, for 'remaining with her majesty, he would not cease until he did her some other evil turn'. She could not sit about waiting to be poisoned.

Mary feared divorce because she did not want to undermine the position of her son, 'otherwise her Highness would rather endure all torments and abide the perils that might chance her'. Her advisors talked of arresting Darnley and then their talk took a dark turn, saying Moray would 'look through his fingers' at what they might do – implying that a criminal act against Darnley would occur, which Moray would be aware of and condone, if not actively be engaged in. Mary refused to hear of it. 'Let us guide the matter amongst us,' said Maitland. He added that they would do 'nothing that was not good and approved by Parliament'.[14]

But while Mary returned to her rooms, they made a further promise to each other: signing a bond that Darnley should be got rid of. The bond does not survive, so we can see it only through the various and conflicting testimonies, but those declared as signatories included Argyll, Huntly, Bothwell and Maitland. Moray was present, although he may not have signed. Maitland was keen on legal measures, such as divorce or even arrest for treason. But for both, Darnley would have to be forced to cooperate. As one document signed by various lords lays out, if there was not a divorce on the basis of consanguity or adultery they might then 'get him convicted of treason because he consented to her Grace's imprisonment' (they meant after Rizzio's death; the original wording was 'hir Grace's retentioun in ward'). This was a good idea, but unfortunately too many other nobles were involved in that episode and a treason trial for Darnley might drag them all into it. And so they ended 'or what other ways to dispatch him, which altogether her Grace refuses as is widely known'.[15]

Mary was unhappy with Darnley and did fear he might be plotting to kill her, but she was staunchly against anything violent or his 'dispatch'. Why did they keep telling her of their plots to kill him when they knew she would not entertain it? As even the Spanish ambassador in London, Diego Guzman de Silva (who had replaced Quadra) had said, 'the displeasure of the Queen of Scotland with her husband is carried so far, that she was approached by some who wanted to induce her to allow a plot to be formed against him, which she refused'.[16] Not only were they telling Mary their plans, but they were also allowing the information to get back to London and the Spanish ambassador – and if Silva knew, then Cecil did too. We have to ask, what possible benefit was it to them that Cecil should know this? The plotters wanted support from England. And they also wanted Cecil and everybody across Europe to know that Mary knew of the plots. She was being framed.

Moray hated Darnley and he rightly saw Darnley's declaration that he had too much land as a threat to his property. With Darnley out of the way, Moray could assume power, for Mary would hopefully be dissuaded from remarrying for a while, now that she had a legitimate heir. But Moray's problem was that even if his friends dispatched Darnley, he would still have Mary, resistant, not Protestant and increasingly ill-disposed to listen to him. After the Chaseabout raid and his failure to rescue her from the post-Rizzio imprisonment, she did not trust him.

The ideal situation for Moray would be both Mary and Darnley dead – for then he could assume the role as regent. But there was no way he was going to kill the queen or persuade anyone else to do it. That would be going too far. But implicate her in the murder of Darnley – so that she was confused, hated, withdrew, put everything in his hands and let him be regent for baby James? Win–win. The question of who benefits leads directly to Moray. He hated Darnley, he had come up with the divorce idea, he was pushing forward the plans and his 'looking through his fingers' had been mentioned to Mary as a way of encouraging her to agree to something on the other side of the law. But there was no way that such a shocking event as the death of the king was not going to be investigated, with culprits hanged and all the foreign ambassadors demanding vengeance (they might have despaired of Darnley's behaviour but killing a king was an affront to all authority and monarchy). What Moray needed to do was to make sure the suspicion was thrown onto anyone but him. And if he threw it onto his sister, he would gain all he desired.

Moray had already rebelled against his sister and tried to seize the throne from her, criticising the foreigners at court, Darnley, Catholicism and questions about selling church lands and the distributions of bene-fices. These grievances were still with him, as everyone knew. In the plot to kill Darnley, Bothwell and the Douglases, along with Morton, would do the dirty work. But even though he would absent himself from the situation, as with the Rizzio murder, people would think he had been involved. So he had to divert their attention – and Mary was the perfect scapegoat.

The christening was to be a great celebration, with the Privy Council offering the queen £12,000 for the ceremony – nearly £4 million today. On 17 December, the prince was finally christened in the chapel royal of Stirling Castle, in a Catholic ceremony that caused much upset among the lords. He was borne from the royal apartments to the chapel by the Count of Brienne, on behalf of the King of France, and the Countess of Argyll stood in for Elizabeth I. The Queen of England had sent a marvellous gold font, weighing exactly 'three hundred and thirty-three ounces' – and had got it to Scotland despite a gang of professional thieves who had tried to steal it in Doncaster.[17] The proud mother gave the nobility gold and silver outfits at her own expense. Mary presided over the balls and banquets that declared James's magnifi-cence to the world, with fireworks and masques written by George Buchanan (who later turned his pen on Mary in crueller ways). One particular guest was pointedly missing. Darnley remained in his rooms at Stirling, sulking. Philibert du Croc, the kind-hearted French ambas-sador who had been told by Catherine de' Medici not to deal with the queen's husband because she thought him treacherous, believed that

Darnley did not want all the envoys to see how low was his status and reputation at court, while the Parisian lawyer Claude Nau (who worked for the Guise family and would later be Mary's confidential secretary) thought that Darnley suspected Elizabeth's envoy would not recognise him as King of Scotland and was resentful that she was a godparent. Perhaps Darnley was trying to threaten, to suggest what might happen if he withdrew his assent to the child's legitimacy, test his power. Whatever the truth, he humiliated Mary publicly and he also undermined Elizabeth by not recognising her proxy. As du Croc fretted, 'His bad behaviour is incurable'.[18]

Mary finally decided to pardon Morton and the others who had plotted against Rizzio – with the exception of Andrew Ker and George Douglas – and did so on Christmas Eve. Morton and most of his associates blamed Darnley for ruining their plot and betraying them. By inviting them back, she was exposing her husband to risk – and Darnley knew it. He was petrified and swept off to Glasgow, where the Lennox family were strong, hoping for better treatment. Left behind, Mary was listening to legal experts continue to talk of the possibility of divorce or annulling the marriage on the grounds of consanguity, pre-existing relation (tricky, as everyone of royal blood was related), or adultery. The latter was difficult to use in such cases and the former would be up to the Pope – who could very well say no. As step-cousins, Mary and Darnley were hardly closely related. On 6 January, Maitland had married Mary Fleming, one of the four Marys, and this brought him closer into the queen's trusted circle. Her secretary of state, her half-brother, her close friends – they were all telling her they would deal with Darnley, but in legal ways.

While in Glasgow, a Lennox stronghold, Darnley fell ill and 'livid pustules broke out' painfully over his whole body. He also lost his hair. It was said he had smallpox, but more likely it was syphilis – and he had had breakouts before. (When his skull was analysed much later at the Royal College of Surgeons, it revealed 'traces of a violent syphilitic disease'.[19]) This was yet more humiliation for Mary, evidence that he had been louche and might even have given her and her beloved son the dreadful disease.

Mary heard her husband was planning to steal Prince James and set up as a great monarch without her – and on 14 January she promptly had James taken from Stirling to live with her at Holyrood. Darnley begged Mary to visit him but she refrained, saying she had fallen and injured herself, although she did send her personal doctor to him. He was seriously ill – but not dying, although the possibility of that gave heart to many around him.

Bothwell – unscrupulous, misogynist and violent – had convinced Mary that he had her best interests at heart and was attempting to secure her affections as well. Emboldened by the queen's trust and convinced of his brilliant effect on women, he felt that his only block to complete power over Mary was Darnley. And thus he agreed to take on the actual business of the plot initially driven by Moray.

Mary's friends told her Darnley was planning her death. The dreaded Andrew Ker had returned from England and was crowing about the revenge he was going to take. He had been issued a pardon, probably by Darnley, without Mary's say-so and he was a clear Darnley supporter. The queen was afraid of her husband.

On 27 January, Mary's envoy in Paris sent her a letter with the news that he had also heard there was a plot against her.[20] Her life was in danger, again, but he had no clue as to the details.

The lords feared Darnley was gathering support in Glasgow and so they needed to strike. Again, Mary said 'she would have no speech on the matter'.[21] She didn't understand – no one had told her – that they were talking of murder. She wanted Darnley brought under control and it seems to be the case that she thought they were going to threaten him and commit a small amount of violence. Darnley had punched and threatened before: it was a language he understood. Some of the lords did think this was what was in the offing. But others wanted him killed. At Holyrood, in dark corners, in private rooms in taverns, late at night in houses, men plotted and laid out how they might dispatch the husband. And yet, the Spanish ambassador already knew – many people did. Silva was not particularly keyed in to the networks of the court and his spies were poor. Someone had told him, fed him the information.

The three big problems of the Darnley murder, which have not been fully accounted for, are *cui bono*, Bothwell's influence, and the question of reprisals. Scotland is too often viewed as a lawless country at this time. Yes, there was violence and nobles punching each other on their sickbeds. But the country was strong on the rule of law and prided itself on justice. Perhaps a few peasants or servants could be quietly murdered. But one could not kill a king, the father of the future heir, a relation of Elizabeth

I, and not expect some retaliation or prosecution. Someone would have to be put on trial – the ordinary people would not stand for anything less. So the men could hardly have imagined that they would not be punished.

Some have theorised that Bothwell was the master of the plot. But he was unpopular – partly because of his gruff character and partly because he had gone the other way to everyone else over the Rizzio plot. He was not liked or supported by the other lords and could hardly have staged the killing by himself. He would have needed help. It is also significant that Moray hated Bothwell and wanted him dislodged. Arran and the Hamiltons detested him as well. But Moray saw that he could be useful. Bothwell could be persuaded to actually carry out the murder along with various accomplices – and cover his hands with blood while the rest looked through their fingers.

Mary was constantly looking for advisors who truly cared for her, rather than what they could gain. Elizabeth had the ever-loyal Cecil and also Dudley, but Mary had arrived in Scotland against the backdrop of long battles between the lords and interfamilial strife that went back decades, even hundreds of years. The only other possible strategy would have been to favour no one, to play the lords off against each other, but that would have been risky too. There was no chance to advance a keen independent lawyer, as Henry VIII had done with Thomas Cromwell. And now, with the plot against Darnley, Moray and the rest could make the ultimate power grab.

Darnley was returning to Edinburgh to complete his convalescence. Mary went to escort him. But he was still too ill and marked to attend court – he wore a piece of taffeta over his face to hide the pocks of syphilis – so he had to go to a place where he could be private. Mary thought he might wish to stay at Craigmillar Castle, not far from Edinburgh, but he took a house just inside the town wall, the old provost's lodgings of the church of Kirk o' Field. The choice was between one owned by his enemies, the Hamiltons, and one owned by the Balfours. He chose the latter. Possibly he suspected a plot and wanted to choose a different house to that offered to him. It was a rather comfortable and well-appointed house at the south side of the quad-rangle, although hardly suitable for the queen's husband. It was quickly furnished with items from the royal apartments at Holyrood – his room was decorated with six pieces of tapestry, a Turkish carpet, red velvet cushions and a velvet-covered chair and table and he had his ornate bed, draped in purple velvet, sent up from Holyrood. The room below Darnley's was appointed and decorated for the queen, when she chose to visit along with her nobles and courtiers. Darnley kept his servants with him but there was no royal guard. This was significant.

Darnley arrived on Saturday 1 February and seemed content. Mary stayed overnight in her room on Wednesday and visited in the daytimes, and by Friday Darnley was so touched by her attentions that he passed on information he had about various plots against her, and she once more stayed for the night. On Friday, he took a medicinal bath and Mary nursed him. On Saturday night, he told Mary that Lord Robert, her half-brother, had told him his life was in danger, but then when questioned Robert denied he had ever said anything. Still, as Darnley was recovering quickly, it was thought that he should move soon and on the next day, Sunday, it was announced that he would return to Holyrood on the following day, Monday 10 February. The day was one of great celebrations across Edinburgh for it was the last Sunday before Lent. And Holyrood was busy with the wedding of Mary's favourite valet, Bastian Pagez. The queen attended his wedding breakfast at midday, and then at four there was a formal dinner for the ambassador of Savoy, attended by all the major nobles. Only Moray was missing – on Sunday morning, he begged permission to leave for St Andrews to attend his sick wife, and so, conveniently, he disappeared.

On Sunday evening, Mary and a large party of nobles and courtiers arrived at Kirk o'Field and crammed into Darnley's rooms. Bothwell was there, resplendent in black velvet and silver-trimmed satin. There was music and conversation – and then Mary was reminded that she had promised to attend the masque to celebrate Bastian's wedding. Darnley was cross and unhappy but the queen gave him a ring and bid him goodbye. The whole party then set off for Holyrood, leaving an angry Darnley to his bath and bed. On the way out, Mary met the servant who had once been Bothwell's, Nicholas Hubert, nicknamed French Paris. 'How begrimed you are!' she said in surprise.[22]

At some point that day, probably while Mary was entertaining the ambassador, dark-clothed men had crept into the house and crammed it full of gunpowder.

Chapter Nineteen
'So Horrible and Strange'

I n the early morning of 10 February 1567, a terrifying explosion shook Edinburgh. The 'blast was fearful to all about and many rose from their beds'.[1] At Holyrood Palace, Mary sprang awake, hearing what she thought was the noise of twenty or thirty cannon, and sent her guards to investigate. The people of Kirk o'Field dashed out and saw the whole house in which the king had lodged blown to rubble. They believed the queen might still be in there too. Mass panic ensued, slightly alleviated when they spotted one of Darnley's servants, clinging to the town wall for dear life. The searchers broke into the garden – and there saw the bodies of Darnley, and his servant William Taylor, lying under a pear tree. The king was wearing only his nightshirt. Beside him was his furred cloak, a chair, a gown, a dagger and a rope. There were no marks of violent landing, blood or bruising on the bodies. It was quite impossible that the two men, sleeping in different rooms, could have been blown out of the building, over the wall and into the garden, a distance of a good forty feet. The watch realised they were looking at a murder scene. Both men had been strangled.

The messengers ran post-haste to the queen and delivered her the news that her husband was dead. Mary was near to collapse, believing that she had been the target of the killers. Bothwell was sheriff of Edinburgh and was awakened (from a sleep that had been very short) and rode to Kirk o'Field with soldiers and took the bodies to the new provost's lodgings. There they were surveyed by surgeons, the Privy Council and then the general public. Those who looked at Darnley discussed the pristine state of his body, and then the gossip spread that marks of strangulation had been visible. English spies were on the site in a moment. Some old women who lived nearby had heard men rushing away, and one, Mrs Mertine, had shouted after them, sure that they were engaged in evil doings. Another woman who lived near the orchard and garden of Kirk o'Field said she heard a man crying, 'Pity me, kinsmen!'.[2]

In Holyrood, sick and panicked, Mary wrote to her ambassador in Paris, stunned by what had happened, the thing 'so horrible and strange'. James Beaton, Archbishop of Glasgow, nephew of the disgraced Cardinal, was a close advisor, a man she really trusted. She still thought Darnley had died in the explosion and that the attack had been meant for her. 'Always, whoever have taken this wicked enterprise in hand, we assure our self it was dressed always for us as for the King, for we lay the most part of all the last week in that same lodging, and was there accompanied with the most part of the lords that are in this town at the same time at midnight, and of very chance, waited not all night, by reason of some masque in the abbey'.[3] She believed that God had rescued her. And she had no idea of the link to her lords. She planned to seek out the guilty men and bring them to justice. 'We hope to punish the same with such rigour as shall serve for example of this cruelty of all ages to come.'

The English spies busied themselves creating the sketches that would inform the incredible drawing of the murder scene commissioned by William Drury, second in command to Elizabeth's lieutenant in the north. It is astonishing to look at it in the National Archives now: the sketch that shows a murder. Darnley and his servant lie in the field, the house a pile of rubble – as Mary put it in her letter to Paris, 'nothing remaining, no, not a stone above another'. It underlines the impossibility that Darnley and Taylor could have died as a consequence of the explosion – unlike the grooms, who did die in the blast. The drawing made clear that Darnley was murdered, to the degree of showing Prince James in his cot praying to God to avenge his cause. The drawing is a very useful plan. But it is not an objective document; every stroke is about vengeance.

The queen was afraid for her own life and that of her son, and she could not believe what had happened. She passed the days in a daze. She slept until noon on the day after Darnley's death because she had been up late and worrying. But the queen appearing to sleep soundly on the day after her husband died did not give a good impression.

Mary ordered the whole court into mourning and embarked on the forty days of grief that was expected of her. But within twenty-four hours, she broke mourning to attend the wedding of one of her bedchamber attendants, Margaret Carwood. She was still in shock and didn't want to break her promise to be present – but it was a very unwise move. For the world was beginning to whisper about the murder and the shadows of gossip were coming very close to the queen. In her grief and terror, Mary fell prey to her old foes of sickness and migraines and the doctors sent her to take the air for a few days at Seton. She was lost, uncomprehending, struggling to think straight, having suffered greatly over the previous year, her mind fragile, her understanding overturned, unable to act. This would have been entirely reasonable and forgiven if she'd been a queen consort. But she was queen regnant, and she was expected not just to grieve for her husband but to act to punish the criminals. She needed to make a great speech to vow vengeance and weep for the crowd. She needed to throw herself into a paroxysm of public grief and say she would not rest until the guilty were arrested. Then she needed to find the guilty – or even the innocent, if needed – and put them on trial.

True grief often does not manifest immediately in such dramatic, visible terms, but our perception, then and now, is that it should, and Mary fell short. Her behaviour suggests that she was not guilty of the plot, for only the innocent would behave with such naivety. And as she appears to have known a little of the conspiracy against her husband, had expected Darnley at some point to be injured and roughed up a little, was in horrified shock because it had been done so close to her and matters had escalated. She could not believe what had happened. If she put anyone on trial, they could implicate the others, say she was told of the 'matter' and so should have stopped it, and pull down the whole house of cards.

The Privy Council did quickly announce a reward for the capture of the criminals and there were questionings carried out, and discussion of an inquiry that was planned to take place during the parliament at the end of April, but this wasn't enough. Mary fell prey to the hypocrisies of the time. Everyone had been intent on her having a husband to manage matters for her – those matters considered by Philip of Spain as 'not in ladies' capacity'. But now that an event had occurred that was so terrible – if anything was outside a lady's capacity, this was it – she was condemned for not acting. Mary wanted someone to help her and rescue her, a knight in shining armour to sweep up the matter. But the lords did nothing for her, for it suited them that little was done. The Privy Council and her advisors should have rallied her to act. But Moray was her chief advisor, Maitland her Secretary of State and they had stuffed the Privy Council with their allies. Moray and the others did not leap up and demand that a trial was launched, announce that the queen was in shock and so they were dealing with matters. Instead, they watched things crash into the wall because this suited their agenda. With every moment of inaction, Mary played into Moray's hands.

With Bothwell as sheriff of Edinburgh, the investigations were flimsy. Everyone knew that it had to be some member or members of the nobility who had killed Darnley, and strong suspicion fell on Bothwell and Moray, as well as Maitland. The Venetian ambassador in Paris heard that 'It is widely believed that the principal persons of this kingdom were implicated in this act because they were dissatisfied with the King' – he thought Moray was the guilty party.[4] Moray, who had returned to Edinburgh five days after the murder, needed to stop that kind of talk and fast.

Within a week of the killings, a placard was hammered up in Edinburgh blaming Bothwell and his associate James Balfour, and moreover stating that the queen had known of and forgiven the murder, thanks to witchcraft.

Mary still did not act.

What exactly had happened on that night? The plot had gone wrong: Darnley had not been strangled in his bed and then blown up to hide the evidence. He was woken at night, perhaps by some noise of men coming for him or heard a shuffling about from those setting out the gunpowder. He looked out of the window, saw men gathering in the east garden, and he clutched his cloak around him and he and Taylor let themselves down from the window, using the rope and the chair that were later found next to their bodies. It is possible that one of the plotters, horrified that this had been turned into a gunpowder assassination, bounded upstairs to tip them off. Darnley and his servant ran for their lives but were spotted in flight and the assassins caught them, strangled them and dumped them in the garden.

Mrs Mertine, who lived nearby, said she had heard thirteen men and saw eleven run up towards the High Street, after the explosion, and bravely shouted to tell them off. Another woman who was in the service of the Archbishop of St Andrews, whose house was adjacent, saw eleven and managed to catch one by his coat, but he ran free. These men were the stranglers, most likely the Douglas family, fleeing. Rather than strangling him quietly in a private home, the killers had been forced to chase Darnley and his man and then run away, and they had been seen.

John Hepburn, Bothwell's accomplice, later confessed that Bothwell supervised the planting of gunpowder and watched it light, even approaching closer when he saw it was not exploding. But why choose such an obvious and public way of killing Darnley? Pushing him down the stairs (as may have happened to Amy Robsart), poisoning him, or even sending a stealthy assassin in by night to stab his heart might have been difficult, but less dramatic than blowing up a whole house. They could have set the house on fire at a time when house fires were common and hope it spread to him quickly. What can definitely be concluded is the outcome – Darnley had nearly escaped and the whole world immediately knew it was a murder. Still, had he been blown up by the gunpowder, it would have been much less easy to trace the matter and there could have been counterclaims that he had had his own supply of gunpowder and lit it by mistake. The perfect plot had failed.

Where had the gunpowder come from? A significant and costly amount was needed to blow up the entire house. It is not impossible that Bothwell had taken it from the royal stores although his servants later said he brought it from Dunbar and hid it at Holyrood. James Balfour was also accused of buying it and storing it in the vaults. He and his servants had also managed to get it through the streets of Edinburgh and into the house while Mary and her court were present. The comings and goings of a big party was cover. But still, there needed to be people in on the plot. Nine accomplices of Bothwell were later rounded up, including John Hepburn, John Spens and his porter, Dalgleish. But greater men also knew.

One of Darnley's servants, Thomas Nelson, who was sleeping in the upper rooms, survived – he was found clinging to the city walls, thrown there by the explosion. Two plots had converged. Some lords thought the plan was for Darnley to merely be exposed to violence, roughed up and told to behave – rather than the horror of murder, which would cause even more enmity and anger. But Moray wanted him dead, as did his supporters and the Hamiltons, as well as Maitland, Argyll and Huntly and plenty of others. Bothwell, his servants and the Douglases were willing to carry out the actual killing. And then Moray edged the suspicion onto Mary, which she made a million times easier for him with her shocked, lost behaviour.

There is no way that Mary, always fearful of being kidnapped and killed and preoccupied with her health, nervous by disposition, would have spent an evening in a house packed to the brim with gunpowder. She knew that some act was compassed, although did not know when – but she also presumed that the 'matter' Moray would be 'looking through his fingers' at was just light violence. Darnley would only suffer a little, be brought to heel. She would have naturally assumed that this would be done while she was apart from Darnley, not close by him as this would expose her to suspicion. She didn't realise that exposing her to suspicion had been the point.

Moray kept a low profile and let Bothwell lead at Court. It was a good strategy – people's curious eyes turned to this man who seemed so close to Mary. 'Everybody suspected the Earl of Bothwell and those who durst speak freely to others said plainly it was he', declared Melville.[5] Mary went on as she had been, living in mourning, trusting that the small measures taken by the Privy Council were enough. She was mired in inaction. Bothwell was furious with Moray for having pushed a plot that had failed and exposed him to risk and the fragile alliance between the two collapsed into acrimony.

Elizabeth wrote to Mary on 24 February, two weeks after the murder, urgently pleading with Mary to prosecute the guilty men:

Madame,
My ears have been so shocked, my understanding so broken and and my heart so frightened to hear the awful news of the abominable murder of your husband and my slaughtered cousin, that I can barely write. And although I would take his death hard, with him being kin, I must tell you honestly, I cannot pretend that I mourn more for you than for him. O, Madame, I would not be doing as a faithful cousin should, or a loving friend, if I did not speak openly and beg you to preserve your reputation. I must and I will tell you what

people are saying. They say that instead of taking measures to arrest those responsible, you are looking through your fingers while they escape, that you will not seek revenge on those who have done what is what you wished, as if the deed had been trusted to be forgiven, so the murderers felt assured to do it. I do not think this way. I would never hold such a miserable opinion of a prince. And even less of you, to whom I wish every good my heart can imagine and you could wish for. For this every reason, I exhort, I counsel, I beg you deeply to take this to heart and even if the guilty is the nearest friend you have, to lay your hands upon him, show to the world that you are a noble princess and a loyal wife. I write thus vehemently not out of doubt, but through the true love I have for you. I know you have other wise counsellors around you. But I remember that even our Lord had a Judas among the twelve. I assure myself that you have no one more loyal than I and you can rely on my affection.[6]

Elizabeth was pushed to desperation – and she wrote with her heart. As she knew the letter would be intercepted, she was careful to present herself as entirely innocent and lay all the guilt on Scotland. In this she was right, although she could hardly claim no involvement in fostering support for Moray and had paid him on other occasions. Elizabeth suggested that Mary had even promised the plotters impunity and raised the possibility that the murderer could be Mary's 'nearest friend' – by which she could have meant Moray, Bothwell or even Maitland. It is very striking that Elizabeth wrote 'regardant entre vos doigts' [looking through your fingers] – a phrase she did not use particularly often. These were the words apparently used at Craigmillar about Moray – when the nobles told the queen that they would quit her of Darnley, one way or another. Coincidence? Or had Elizabeth's spies managed to get hold of the document or reports – and the phrase was used here, pointedly, to remind Mary of who else might be looking through their fingers at the matter? But whatever Elizabeth thought, Cecil was working to protect Moray and made it clear to him he would be welcome in England.

Catherine de' Medici wrote to advise similarly: the queen should prosecute the killers immediately, and thus reveal her innocence to her subjects.

Mary should have chosen someone – anyone – to be scapegoated. There were no witnesses, and those who saw the men running away, like Mrs Mertine, could not identify who they had seen. Trials had risen and fallen on less in the period and Mary needed to be ruthless to preserve her position. The people may have seen it as a show trial, but at least it would have given the impression Mary was taking the matter seriously. In her letter to Ambassador Beaton in Paris, she had promised to prosecute the murder swiftly. But a week, two weeks passed. She did nothing – and this suited Moray, Bothwell and the rest of his circle well.

Mary's belief that she had been the main target of the explosion was blurring her judgement. For, as she saw it, Bothwell could never want her killed (and in this she was right, he had too much to gain with her alive) and so could not have been part of the plot. But whether she was too fearful, too loyal or too dependent on Bothwell to move against him, she should have accused someone else. The problem was that many high-born lords were complicit or had known something of what was going to happen. And Mary too had some knowledge that Darnley was about to be set up, and was plunged into guilt that he had died.

If Mary had been guilty, she would have tried to foist the blame onto someone else. Instead she walked as in shock, fearful of what the other lords had done and aware that all her prior refusals to hear about 'the matter' or assent to Darnley's removal could count in some eyes as an awareness that it would be done. Mary had told her lords over and over again that she would not hear of them dispatching her husband. And yet they had all disobeyed her, even Moray, even Bothwell. Never had her powerlessness been more blatantly obvious to her.

As the days dragged on and still nothing happened, the outrage grew. Darnley, who had been little liked, was transformed into a saint, a sacrificed martyr, and the public screamed for justice. He should be avenged but also the reputation of Scotland was under threat. Despite the violence between the lords, the Scots liked to see themselves as a fair people, rather than the blood-mad French or Spanish or the aggressive English. But this – who had ever killed a king before?

The first placard had accused Bothwell and his servant Balfour and noted the queen had known of it. Another placard, two days later, blamed Mary's foreign servants. One included words as if written by the queen, declaring 'I and the Earl of Bothwell were doers of it'. There were drawings of Bothwell and the words 'Here is the Murderer of the King'[7], as well as slurs against Mary and the whole court. At church, ministers begged God reveal the guilty, for they knew their congregations demanded justice. The placards and posters were seized and taken down – but appeared again overnight. Bothwell thought it was his enemies at court and others thought Cecil was to blame – if he had a hand in it, he would have been protecting Moray. The Spanish ambassador worried that Elizabeth might interfere to ferment unrest 'more for her own ends than for any love she bore the king'. He was right – and some of the placards probably were posted by English spies.[8]

Moray himself probably had a few put up. But although both men might have been involved, the movement was too organic, too widespread, to be laid at the door of one person. The people were stunned and wanted answers. Unfortunately, the government then began to investigate the posters, arresting painters and scriveners and testing their handwriting and drawing style. Seeing the government arrest ordinary working men, while letting the killers of the king go free, only inflamed the public further.

Archbishop Beaton wrote from Paris to Mary telling her she must take vengeance, pleading with her to show 'the great virtue, magnanimity and constancy that God has granted you' and urging that she should 'do such justice as the whole world may declare your innocence'. He didn't hold back, telling her it was God's will, and even went so far as to suggest that if she didn't take action, 'it appears to me better that you had lost life and all'.[9] He was a kind and wise friend to her, but she was still listening to her Privy Council instead. They and Mary were still following due process, however slowly. Bothwell had appeared in Edinburgh surrounded by his heavies, near fifty of them, declaring that 'if he knew who were the setters up of the bills and writings, he would wash his hands in their blood'. The people prided themselves on living in a fair country, where honest speech was valued. Their hatred increased – and more posters appeared accusing him.

By the end of February, the Countess of Bothwell was very unwell and afflicted with swellings. Had she been plunged into illness after suspecting her husband of the terrible crime? Or had she been poisoned by Bothwell to get her out of the way? The English spies thought the latter and certainly Bothwell had hardly rushed to spend time at her bedside. Her brother Huntly was supposed to be Bothwell's ally, and if Bothwell had poisoned his sister, it showed how confident and foolhardy he had become. Huntly was pressing her to end the marriage and the countess was giving the matter serious thought. She had always been in love with Alexander Ogilvie of Boyne, even though he was married to Mary Beaton. But still, she was young and could marry again, ideally to someone who hadn't got himself mixed up in plots to kill the king. Yet, it seems unlikely that Jean had been poisoned, for that would be going too far, even for Bothwell.

Mary wrote to Darnley's father, the Earl of Lennox, on 1 March promising that she wanted to find the culprits and answering his declaration that she should arrest 'names contained in some tickets affixed on the Tolbooth'. But, she said, there were so many different posters and various names that they barely knew where to start. If he could name an actual guilty party and 'stand to the accusation'[10], she could authorise a private prosecution. In doing so, she laid all the responsibility on Lennox – and how could he dare? On the same day, she gave Bothwell more financial benefits and privileges linked to the role of sheriff of Edinburgh. He had no doubt been demanding them to secure his position. For who would accuse a sheriff who had the favour of the queen? The Spanish ambassador was beginning to panic: 'the queen must take steps to prove she had no hand in the death of her husband, if she is to prosper in her claims to the succession'.[11] There was no evidence that Mary had been involved in the murder plot, and her hatred for Darnley was less than that of many of the lords, who feared him taking their lands. But her continued failure to scream vengeance and prosecute was making people think that she knew more than she said. And thus she fell into Moray's web, wrapped herself up in the strands.

If the Spanish ambassador hoped that Philip would write to Mary, he hoped in vain. Philip had still not made any public comment or written directly, as Elizabeth and Catherine de' Medici had. He was surely attempting to hold himself clear from any suggestion of a Spanish plot. And even if he had written, Mary would have probably consigned it to the same basket as the letters from her cousin and her former mother-in-law. For Mary, due process and Parliament would attend to the matter and she was doing all she could. Her lords and her Privy Council were most pleased that she was so slow to act, so bound by the process they had recommended.

Later on 1 March, surely prompted by the news of the fresh benefits heaped on Bothwell, a new placard appeared. This was the worst yet, with a picture of a mermaid, breasts bared, with beautiful hair and a crown, 'MR' for Mary Regina on either side. She bore a rolled-up net in one hand and a large sea flower with petals that resembled the female genitalia. The mermaid represented a siren – with her net to catch unsuspecting soldiers – or even a prostitute. Under Mary was a hare surrounded by daggers. The hare was Bothwell's symbol and it bore his initials, 'JH'. The daggers referred to Mary's protection of him and to his violent acts, as well as being positioned as phallic symbols pointing towards the mermaid. 'Destruction awaits the wicked on every side'[12] were the words. Mary was being depicted as one of the 'wicked' and she was devastated by the slur. It was the creation of an educated artist, and could possibly have been generated by the Lennox side. Mary had been publicly slandered as a prostitute and there was no going back.

Chapter Twenty
The Mermaid

The council proclaimed that James Murray, loyal to the Lennoxes and against Bothwell, should be arrested for the placards. As the council contained Moray, Argyll, Huntly and Bothwell, it could hardly be trusted. Murray fled to England – perhaps with the help of Moray or one of his network. The whole thing looked dreadful. Mary seemingly refused to find a culprit for her husband's murder, but was happy to pursue a placard artist. Catherine de' Medici was so angered by events that she wrote again to Mary that if she didn't hunt down the killers, she should both think herself dishonoured and understand that Catherine and Charles IX would 'be her enemies'[1]. On 8 March, Elizabeth's envoy, Henry Killigrew, visited Mary and found her deep in despair. As he wrote, 'I could not see her face but by her very words, she seemed very doleful.'[2]

Moray knew he was suspected and, still considering fleeing to England, decided to throw off the scent of crime and joined with Morton and others to declare he would give support to Darnley's father Lennox in bringing the guilty to trial. Servants were beginning to talk and say that lords had banded together to kill Darnley. The discussions at Craigmillar Castle in late 1566 about Darnley between Maitland, Huntly, Bothwell and Argyll were being talked of, as well as the involvement of others. Bothwell clung harder to the queen. After all, he was the only one of the lot who had never conspired against her.

Lennox begged Cecil for help in prosecuting Bothwell – but the statesman was torn. Elizabeth wanted her cousin to act for herself, to prove that a queen could govern. Lennox decided to take action, come what may, and wrote to Mary telling her who he felt was guilty: Bothwell, Balfour, Rizzio's brother, Joseph, and others. Matters had got to such a head that even Bothwell was arguing he should be sent to trial, to dispel the rumours. Mary was, by this point, struggling and ill from the terrible strain. She was pale, suffering from insomnia and fainting fits.

She could hold off no longer. The placards, the desperate pleas of her advisors, the panicked importuning of foreign diplomats and their royal masters; she had to submit. On 22 March, Mary wrote to Lennox, promising him the trial he longed for. As she wrote, 'the persons nominated in your letter shall . . . undergo such trial as by the lords of this realm is accustomed'. She promised him her 'earnest will and affectionate mind to have an end to this matter, and the authors of so unworthy a deed really punished'.[3] On 23 March, her official forty days of mourning for Darnley was ended, with prayers for her dead husband's soul.

Mary was still in shock – as we know, matters suggest she had heard that Darnley was going to be threatened, although she expected it would not be done when she was nearby. Everything else she had forbidden and refused to hear talk of – thinking her lords would obey her. Her fear was that she would be implicated by any trial. Perhaps, had she initiated a trial straight away, there would have been sympathy for any involvement of hers that might surface. Darnley was, after all, a bad husband, a plotter of murder, and violence was a language he understood – plenty of families would have made physical threats to a new husband who was treating one of their female relations so badly. But by this point, any awareness of Darnley's fate damned her in public eyes and made her a murderess too. So Mary had to put men whom she believed had been most loyal to her on trial, and thus was naturally fearful that she would be incriminated and pulled down with them – an eventuality that would be most gratifying to Moray and the others, who would gain with her fall and could deny all involvement. Mary again fell ill almost as soon as she had made the announcement and it was reported back to England that 'she has been for the most part either sickly or melancholy ever since'.[4]

Still, she rewarded Bothwell. It was Easter week and she gave him some priceless vestments originally from Aberdeen Cathedral that were said to be made of cloth of gold. She used the other vestments from the collection to ornament a memorial bed for Darnley. The gift was scandalous: not only was Bothwell about to stand criminal trial, and was a Protestant receiving Catholic objects, but the fact that the vestments were being divided between her dead husband and the man who many suspected to be her lover – it was too much. What was Mary thinking? It looks like a terrible lapse of judgement, an open mark of affection for a suspected criminal. But if it was a present to keep him onside and keep her name and complicity out of the trial, it makes sense and is reasonable. The most important thing was to stop herself being implicated.

The gossip swelled. On the day before Mary had written to Lennox, 21 March, the Countess of Bothwell had begun divorce proceedings against her husband, on the basis of his adultery with sewing maid Bessie Crawford, over a year earlier. She wanted to release herself from someone who might go on trial for killing the king but she was also obeying her brother Huntly's suggestion that she divorce. Her act only fuelled the gossip that Mary and Bothwell were lovers.

In Paris, James Beaton, Mary's ambassador and devoted friend, was saying that 'the Lord James [Moray] was the author of the King's death, and Lord Lennox is deluded and mocked by him'.[5] People in Scotland must have told him. Or perhaps it was Mary, through secret messengers. If so, this explains some of her shock and panic. She'd understood her half-brother had been involved. Yet she couldn't prosecute him: not only would he bring her into it, but he was too powerful, and she would suffer greatly for accusing him (not least from Cecil). Perhaps, at the beginning, Mary might have thrown Moray to the wolves and survived. But she did not, and now he had caught her in a mire from which she couldn't escape.

With the trial imminent, Moray did what he always did when matters became too hot. He disappeared. On 13 March, he had written to Cecil asking for a passport to come to London and he set off at the end of the month. It is significant that Cecil granted a passport so quickly; he had protected Moray and did not want him exposed to a trial. Mary wept as he left. Her half-brother was deserting her in her hour of need – and leaving her with all the guilt and the pain of her husband's death. When he reached England, he headed for London and started talking to anyone he could think of. He told the Spanish ambassador Silva that he had left Scotland for fear of Bothwell, who he made clear was guilty of Darnley's death. He also said that Bothwell wanted a divorce so that he could marry Mary. That she and Bothwell were in cahoots.

He played the terrified innocent, afraid of Bothwell, told everyone that he had done it. His plot had worked. Mary was well and truly framed.

Moray had won. Even though the plot for the perfect murder had failed at the last minute when Darnley had jumped out of the window, it had still had a magnificent effect. Darnley was dead. Mary was hated. Bothwell was blamed. All Moray had to do was lie low and brief against his sister until Bothwell was put on trial. He had no idea that Bothwell's anger at being betrayed and his fury against the other lords was going to explode into terrible violence – and unsuspectingly play right into Moray's hands.

Some might think a brother could never do such a thing. But for Moray, Mary's presence blocked the money and power he wanted for himself and his family, and she was also the barrier to the Protestant Reformation he desired. As she was a Catholic queen, a woman who'd married a terrible husband, he could easily justify it to himself that he had been acting in the interests of the country.

On Good Friday, the council decreed that the men named by Lennox would be tried on 12 April. Bothwell was present for the decree. This was surprising speed for the sixteenth-century legal system, and Lennox didn't like it. He begged Cecil to ask for a postponement, convinced it would be a show trial, because there was no time to gather evidence. Lennox himself set out for Edinburgh with 3,000 retainers, but was told at Linlithgow that he could only proceed to Edinburgh with six – and he was naturally too afraid to continue.

Elizabeth considered her position and finally wrote to Mary asking for a delay, but when it arrived at Holyrood at 6 a.m. on the day of the trial, the messenger was sent away because Mary was said to be asleep. He came back and was once more rebuffed, waited until ten, saw Bothwell's men assembling and tried again, but was refused and then everybody pretended not to hear him. One of Bothwell's relatives then brought a message from Bothwell saying Elizabeth's letter would not be received because the queen was 'so molested and disquieted with the business of that day'.[6] Finally, Maitland came out, spotted the messenger and took the letter. The messenger asked for an answer and he was told Mary was still asleep, even though she had just appeared at the window. The messenger lost patience and demanded an honest answer – and Maitland said he had not delivered it to the queen and would not do so until after the trial. Did Mary know there was a letter arriving for her from her cousin? Almost probably. She dreaded, no doubt, reading her cousin's criticism. And stopping the trial at this point might have caused a surge of anger in the common people, since they had waited so long.

But, also, Bothwell was dominant and she was increasingly afraid of him. There was simply no comparing the positions of Elizabeth and Mary. Men on trial in London wouldn't have expected to be able to take thousands of retainers with them, neither would witnesses. But Bothwell set off from Holyrood with 4,000 retainers, riding Darnley's favourite horse, with Morton and Maitland riding beside him and Hepburn's relatives bringing up the rear. Mary watched him depart from her window, accompanied by Mary Fleming. When Bothwell arrived at the Tolbooth and all had entered, his men were put to guard the door so that Bothwell's enemies could not enter.

Lennox's and Cecil's fears had been correct. The trial turned out to be a sham. Although Bothwell was correctly accused of killing Darnley and causing the explosion, there was no evidence given on either side. Lennox's plea for an adjournment was considered and dismissed. After eight hours, the court declared Bothwell not guilty. He promptly pinned up a notice on the door declaring his innocence and set off back to Holyrood. Mary was now officially spared.

Bothwell had his crier put it out across Edinburgh that he was innocent and put bills up on the Tolbooth announcing he would fight anyone who now accused him. Four days after Bothwell's sham trial, Mary rode to Parliament, and Bothwell carried the sceptre beside her. Her guards were no longer the usual bailiffs of Edinburgh but his personal musketeers. He used his acquittal to influence her, told her that only he cared for her, and insinuated that everyone else would kill her if they could. Parliament confirmed the judgement of Bothwell as not guilty and also gave him more: confirming and enlarging his rights as Lord Admiral, awarding loyalist Argyll some of Darnley's former estates and ensuring other lords had their possession of estates confirmed. And then they produced an 'Act against the Makers and Setters Up of Placards and Bills'. No one would be allowed to paint Bothwell as a hare with a sensual mermaid again. On the last night of the parliament, Saturday 19 April, Bothwell took twenty-eight lords to dinner at Ainslie's tavern and asked them to sign a bond declaring his innocence of the murder and expressing their support for him and noting that the queen was 'now destitute of a husband, in the which solitary state the common-wealth of this realm may not permit her to continue and endure'. That was bad enough. But then, the Ainslie bond continued, 'at some time her highness in appearance may be inclined to yield unto a marriage' and, as she might prefer a native-born subject to a foreign prince, 'to take to husband the said earl'.[7]

Eight bishops, nine earls and seven barons signed but many of the lords managed to escape the pen. Four refused at the tavern, some had cleverly declined to attend, and Moray was on his way to France. The various copies have different signatures but it seems as if Huntly and Morton signed and Argyll probably did too, despite qualms.[8] It was hardly conclusive. But Bothwell was now power-hungry, emboldened to grab what he wanted and willing to do anything to get it. And the more he said that Mary was going to marry him, the more people believed it. They couldn't draw Mary as a mermaid anymore, but they still whispered. As one put it, she would 'go to the world's end in a white petticoat ere she leave him'.[9]

But Bothwell was already losing supporters. Balfour, who was suspected of having transported the gunpowder that killed Darnley, asked Mary for a similar trial but was refused. He was nervous – one of his own servants had already threatened to inform and Balfour had ordered him murdered. A trial would dispel all the gossip. But Mary did not want the matter discussed any further. Morton, too, felt excluded and as if he hadn't been sufficiently rewarded for his role, and Argyll now felt shocked by the signing of the paper and was keen to leave his old friend's camp.

The day after the parliament was over, Mary fled to the better air of Seton and Bothwell followed her, proposed marriage and said that her nobles wished it, citing the Ainslie bond. Bothwell wrangled all his supporters out in force and they besieged her with letters encouraging her to marry him. But Mary refused, on the grounds that there was too much scandal surrounding the death of her husband. Had she really wanted to marry Bothwell, then this moment, following a document held and agreed to by many lords, would be the one. And yet she did not.

Mary later said that her country needed male authority. It was, as she said, 'being divided into factions as it is, cannot be contained in order unless our authority be assisted and set forth by the fortification of a man'.[10] But she was growing less convinced that Bothwell was that man. After all, he had been no protection from the horror and humiliations she had been exposed to, and Elizabeth and Cecil still meddled in her country. Perhaps a foreign prince might add to her power – he'd certainly have more troops to send over in support of her. Bothwell ventured his suit and Mary discouraged him. She thought that would be an end of the matter.

She needed the protection of her son, now ten months old, who had been moved from Holyrood in the previous month. On Monday 21 April, Mary rode to Stirling. She took with her comparatively few men because it was supposed to be a private visit – she had Maitland, Huntly, Melville and about thirty horsemen – a small number for the queen. There, the Earl of Mar told her she was allowed to enter with only two female attendants and forbade her to take little James for he feared the child would be put into Bothwell's clutches. Mary was incensed but she had no choice. She spent two days with her child and set off back for Edinburgh. Just out of Stirling, she fell ill with stomach pain and had to rest in a cottage. They arrived late at night at Linlithgow and resumed the journey the next morning. Next day, a few miles outside Edinburgh and crossing the river Almond, Mary and her men were ambushed. Bothwell leapt out, grabbed the bridle of Mary's horse. He had 800 soldiers with him, all with their swords drawn. Holding tight to her horse, he said danger was threatening her in Edinburgh and offered to escort her to Dunbar to ensure her safety. She told her servant, James Borthwick, to ride to Edinburgh to get help – and then turned to Bothwell and agreed to go with him, for, she said, there would be danger and bloodshed if she did not. What could she do? She had only a few men, he had hundreds and he could have overpowered her easily. He had been so sure of success that he had told the lords his plan. In the words of Kirkaldy of Grange, who was passing on information to Elizabeth's man, the Earl of Bedford, 'he is minded to meet the queen this day, Thursday, and to take her by the way, and bring her to Dunbar.'[11] Mary had sent Borthwick to Edinburgh to raise the alarm, but otherwise she trusted her captor to treat her as a queen.

As planned, Bothwell took Mary on a forty-mile ride to Dunbar – which she had given him as a reward for his support after the Rizzio murder. He bundled her into the castle and slammed shut the gates.

Chapter Twenty-One

'Whether She Would or Would Not'

At Dunbar, Bothwell took the queen to a room and he raped her. Melville, who was with Mary in the castle, wrote that 'he had ravished her and laid with her against her will' and that Bothwell was boasting that he would have her whether she 'would or would not'.[1] He did not care that she was a queen. She was a woman and to him, women had one use only. He would force her to submit. As soon as she arrived, he dismissed her attendants and began pressing her to marry him, as had been provided for by the council. She refused and sent a secret message out to the Governor of Dunbar to come with his men to rescue her. No rescue came.

Mary was caught in a web, all of it spun by Bothwell. For some historians, the fact she did not scream and resist, much less fight to the death, was evidence of complicity. But Mary considered Bothwell a friend and an ally. She expected to be taken to a castle and treated well. But most of all, we view the incident with the benefit of hindsight. Mary trusted him as she always had done and she thought he was saving her from riots in Edinburgh.

Bothwell's crime was dreadful. Even though the code of gallantry in Scotland was not always strong, to seize a lady from the road was seen as shocking behaviour. And a queen anointed by God was a sacred being. To take her was enough – and a rape was beyond imaginable. Bothwell raped Mary to attempt to reduce her into marrying him, to gain power over her, to show her that despite her riches and authority and God-given crown, she was nothing more than a body and reducible to subservience by a man's act on her. Most of all, he wanted to impregnate her so she had no choice but to marry him. And once Mary was married and pregnant, everyone would forget the method. He deluded himself into believing he had the lords' support, clutching the Ainslie tavern bond, signed by nobles, saying they would support the marriage.

Bothwell had precedent in mind. Men kidnapping and raping women who had refused to marry them or whose fathers had resisted their overtures was not uncommon. Heiresses were often at risk of being abducted. In such cases, the rapist would be allowed, even encouraged, to marry the girl, perhaps after a small fine had been paid to the father. Women in the sixteenth century were constantly exposed to the possibility of sexual assault – and Scotland, where there were long and dangerous roads without settlements, was a dangerous place for female travel.

In Spenser's *The Fairie Queene*, nearly all female characters, including those standing for Elizabeth, are threatened with rape, which Spenser tends to denote with the word 'spoil'. But although these encounters are demarcated as forced, they are represented as vital for the founding of the world they create: the women give birth to children, and Agape, who is raped and bears three sons, is described as 'full blessed' for producing such brave young men. Rape comes to seem a necessary part of the dynastic creation of a strong race of warriors. For many men committing rape, such language could function as a pleasing cover: they committed the assaults to create a dynasty and sons. As the historian and sociologist Georges Vigarello shows in his study of sexual violence in France in the early modern period, trials, even of child victims who were victims of rape, ended up with the child castigated and seen as spoiled, and if the man was more powerful, recourse was rarely possible.[2]

But to do this to the queen? Too many historians have found it impossible that a man would dare, and thus judged her complicit. Others have argued that because Mary did not fight back, she must have consented. We have a much greater understanding of sexual assault and consent these days: many victims panic or fear that if they do not submit, they will be killed. Bothwell was furious that she was refusing to marry him, and he took his revenge on her in the cruellest and most devastating way, using his physical force to intimidate her. If Andrew Ker had been happy to hold a gun to her stomach during the Rizzio murder, it is possible that Bothwell's men threatened her with guns to submit to him – and witnessed her horrible assault.

Those who say she could have then escaped – and should have done so – reflect a misunderstanding of the effect of trauma on the mind. Mary was excessively proud, obsessed with her status as a queen. She had been tormented and attacked by a former friend, and this may have been witnessed by his servants – most things were at the time. She was deeply distressed, may have been too physically injured to move, and was consumed by fear. Moreover, it was possible that she thought she was pregnant.

As Mary knew, women who had been raped were generally expected to come to terms with their rapist and usually marry him. As Melville, her supporter, put it, 'The Queen could not but marry him, seeing he ravished her and laid with her against her will.'[3]

Exodus and Deuteronomy suggested the father of a single woman could agree her marriage to her rapist. Catherine Howard, fifth wife of Henry VIII, was assaulted and groomed by her tutor, but was blamed for it. And heiresses who were seized were blamed for having been too friendly to the man – wearing certain gowns, looking at him in company, walking in the garden alone with him. Later fiction was filled with heroines who were raped, married their assaulters and then managed to 'reform' the man into love and piety.

Mary, who had encouraged Bothwell, given him presents and let him remain at Holyrood, had given him so much that she knew the world would blame her. And, like most victims, she no doubt castigated herself when there was no reason to do so. Historians who claim Mary did not flee the castle and so wanted the rape, enjoyed it, or had even colluded with Bothwell all along, ignore the fundamentally sexist nature of sixteenth-century society: a woman who was raped was to blame for it. And since the Governor of Dunbar had not come for her and the Ainslie bond had been signed by so many, she felt she had no one to support her.

Mary was in fear of her life, possibly injured and afraid of another rape at Bothwell's hands – one that he might make even worse this time. She remained at the castle and submitted to him. Today, our notions of consent are undergoing a fundamental shift, with the whole understanding of rape being re-evaluated in terms of the power structure between men and women. I write in modern times and we are dealing with the sixteenth century here – but one thing that does not change is the pain and suffering and struggle with self-blame that survivors feel, often years later. Some women, after they have been attacked by someone they know, attempt to get a handle on the situation and get some power back by contacting the rapist or even attempting to seduce him on their terms. Mary had often used sex or the promise of it to gain some control over Darnley. Perhaps she hoped that by promising to marry Bothwell, she could encourage some sort of rapprochement or at least equality.

The worst arguments have come from historians who argue that after the effete Darnley, Mary was thrilled to receive sexual satisfaction from a 'real man'. But Bothwell was no romantic hero – he was gruff, violent and opportunist, unloved by his wife and mistresses. Even consensual intercourse with him was unlikely to be tender. Such notions of him as being sexually a 'real man' rest dangerously close to notions that all women want to be overpowered and attacked, that having rape fantasies (a way of gaining control over what is for many a perennial fear) is the same as wanting to be assaulted. As was entirely the case here, rape is about power not sex. Bothwell didn't assault Mary because he was overwhelmed with sexual desire for her and had to act on it. He wanted to be king, he was furious that she would not marry him, and wished to force her submission.

Mary was never going to forgive a man who had attacked her, so keenly wanting to humiliate her and debase her. She could never bear to speak of what had happened, such were her feelings of shame, and she could only refer to 'doings rude' – 'rude' being a word applied to rape. Later, when in captivity, she did not talk of him or write to him – which hardly suggested she was in love with him. But, exhausted, afraid and fearful of the consequences, she agreed to marry him. 'As it is succeeded, we must take the best of it', she said. She might be pregnant. And, moreover, she thought she was doing what her nobles desired, since so many had signed the Ainslie bond. As she wrote, 'seeing ourselves in his power, sequestered from the company of our servants and others, of whom we might ask counsel, yea, seeing them upon whose counsel and fidelity we had before dependene, already welded to his appetite and so we left alone, as it were, a prey to him'.[4]

She was utterly isolated and friendless and saw, as she said, 'no way out'. She was perhaps hoping that if she married Bothwell, no one would hear about the rape.

However, the news got out fast, and because Mary was no ordinary woman, sympathy was with her. Taking an heiress? Unfortunate, but her father should have been more careful and she should marry the offender quickly. Seizing a queen? A scandal that would damn Scotland in the eyes of the world. A petition from Aberdeen on 27 April asked what could be done since she had been 'ravished by the Earl of Bothwell against your will'. Morton, Argyll and Mar met urgently at Stirling three days after the abduction and agreed to free the queen, safeguard little James, and kill Bothwell 'the barbarous tyrant'.[5] Robert Melville requested English support and urgent letters were sent to Moray asking him to return.

Of course, as well as sympathy for Mary, the lords were motivated by horror at the vaunting power of Bothwell. But still, Scotland saw her as an innocent victim of Bothwell's criminal acts. Even at this point, Mary could have turned things around by waiting until it was possible and then fleeing back to Edinburgh, throwing herself on her people for help. But Mary did not know what support she had in the capital. Bothwell watched all her messengers and later she said that she never heard from her nobles, even though the nobles at Stirling said they had written to her and she had replied that she had been 'evil and strangely handled'.[6] Even if she was lying and they did write to her and she replied, still, she could see no effort to rescue her. And she believed that they had all wished her to marry her attacker. She was caught in Bothwell's trap and could not escape.

All her life, Mary had believed that she was special because she was a queen. The one and only time that this belief could have served her well – in believing that she would be better treated than the average woman and public sympathy would lie with her – this confidence deserted her. There was not a single lord, it seemed, who had not tried to imprison her, capture her, demean her or undermine her. Bothwell had killed her spirit.

On 6 May, Bothwell's divorce still not completed, Mary and Bothwell rode back to Edinburgh. On the arrival at the gate, Bothwell took Mary's horse and led her up to the castle. This was Mary's moment to show displeasure for Bothwell and her desire to escape. The crowds would have supported her. But all the other lords had plotted against her in one way or another and she had no one left to trust. On the same day, John Craig of St Giles Kirk was asked to pronounce the banns of marriage between the pair. He refused. Next day he was given a writ in which Mary said she had not been raped nor held by Bothwell. But, as he put it, if she had not been assaulted, she had committed adultery with a still-married man. He was compelled to read the banns but he made it clear that he found the marriage a disgrace. Bothwell summoned him and asked for an apology. But Craig, loyal man of Knox, was not easily cowed and launched into what everyone was thinking, declaring Bothwell guilty of breaking 'the law of adultery, the ordinance of the Kirk, the law of ravishing, the suspicion of collusion between him and his wife, the sudden divorcement and proclaiming within the space of four days and the last, the suspicion of the king's death, which her marriage would confirm'.[7] Bothwell should have realised that if the minister dared say this to his face then he was losing his grip. Craig repeated the lot in his sermon the next day and Bothwell was apoplectic, threatening to have him hanged.

Mary was desperate now. She felt that if she, the most injured, had forgiven Bothwell then everybody else should too. But the church was scandalised, the ordinary people distressed, and Mar and Argyll and the rest had begun to create a separate court of James at Stirling, going so far as performing a masque in which Bothwell was hanged. The implication was clear: Bothwell should die and Mary should be deposed for James. They feared – rightly – that Bothwell would try to make himself king. The foreign ambassadors watched matters in shock and disbelief. As Cecil had put it, Scotland was 'in a quagmire'.[8] Elizabeth was deeply distressed and appalled. Mary's acts were to her horrific and wrong – and the possibility that she would be deposed for her son was an implicit condemnation of all female rule. Still, Mary made Bothwell Duke of Orkney and Lord of Shetland on 12 May. She commissioned a beautiful wedding gown and set her seamstresses to work.

In France, Moray read reports of what was happening in Scotland. Mary's actions were playing more into his hands than anything he could have imagined. The suspicions that he had been behind her husband's murder had drowned under this new scandal.

Mary signed the marriage contract, which was all written to support Bothwell. Much of the language seemed to have been copied directly from the Ainslie bond, as it noted that Mary was 'destitute of a husband'. As it put it, Mary was 'living solitary in the state of widowhood, and yet young and of flourishing age, apt to procreate and bring forth children, has been pressed and humbly require to yield to some marriage'.[9] The latter was guaranteed to outrage everyone. The last thing anyone wanted was Bothwell fathering a child he could then claim was a legitimate heir to the throne and unseat Prince James – or even kill him. Mary's friends begged her not to marry but she said that 'her object in marrying [was] to settle religion by that means'. She was desperate, felt she had no choice and believed that Bothwell must be able to cow the lords, as he had attacked her. And she – or more likely he – had clearly created some kind of great fantasy, where their differing religions might represent religious co-existence, a king and queen who were both Protestant and Catholic respectively, representing union and unity. This might just possibly have worked, if Bothwell had not been universally hated and he hadn't sexually assaulted the queen in order to force her into marriage.

The contract noted that all documents must be signed by Mary alone or in joint signature, but this was scant consolation to the lords, the Scottish people and the foreign crowns. As soon as Bothwell had managed to beget a child, he would be demanding unlimited powers. Du Croc declared he had no mandate from France to recognise Bothwell as Mary's husband and would not attend the wedding – and encouraged others to do the same.[10] The stage was set for the most scandalous marriage in royal history.

Chapter Twenty-Two
'So Wearied and Broken'

On Thursday 15 May, Mary and Bothwell were married in the great hall at Holyrood in a Protestant service. There were few witnesses. The four Marys were present, along with Bothwell's men, and Huntly and Maitland, but nearly everybody else had stayed away. The bishop presiding mumbled about Bothwell's penitence for his sins as an 'evil liver'.[1] The queen was resplendent in the old black gown that her seamstresses had converted and embroidered in gold and silver thread. Once more, she was showing that she came to her husband as a widow, not a virgin.

Stately as ever, her auburn hair set off by the black, many thought she had never been so beautiful. And yet she was marrying in a ceremony that she would never ordinarily have recognised. The horrifying events of the last months had left her cowed. There were no masques or plays or celebrations, which always followed a royal wedding and indeed those of many ordinary people – she had been at a masque for the wedding of Bastian Pagez, just before Darnley died. There was merely a rather sombre wedding dinner, to which the public were invited to watch Mary eat.

Some historians have stated there was no wedding banquet – but this was not the case. There was a dinner, it was just no comparison to the great events in the past, lesser even than the marriage festivals of the courtiers and certainly much less than that of the Earl of Moray. It was a sad contrast to the astonishing tableaux of her first wedding with its mechanised boats and royal glory. Mary gave no wedding presents to Bothwell and barely attended to her own wardrobe. Later, she burst into tears about the heretical ceremony and told the Bishop of Ross that she would never again do anything to harm the church. She summoned the French ambassador, du Croc, who was always sympathetic, and he found her heartbroken. She was distressed at how little support she had for the wedding, from noble and commoner alike, was suffering at the thought of the Protestant ceremony, and was haunted by the shame and pain of the rape and news of the nobles who were creating a court around her son. As he reported to Catherine de' Medici, 'if I saw her sad, it was because she did not wish to be happy, as she said she never could be, wishing only to die'.[2] A new placard appeared in Edinburgh noting 'Only harlots marry in the month of May'.[3]

Mary sent ambassadors out to tell Catherine de' Medici and Elizabeth her reasons for taking Bothwell to be her husband. Her man, the Bishop of Dunblane, was to tell the French court that Bothwell had been loyal and 'dedicated his whole service to his sovereign' but also to explain the truth: that he had behaved with 'plain contempt of our person and use of force to have us in his power'. She said that she was compelled to marry in a Protestant ceremony because Bothwell was more concerned about pleasing his Protestant allies than 'regarding our contention, or weighing what was convenient to us'.[4]

She begged the pardon of her 'dear sister' for not 'asking her advice and counsel' about the marriage. She said only a Scottish man could stop the division, saying that the 'factions and conspiracies . . . occurring so frequently had already in a manner so wearied and broken us' that he seemed a proper option. She noted that Bothwell had been cleared of Darnley's murder by Parliament. She also added a graceful letter to Cecil, asking him to speak to his mistress on her behalf. But the letter took some time to reach Elizabeth.[5]

Mary emphasised the Ainslie bond and how the nobles had wished her to marry Bothwell. Most of all, she wrote, she needed a man, since the realm was so 'divided into factions' that it 'cannot be contained in order unless our authority be assisted and forthset by the fortification of a man who must take upon his person in the execution of justice'. Mary said all the correct words, but she wrote to Beaton in France from the heart. 'The event is indeed strange and otherwise nor (we know) you would have looked for it. But as it is succeeded, we must take the best of it.'[6] But the truth was that Bothwell was a brutal husband, shouting at Mary and treating her cruelly.

But by this point, Mary was not giving up Bothwell. She was pregnant.

When exactly did Mary conceive her child by Bothwell? She said that it was after her marriage, dating a pregnancy of seven weeks on 16 July, suggesting conception at around the end of May. But Bedford noted that the queen was pregnant on 15 June. Either he was making a lucky guess or Mary was pregnant before marriage. Granted, the knowledge of pregnancy and the female anatomy was poor and dates were sometimes wildly out, but if the queen knew she was pregnant before her marriage, this would explain her misery and desperate submission. But Mary had suffered from vomiting and fainting fits and even fake pregnancies before. Even if she actually conceived after marriage, it is very likely that, tortured, miserable and suffering from real and psychosomatic pain, she imagined that she was pregnant after the rape. A pregnancy outside wedlock was not only a scandal, it would mean her child was illegitimate. Rape was near impossible to prosecute anyway, but if the woman fell pregnant, it was even more problematic, for the conception might suggest that she had enjoyed it (some believed ovulation was the consequence of arousal) thus it was not defined as rape.

Whether she was pregnant or not on her wedding day, Mary was constantly ill and weeping. Once Bothwell had secured the queen, his behaviour worsened. He was madly jealous and flew into a rage when she even dared look at a man, refused to allow her ministers to speak to her alone, had his men guard her chamber, was equally obsessive about and resentful of her female confidants, and he was in a fury about a horse she had given to the younger brother of the Earl of Arran, an old enemy of his. Every day, he said cruel things and made her cry. Mary's friends told her he still visited his former wife, Lady Jean Gordon, at Crichton Castle not far from Edinburgh, and even that he had written to Jean telling her he thought her his lawful wife still, and Mary was just a concubine. As the French ambassador put it, it was said he 'loves his former wife greatly more than he loves the queen'.[7] As it was becoming clear to Mary, he'd never had any affection or even sexual desire for her. She was a mere tool for him to advance himself.

Perhaps, had he been madly in love with her, or sexually obsessed with her, the argument proposed by some historians that she stayed with him because she loved him might be more understandable. A woman knows when a man is only pretending to desire her – but the only thing he wanted was power over her. She was never his type – he liked jolly servant girls. He was spiteful in public and cruel in private. In the words of Sir James Melville he 'mishandled' her – giving the lie to the view held by those historians who argue that Mary found sexual satisfaction with him. Only two days after the marriage, still firmly in what should have been the honeymoon period, she was alone in a room with Bothwell and screamed out for someone to bring her knife so she could kill herself. Otherwise, she said, she'd drown herself. Those around her believed she was serious: 'if God does not aid her she will become desperate'.[8] As poor du Croc, saddened by the terrible state of a monarch he respected, said in a letter some three days after the marriage, it was 'already repented of'.[9]

Bothwell stepped up his campaign. He put guards outside the queen's door so she could not speak to anybody without him being present. Had he attempted to bring the lords together, spoken to those at Stirling and invoked the Ainslie bond, offered sweeteners and treated Mary fairly, he might have managed to win the other lords to his cause, as well as Cecil. After all, he was Protestant and plenty of them could be implicated in the death of Darnley. He had the good sense to write with humility to England, 'albeit men of greater birth and estimation might well have been preferred' to him, 'yet none more careful to see your two Majesties' amitie and intelligence continued by all good offices',[10] and was equally polite with France. But in Scotland, he swaggered, threatened and shouted, and so those who had once tolerated him or even been friendly with him turned to plotting. As du Croc said, he 'will not remain so long, for he is too much hated in this realm, as he is always considered guilty of the death of the King'. Balfour, who had got the gunpowder used on the night of Darnley's murder, was now entirely gone to the other side. He offered the rebels his possession of Edinburgh Castle and his support, as long as all past crimes were forgiven.

Elizabeth wrote a letter, dismayed and outraged. 'To be plain with you, our grief has not been small; for how could a worse choice be made for your honour than in such haste to marry a subject who, besides other notorious lacks, public fame has charged with the murder of your late husband, besides touching yourself in some part, though, we trust in that behalf, falsely.'[11] She said that England would now 'procure the punishment of that murder', whoever was guilty. Safe in a country where no one would kidnap her, Elizabeth could not believe what Mary had done. She did not say in the letter, but she hardly needed to: there was no possibility that she would give Mary the position of heir now. As Melville put it, the marriage 'was at last the Queen's wreck, and the hindrance of all our hopes in the hasty obtaining of all our desires concerning the crown of England'.[12] Catherine de' Medici told Beaton that France would no longer give the queen advice or counsel.

In public, Mary tried to put a brave face on things. She planned a great water pageant for the court to celebrate their marriage. She was graceful and beautifully gowned. But, crucially, she made no effort to reconcile with the lords at Stirling and bring them into her fold. Bothwell added to his men and planned to lead an army against his enemies. He was high-handed with those who remained and finally was so aggressive with Maitland that his old ally stormed off for Stirling. With him he took his wife, Mary's beloved Mary Fleming, much to the queen's shock. Maitland wrote to Cecil that Bothwell had been so angry with him that he had tried to kill him, and only Mary's inter-vention had saved him.[13] The lords ranged against them had now reached thirty and public opinion was very strong. Mary was told it was said she would be burnt as a witch or die. Desperate for money, she melted down the pure gold font that Elizabeth had sent as a present for the christening of Prince James.

The lords were planning to attack Holyrood and seize her. And many of those in Edinburgh, even though they had assented to the marriage, were now opposed to it. When Bothwell heard, he realised how friend-less he was. He might have written polite letters to France and England but neither Charles IX or Elizabeth were about to send troops to support him, and Cecil, at least, was probably giving funds to those who planned to bring Bothwell down.

Bothwell forced Mary to flee and she bundled up some belongings, a silver basin and a kettle for heating water, a small lockable box for her papers and pins for her beautiful hair. The queen who had brought back dozens of boats filled with tapestries, silver, books, jewels and clothes from France was now reduced to a few poignant items. They shifted to Borthwick Castle, which was strongly fortified, almost impossible to enter. It was superbly safe – but Mary had made a terrible mistake in quitting her palace and castle. Four days later, the lords attacked, Bothwell galloped away, claiming he was going for reinforcements, and Mary stood on the battlements of Borthwick and shouted down at them to leave her. Once more, she could have saved herself if she had claimed to have been tormented by Bothwell and desperate to be free. Elizabeth might have played such a game. But Mary had no idea of the danger approaching. As she saw it, she was the rightful queen, put there by God, and the lords must understand it. She refused to go with them because she did not trust them. When they shouted up at her with 'undutiful and unseemly speeches' she defended herself valiantly.

The lords set out for Edinburgh with 2,000 men, broke through the fortified gates and took control of the city. Their call to arms was clear: everybody should accompany them to revenge Bothwell and take the queen from him. For he 'having put violent hands on the queen's person and shut her up in the castle of Dunbar', marrying her dishonestly and 'already murdered the late king and now attempting by his gathering together of forces to murder the young prince also', they commanded 'all the lieges to be ready on three hours' warning to pass forward with them to deliver the queen's person and take revenge on the Earl Bothwell'.[14] Morton and his men sacked the royal mint for funds and so potential soldiers were offered the stunning sum of twenty shillings a month.

Mary was fearful of what might happen. She dressed as a man and fled Borthwick Castle to meet Bothwell in the middle of the night and hurry back with him to Dunbar. There she received a letter from Balfour, who asked her to return to Edinburgh, where he would support her and the guns at his castle would be at her disposal. Mary believed him and Bothwell and she set off with 200 musketeers, along with cavalrymen and guns from the castle. She had left all her clothes at Holyrood and Borthwick and so rode forth in a borrowed red skirt made for a much shorter woman, and a velvet hat. She gathered men as she went, promising lands to those of gentle birth who assisted her. They did not accrue as many people as they hoped.

The lords set out against them, bearing a banner of Darnley dead under a tree, with Prince James kneeling before him, crying, 'Judge and Avenge My Cause O Lord,'[15] exactly the words written on the sketch of the murder scene sent to Cecil. Most of them rode under family banners. The stage was set for war.

The forces came together at Carberry Hill, about two miles from Edinburgh, on 15 June, an extremely hot day. And then it was a standoff.

Du Croc helpfully offered to negotiate a truce – hardly the French ambassador's job, but the world had been turned upside down. He was deeply distressed at the thought of engaging a queen in battle and he begged the lords to reconsider. They argued that Mary needed to leave Bothwell or hand him over. As Morton put it, if she would either give him up to be 'punished or remove him from her company, she should find them in continuation of all dutiful obedience'.[16]

Du Croc rode over to Mary, who was sitting on a stone in her red dress. Mary had been broken and blown back and forth by the winds of betrayal and treachery, old friends changing sides and being lied to. She believed that the lords had once supported Bothwell – which they had – and would do so again. She could not believe that he had been guilty of the murder. She had thrown in her lot with Bothwell, the father of her unborn child, a child that would have rights over the succession. She said they had already acquitted Bothwell of the murder and were very wrong to ask for vengeance again. But she offered that if they begged for her pardon, she would be merciful. Bothwell vowed he would fight anyone of sufficient rank. Du Croc told the lords that Mary would pardon them if they asked for it and they were furious. The poor Frenchman had only made things worse. As the hot day wore on, the soldiers began to demand why Bothwell did not just simply fight – and save them all the misery. Some began to desert. Finally, Bothwell agreed to fight Morton, his fellow murderer, a man both fifteen years Bothwell's senior and very unfit. Lord Lindsay, strong, younger and a good fighter, offered to be surrogate. But no fighting came to pass – and the whole palaver was probably a delaying tactic. The lords hoped that the royalist forces would weary of waiting and leave their mistress.[17]

Mary's men were deserting her. There was some talk that this had been her plan all along, she wished to escape Bothwell but was too afraid to do it. She asked the lords how she would be received if she surrendered and they agreed to let Bothwell go. As he wished her goodbye, he thrust into her hand a bombshell: a copy of the bond in which the lords promised to despatch Darnley – and she saw the signatures of Morton, Maitland, Argyll, Huntly and the others. Mary was devastated. They had lied to her all along, telling her that they would chastise Darnley, and instead they had always wanted to kill him. Mary hardly had a moment to process the horrific news before she was taken off to the lords. She had expected polite treatment – in Bothwell's words, she could go to them in 'perfect safety' and the men would be 'offering to the Queen, as their rightful superior, their true allegiance . . . that each single one of them wanted no more than to accord her all honour and obedience'.[18] Mary believed that the lords would conduct her back to Parliament, which would restore order. Morton and the other leaders greeted her with respect but from the army there were shouts about burning the whore and cruel insults. Mary turned on Morton.

'How is this, my Lord Morton? I am told all this is done to get justice among the King's murderers. I am also told you were one of the chief of them.' Morton refused to listen to her, shuffling away. Mary was courageous, but it was a terrible mistake to expose to the lords how much she now knew. They had to keep her quiet and stop her speaking. The paper of the Craigmillar bond was taken from her, probably at this point. She was given to two rough young guards and rudely jostled about. She was pushed forward, to ride back to Edinburgh, with men yelling insults, and the Darnley banner borne in front of her. Exhausted, in shock at what she had learned, terrified by her treatment, she wept all the way.

In Edinburgh, groups shouted insults against her, some of them planted by the lords. Instead of going to Holyrood, she was taken to the Provost's house. She was now a prisoner. The guards accompanied her to her bedroom and she could not even undress in privacy. The white banner was hung in front of the window, depicting Darnley dead and her baby son begging for vengeance. After a miserable night, in horror and distress, she came to the window the next morning, her beautiful hair wild and her bodice unlaced so her breasts were revealed, begging for assistance. Mary as Queen of Scots, as the most powerful woman in the country, and Queen of France, she who had claimed the English throne, was no more.

Chapter Twenty-Three
'They Have Robbed Me of Everything I Have in This World'

T he lords had expected that the people would attack and mock their queen, but the people of Edinburgh were outraged to see her so treated and flocked to the Provost's house to shout that she should be freed. And even those they expected to be loyal were complaining that she had been promised good conduct and was instead being treated as a common prisoner.

From her awful captivity, Mary spotted Maitland in the crowd and managed to persuade him to speak to her, even though he was too ashamed to meet her eye. Her old friend, Secretary of State and husband of her beloved Mary Fleming rebuffed her cruelly, telling her that 'it was suspected and feared that she meant to thwart the execution of the justice demanded on the death of the late king'. He talked on about the sins of Bothwell. Mary countered that the lords were engaging in 'false pretexts' and trying to hinder 'justice done for the murder which they themselves had committed'. As she had with Morton, she revealed to Maitland that she knew he was guilty: 'She told him that she feared that he, Morton and Balfour, more than any others, hindered the inquiry into the murder, to which they were the consenting and guilty parties.' She told Maitland that Bothwell had shown her the bond. If she was treated thus for attempting to prevent the investigation into Darnley's murder, how much harder would the inquiry be against Maitland, 'with how much greater certainty could they proceed against him, Morton, Balfour and the rest who were the actual murderers?'[1]

Again, Mary rushed to speak when she should have stayed quiet. She should have published the truth herself, engaged her lawyers or used the knowledge she now had to get other lords on her side before going public. Instead, she gave the lords even more reason to try to silence her and lock her away. Maitland, the man she had thought of as a friend, was terrified. He told the queen that if she said he was responsible, it would 'drive him to greater lengths than he yet had gone in order to save his own life'. He suggested too that her own life was under threat but that he could save her – he blackmailed her to stay quiet. She was making a great mistake in telling them what she knew.

It does not seem, however, that Mary told them she was pregnant. Even if she had not been with child, arguing that she was would have been a protection for her. If it had reached the public that the queen was pregnant with an heir to the throne – even by the hated Bothwell – there would have been a heavy surge of support for her. For Mary could do the one thing that the lords could not: give birth to a future king. And James was still only a toddler. He had not reached the golden age of five, when the mortality rate was much reduced. But she appears to have said nothing and the chance was lost.

Maitland went straight to the others and told them that Mary knew about their involvement and was talking. They had to act. They could not put her on trial because she would speak of their guilt. A few lords proposed she might be put on the throne as a figurehead, but that idea was shouted down: she might put the signatories to the bond on trial and give power to her old supporters. In the mire of her life, unloved by the lords, her best friend was the French ambassador, and du Croc tried valiantly to save her, suggesting that if she were sent to France, the king would put her in a convent. Du Croc tried to help but the lords did not trust Charles IX and suspected that if Mary was put in a convent, she would be allowed a certain liberty (which was likely) and start plotting against them.[2]

As for asking Elizabeth for help or sending Mary to an English prison, the lords knew they would be playing into the hands of the English. Elizabeth would hold Mary's presence over them, using it to reduce their power and blackmail them into doing as she wished. As they saw it, there was no option but to keep Mary captive – but away from Edinburgh and all her supporters. The last thing they wanted was the queen, dishevelled and weeping in the Tolbooth again, gathering sympathy, constantly talking of how the lords had killed her husband. A harsh warrant for Mary's incarceration was produced, noting that her indefinite imprisonment was because she had been 'fortifying' Bothwell in his terrible acts. She simply had to be stopped for the good of Scotland for she was in thrall to following her 'inordinate passion, to the final confusion and extermination of the whole realm'.[3] It was signed by Morton, Mar, Atholl, Lindsay and others, some of whom had also signed to support Bothwell's claim of marriage, only two months earlier. Thus far, one might be able to excuse the lords on the basis that they were attempting to secure the country after a period of bloodshed. But locking up the queen indefinitely was nothing more than a blatant grab for power. They wanted the crown and the fact that she was a woman more emboldened them to seize it.

That evening, Mary was escorted to Holyrood with the Darnley banner carried in front of her. The lords were keen to make a show of her, like the conquering Romans displaying a captive queen, and so she was escorted on foot, guarded by 200 soldiers and 1,000 of the lords' own servants, insulted by the crowds as she walked. Exhausted and dishevelled, she was the single woman in the midst of over 1,200 men, the power imbalance never more evident.

At Holyrood, Mary was overcome with relief. Two of her Marys, Seton and Livingston, tended to her and she was given the first meal she had eaten since she had given herself up at Carberry Hill. Morton was standing behind her chair, an impatient gargoyle, and he grew cross at Mary's lengthy dinner of various courses. Halfway through, he roughly told her that she must leave on the instant, and she would be forbidden from taking her ladies with her. She was wearing only a thin silk gown and she seized a rough brown cloak to warm herself and was ushered to the dreaded lords Lindsay and Ruthven, who were waiting on horses outside. Still trusting the lords would protect her due to her surrender, she gathered from Morton she was going to Stirling to see her son. Instead, they forced her out and headed north, towards Loch Leven, just over thirty miles from Edinburgh. There poor Mary was shoved onto a boat and taken to Lochleven Castle, on an island in the middle of the loch. The laird received her and took her to a meagre room on the ground floor.

None of the royal furniture that she might expect was there. She collapsed in exhaustion and shock. As Mary herself wrote: 'They have robbed me of everything I had in the world, not permitting me either to write or speak, in order that I might not contradict their false inventions.'[4] She was right. While she was being whisked away from Holyrood, the lords looted her rooms and tore down the religious decorations in her private chapel. Still concerned about the force of public opinion, they told preachers to rail against her from the pulpit. Lochleven had long been selected as a jail: Mary had been on a fast track to her isolated captivity from the moment she had given herself up at Carberry Hill.

The Queen of Scots was now a prisoner. There was only one person who could save her and that was Elizabeth. She wrote in secret to 'my Good Sister', pleading for assistance. Mary was still dreaming of the romantic meeting between queens, in which they would speak in perfect sympathy and all Mary's problems would be at an end.

The length of my weary imprisonment and the wrongs I have received from those on whom I have conferred so many benefits, are less annoying to me than not having it in my power to acquaint you with the realities of my calamities, and the injuries that have been done to me in various ways. It may please you to remember that you have often told me several times 'that on receiving the ring you gave me, you would assist me in any time of trouble'. You know that Lord James [Moray] has seized all I have. Melville, to whom I have sent secretly for this ring as my most precious jewel, says that he dare not let me have it. Therefore I implore you to have compassion on your good sister and cousin, and believe you have not a more affectionate relative in the world. You should also consider the importance of the example practised against me.[5]

Mary begged Elizabeth not to let anyone know that she had written, 'for it would cause me to be treated worse than I am now'.

Elizabeth was shocked when she heard that Mary had been whisked away secretly to an extremely secure fortress. She was scandalised by the rough treatment of a queen and deeply worried that they had had the audacity to put Mary in prison, without a trial. Even the lowest peasant was supposed to be allowed to stand trial. But Mary had been flung into jail by the exercise of brute force. She started talking of war and Cecil dissuaded her, told her to wait to see if diplomatic efforts might succeed.

Elizabeth wrote to the lords of her horror and dictated a letter of support to Mary. Her words couldn't have been plainer. She declared of the lords that 'They have no warrant nor authority, by the law of God or man, to be as superiors, judges or vindicators over their prince and sovereign,' and decreed, 'We are determined we will take plain part with them to revenge their sovereign, for an example to all prosperity.'[6] But Moray and the rest were not burned by Elizabeth's fiery words. Their men were sorting through the queen's jewellery and choosing pieces for him and Agnes and setting aside other jewels to sell. They guessed that England would not be invading Scotland any time soon – Moray expected Cecil to support him and his pro-Protestant government. Elizabeth sent Sir Nicholas Throckmorton to try to reconcile Mary to the lords and get her back on the throne, even if by force, as well as to hunt down Darnley's killers and persuade the Scots to send Prince James to be brought up in the English court under Elizabeth's guardianship (the French also wanted the prince).

Elizabeth had set her man the most Sisyphean task imaginable. How on earth was the English ambassador to force Mary back into power when she was imprisoned and the lords were all-powerful? If Elizabeth had told Throckmorton to engage in long-term sedition, dividing the lords one by one from their cause and over to Mary's, promising money and support to those who did, that could have been successful. Plenty of the lords were wavering or already aggrieved at not getting what they perceived as their just desserts. But to tell him to get Mary back on the throne without the back-up of a full threat of war was as incredible as sending her to the moon.

Elizabeth was preoccupied by the sanctity of royal blood. But Cecil undermined her by sending his own set of instructions to the envoy. He decreed that Mary should become a figurehead, divested of all authority, named queen, but the power would lie with a council of nobles. No doubt, as politic as ever, he felt that this much-reduced offer was the only chance of getting Mary restored and doing what Elizabeth wanted. But he also despaired of Mary and thought she didn't deserve to rule. He scribbled on his letter in Latin, 'Athalia was killed so Joash could be king',[7] an example from *Chronicles* that Knox had used against poor female rulers. Athalia had been a bad and idolatrous queen, deposed by her elites in favour of her seven-year-old son, for whom they ruled as regent. Although it is unlikely that Cecil at this point supported the idea of killing Mary, he certainly wanted her out of the way.

For everyone other than Elizabeth, the easiest eventuality would be if Mary was found dead. As the lords had rued, a trial and execution would be a hornets' nest, for Elizabeth and other monarchs might protest the queen going on trial, there was no real evidence against her, and plenty of the lords had been involved in the various plots and Mary had already threatened to talk. Moreover, if Mary appeared at trial, she would very likely win over sympathies and the ordinary Edinburgh people would protest the process vociferously. So it would be easier simply to kill the queen off in a secret execution, by poison or even by gunpowder or strangling, as with Darnley. Mary was in danger – and she knew it. But by sending Throckmorton and writing incensed letters, Elizabeth made it clear that she was watching and her spy networks were doubling their efforts. If Mary was found murdered, Elizabeth would very likely insist on war.

Throckmorton met Maitland, told him of Elizabeth's fury and demanded to see the queen, but he was denied. Maitland threatened Throckmorton that if he caused trouble, it would expose Mary to more risk of her life. Mary's old friend insisted that she was in prison to save her from the wrath of the common people. He said that as soon as she prosecuted the murderers and relinquished Bothwell they would 'restore her to her estate'.[8] Throckmorton knew he had to find more surreptitious means of contacting the queen.

Lochleven, on one of four islands in the loch, felt utterly isolated. The castle was owned by Sir William Douglas, nephew of Mar and half-brother to Moray, and Ruthven and Lindsay had been left in charge of Mary. There had been no preparation of her crude downstairs room – a calculated insult to a queen. For the first two weeks after her arrival, Mary sank into a stupor of shock and inaction, unable to drink, speak or eat. In private, she must have drunk a little. But to Sir William, she would give no sign of submitting. She feared that she might be poisoned. Mary Seton, in attendance on her, was the only person she could trust.

Mary came round: she realised her best chance of escape was by using her legendary charm. She began to 'take both rest and meat and also some dancing and play at cards'.[9] Her captor also noted, on 17 July, that she was growing fat – her pregnancy was continuing. She attempted to win over Ruthven – which unfortunately worked too well, as he became infatuated with her, promising to help her if she became his lover. She might have tried to string him along and see what promises he might make and what information she might extract. But Mary, powerful beauty, was no manipulator of men and wished above all to be honourable. She was already married and would not escape in any low manner. Agnes Keith, wife of Moray, was sent to accompany her, softening Mary up for what was to come. The queen was grateful for the friendship of her sister-in-law and it gave her hope that she might be better treated. But Agnes was reporting back to her husband, who had the regency in his sights now.

In mid-July, the intrepid English envoy Throckmorton managed to smuggle in a secret letter to Mary. He begged her to publicly relinquish Bothwell and made it clear that he wanted to help her. She replied that she was in despair and constantly in fear of death. But she would not give up her husband. She didn't declare love for him or try to claim again that it had been necessary to marry him to prevent factionalism among the nobles and the court. Instead she needed him because she was pregnant, 'taking herself seven weeks gone with child, she should acknowledge herself to be with child of a bastard and to have forfeited her honour' if she divorced him.[10] The reference to seven weeks dated the conception safely after the marriage, just as should be the case, in a letter that would be communicated straight to Elizabeth. But it certainly seems as if Mary thought herself pregnant before that date. A pregnancy of seven weeks is a fragile thing. Even at this time, due to anecdotal knowledge, most women and doctors understood that passing two months improved the chances of carrying a pregnancy to term and three months was the golden line. Mary was probably much further along than she stated – and so it seemed to her that the pregnancy would be carried to term and she would bear Bothwell's child.

The letter cast Throckmorton into a panic. If Mary could not be induced to give up Bothwell, then he could not see how he could help her. The lords had repeatedly justified her imprisonment by saying that it was to keep her from Bothwell, and they were stopping her from writing to him in order to allow them 'leisure to go forward in the prosecution of the murder'. He did not believe them, ruing that 'when they have gone so far, these lords will think themselves unsafe while she lives and take her life'.[11] He guessed the truth – the lords would not release her even if she relinquished her husband. But their excuse of holding Mary in order to pursue the murderers had a fair appearance to the rest of the world and Throckmorton could not see how he could contest it.

Mary's former friends were fully occupied dividing her belongings and encouraging sermons against her. They summoned Bothwell to answer for murdering Darnley, abducting the queen and forcing her to agree to marriage, and when he did not appear, he was declared an outlaw. He fled to Orkney, where he hoped to raise ships to fight. Next, the lords attempted to hunt down all of those servants and men of ordinary stature who had helped to kill Darnley. William Blackadder, who said he had only been in a nearby tavern, was hanged, drawn and quartered and his limbs were placed on the gates. Bastian, the groom whose masque Mary had attended, was imprisoned in the Tolbooth. Cecil demanded to interview one man who claimed he had been bullied into committing the murder, but the lords hanged him, keen not to see him sent to England. A tailor who had watched Bothwell change his celebratory outfit for a dark dress that would mean he was not so easily found was captured and hanged. The lords were engaging in a wholesale mass killing of the minor players.

George Dalgleish, a tailor and one of Bothwell's servants, was arrested. It was later said that he had broken into Edinburgh Castle on the orders of Bothwell to get possession of a small silver casket containing incriminating letters from Mary to Bothwell. Once arrested, Dalgleish was shipped off to the Tolbooth and threatened with torture. He quickly caved in, and on 20 June took the investigators to a house where he showed them the casket, hidden under a bed. This was the item on which all accusations of Mary's guilt about the murder would hinge, and all our evidence for it comes from a statement from Morton to Cecil. Even at this point, the story has an oddly fairy-tale ring, chiefly because it would be a poor hiding place for such a vital item. According to Morton, on the following day, the casket was broken open in the presence of Maitland and Atholl and others, and the letters were 'sighted'[12] – but the Scots word does not indicate whether they were read or simply seen. Did the casket even exist? Or did it exist but contained nothing more incriminating than notes – and gave Morton an idea of how to throw opprobrium at the queen? Oddly, in a council meeting on the next day, there was no mention of the casket or its contents. On 26 June, Dalgleish was interviewed by the council and made a confession about Darnley's murder. Even stranger, he did not mention the casket at all and was not questioned on it. He was hanged for being part of the murder along with some other accomplices in early 1568 – and surely if his evidence was so material to Mary's guilt, they would have kept him alive.

The lords were hunting for documents. Mary had not taken her papers with her – so where were they? Either she or a quick-thinking attendant such as Mary Seton had destroyed them or, simply, there was nothing particularly incriminating. The lords did find another casket at Edinburgh Castle – but, unfortunately for them, it seems to have contained evidence that other lords knew of the plan to kill Darnley, probably the Craigmillar bond. That was the sort of evidence the lords didn't want in the public domain.

Still, the lords were delighted with the course of events. They declared they had evidence of Bothwell's guilt, although they refrained from showing it. A deposition was sent to the French king and to Elizabeth explaining their acts. Happily for them, the Pope was scandalised to hear about Mary's marriage to Bothwell and decided he could no longer assist her, complaining that he couldn't decide which of the two queens in Britain was worse.[13]

Chapter Twenty-Four
'The Conspiracy for Her Husband's Murder'

On 20 July, in her dismal rooms at Lochleven, Mary began suffering pains. Within a day or so, she realised she was miscarrying. Her secretary later said she had been carrying twins – if she was miscarrying at only eight weeks, this would have been difficult to see although, perhaps if identical, two sacs might have been visible, but it was probably more likely that Mary was further along, perhaps even around the three-month mark, and thus could see what she was losing. This dating makes it seem more likely that she conceived before her marriage – and so she felt she had no choice but to go ahead with her marriage to Bothwell. Now, however, the reason she had given to Throckmorton as to why she would not relinquish her husband was no longer valid. The child – or children – were no more.

The news was quickly sent to the lords that Mary was suffering and sick and appeared to be losing her pregnancy. For the lords, this was fraught with danger. If she rose from her sickbed to declare she would divorce Bothwell, as was not unlikely, there would be little reason not to restore her to the throne, as they had told Throckmorton they would. By giving up Bothwell, Mary would win back the support of Elizabeth – and most likely of the Pope as well. The ordinary people of Edinburgh had come to hear that other lords had been involved in the murder, and they were restive that only the lesser men were being prosecuted. They still loved and pitied their queen. Moray and the rest had to act swiftly to prevent Mary regaining her position.

On 24 July, only a few days after the miscarriage began, Mary was collapsed on her bed, exhausted and suffering severe blood loss and pain, in what she called 'a state of great weakness', when Lindsay and a group of other lords burst in. They gave her documents declaring she was too enervated in body, mind and spirit to continue to reign and thus would abdicate in favour of James.[1] Moray would be regent and Morton and the others act as a temporary regency council until he returned from France. Mary refused. Lindsay cruelly ordered her to stand and said she'd be sent to the most isolated island or cast into the loch. Then he told her he'd cut her throat.

Mary, shocked and humiliated, in fear for her life, agreed to sign, weeping at how she was 'vexed, broken and unquieted'. Brave until the end, she told the men that when God had returned her to liberty she would disavow the documents for 'it is done against my will'.[2] She fell into a terrible state of illness, with swelling in her limbs and boils over her body – and believed she had been poisoned. The lords rushed off to prepare for crowning the child James, aiming to get the job done before Elizabeth or any foreign power could intervene. Five days after Mary had signed the documents under duress, Morton swore the coronation oath in place of the gurgling baby prince at the first Scottish Protestant coronation ceremony. The lords had organised bonfires and celebrations in Edinburgh but the people had no desire to celebrate. They still supported Mary and they were sick of fighting. In Lochleven, the cannons were fired and when Mary asked why, the laird told her and cruelly asked why she was not celebrating the coronation of her own child.

Poor Throckmorton, trounced at every turn and shocked at the violence he had seen from the lords, begged to return to England, two days after Mary's forced abdication. 'I see no likelihood to win anything at these men's hands', he complained to Cecil.[3] It was the greatest admission that mere legal and diplomatic threat simply didn't work – when Lindsay could threaten to throw the queen into the loch and cut her throat if she didn't obey. To Leicester, Throckmorton was even more blunt, fearing the 'tragedy will end in the queen's person', in the same way as it began with Rizzio and Darnley.[4]

Elizabeth received the news of Mary's abdication at the beginning of August with rage. She demanded to see Cecil and railed at him in, in his words, 'a great offensive speech'[5] about his inaction and declared she would go to war. She was distressed for her cousin and infuriated by the lies of the lords and blamed Cecil for the disaster. Elizabeth was scandalised and also conscious of her own position: if an anointed queen could be abducted, raped, imprisoned and then deposed and no one protested, then what of the right of any queen to be on the throne? She naturally feared that her enemies might be emboldened to treat her similarly. It would go through a more openly legal process in England, but her detractors could easily vaunt that Mary's fate proved that Elizabeth would fail too – and should be removed from the throne before the country fell into ruin.

Cecil recoiled at the idea of sending in the army. He disliked Mary and thought her a threat to his queen and had no time for female rule, other than that of his mistress. Also, he was a behind-the-scenes man. He was happy – and indeed expert – at raising sedition backstage or harrying on the borders, but the thought of all-out war on the outskirts of Edinburgh was terrifying; expensive, unpopular and there was the possibility of losing, which would be roundly humiliating and bad for their international standing. Moray was running a friendly Protestant government and restoring Mary would mean a return to some power for Catholics. Cecil told Elizabeth that if she announced war, the lords might try to avoid it by simply assassinating the queen (because if she were dead, there was no point fighting to restore her). With the Privy Council, he tried to persuade Elizabeth to negotiate with Scotland.[6] On this, the queen was steadfast. She would not speak to the lords while Mary was in prison, and if any harm came to Mary, she was ready to send in the armies.

Elizabeth still could have saved Mary at this point with a viable threat of war, even if she only proposed that Mary occupy a reduced role as a symbolic queen. Invading Scotland would be difficult and dangerous and Mary had signed the deed of abdication allowing the lords to crown James. But if Elizabeth had made a serious threat, the lords, isolated from any allies and already riven by internal divisions, would have possibly agreed to give Mary a limited symbolic role, alongside her son, if they could guarantee she never saw Bothwell again (a condition that Elizabeth would also expect). Mary would have had little choice other than to accept and assume a position that was more akin to the 'queen mother', a reduction but at least better than permanent imprisonment on a chilly loch. And Elizabeth would be spared the painful problems of Mary's exile that awaited.

Cecil, not for the first time, was wrong. A letter of horror from Elizabeth, implicit threat and possibly even the suggestion of collaboration with Spain or France could have had some impact. No one wanted to see a queen pushed off her throne. There was no way that the lords, embattled and exhausted, would have rushed to war against England, the wealthy, well-oiled fighting machine. People had suffered so much under the previous English invasions and they would blame the lords for subjecting them to harrying and bloodshed once more. And after months of fighting, the lords' retainers were weary and there was no money to pay them. If Elizabeth had made a serious warning, the lords would have sent a team to negotiate with her. For, as the sensible ones among them knew, keeping Mary a prisoner was continuing to prove deeply unpopular with the common people.

Elizabeth held all the cards. But Cecil convinced her not to use them. All she could do was to insist that he made it clear that if Mary was mistreated or killed, then the English would invade. Battling to make the best of his impossible task, hated and suspected on all sides, Throckmorton did force Maitland to promise that Mary 'shall not die any violent death unless some new accident chance'.[7] One might argue that there were many possible deaths that were not violent. And 'accident chance' could be easily simulated. Throckmorton and Elizabeth pretended to themselves they were protecting Mary. But although many lords would have preferred her dead, the actual act would have been a shocking one. She was an anointed queen and thus touched by God, and many lords naturally feared that God would take vengeance. Mary was frequently threatened with death. But had she died mysteriously, poisoned or pushed down the stairs, Scotland would have been aflame.

On 11 August, Moray arrived back from France, after long manipulating matters behind the scenes. Everything had worked out perfectly for him. Darnley had been killed, and Bothwell had fled – and now his troublesome sister had lost all power. He had gained everything and he could push forward the Protestant Reformation and reward himself and his followers with money, jewels and land. Cecil had backed the right horse.

Five days after his arrival, Moray visited Mary in her prison, where she was sick and suffering. She flung herself towards him, weeping passionately. She had hoped for words of comfort or outrage at how she had been treated. Instead, he was cold and cruel, telling her the people were angry with her and she had been careless about her reputation, words that must work to 'cut the thread of love betwixt him and the queen forever'.[8] She pleaded her innocence but he shrugged her off. Next day, he returned and told her she must not apply for help to England or France, threatening her and then offering to make her life easier if she submitted to accepting him as regent. He also told her that he could not protect her life if she contacted Bothwell. In other words, she could be put on trial and executed. She had no choice. She was so desperate that she agreed to it all without asking for anything in return. Moray relented somewhat, lying to Mary to stop her from making him feel guilty, telling her that if she showed abhorrence for the murder of Darnley but agreed not to take any revenge, she might 'one day be restored to the throne'.[9] Poor Mary clutched at his lies with hope. On 22 August, Moray was pronounced Regent of Scotland. He took up Holyrood, revelled in her jewels. He rewarded his beloved wife, Agnes, with Mary's beloved giant diamond, 'the great H', her wedding gift in 1558 from the King of France.

Moray had won, once again, and the winner had taken all.

The new regent didn't want to be challenged about his sister's treatment and so she was moved to better quarters of two rooms in September and allowed to take occasional exercise in the castle gardens, and Mary Seton came to attend her. Unfortunately, the unsympathetic Lady Douglas slept in her chamber. Mary was allowed to order clothes, embroidery thread, boxes of sweets and, in November, a striking clock with an alarm. She had few other comforts.

Elizabeth refused to recognise Moray as regent or James as king and recalled Throckmorton, officially breaking off diplomatic relations.

Moray tried to win over the English queen by sending her Mary's famed black pearls, six rows of them as large as grapes. He then reviewed the evidence his friends had found against Mary. If placards started appearing, the people became restive and lords began complaining, and England, France or Spain threatened invasion, he had the perfect answer. He would put Mary on trial for part of the conspiracy against Darnley. But they had to ensure that none of the lords were implicated. There were copies in circulation of the Craigmillar bond – and it was so widely discussed that even an English informer, William Drury, heard of it and reported it back to London.

Lady Lennox, mother of Lord Darnley, said that Moray had been told by the queen that she 'knew the conspiracy for her husband's murder'.[10] Moray lied. What Mary had known was that Darnley would be threatened, and it was the guilt over this that had shaped her life and her terrible situation. What she now knew was that Bothwell had lied to her all along and had always planned to kill the young king, with the backup of the other signatories to the Craigmillar bond. Moray's use of the word 'knew' indicated the project upon which he was now set: collecting evidence to condemn the queen in a show trial.

Mary wrote to Moray asking for the opportunity to speak in front of Parliament to 'answer the false calumnies that had been published about her' and 'submit herself to all the rigour of the laws', as well as pursuing 'the punishment of all persons who might be found guilty of the murder of the late king'.[11] Of course, Moray refused.

It seems astonishing that the queen had lived through so much and was still only twenty-four. Her twenty-fifth birthday on 8 December was a dangerous and fast-approaching moment for the lords, for it meant that she had officially reached her majority. Most significantly, she could take back any land grants she had made during the previous years and she had made a lot of grants to those who were now putting her on trial. If she attended Parliament, she could potentially take them back. The lords dashed to produce conspiracies and on 4 December they produced an Act of Council that accused Mary of Darnley's murder and wishing to kill her son, on the basis that there were 'letters written and subscribed with her own hand' sent to James, Earl of Bothwell, chief executioner of the horrible murder, that revealed she was 'privy, art and part, and of the actual devise and deed of the murder of the king'[12] – and thus the lords had taken her into custody on 15 June. The letters themselves were not produced and no quotations were read from them.

If such overweening evidence of Mary's guilt existed, then why had the letters not been mentioned earlier? Surely Lindsay and his fellow henchmen would have used them against Mary when they forced her to abdicate at the end of July, just after her miscarriage. And why would Moray not have shown them to Throckmorton or even sent them to Cecil, in their private exchanges? Or even taken them with him to confront his half-sister when he visited her to force her to accept his regency in August? One can only conclude that these letters did not exist on 15 June, either because they had not yet been found, or because they had not yet been written. Equally suspicious was the fact that the casket letters were said to have been found after George Dalgleish, Bothwell's servant, had been arrested. But, as already noted, very strangely the casket letters were not mentioned around the time of Dalgleish's capture. And even if they had been found via Dalgleish, that was after 15 June, not before.

Moreover, if at the trial they referred to the casket letters, none of these were signed. Mary was being accused by the flimsiest of fake evidence – for who would defend her? The Parliament of 15 December that Mary had so hoped to address passed an Act enthusing that Mary's abdication, James's accession and the regency of Moray were all 'lawful and perfect'. The terrible accusations that Mary had manipulated the murder were then ratified. Everything had changed. The lords had said they captured Mary at Carberry Hill due to Bothwell's perfidy and murder of Darnley, telling her they wished only that she give up her husband. Now, she was being accused of the murder herself.

The whole story would be that Bothwell and his servants killed Darnley, with Mary's connivance. Moray had outwitted Mary at every turn, creating alliances, flattering Lady Lennox, promising money and now planning her trial.

In exile, Mary was devastated at the betrayal of so many, and constantly ill. She knew that she was not going to be released and she feared poisoning or being brought to death. She started to plan her escape, aware from secret letters that some of her old supporters were keen to assist her. At the same time, her subjects were growing increasingly resentful at the continuing mass execution of minor servants for Darnley's murder. In early January, another set of men were killed, including poor George Dalgleish and John Hepburn.

When Hepburn was about to mount the scaffold to be hanged, he shouted to the crowd that Huntly, Argyll, Maitland and Balfour had all signed the bond to support Darnley's murder, to much public consternation. John Hay, another conspirator, apparently also named Balfour and Maitland. The old placards came back, but this time demanding why Hay and Hepburn had not been allowed to publicly explain 'the manner of the king's slaughter'[13] and who had been involved. The lords accused made a sharp exit from Edinburgh.

The pattern of loyalties was beginning to shift in Mary's favour, and her supporters – including Huntly, Argyll, Fleming, Seton and the Hamiltons – believed she had been in prison for long enough. Maitland, who had once been so cruel and dismissive, had now changed his mind. He was resentful of Moray's high-handed behaviour and surreptitiously sent Mary a ring as a pledge of support. Argyll, too, had defected from the other side. He seems to have genuinely believed that the lords had been trying to rescue Mary when they had seized her the previous June, and he was shocked at her rough treatment and forced imprisonment.

Emboldened by support from outside, Mary continued to work towards freeing herself. She managed to charm George Douglas, the younger brother of Sir William, the laird of Lochleven, and he helped her get letters to her supporters, including Huntly. Nine months after she had first been confined, she set off disguised as a laundress in a boat across the loch. Unfortunately for her, the boatmen grew suspicious, tried to pull off her muffler and saw that she had beautifully white hands – not those of a laundress. Mary's fine skin, always a source of pride to her, had betrayed her. The boatman took her back, but chose not to report the flight to the laird. Six weeks later, on 2 May 1568, she made another attempt. Willie Douglas, a young page, had been won to her cause and he'd agreed to help her. He spoiled all the castle's boats except one and that evening, when the family were at dinner, he stole the key to the castle, whipping it away from under the laird's nose while he enjoyed his meal. In her room, Mary changed clothes with the ever-faithful Mary Seton. There, her old friend stood at the window dressed as the queen, so that anyone would think it was her – a courageous act.

Mary and Willie hurried from the castle and as they left, he ingeniously locked the castle behind him and cast the key into a cannon. As the family continued to eat and drink, happily unaware, Willie rowed Mary over the loch and met George Douglas at the other side, riding on horses he had stolen from the laird. Mary rode to the castle of Niddrie, owned by Lord Seton, and from there set off to Cadzow Castle, near Hamilton, the headquarters of the Hamilton family – who expected a hefty payback for supporting her escape. She would always be grateful to Willie Douglas too, keeping him in her service until death. At Cadzow, she met Lord Seton and the others and began to plan her next move. All the while, through her imprisonment, assault and final escape, she carried with her the belief in the precious diamond ring that Elizabeth had sent her in 1563, which had been left behind at Holyrood. She clutched the remembrance of it like a talisman, as if it had magical powers to protect her.

Chapter Twenty-Five

'Forced Out of My Kingdom'

Mary regained her spirits. She wrote to Moray instructing him that she had been forced to abdicate and thus his position as regent was false. In shock that his half-sister had escaped, he refused to discuss the matter. So the only solution was war. Many Scots, who had been uneasy about the abdication and imprisonment, were keen to support their queen and she soon had around 6,000 men. 'By battle let us try it',[1] she said. On 8 May, nine earls, nine bishops, eighteen lairds and one hundred other men of influence agreed to support her in a proclamation called the 'Hamilton bond'. Argyll agreed to lead her army into battle against Moray, who had once been his friend. And now that Mary was claiming she had been compelled to abdicate, Moray's position was looking very close to treason. This was fighting talk from her but it pushed her half-brother into a corner. If she won, then he could justly be executed and so his side was fired and strengthened in their desire to fight until the death. After all that she had suffered and his cruel treatment of her at Lochleven, where he'd made it clear her life would be in danger if she didn't sign the deed of abdication, Mary had no more love for him and she was ready to see him die.

Mary had a third more men than Moray and she had public opinion behind her. Melville had finally brought her the diamond ring that had been Elizabeth's promise to her – and Mary held tight to it. She was confident of success. But when the half-siblings met on 13 May at the village of Langside, near Glasgow, Moray proved the better commander and gained a swift advantage. William Kirkcaldy of Grange, acting for

Moray, proved the decisive factor when he saw that Moray was failing and galloped to his aid with so many men that Moray was able to charge. After a mere forty-five minutes, Mary had lost and over a hundred of her men had died. Over 300 of the rest were seized, including Lord Seton and Sir James Hamilton. Mary fled, shaved off her magnificent hair so she would not be recognised and rode her horse without stopping towards Dumbarton Castle, still clutching the diamond ring that Elizabeth had given her. She was right to choose Dumbarton: resting in a secure castle, she could send word to France or simply wait to see how many lords turned to her cause. As she recalled to her uncle in France, 'I have endured injuries, calumnies, imprisonment, famine, cold, heat, flight not knowing whither, ninety-two miles across the country without stopping or alighting, and then I have to sleep on the ground and drink sour milk and eat oatmeal without bread, and have three nights like the owls.'[2]

She stopped first at Dumfries and travelled to the castle of Terregles. There she made a fateful decision. Dumbarton was difficult to reach as she would have to pass Lennox strongholds, so she decided against it. There were other castles she could have aimed for. But Mary was convinced Elizabeth would support her and she should go to England to raise an army. Her supporters at Terregles begged her not to – reminding her that even her own father had been too concerned about imprisonment to meet Henry VIII at York. They pleaded with her to stay in Scotland or at least think of France, where she had valuable lands. And although relations with Catherine de' Medici were hardly cordial, she still had her Guise family, and Charles IX was said to be sympathetic. For even if Elizabeth was well disposed to Mary, there were all her Protestant churchmen and advisors to reckon with, who would likely prefer a Protestant government in Scotland, even if they were usurpers. But Mary was convinced that Elizabeth could help her and, as she dolefully put it later, 'I commanded my best friends to permit me to have my own way.'[3]

Wearing a cloak and hood borrowed from the laird of Lochnivar, Mary rode to the abbey of Dundrennan. There, she wrote a desperate letter to Elizabeth 'my dearest sister', and finally relinquished the diamond ring as a 'token of her promised friendship'. It was a short letter in which Mary set to 'acquaint you as quickly as I can' of her latest misfortunes, that 'some of my subjects who I most confided in, and had raised to the highest pitch of honour, have taken up arms against me, and treated me with the utmost indignity'. She continued:

> I have since lost a battle, in which most of those who preserved their loyal integrity fell before my eyes. I am now forced out of my kingdom, and driven to such straits that, next to God, I have no hope but in your goodness. I beseech you therefore, my dearest sister, that I may be conducted to your presence, that I may tell you everything that has happened.
>
> Meanwhile, I beg God to grant you all heavenly blessings and to me patience and comfort, which last I hope and pray to gain by your means.
>
> To remind you of the reasons I have to depend on England, I send back to the queen, this token, the jewel of her promised friendship and assistance.[4]

She sent the ring and letter via John Beaton, imagining its effect on Elizabeth. Mary was convinced that she would return with English fighters behind her, ready to seize her rightful throne. She had reason: although she didn't know it, Elizabeth had actually written her a letter when she heard of her escape, congratulating her and offering support. But this support was in words only. As had been made clear by the events of the previous year, Elizabeth would exert pressure behind the scenes, argue for reconciliation, but no more. Had Mary remained in Scotland, gathering her army, Elizabeth would have probably sent Throckmorton to press Moray and the lords to negotiate and reach a settlement. That was the kind of support she meant. Not a full-fledged army, riding behind the woman who was the greatest threat to her own claim to the English throne.

The final battle had been between half-brother and half-sister. At its heart, Mary's story had always been one of family. Relations had fought to exploit her, families had battled over her, male relatives struggled for control and Darnley had wished to be king. Mary had been betrayed over and over by her family – and the first mistake had been by Mary of Guise, treating her more as a royal brood mare to be married off than a queen. Mary of Guise was motivated by good, hoping to keep her daughter safe and strengthen an important alliance with France. But Mary grew up far from the country of her birth and was always mistrusted for foreign influences. At every score, even when trying to help, Mary's family had created destruction – and finally, in a brief May afternoon, her half-brother took everything from her.

Mary imagined she could rely on Elizabeth's support and the anger of those on the borders. She was right that the area would have been a good recruiting ground. But she was fascinated by England, convinced the queen was her only hope, and acted rashly. Instead of waiting for Elizabeth's reply (which, granted, might have taken some time to arrive), she decided to cross the border herself. At three o'clock in the afternoon on 16 May, only three days after losing her battle, she and a few loyal followers, and about sixteen attendants, took a fishing boat over the Solway Firth. And so she left the country of her birth, the place of her queenship, for England and Elizabeth, a country and a queen she had never seen.

The journey took four hours and there was one tale that the queen begged to turn around and travel to France, but it was too late and the wind was against them. But when she arrived at the small Cumberland port of Workington, she was in high spirits and talkative. She stumbled when arriving on English soil, read by some as an omen. Lord Herries sent a message to Sir Henry Curwen of Workington Hall asking for safe harbour – also offering a young Scottish heiress as a bride for Sir Henry's son. Sir Henry was not present but the party was allowed to use his house – and there Mary wrote again to Elizabeth. In it, she poignantly explained what had happened and how she had been captured and denied the chance to 'write or speak, in order that I might not contradict their false inventions'.[5] Mary believed that Elizabeth had not come to her rescue because she had believed the words of the lords that Mary had wanted to abdicate due to exhaustion. It had not occurred to her that Elizabeth already had known the truth.

The two rival queens had never met. Now, finally, Mary expected to have the meeting with Elizabeth she had desired for so long. She imagined an honest conversation, emotional and truthful, in which she explained to her horrified cousin everything about the lords' lies. Elizabeth would then give her money and soldiers and Mary would make a glorious return to power. Mary had left Scotland behind, but she thought she would be back within a month or two, heading a magnificent army.

The local officials in Workington panicked when they realised that the Scottish queen had crept in. On the following morning Richard Lowther, the deputy governor of Cumberland, rode over with 400 men and requested to escort the queen to Carlisle. Mary was taken first to Cockermouth and then on to Carlisle Castle. Lowther was somewhat confused at how to treat his new visitor: was she captive or queen? At any moment, Elizabeth might summon her to London and she would be conducted in safe passage. And she had not been captured or taken hostage, but instead arrived in the country as a visitor and supplicant. He ordered her expenses to be met and lent her horses to convey her to Carlisle. Mary was dubious about the armed guard put over her there, but still confident. In a letter to one of her supporters on 20 May, Mary wrote that she had been 'right well received and honourably accompanied and treated' and expected to be back in Scotland at the head of an army on about 'the fifteenth day of August'.[6] On the 30th, she sent Lord Fleming to London to tell Elizabeth that if she did not help her, then Mary would move quickly to France.

When Cecil heard the news of Mary's arrival, he struck. He believed her a failed queen, a Catholic rebel, and he had never forgiven her for her claims to be the Queen of England when she was young. After all, as he saw it, Mary had failed to keep her own throne and perhaps instead she would try to capture Elizabeth's. And the queen was still under suspicion for murder – and in one sense, it might look as if England was harbouring a fugitive from justice. Most of all, he wished to support his old associate Moray and his Protestant government of lords.

Elizabeth was shocked that Mary had arrived in England. Her vague promises of help had never been intended to lead to this. But, as Elizabeth knew, a bad king is simply a bad king, a rotten egg who has no bearing on all the others, but a bad queen makes all women rulers look bad. If a woman was too weak to rule Scotland, then what did it say of Elizabeth? She was constantly being importuned to marry, told it was irresponsible to remain single and that the security of the country depended on her taking a powerful husband. Mary's example gave Elizabeth's detractors even more ammunition against female monarchs. One might think that the tribulations of Mary at the hands of her husbands would have encouraged Cecil and others to rethink their constant complaints that their mistress should marry. But Darnley and

Bothwell were just seen as individual failures rather than a reflection of what happened to men when they got the power of being the queen's husband. Mary's weakness was directly relevant to Elizabeth, and it undermined her position. She wanted to punish subjects who rebelled against their monarch.

But still she was concerned about the lack of a trial for Darnley's murder and the taint of suspicion. And she knew that it was possible that Catholic rebels might gather around Mary, or even that Philip of Spain might attempt to support her to gain the English throne. Cecil was constantly afraid of invasion, obsessed with the insecurity of the realm. Mary would be a talisman for those wanting to throw Elizabeth off her throne and restore a Catholic monarchy. It is difficult for us to understand now, with hindsight, how much the council – and indeed the ordinary Elizabethan – feared foreign invasion. Those living in the coastal regions looked out for enemy ships. The presence of Mary tripled the threat of invasion overnight.

The Guises had pushed Mary to claim the throne when she had been a young woman. If only she had resisted their importuning. Their rash act condemned her in the eyes of those such as Cecil for ever. The Guises had used her for power and then abandoned her to her fate.

Elizabeth called an emergency council meeting and said that she wished to meet with Mary and discuss how she might regain her throne. Cecil and the council were horrified. Not only was Mary a Catholic who had laid claim to the English crown, but she was also a woman who had been condemned as an adulterer – and Elizabeth was supposed to be the Virgin Queen. Cecil wanted to send Mary back to Scotland. Elizabeth refused, for Mary would surely be captured and killed. As was always the case in sixteenth-century England, when in doubt, the queen turned to the law. Cecil persuaded her that the case of Lord Darnley's murder should be fully investigated to clear Mary's name. Then Mary could be restored, although perhaps rather more as a figurehead, with Moray in charge.[7]

Cecil wrote urgently to Moray asking for proof of Mary's involvement with Bothwell and the conspiracy to kill Darnley.[8] Implicitly, he was telling Moray he would support him, could do business with him. For if Cecil supported Moray in his hour of need, then in return Moray would ignore Prince James's claim to the English throne. And if Mary had left the land where much was settled by battle and knives, she had arrived in the one in which all was agreed through (often equally unfair) legal trials. Cecil had provided for every outcome. If guilty of some knowledge, Mary could be sent into exile, as long as she never challenged Moray. If her complicity was judged to be more serious, she would be imprisoned and possibly worse. If innocent, Mary would be allowed to return but she would have to ratify the Treaty of Edinburgh. It was up to Moray to find the damning evidence of her guilt.

Mary's flight to England was a brilliant stroke of luck for her enemies. In a flash, the existence of the anointed queen in her own land where there was another king, the likelihood of Mary continually escaping her prisons and collecting supporters, an endless game of cat and mouse — all was over. She was Elizabeth's problem now.

Chapter Twenty-Six
'Pain and Peril Seem Pleasant to Her'

At Carlisle Castle, Mary's accommodation was much lacking. She had only two ladies to wait on her, and these were 'not of the finest sort'.[1] She did not have enough horses and felt the lack of exercise. There were iron grilles over her windows, and whenever she went out she was accompanied by a hundred men. Some of her old staff came to join her and she was allowed out to walk and cheer on her male followers as they played football against each other on a nearby green.

Elizabeth sent her loyal long-time counsellor and Treasurer of her Household, the fifty-seven-year-old Sir Francis Knollys, north to speak with the queen. He thought her brave and engaging and reported that 'for victory's sake, pain and peril seem pleasant to her'. In late May, Knollys was told to tell Mary that she could not be received by Elizabeth until she was proved innocent of Darnley's murder. Mary burst into tears and in a 'great passion of weeping', declared that 'no one but God could take it upon themselves to judge princes'. She angrily reminded Knollys that both Maitland and Morton had been part of the conspiracy against Darnley. And she blamed the forced abdication on the fact that she had been approaching her majority, so they deposed her to 'keep by violence that which she had given so liberally, since by her revocation thereof within full age, they could not enjoy it by law'.[2]

Knollys reported back to the queen, impressed by Mary's strength and claims of innocence, and suggested that Elizabeth might offer Mary the choice of remaining in England and submitting to trial or returning

233

to Scotland. Elizabeth refused to let Mary return to her home country. Most likely, she knew that Mary would be taken captive by Moray and wished to save her. She still believed that Mary could be cleared and then the lords persuaded to accept her. But she could have given Mary the choice.

When Knollys returned a few days later, he brought little comfort for Mary. He told her that the queen would be the 'gladdest in the world' to see Mary cleared, but first Mary must submit to the inquiry.[3]

Elizabeth herself sent a letter along the same lines, telling her cousin that she was greatly desirous of a judgement on Mary as innocent, but she could do nothing before then. She told her that she would receive her at court and assist her to gain her throne. It was the most glittering promise, holding out everything that Mary could desire:

'Oh Madam, there is no creature living who wishes to hear such a declaration more than I do. But I cannot sacrifice my reputation on your account. To tell you the truth, I am already thought to be more willing to defend your cause than to open my eyes to see the things of which your subjects accuse you.' She pledged Mary would receive everything: 'once honourably acquitted of this crime, I swear to you before God that, among all worldly pleasures [meeting you] will hold the first rank'.[4] Even if she were not allowed back to Scotland, here was a possible vision of life at the English court with Elizabeth.

When Mary received the letter, she was infuriated, still resistant, declaring again that God alone could judge a sovereign and there were matters she could tell Elizabeth only in an intimate meeting. Why, she wondered, was it just her who was to be attacked and blamed? Why could the English not summon Moray and Maitland and ask both of them to explain themselves? Unbeknownst to Mary, Elizabeth had done so: she had written to Moray demanding his explanation of his 'strange doings' against a monarch and requiring his explanation and defence of the 'weighty crimes' that Mary had accused him of.[5] But she did not have the power to summon him and of course he would not have come.

Mary lost all patience. She wrote a passionate letter to Elizabeth, begging her and accusing her: 'do you not wrong me by keeping me here, encouraging by that means my perfidious foes to continue their determined falsehoods? I neither can nor will answer their false accusations, although I will with pleasure justify myself to you voluntarily as friend to friend, but not in a form of process with my subjects.'[6]

Elizabeth would not receive her. Mary sent her men who had come to Carlisle, Herries and Bishop Leslie, to speak to Elizabeth, who then asked them for a better reply from Mary, as if she had been making a great concession, and said she would call Moray forth to answer for himself. She said if Mary were found innocent, she would defend her and if not, she would try to create a good relationship between Mary and her subjects – or send her back. Herries was suspicious and declared that she was dissembling. Elizabeth, he said, gave fine words but he had heard she had been 'boasting in private of the great captive she has made without having incurred the expense of a war'.[7]

Elizabeth's demand that Moray appear had caused some panic in Edinburgh. The last thing Moray wanted was to accuse Mary in public in an English court – for if Elizabeth chose to attempt to put her back on the throne, he would be damned. He wrote angrily, asking what would be the consequence if Mary were found guilty. Elizabeth did not reply. She told Mary that 'I assure you I will do nothing to hurt you but honour and aid you.'[8] At the same time, Cecil told Moray through an intermediary that there was no way that the English would reinstate Mary to the throne, no matter what was found in the inquiry. Did Elizabeth know this? For if Mary was not going back on the throne then the only alternatives for her were exile – which Cecil would block in case she gathered the support of disgruntled Catholics for a bid for the English crown – or more likely a life in England. And this life had to be under protection, for Cecil and the council so feared her attempting the throne. The Spanish and French ambassadors were reporting back to their masters that the English wished to keep Mary under lock and key, so Cecil's aims were hardly secret.

So was the queen lying, promising Mary protection to soften her to agree to the inquiry, when she had no intention of helping? Or was she unaware of Cecil's tough approach? As Cecil's attitude to Mary had always been hard-hearted, Elizabeth probably did know what he'd been saying, although she did not expect that this had been communicated to Moray. They had always clashed over Mary and she no doubt hoped to change Cecil's mind. She would have expected to follow public opinion after Mary had hopefully been cleared by the inquiry – and establish her as a type of royal figurehead. But unfortunately, Cecil had a network of spies and influencers at his fingers and he was driving operations.

In the early months of 1569, Cecil believed England was menaced on all sides. As he put it, 'Perils are many, great and imminent, great in respect of Persons and Matters.'⁹ Enemy number one was Catholicism. In Cecil's gloomy view, they faced a conspiracy of the 'Pope, King Philip, the French king and sundry potentates of Italy to employ all their forces for the subversion of the professors of the gospel'. Across Europe, the Protestant cause was under threat. There was war in France between Huguenots and Catholics, and the Protestants in the Low Countries were threatened by Spanish forces. The English were genuinely afraid that the Catholics would soon attempt to conquer England. Elizabeth did not help matters by having her forces seize Spanish ships bound for the Netherlands that had taken shelter in English ports, which infuriated Philip and threw him into a desire for revenge.

Cecil, fearful and threatened, felt that Mary's presence held the potential for the greatest danger of all. If Elizabeth suceeded in her attempts to put her back on the Scottish throne, England would be surrounded on all sides by Catholic powers. He doubted that a restored Queen Mary, if offered the possibility of converting England to Catholicism by a crusading Philip of Spain, would be so mindful of gratitude to her cousin that she would refuse. He had to persuade Elizabeth not to try to restore the queen. The only way to do so was by proving that she had killed Darnley.

George Buchanan, scholar and once Mary's friend with whom she had read Latin and discussed books, set to work and, within a few weeks, Cecil had a document declaring that the Scots queen was not only 'privy of this horrid and unworthy murder' but was also the 'instrument, chief organ and cause of that unnatural cruelty'.¹⁰ Apparently, she had begun the affair with Bothwell a few weeks after the birth of her son (the lords of course did not want to imply that James was not Darnley's child and thereby bring his claim to the throne into question). Outrageously, Buchanan wrote that her sexual behaviour 'exceeded measure and all womanly behaviour', allowing Bothwell to 'abuse her body at his pleasure, having passage at the backdoor – the which she excused on the basis that one of his former lovers had given him the same'.¹¹ He did not mention that Moray had been present at this time, apparently missing such blatant adulterous behaviour going on under his nose.

Darnley, weak, syphilitic and cruel, was now a saintly victim, cuckolded and ill-treated by his Bothwell-obsessed wife. Buchanan conveniently forgot that all the lords had hated Darnley too and had encouraged Mary to divorce. In his view, Mary wanted to be with Bothwell but didn't want to harm her son's chances and so she 'devised how to cut [Darnley] away', showed no sadness and got back to openly sporting with Bothwell. Then to feign that she wasn't wildly in lust with him, she 'pretended herself ravished'.[12] So it went on. The problem was that it was all very purple and enthusiastically damning, but it was hardly proof – it was entirely lacking in witness statements, heard speech or even reports of who exactly had been there at the time. There was no way Cecil would persuade Elizabeth, let alone a panel of judges, with this ludicrous piece of creative writing. And there was zero possibility of extracting a confession out of Mary. He needed hard evidence and he needed it fast.

Moray scrabbled to oblige. At the end of June, he wrote that he had laid his hands on a box of letters from the queen that 'sufficiently in our opinion proves her consenting to the murder of the king her lawful husband'.[13] He was going to make copies of them, translated for the Scots Lords. One might have expected Throckmorton or another would be sent to check the originals. Still, Cecil decided it was enough. A court of inquiry was instigated to be held at York. Mary was a sovereign and the English court had no right to try a foreign queen – and it would have been a dangerous precedent. But there could be an inquiry into the queen's conduct and this Cecil intended to win. Through it all ran a wider message to Europe from Cecil and Elizabeth: English justice is official, it can solve problems, it is superior.

Cecil also asked Lennox for a written request for an inquiry – and Darnley's father obliged with a lengthy description of events, which was overheated in the extreme, even suggesting that Bothwell and Mary began their affair when she was pregnant with Prince James. Bothwell himself had been caught off the coast of Norway with his ships, probably attempting to reach Denmark and beg the king, Frederick II, for support. He was taken to Bergen, where Anna Tronds sued him for abandonment and her dowry but agreed to take his ship as compensation, perhaps because she saw he had no other assets to give. He was on the brink of freedom – but then King Frederick had him arrested, guessing he would be a good political pawn to hold over Scotland or even England. Moray sent to Denmark to retrieve Bothwell and bring him back to Scotland, dead or alive.

Mary knew nothing. When she finally heard that the lords were using letters of hers in the inquiry, she collapsed. As she wrote to Elizabeth, 'these letters, so falsely invented, have made me ill'. She well understood: the lords and Moray wanted her found guilty and it seemed as if all the evidence to the inquiry was coming from them – she was not able to make any accusations of her own. She could be saved if a lord turned against the rest – or if Bothwell was called to evidence, and told the truth. But Moray was trying to stop the English getting their hands on Bothwell and the lords were being held together with threats and promises. Desperately, Mary once again started begging Elizabeth to see her, writing over and over with frantic pleas in beautifully composed letters, describing her innocence, reasoning out the evidence, and reminding Elizabeth she was her 'sister and cousin'.[14] She even sent a poem to Elizabeth, comparing herself to a lost ship:

> A sole thought keeps me, day and night,
> Bitter and lovely, rocks my heart without end.
> Between doubt and fear, it oppresses me
> And while it is here, rest and peace flees from me.
> Ah! I have seen a ship freed from constraint
> On the high seas, very close to port,
> And peaceful times turn to difficult.
> But yet I am, in fear and worry,
> Not afraid of you but that I will be the toy
> Of fortune that rents the strongest tied chain.[15]

Elizabeth was not swayed by the poem. She began to complain that Mary's letters were distressing and importuning her. Mary was lost, isolated, friendless and – Elizabeth knew – on a rapid straight line to a show trial.

The very fact that Cecil had accepted the transcriptions of the so-called casket letters as viable evidence in the inquiry suggests what a travesty of justice the trial was. Not least because none of them were signed and there were no seals or marks to suggest they definitely came from the queen. Moreover, they had not even been found among her belongings. As she was whisked off to Lochleven with only the clothes she stood up in, leaving behind all she owned, the lords had plenty of opportunity to rifle through her rooms in

Holyrood and her other residences. It appears that they found nothing except jewels and treasures that they divided between them or sold, and trinkets to give to their wives. Bothwell's belongings had also been searched. But when Cecil asked for harder evidence than Buchanan's flight of fancy, Moray conveniently found the letters. He gave them a good back story. As we have seen, according to a statement by Morton in December 1568, after the inquiry, they had heard while Mary was at Lochleven that Bothwell's servants had entered Edinburgh Castle. Morton sent his men off to capture the servants and found George Dalgleish. Dalgleish claimed he had only entered the castle to retrieve Bothwell's clothes but when he was arrested and taken to the Tolbooth for torture, he panicked, took the men back to a house in Potterow, Edinburgh, and retrieved from under the bed a locked silver casket that had been Bothwell's. And yet surely any servants of the lords would have searched under the beds after Dalgleish was arrested. According to Morton, the casket was opened by various lords on 21 June and then sent to him. But no mention was made of the casket in the minutes of council that day.

Oddly, there were no other accounts of finding the casket. And Moray's statement to Cecil was full of holes and discrepancies. He said the letters were found on 20 June. But the Act of Council of 4 December accusing Mary of Darnley's murder declared that the letters denoting Mary's guilt had been seen before 15 June. The Act did not explicitly state they were the letters from the silver casket. But if not, where were those letters? And if they had obtained this evidence in mid-June, then surely Lindsay and his fellow henchmen would have used it against Mary when they forced her to abdicate at the end of July, just after her miscarriage. Moreover, they would surely have handed such letters to Throckmorton. As no one but the lords seems to have seen the letters until Mary fled to England and Cecil started talking about a trial, it is hard not to conclude that they were cobbled together, possibly forged. That the evidence had been at least tampered with was clear: Drury wrote on 28 November, just before the Act of Council, that the lords had been discussing the letters that proved Mary guilty, but that 'the writings that did comprehend the names and consents of the king for murdering the chief are turned to ashes'[16] – i.e. the much-discussed Craigmillar bond.

In mid-July, Mary was moved to Bolton Castle in Yorkshire, under the charge of Knollys and Lord Scrope. As the spies told Cecil and his council, support for Mary was increasing in Scotland and there had been some anger against what was perceived as her imprisonment in England. The last thing anyone in England wanted was enthusiastic Scottish supporters attempting to rescue their queen – and so she was moved further from the border. Lord Scrope was not often present and Mary grew friendly with Lady Scrope, the sister of the Duke of Norfolk.

Knollys spent thousands on keeping Mary in a properly royal state and she was allowed to go hunting, with a guard. The devoted Mary Seton arrived – as the only one of the four Marys still unmarried, she had the freedom to do so, and assisted her queen with the dressing of what was growing back of her hair, as well as finding elaborate curled wigs that looked very realistic. As Knollys marvelled, 'every day, she has a new way of head dressing, setting forth her woman gaily but with no cost'.[17]

Elizabeth was asked for help with a few gowns but sent only a few pieces of black velvet and dresses so worn that her advisor blushed and said they had been meant for Mary's maids. Knollys asked for the clothes that had been brought to her at Lochleven and Moray was asked to send her wardrobe from Edinburgh. Little had survived the rampages of the lords at Holyrood, for what arrived were a few old cloaks and covers for saddles, with only one taffeta dress. Other women in Scotland had long ago been wearing Mary's gowns. She was later sent some gloves, veils and assorted small items by her former chamberlain, but, still, it took some time and ingenuity to dress and style herself as a queen. Along with Mary Seton came Willie and George Douglas, who had engineered her escape from Lochleven. Mary was allowed her own horse, her own staff to care for her things and cook her food, and she had some of her old belongings. She had her Book of Hours, given to her as a young girl in France, beautifully and elaboratedly illuminated, both her book for daily devotions and reflections and a memory of a different time.

But even though she lived in more comfort, Mary did not have the one thing she desired: an audience with Elizabeth. She was angry and miserable, and she constantly importuned Knollys with her distress. She knew that she was surrounded on all sides by enemies and spies and her only hope was that Elizabeth would find for her. But, so far,

Mary still had not agreed to the inquiry, and this Elizabeth urgently needed. Elizabeth gathered together all her most persuasive words. Using the same language of affection and 'cousin' that Mary had sent to her in her pleading letters, Elizabeth wrote that if Mary would agree to 'her case to be heard by me, as her dear cousin and friend, I will send for her rebels and know why they deposed their queen. If they cannot allege some reason for doing so, which I think they cannot, I will restore Queen Mary to her throne', even by force – as long as Mary reneged her claim to the English throne, abandoned the Catholic Mass, received the Book of Common Prayer, no longer felt herself in league with France, and agreed not to punish the lords for their actions.[18]

Mary was distressed at the suggestion she should relinquish the Mass and, at least in outward form, agree to the Protestant rites. But Elizabeth, it seemed to her, had promised that she would be restored, as she had promised to do so if the rebels could not give a 'reason' and she thought 'they cannot'.[19] Mary agreed to Elizabeth's request and, even more importantly, sent word to her supporters in Scotland that they should not assemble to fight in her name. Was Elizabeth lying to Mary? Or did she really want to restore Mary to the throne by force, which could be a bloody battle? Cecil, of course, wanted Mary in prison in England so he could use her presence to threaten the lords and keep Scotland at heel. If Moray was allowed to continue as regent, he would be much in England's debt. And sending off the army to restore Mary might create a power vacuum in England that Spain or France would rush to exploit. And Elizabeth's own Protestant subjects, who cared not who ruled in Scotland as long as the Protestant church was ascendant, would turn against her for restoring a Catholic queen. Elizabeth was torn. Her heart wished to see Mary returned as the rightful queen. She still hoped that the lords might take Mary back as a figurehead, while Moray continued as the (Protestant) regent for James's reign. But she was not creating a system to put that in place, instead she was rather hoping for the best. Elizabeth was coming to realise that she had promised too much.

Mary was not allowed to look at the so-called casket letters, and nor were the commissioners for her defence. And in addition to having declined to be questioned at the inquiry, she was also forbidden to attend and thus would be unable to hear the letters read out and contest them. Cecil and Elizabeth did not want the queen's legendary charisma being witnessed and winning people to her cause. Also, if Mary heard the letters read out, she might very well be able to disprove them on the basis that she had not been in a place specified or had not spoken to a person named. Thus the Scots queen had to write to protest her innocence without knowing exactly what the details were of her 'guilt'. She declared that if there were any 'writings of mine which may infer presumptions against me, ye shall desire that the principals be produced and that I myself may have inspection thereof, and make answer thereto, for ye shall affirm in my name I never wrote anything concerning that matter to any creature, and if any writings be, they are false and feigned, forged and invented by themselves'.[20]

Mary noted that there were many across Scotland, both male and female, who could forge her handwriting and said that 'if I had remained in my own realm, I should before now have discovered the inventors and writers of such writings, to the declaration of my innocence'.[21] She was right that she should have stayed in her own realm. Who was she referring to as a forger? Maitland's wife was Mary Fleming and she was familiar with her mistress's handwriting. Could the pair together have forged the queen's writing? In Scotland, the queen's supporters declared the letters forgeries, but they too were unable to look at them. When Moray left for England, he gave the casket to Morton for safe-keeping. Thus, he would not be bringing the originals with him and no one impartial had seen them. This hardly suggests that they were the most robust of evidence. And Moray was naturally worried that a commissioner might protest that they were insufficient. Elizabeth – no doubt to ensure that he appeared at the inquiry – wrote to him privately that Mary would not be restored if she were found guilty. Cecil was sent his own set of copies of the letters, just in case he needed them. Cecil had to hold on to his own position, and treating Mary harshly was one of his efforts to distract attention from internal politics and other foreign affairs. Elizabeth relied on him but most of her nobles were deeply resentful of his influence and many found his policies towards Catholic Europe too aggressive and anti-trade.

On 29 August 1568, Thomas Howard, Duke of Norfolk, first aristocrat of the country and a Protestant widower, was appointed as head of the inquiry with the Earl of Sussex and Sir Ralph Sadler. They were told to press Moray to appear and given the instructions that Mary would be restored if she were found innocent – which was not what Moray had been told by Cecil.

Cecil should have ensured the Duke of Norfolk had been married off before he was thrown into Mary's orbit. Maitland made a suggestion to Mary that reached her no doubt through Lady Scrope, sister to Norfolk: if she married a great English aristocrat, ideally Lord Norfolk, Elizabeth might believe her a supporter. And perhaps if the lords saw that she was married to a Protestant peer, they would wish her back on the Scottish throne. This might have been an effective idea some years before – as with the possible marriage to Leicester. But now? It was wildly misguided. Elizabeth did not want her great noble marrying someone who might be her enemy. Although she had considered him as a husband for Mary years ago, when she had been wondering about Dudley, things had much changed now. A marriage between Mary and Norfolk directly threatened Elizabeth, for any son of theirs would be a very inviting heir to the throne. And Norfolk, who had lost three wives to death in quick succession by the tender age of thirty-three, was lonely, had Catholic sympathies, and was always susceptible to damsels in distress. If Maitland was hoping to encourage Norfolk to look kindly on Mary and eventually clear her in the hope of marrying her, his was a very effective strategy. After all, Norfolk genuinely believed that if Mary were cleared, she would be restored to the throne. And the anti-Cecil faction of nobles would support anything that undermined his interests. Mary expressed an interest in the possibility of marrying a kinsman of Elizabeth (Norfolk was Elizabeth's second cousin) and this was enough to win him to her side.

The trial approached. Mary stayed majestic. She told her commissioners to treat Moray and anyone else who popped up as 'disobedient subjects', not accusers. As she told Elizabeth, 'I will never plead my cause against them unless they stand before you in manacles.'[22]

Chapter Twenty-Seven

'With Her Own Hand'

The inquiry at York began on 4 October 1568 – and all turned on the eight unsigned 'casket letters' from Mary to Bothwell, two draft marriage contracts and twelve love sonnets. Then, at the last minute, Moray declined to submit them or accuse Mary. He refused to do so without a promise of protection from her vengeance and affirmation that she would not be restored if she was guilty. Essentially, he was asking if his evidence was enough to condemn the queen. And if he received such an assent in official form, then what did this mean for the trial? Norfolk sent the demands to London. Nothing appears to have been forthcoming, but clearly Moray's mind was laid at rest somehow, presumably by Cecil moving clandestinely. The letters were shown to the English commissioners, although not to those representing Mary.

The paper that Elizabeth received from the inquiry survives in manuscript in the British Library. But in it, the extracts of letters are in Scots. Mary tended to write in French. The lords swore they were genuine and the English commissioners found these copies of originals they had not seen to be persuasive evidence. As they saw it, they had to be genuine because they 'could hardly be invented or devised by any other than herself' and 'they discourse of some things which were unknown to any but herself and Bothwell'.[1] How could they know what was and was not known by anybody other than Mary and Bothwell, without interviewing either party or questioning others about what they knew? Their other proof that the letters couldn't be forgeries was because 'it is hard to counterfeit so many' – but how hard would it be to counterfeit a series? And finally they were moved by the 'manner of them' and how they were obtained. The reasoning was all ludicrously vague. No matter, they were evidence enough and, the commissioners decreed, 'if the set letters be written with her own hand', then they were 'sufficient to convict her of the detestable crime of the murder of her husband'.[2]

The caveat 'written with her own hand' was crucial. They were most likely looking at Scots translations of the 'original' letters, in the hand of the translator, and then supplied a simultaneous copy in English. It was possible for an Englishman to read and understand Scots – but it was not easy to decipher lengthy documents, and they most likely relied on translations. And, if so, how could they assert the 'manner of them'? One has to conclude that they took the word of the lords that Letter II, for instance, revealed 'inordinate love' from Mary for Bothwell and 'abhorrence' for her husband.

So what were these letters? Unfortunately, the originals – whether real letters or spliced-together forgeries – have been lost. Elizabeth sent her man to find them after Mary's death and he was told that they had been destroyed, conveniently, and we have only the transcripts, notes of what was shown in York and copies sent to Cecil (some still bearing Cecil's annotations) kept by Cecil's descendants along with other copies made at Westminster.

The sonnets were supposed to prove Mary's lust for Bothwell, but one might just as easily read them as a promise of constancy to God:

I have no other desire
But to make him perceive my faithfulness;
For storm or fair weather that may come,
Never will it change dwelling or place[3]

It could not be said to be erotic. Cecil discounted the poetry as irrelevant. The marriage contracts were equally ambiguous. One used the language of the Ainslie's tavern bond, but was noted as written two weeks earlier. It was an obvious forgery. The other was a written promise from Mary to marry Bothwell, which noted that she was a widow and he was divorced. This may well have been genuine but was hardly damning – the fact that Mary agreed to marry Bothwell when she was a widow (and after he had raped her) hardly made her guilty of murder.

Moray desperately flustered that although there 'was no date and though some words therein seem to the contrary, yet it is on credible grounds supposed to have been made and written before the death of her husband.'[4] What grounds? He had none. This was poor stuff and not even Mary's keenest enemy could have put it in front of a judge.

The letters were a different matter. They are all unsigned and un-addressed and only one has a date – so we first must trust that Mary would have sent off letters undated, unsigned and without even an address. Letter I, often called the 'short Glasgow letter', 'from Glasgow this Saturday morning', written apparently while Mary was visiting Darnley when he was ill and Letter II, the 'long Glasgow letter', the longest letter of them all, were the most lurid. Letter I is apparently written by a woman suffering with illness who chides her correspondent for being away and says she will bring 'this man' to Craigmillar by Wednesday. She tells the unnamed correspondent he has forgotten her and asks for 'word from you at large, and what I shall do if you be not returned'.[5] The writer talks of the pain in her side and how she needs bloodletting. It could, conceivably, have been a draft from Mary to Bothwell or even to another, perhaps to Moray himself at another time, and the date and place are most likely forged. Would Mary have sent an unsigned and unaddressed letter off to a lover? The lords declared that the man addressed was Bothwell. But there was no proof. And 'this man' could be a reference to Prince James – as historians including Alison Weir have suggested – for the Guises often used 'man' to refer to a boy child, and John Guy points out that Mary's son fitted much better than cross old Darnley the description of the 'man' as 'the merriest you ever saw'.

But even the timing of this one was wrong, if the Saturday meant was 25 January 1567. The woman complains that her correspondent has been too long away and she expected him back. But Bothwell left Edinburgh on the previous evening, to target so-called thieves on the border. Mary often went to Craigmillar as it was a convenient and pleasant retreat near Stirling. It is most likely that this was a genuine letter, probably to Darnley himself, probably from Stirling, complaining of his absence and her poor health and talking of bringing their son to them, and the lords simply changed the date and place. It was more likely written on 11 January, when Mary was at Stirling. On 12 January, she travelled with James to Holyrood, stopping at Falkirk on the way to stay with Lord Livingston, rather than Craigmillar.

Letter II is more convincing. It is a lengthy, rambling letter in which a woman complains to a mystery correspondent about the king, who is importuning her for relations, despite his foul venereal disease, and how she deals with his various demands. 'Cursed be this poxy fellow,' she declares. She is making her lover a bracelet and says, 'God forgive me, and God knit us together for ever the most faithful couple that he ever did knit together. This is my faith. I will die in it.'[6] Even if Mary had been overwhelmed with passion for Bothwell – and there is no evidence that she was – she would not have gone so far as to blaspheme.

That Mary had written to complain about Darnley is not unlikely – and it could have been a diary entry. The – again unnamed – woman tells her lover she is missing him and 'being gone from the place where I have left my heart, it may be easily judged what my countenance was'. She complains that the man she is with – Darnley – wants relations and 'I have refused it', on account of his health. And she tells her lover that she writes to him when asleep because she so wishes to be 'according to my desire, that is between your arms, my dear life'. She even tells him that 'you make me dissemble' and 'you make me almost to play the part of a traitor. Remember that if it were not for [your sake – crossed out], obeying you, I had rather be dead.' We have seen Mary threaten to wish to die throughout her life. But many women did use it as a threat – it was hardly unique to her. She begs her lover for instruction and says 'whatsoever happens to me, I will obey you'.[7]

The letter is convincing for its intimate representations and is much more damning than a few bits of rather dull poetry and a marriage contract. Sections of it are very like Mary's voice. But although it clearly reveals adultery, the murder it suggests is the wrong one. Mary – if it was her – talks of poison, which Bothwell was believed to be no stranger to.

The most damning entries come at the close. The writer talks about 'some invention more secret by physick', says that 'I shall never be willing to beguile one that putteth his trust in me. Nevertheless, you may do all and do not esteem me the less therefore, for you are the cause thereof. For my own revenge, I would not do it.'[8] If this is read as referring to a murder, then it seriously and obviously implicates Mary. But, if it was truly written by her – which of course we will never know – she does not mention any of the other conspirators.

We know that there were many men involved with Bothwell, some who had signed the Craigmillar bond and some who had not – why would Mary not mention them? The reference to poison jars oddly with the rest of the letter, and is blunt and forthright where Mary was circumspect and fond of allusion. It was most convenient for the lords and Cecil. They wanted the whole matter made into a simplistic caricature of Mary and Bothwell versus Darnley, and they could not have shown any letter that implicated even one further lord in the death.

Moreover, when Mary's movements are reviewed around the time, there was no moment when she could have written to Bothwell, sent it to him via Paris and the letter return in time for her to send back Letter II, on the basis that all was arranged for the death. It is more likely that the letters are a collection of extracts from original letters and notes from various dates – which the lords found when Mary was taken off to Lochleven – spliced together with some bits and pieces of forgery. The letter contains a note at the end which states 'Of the Earl Bothwell'.[9] But why put this to a postscript when the whole letter is meant to be to him? Mary Beaton, among others, had written for the queen and her handwriting was easy to counterfeit. The casket letters were rambling, odd, hardly conclusive, muddled. Any lawyer could pick holes in them. And so they were not permitted to do so. The casket letters had been found in a confusing, invented story and the letters themselves were poor evidence. But Moray and the English wanted Mary kept in prison and so these flimsy and ambiguous scribblings had to be damning for they had nothing else.

Mary's commissioners defended her vigorously, saying that if Bothwell did commit the murder, she did not know at the time of the wedding and that the lords had encouraged her to marry him. Norfolk, who was meant to be adjudicating, was growing increasingly frustrated by the political machinations behind the scenes.

On 11 October, Maitland sent Mary a copy of one of the casket letters so she would know what she was up against and told her that the English commissioners had seen it and others. He then went to Norfolk and told him that the letters were forged and Mary's handwriting was so easy to imitate that he had even had a go himself. He also pushed the idea of Mary marrying Norfolk. Norfolk was charmed by the plan. As he saw it, he could win the gratitude of Elizabeth for sorting out the problem of Mary and gain great power and riches for himself, not to mention a famously beautiful and accomplished wife. And he was deeply conflicted over the letters and whether they indicated guilt.

At the same time, Mary had won over Knollys to her side, who felt sorry for his royal captive and decided that her imprisonment was unfair and unjustified. A marriage with Norfolk could mean her escape. On 21 October, she told her commissioners to begin the divorce of Bothwell, and men were despatched to Denmark to ensure his assent. Optimistic, Mary wrote to Elizabeth enthusing and implying that the inquiry would find for her and thus 'we may be perpetually indebted to you'.[10]

Norfolk said he was struggling to find the truth in all the lies. With so many lords involved, the ambiguous letters and her own keen self-defence, he judged it the 'doubtfullest and most difficult that ever I dealt in'. He was lost in the dark. 'You shall find in the end as there be some few in this company that mean plainly and truly, so there be others that seek wholly to serve their own private terms.'[11] Moray and the rest were less concerned with justice than pursuing their own ends – thrusting Mary off the throne and hiding the fact that so many of them were implicated in the murder of Darnley. Their argument that Darnley was killed by Bothwell with Mary's assent and assistance, and that then the lords proceeded to deprive Mary of the throne due to her scandalous behaviour, was looking more impossible to prove by the day.[12] Norfolk was of course biased towards Mary as the wild scheme for their marriage advanced. But his basic criticism was fair: there was no definitive evidence.

Norfolk was hoping, perhaps, that the matter could all be laid to rest and Mary released. But Elizabeth and Cecil had also grown frustrated by the manipulations of the Scottish lords and feared they were being outfoxed by both them and Mary. Elizabeth did not like the sympathy expressed for Mary from Norfolk and Knollys, and she was distrustful of her 'sister and cousin'. Sussex, who had been assisting Norfolk, summed up the matter: either the queen was found guilty of murder on the basis of the casket letters, or the whole matter was bundled up 'with a show of saving her honour'.[13] The problem was that if Mary was found guilty on the basis of the letters, fair treatment involved her being shown them and questioned upon them – and, as he noted, 'she will deny them' and openly accuse the other lords of 'manifest consent to the murder'. The only solution was that Moray might present some indisputable evidence of her guilt, but what that might be no one knew, and surely if he had any, he would have shown it before now.

Elizabeth too saw that the inquiry was getting nowhere and was subject to leaks. Influenced by Cecil, she decided to move the conference to Westminster and appoint further judges, including Cecil and his brother-in-law, Nicholas Bacon. She was perhaps suspecting Norfolk of being too kind to Mary.

If this was not enough, one of Mary's supporters told her he believed that even if she were found innocent, she would not be released and restored to the throne. As she was informed, Elizabeth would not pass judgement but would 'transport you up in the country and retain you there till she thinks time to show you favour'. This favour was 'not likely to be hastily' because Elizabeth feared Mary was 'her unfriend'.[14] In all the months leading up to the trial, Mary and her supporters had not entertained the horrific possibility that there might never be any verdict at all.

Chapter Twenty-Eight
'You Have Promised to Be Mine'

Norfolk sent Mary a glittering diamond and she replied promising to keep it to her, wearing it in secret 'until I give it again to the owner of it and me both'. As she put it, 'you have promised to be mine and I yours'.[1] Mary said clearly that she would not marry without the consent of Elizabeth, because she had caused herself 'hurt' by not gaining her cousin's assent for the marriage to Darnley. But despite all this high speaking, she agreed to a correspondence with him and turned the full force of her charm to appealing to him. Norfolk was not particularly handsome and he was something of an innocent abroad, easily overwhelmed by events, but he was young, single, wealthy, a trusted member of Elizabeth's government and the only duke in England. Mary addressed him as 'My Norfolk' and wrote, 'I trust that none shall say I have ever mind to leave you.'[2] The inconvenient obstacle that Mary still had a living husband in Bothwell was overlooked in all the rush to romance.

Mary should never have corresponded with Norfolk or implied she might marry him. But if she had not, and had obeyed Elizabeth's every word, would Elizabeth have been more sympathetic? She would not. Mary was a political problem, a rival queen in the same land, and could easily become a separate power to challenge her cousin. Elizabeth had initially been sympathetic but then grown more concerned about her own position, and that was what mattered. She called Norfolk to her, demanding to know if he'd been trying to marry Mary. He had the good sense to lie, saying he would rather go to the Tower, declaring rather vividly that 'Should I seek to marry her, being so wicked a woman, such a notorious adulteress and murderer? I love to sleep on a safe pillow.'[3] Elizabeth was left unsatisfied, sure of his duplicity but unable to prove it. She then received Moray in mid-November, much to the horror of Mary, who was heartbroken that her 'cousin' would see Moray but not her. Elizabeth did not want the responsibility of putting a queen on trial like a criminal – if he made the accusation, it would be at his behest, and thus Scotland, not England, risked the vengeance of France and Spain.

The run up to the trial was a cat and mouse power game between Elizabeth and Moray. Both wanted the other to make the final accusation against Mary. Moray knew that he would have to do it. But he was holding out to get as much as he could as a surety beforehand.

When the enlarged commission came together, they met with Moray and told him that if he produced the proof of Mary's guilt, Elizabeth would recognise Prince James as king and Mary would either be given up to Scotland for trial (which raised the possibility of her execution) or imprisoned in England. Mary was bound on every turn.

On 26 November 1568, Moray rose at the inquiry and finally accused Mary publicly of being party to the murder, and named Bothwell as the murderer. As he put it, Bothwell was the 'chief executor of that horrible and unworthy murder' and Mary had 'fore-knowledge' and was the 'counsel, device, persuader, and commander of the said murder to be done', then refused to prosecute the 'executors' and married Bothwell, 'the universally esteemed chief author of the murder'. It is notable that Bothwell was the 'chief executor', not sole, and he was 'universally esteemed' the chief author – for there was, strictly speaking, no evidence. By this point, the inquiry was a club, a comfortable circle of accusations, expectations and protections. No more did Moray declare that Mary had simply been imprisoned so that the investigation could be best continued because she was too loyal to Bothwell. Instead, he said, she did not deserve to rule. And thus 'the estates of the realm of Scotland, finding her unworthy to reign, discerned her demission of the crown'.[4] In other words, they had judged her and found her a failure – even though she had made clear that a sovereign could not be judged by earthly court or council. Previously Moray had maintained the fiction that Mary had voluntarily abdicated, but with these new words, the onus on England was much less. Scotland had already judged her and found her to be unworthy and had 'universally esteemed' Bothwell the murderer and so deprived her of her crown.

Mary had made many mistakes, it was true, and one was her refusal to put people on trial. The lords had engaged in cruel dishonesty in executing a collection of servants on no evidence other than that discovered by the threat of torture. Mary had shied away from such a show trial, in shock and unable to think straight, and she had been subtly influenced by the lords who knew that the Craigmillar bond could implicate them. She had failed to win over public opinion immediately after the murder by demonstrating hysterical feminine grief. And she had trusted Bothwell too much, until the last minute. But overall, what was happening was a naked power grab by men of a woman's crown, by her former friends and half-brother, no less. Of course, plenty of bad male monarchs had lost their crowns, but Richard III – for example – had lost in battle, a fair fight.

Mary, too, had lost in conflict, but only after she had already been wrongfully imprisoned in the guise of rescuing her from Bothwell. It is hard to argue that the lords would have taken power with such confidence had Mary been a man. Such was the structure of society that even a baby male was above her in terms of his right to rule, and she was easily pushed out. Mary succeeded in continuing the line of succession, unlike Elizabeth and a good number of male monarchs, before and after. But without James, it would have been difficult for the lords to depose her, for the blood claim of Moray or anyone else was much diluted. And, simply, it was believed that women were weaker, physically and mentally, and ruled only as an anomaly. At the same time as Mary was deprived of her crown by physical force, so Elizabeth was constantly fighting to keep hold of her prerogative. As Elizabeth saw, if the lords could simply deem Mary 'unworthy to reign', Parliament could do the same to her or anyone who succeeded her.

Mary had lost all trust in the process and had told her commissioners to only make a short address and withdraw, unless she was allowed to speak. If Moray was allowed to accuse her in front of everyone, it was surely unfair if she could not argue her side, so she instructed them to avoid engagement. But her commissioners could not let such a shocking affront go unanswered. On 1 December, after a few days of discussion, her commissioners argued that it was an usurpation: the lords had simply rebelled so that they could stop her reaching the age of twenty-five and thus cancel the grants of land. They made the acute point that the English should think about how dangerous it was for subjects to bring wrongful accusations against their monarchs, and noted that some of the accusers had themselves made bonds for the death of Darnley. They also argued that, as Moray had been present and made his case, Mary should be able to attend and also to protest her innocence in front of the queen and her nobles.[5]

It was an excellent defence and they had done all they could. They were invited to speak to Elizabeth on 3 December at Hampton Court and gave Elizabeth a written request that Mary should be allowed to defend herself. Elizabeth replied to them in a way to give them hope: she said it was 'very reasonable'[6] she should be heard, but first wished Moray to give his proofs of what he accused Mary of; they needed the original letters from the silver casket, or something better. Before she could tell them when or where or by whom Mary would be heard, she first must speak to the Scottish commissioners. But, as she did not tell them, if Mary were to be received, it would not be by her. Elizabeth told her commissioners and Privy Council that she would not meet Mary until she was proved innocent. Mary might have agreed to defend herself in front of a set of nobles and Elizabeth's proxy, but it was unlikely she would be offered even this.

Unfortunately, Herries and the others of Mary's defence then lost their nerve. Convinced, not without reason, that Mary was in a hopeless situation, Herries and Leslie asked for another private meeting with Elizabeth at which they suggested they might come to terms with Moray. Elizabeth would have none of it, and said Mary's honour was so impugned by the accusations that her commissioners should wish the evidence exposed to public scrutiny and so refuted, and Moray and the rest then accused of 'so audaciously defaming'[7] their queen. Of course, Moray had been promised that he would not be punished, even if Mary was found innocent, so this was all castles in the air. Herries and Mary's other defenders would have been better trying to meet Moray privately to discuss the matter. After all, Moray had not yielded up the evidence and was still demanding assurances that he would be protected if he did so. Had Herries moved swiftly at this point and told Moray they might come to terms, Moray might possibly have withdrawn. But what would these terms have been? Most likely, that

Moray would be allowed to continue as regent for James and Mary would go free, probably to live in France. But Elizabeth and Cecil would never have allowed Mary to live there, even if, as the ambassador had already promised, the king kept her shut up in a convent. She might plot against them both, particularly if she was in the Guise convent of her aunt.

Elizabeth saw this plea of Herries as a sign of weakness and moved quickly. She told Herries and the others that Mary would not need to appear in person to give her defence. No proofs had been shown and it would be a long and arduous journey through snow. She said that they must answer for her, for if they did not, people might suspect that the accusations had substance. Mary would surely put up a brilliant defence, winning the court with her beautiful, powerful presence and the sheer reason of her argument. It was also likely that Mary would name the other lords who had been involved in Darnley's death and then Cecil would have a huge problem on his hands. Over and over, the English tried to simplify the case to Bothwell killing Darnley, with Mary's knowledge, rather than the truth: that Darnley's death had been another instance of the endless and violent shifts of power in the Scottish nobility.

Herries and Leslie played the one card they had left: they withdrew from the inquiry on the basis that Mary had been forbidden to appear. They naturally thought that this would bring the commission to a close. But, instead, Cecil found a legal loophole and Herries' statement was discounted on the basis that it had not been a true summary of what Elizabeth had actually said as regarding Mary's appearance. And so, Moray came with his evidence, some witness depositions, the Act of Parliament, the complaint of Darnley's father Lennox, and other inconclusive materials. Some of the casket letters had been shown at York (most likely in the Scottish copies) and copies had been sent to Cecil, but the court needed a public showing of them.

Finally, Moray gave the inquiry a transcript of Bothwell's trial and what he claimed were the original first and second casket letters, in French. On the next day, he gave them the rest of the letters and the love poems. The timing was no coincidence – Moray and Cecil both waited until Mary's commissioners were out of the way before the letters were finally revealed.

For Moray, there was no going back. He had accused Mary of murder and given letters that 'proved' it.[8] The half-siblings were in a battle and only one of them could get out alive.

In 1571, Morton gave Lennox a receipt for the casket letters and wrote that they contained 'missive letters, contracts or obligations, sonnets or love ballads, and other letters to the number of 21'.[9] But we have only ten, and these are not the original French, nor the Scottish translations from the French, nor the copies made in Edinburgh. What remains are the copies in French and English translations from Westminster, and as they are written in the hand of the secretary, there is no use comparing them to Mary's handwriting. It is doubtful that any of the English commissioners or politicians saw any originals in Mary's hand-writing – if they ever existed. They were supplied with Scottish copies at York and then French copies at Westminster – and both times were told that these were the originals, and both statements could not be true. We have various claims that they were in her handwriting, but these came from the virulent supporters of Moray. It is indeed fortui-tous that the letters lack signatures.

As we know, there was a huge search for documents in the early days of Mary's incarceration. Some of Mary's papers were found and used and it is most likely that the lords, finding no admission of guilt, did the sixteenth-century equivalent of cutting and pasting and created the most damning missives out of pieces of original letters along with additions. As Maitland and others had pointed out, it was easy to forge Mary's handwriting. Not only do the letters at times sound nothing akin to her own expressions used in the correspondence of hers that does survive, but we also know that Mary tended to date and sign her letters.

Elizabeth herself, always shrewd, never pronounced on the letters and their authenticity, only saying they contained shocking contents and that it was regretful that Moray had produced them to the public (even though she had compelled him to do so).

It is a vital point that neither Mary nor her defenders were allowed by the inquiry to see the letters. Mary could have argued against many of the points contained within them and publicly noted that they were forgeries. But she was never permitted to do so. Surely, if they were indisputable, Moray would have shown them to Herries and Leslie. He did not. As we saw, the judges and nobles at York believed the lords' assertions on what the letters contained. Repeatedly, the English judges took the lords' word for it, either because they could not believe that anyone would do anything so low as forge the hand of a queen, or because it suited them to do so.

Dalgleish, who had 'shown' the investigators the casket under the bed, had been executed in early 1568 and could not be questioned – when surely the lords should have kept him alive as a witness, if he had truly been the possessor of the casket. French Paris or Nicholas Hubert, the servant of Bothwell who had then gone to work for the queen and carried her letters, had fled to Denmark after his mistress had been taken to Lochleven but the lords were chasing him down. When he was finally brought back and interrogated in the summer of 1569, he stoutly said that he did not carry Letters I and II to Bothwell at Mary's instigation. He was promptly tortured and confessed. But the confession was so weak that when Cecil read it, he wrote instantly to say that any execution should be delayed and the man sent for interview in England. Elizabeth wished him interrogated about the role of other lords in the conspiracy and how much Moray had known. But Paris was hanged without trial almost immediately after the confession had been wrung out of him. On the scaffold, he shouted that he had never delivered the letters.

What Mary's accusers needed was a letter from her directing Bothwell to kill Darnley. But instead, there was a very vague unsigned love poem that could have been to anyone, and undated copies of letters that were inconclusive. As we have seen, the dates were entirely wrong on Letter I, and Letter II has incorrect timing as well – as well as no mention of anybody else being involved.

Mary had been investigated on perhaps the flimsiest evidence conceivable. But the judges believed they had done their job.

Then Elizabeth had another change of heart. The whole pantomime of judges looking at letters when Mary was denied them, and which her commissioners could not defend, smacked of unfairness, and the English queen had come to suspect that the casket letters were unreliable. She was not only concerned with upholding the rule of law, but she also worried that if a trumped-up court and accusations based on false letters took place under her watch then she would be damned in the eyes of the world. Elizabeth suspended the tribunal, added further dignitaries to the group of judges to balance out the bias and decreed she would supervise proceedings herself. Cecil took the minutes and noted that when the casket letters were compared to those written by Mary to Elizabeth, 'no difference was found'.[10]

This was a lie. Not only were they looking at copies, but Mary, when writing to Elizabeth, as the archives show, would write in her most perfect script – as people tended to do when writing on official business. She no doubt copied the letter out more than once to ensure a good impression. Letter II declared that it was 'scribbled' and that the writing was 'evil'. Moreover, Mary's handwriting, when examined in the archives, was not particularly distinctive. It was actually rather round and almost schoolgirlish, unlike Elizabeth's charismatic hand. As she herself had said before, it was easy to forge. Not all the nobles were convinced. The Spanish ambassador heard that some had dissented and found Cecil too aggressive in his attitudes towards the Scots queen.

Mary's commissioners were despairing when they heard that the inquiry had proceeded without them. Elizabeth agreed to meet them and said that Mary could send someone to answer on her behalf or that a deputation would be sent to question her (but they would probably not bring copies of the letters). Herries and Leslie advised Mary to compromise. But she was infuriated and she wrote to Elizabeth that she would not answer accusations based on evidence she had not been shown. She requested again that her commissioners should receive copies of all the documents that were ranged against her and should also be allowed to see the originals. Mary made her points clear: Moray and the others had blamed her for the murder when 'they themselves are authors, inventors, doers and executors', and any writings that might exist were 'false and feigned'. She made a proud declaration that she was not 'equal to her rebels' and 'neither will I submit myself to be weighted in equal balance with them'.[11] Finally, she had openly accused her half-brother of Darnley's murder.

Before Elizabeth could receive the letter, she wrote again to Mary that she had been 'very sorry of long time for your mishaps' and was even sorrier now 'in beholding such things as are produced to prove yourself cause of all the same'. But, she said, she would wait for Mary to provide her defence – 'we are moved to stay our judgement before we may hear of your direct answer thereunto'. Elizabeth told her that she should reply quickly, 'as earnestly as we may, require and charge you not to forbear answering'.[12] The inquiry could hardly find Mary guilty of the charges if she had not given her response. To reach a conclusion and a verdict, it was necessary that Mary should speak – and she refused to do so unless she saw the letters.

Herries and Leslie also tried to offer a compromise to Moray but he would only consider that Mary might assent to her abdication and live in England. They then told Elizabeth that they were acting on Mary's behalf and were now accusing Moray and the other lords of Darnley's murder. They asked again to see the letters that had been given as proof of Mary's guilt. Elizabeth received their requests but still the copies were not forthcoming. Then in mid-January, Herries and Leslie were told that Elizabeth would allow Mary to see the letters, but only if she agreed to submit to a trial, after which she would be pronounced innocent or guilty.[13] It was the most enormous travesty of justice – but to whom could Mary complain? The French ambassador attempted to get the letters for her.[14] Elizabeth told him that she would show them to him but then promptly did not.

Elizabeth was reluctant to openly pass judgement on a queen. And finding Mary innocent was anathema to Cecil, who continued to believe she aimed to seize the English throne. Elizabeth adjourned the inquiry, swearing all the judges to secrecy over the letters. She agreed to recognise Moray as regent, although she did not trust him. It was a hopeless stalemate.

Mary was begging again to see her, declaring Elizabeth her 'nearest kinswoman and perfect friend', expressed her bitter disappointment that her cousin was not the 'queen restorer' she had hoped and blamed Cecil for everything. Although Elizabeth had suspended the inquiry, the stench of suspicion still hung around Mary, and if Elizabeth would not meet her, it was a signal to the rest of the world. Mary saw that no hope lay with her cousin and instead turned to Philip of Spain, begging him to take pity on her because she was 'deprived of my liberty and closely guarded'.[15] She wished that he would push for her release. The new Spanish ambassador went swiftly to his French counter-part and declared Cecil the greatest enemy to Catholicism possible and that they should work together to 'make him lose his office'.

On 12 January 1569, Moray was formally allowed to return to Scotland, even though Mary had accused him of murder. He set off with a large loan from England and the crown. As both Elizabeth and Cecil knew, Moray was entirely under their control.[16] If he rebelled, threatened or attempted a foreign alliance, they could remind him of the accusation of regicide to bring him back into line and even expose the letters as full forgeries.

On 20 January, Elizabeth wrote to Mary without the usual expressions of emotion, sympathy or desire to see her cleared. She told her: 'Your case is not so clear but that much remains to be explained.' This state of ambiguity and confusion was exactly what Elizabeth wished to continue. Mary was to remain, as it were, in suspended animation.

At the end of January, Mary was moved to Tutbury Castle in Staffordshire, ensconced in the landlocked Midlands, far from Scotland and the sea. She had begged not to be moved from Bolton Castle in Yorkshire, declaring she would have to be 'bound hand and foot'[17] to be shifted. But she had no choice. After an arduous journey, she arrived on 3 February to a solemn and miserable place. It was derelict, admitted every draught, was damp and situated on a marsh that was very unhealthy. Although her furniture followed her there, no money had been provided to make her home habitable. Mary finally realised she was a prisoner. As she wrote in her Book of Hours, pitifully, '*Qui jamais davantage eust contraire le sort, Si la vie m'est moins utile que la mort*' ('Who has ever been dealt with by a more hostile fate, if my life is less useful to me than death').[18]

Then she was handed over to her new captor, George Talbot, Earl of Shrewsbury, who had recently become the fourth husband to the formidable Bess of Hardwick. Between them, they had a dazzling array of properties including Sheffield Castle and Chatsworth House, and Tutbury was the least appealing. Elizabeth had sent beds and furniture to make it more comfortable, but it was hardly fit for a queen, and Mary, exhausted after a damp and cold nine-day journey, collapsed into bed with rheumatism and fever. Talbot was sympathetic to Mary and her position, and, like many nobles, was resentful of Cecil and his power. He had no desire for a sickly queen on his hands and Tutbury was not suitable for Mary's ever-growing entourage, so he wrote to Elizabeth requesting permission to move her to another of his homes.

Notwithstanding her illness and imprisonment, the insults to Mary didn't stop. She was visited by Nicholas White, one of Cecil's men, who, despite a pleasant conversation about art, informed her that she had been responsible for the death of Francis Knollys' wife, Catherine – favourite and chief Lady of the Bedchamber to Elizabeth, daughter of Mary Boleyn – who had died in mid-January, just before Mary was moved, her suffering increased because her husband was away. It was of course unfair – Cecil could have relieved Knollys of the job of jailer so he could have been with his wife. For White, Mary was still a serpent. Despite being reduced, heartbroken, ignored by her relations overseas, deprived of money and associates, imprisoned and watched on all sides, she was to him a terrible threat, a seductive beauty who could send men to their doom. As he warned, she had an 'alluring grace, a pretty Scots accent, and a searching wit, clouded with mildness. Fame might move some to relieve her, and glory joined with gain might stir others to adventure much for her sake.'[19]

Elizabeth wrote a letter to Sir Ralph Sadler, one of the three grandees who had headed the inquiry, that she intended to be read by Mary. Elizabeth employed the romantic language that Mary had used – against her. She wrote that she had vowed not 'to write to her with my own hand until I have received better satisfaction from her to create my contentment than I have received so far'. As she told Sadler, 'you may let her understand that I wish she had been as careful in the past to have avoided the cause and ground by her given of the just jealousy that I have conceived, since she now appears to dislike the effects that the same has bred towards her'.[9] It must have been painful for Mary to read, for Elizabeth does not spare her words. The Queen of Scots knew 'how great contentment and liking we had for a period of her friendship, which I then esteemed as a singular and extraordinary blessing of God to have one so nearly tied to us with blood and kin'. The 'just jealousy' was not so much Mary's claim to the English throne but the whole avalanche of activities around Darnley's death. Elizabeth claimed she was sad to see the break in the amity, but, as she put it, it was not her fault. 'So I am now much grieved to behold the alteration and interruption in the matter, taking no pleasure to look back on the causes that have bred such unpleasant acts which I wish that either they never had been or at the least we could never remember, and that she were as innocent of them as she works so hard to convince both me and the world that she is.'[20]

Elizabeth was refusing even to write to Mary unless she submitted to the English judges. And to Mary, Elizabeth's sentiments in this letter were barely distinct from those of the lords. They had changed from saying they would rescue her to declaring she was unfit for the throne because she had been part of the murder plot. Now Elizabeth was declaring that Mary was at fault for what had occurred, and consequently she could not treat her as kindly as she wished. When Elizabeth wrote that she wished Mary 'were as innocent of them as she works so hard to convince both me and the world she is', she questioned Mary's innocence. This was something of a new turn. Did Elizabeth truly believe Mary had played a part in the conspiracy? Was she simply trying to attack and reduce her? Or did she dread foreign criticism and was therefore trying to make herself seem less to blame by throwing guilt on Mary?

Typical of Elizabeth, the letter did not choose either way. It cast doubt on Mary's innocence and yet suggested how much Elizabeth wished her to be innocent. But the import was clear to Mary – her situation could not be worse.

Chapter Twenty-Nine
'Unnatural Sister'

Keeping Mary in the state of royal grace that a queen required was dazzlingly expensive and Elizabeth was reluctant to pay the bills. Talbot was begging Elizabeth for money. His allowance for the Scottish queen was £52 a week – a pitiful sum when her servants often numbered fifty, she had ten horses in her stable along with grooms in livery, and the household consumed an eye-popping amount of food. Poor Talbot complained that the queen's gentlemen ate eight courses at every meal and he could barely afford it. But Mary sailed on regardless, expecting money to appear, and Elizabeth ignored Talbot's begging letters. As with so many government payments in the sixteenth century, the sums Talbot was promised took months to turn up. He paid for Mary out of his own pocket. He possessed the most marvellous exotic captive in the whole of England, a woman who thousands were desperate to see and he tended to promise overexcited Midlands visitors that they might glimpse her or even meet her if they came to his home. The great local families came to visit for musical entertainments and dinners and Mary was allowed to attend.

Elizabeth agreed to have Mary moved, first to Wingfield House, then to Chatsworth, and finally to Sheffield Castle, where she lived in great state, her apartments hung with tapestries and lit with chandeliers, thick carpets on the floor and the chairs upholstered in gold and crimson. Mary Seton dressed her hair to dazzling effect and Mary's cosmetics bill would have sunk a lesser host. She sent to Paris for the latest designs and 'cloth of gold and silver, and of silks, the handsomest and the rarest that are worn at court' and 'crowns of gold and silver, such as were formerly made for me'.[1] Such orders of splendour were hardly calculated to win over Elizabeth. Moreover, Mary sometimes used these consignments as ways of sending letters back and forth to Paris, secretly tucked into the folds of dresses or in between the boxes.

For Mary, maintaining a royal lifestyle was the way in which she helped persuade the world that she was a queen who deserved to keep her throne. She dined off silver dishes and expected two courses at meals, both with a selection of sixteen dishes from which she would choose, washed down with crystal glasses of wine, along with plentiful bread, salad and fruit. A typical menu might be soup, with meats such as veal, chicken, beef, mutton, duck and rabbit, followed by substantial dishes of pheasant, lamb, quails and a baked tart. Her ladies were allowed nine dishes per course, the secretaries six or seven, so there was a lot of wasted food. Mary lived in such grandeur that her court was second only to Elizabeth's. Bess of Hardwick and Mary struck up a friendship in the early days and sat and worked on their embroidery together, accompanied by Mary Seton. The captive queen had companions, riches and grandeur.

And yet she was still not at liberty, watched by armed guards who marched under her windows and followed her closely when she rode out or went hunting. Talbot promised Cecil that Mary was very restricted, telling her he refused her and her company any exercise out of the gates, 'for fear of many dangers needless to be remembered to you. I do suffer her to walk upon the leads [i.e. the roof] here in open air, in my large dining chamber and also in this courtyard, as long as both I myself or my wife be always in her company, for avoiding all others talk either to herself or any of hers. And sure watch is kept within and without the walls, both night and day.'[2] Mary was not even allowed to talk to people whom Talbot had not approved. As Talbot's son gleefully put it, 'good numbers of men, continually armed, watched her day and night, and both under her windows, over her chamber, and of every side of her, so that unless she could transform herself to a flea or a mouse, it was impossible that she should escape'.[3] The trapped flea was forbidden to write to her son and she was heartbroken to think he was being brought up by those who hated her and who she feared were turning him against her. She kept his miniature always beside her. She still held tight to her much-loved Book of Hours, from her days in France, and began to write in it sad little poems.

Apart from the unhappy letters and demands for money from Talbot, Elizabeth could just about pretend that Mary didn't exist. And as the months went by and Moray and Scotland were quiet and caused Elizabeth no problems, the queen felt less enthusiasm for restoring Mary to her throne. Though Elizabeth met Leslie, Mary's commissioner, and told him she 'fully intended to bring this about, without any mention of the murder of her husband'[4] – she was just fobbing Leslie off. As Cecil himself had written in a private memo, the best thing for England was if the Scots queen lost her throne and the state continued as it was. At about this time, the brilliant Sir Francis Walsingham gained the position of spymaster, working with Cecil to head off threats to Elizabeth. Walsingham's arrival meant the end of cack-handed, easily unmasked plots like Rokesby's. Under him, spying and surveillance became a labyrinthine, sophisticated business, a weaving of webs with Mary as the chief fly.

Mary was still hopeful of being rescued. Nothing had been proven against her, so why should she not be freed? But Philip of Spain did nothing for her and Catherine de' Medici was equally reluctant and did not answer Mary's letters. Mary wrote to everyone she could think of, scribbling missives to the Cardinal of Lorraine, her aunt, the Duchess of Nemours and her cousins.[5] Although the duchess offered kind words, there was little she could do, and the cardinal rarely answered. When so many of Mary's problems had come from the fact that the Guises had pushed her to stake her claim to the English throne, it was even more pitiful that they appeared to care little for her now she was no longer of use. Their ascendancy was waning too, and if Catherine de' Medici had any favour to give, they wished it for themselves, not for far-away Mary in her sumptuous isolation. To her annoyance, there was no movement on the dissolution of her marriage with Bothwell. Although she had promised her heart to Norfolk, she was still married to the man she hated.

And Norfolk was moving ahead with his plans, having secured the support of various nobles including Dudley, the Earl of Arundel, and the Catholic noblemen of northern England, the earls of Northumberland and Westmorland (who was married to Norfolk's sister, Jane Howard). By early July, Norfolk had lost patience with the slow pace of the negotiations and he entered into direct correspondence with Moray over dissolving the marriage – a dangerous move.

In July 1569, Moray and the lords were given three proposals by Elizabeth. Mary should continue to live in England, after agreeing her abdication; or she should be joint ruler with her son; or she should be restored with promises to protect the reformed religion and with Moray's safety guaranteed. Led by Moray, the lords voted by forty to nine against Mary returning. They also denied the dissolution of her marriage. Not long afterwards, Mary's valet, Paris, was hanged without trial, in spite of Elizabeth's request to have him sent to England for interrogation. By killing Paris, the lords had eliminated the final witness who might have saved the queen. Her only hope now was if one member of the association broke down and confessed his own part and implicated others, which they would never do for fear of the retribution against their family.

In the late summer of 1569, Elizabeth was given evidence that Norfolk and Mary had talked of betrothal, first by spies linked to Moray, who also had the correspondence from Norfolk pushing for a divorce, and then apparently by Dudley himself, who had supported the plan. The queen was shocked that Dudley had been involved, and emotively declared any marriage would result in her being overthrown. Norfolk was flung in the Tower and his allies put into disgrace. Northumberland and Westmorland were not arrested. But both feared that the investigators would come for them as having conspired for the marriage and against Elizabeth.

Elizabeth had Mary's entourage reduced, forbade correspondence and commanded no lassitude or kindness. She appointed a new guard, Henry Hastings, Earl Huntingdon, who she thought would be harder on the beautiful queen than Talbot. Mary, ever determined, began to develop a system of codes and secret letters. At the beginning of 1569, she had written wildly to Philip of Spain suggesting that she could gain the English throne with his help.[6] At that point, she had been merely posturing, attempting to win his support. But now, with Elizabeth cold and seemingly allied with Moray, Mary was lost and began to listen to the schemes of her supporters.

She wrote to her son, now three and a half, sending him presents and loving notes. But Elizabeth's men confiscated the letters and gifts and little James was left to the ministrations of the Countess of Mar, who hated Mary, and given George Buchanan as his tutor, the man whose pen had dripped venom against Mary. Mary Seton had fallen ill and her mother sent a messenger to Mary, Queen of Scots, asking if she might be sent back to Scotland – for this, the mother was thrown into prison for daring to write to the captive – she was released on a promise never to write again. Mary Seton remained with her mistress, following her wherever she went.

Still, Mary was living in state. When Huntingdon took over, he was informed she had thirty people officially in her train, including Lord and Lady Livingston and their servants; three bedchamber women (her favourite was Jane Kennedy); the ever-faithful Seton, who had her own personal maid and groom; Willie Douglas; and others including Bastian Pages and a master cook, cupbearer and physician. On top of the official collection was a various group of over ten further servants, to whom Talbot turned a blind eye.

In late 1569, the East of Westmorland, part of the original marriage plot of Mary and Norfolk, wrote to the Spanish ambassador that he feared he would have to rebel for 'I know the queen's Majesty is so highly displeased at me and others that I know we shall not be able to bear it, nor answer it'. On 14 November, Westmorland, along with the Earl of Northumberland and thousands of supporters, entered Durham Cathedral by force and ripped up the Protestant prayer book. They were fighting for the Catholic cause. As they put it:

> Forasmuch as diverse, evil-disposed persons about the queen's Majesty have, by their subtle and crafty dealings, to advance themselves, overcome in this Realm the true and Catholic religion towards God, and by the same abused the queen, disordered the realm and now lastly seek and procure the destruction of the nobility. We, therefore, have gathered ourselves together to resist by force, and rather by the help of God and you good people, to see redress of these things amiss, with the restoring of all ancient customs and liberties to God's church and this noble Realm.[7]

It was a desperate scheme. Elizabeth sent nearly 15,000 men north and increased her bodyguard. Westmorland and Northumberland fled over the border and the rebels were hunted down. In awful scenes, 800 were executed on gallows that had been quickly mounted, rudimentary and rushed. Elizabeth said Norfolk must remain in the Tower and she demanded that Mary be sent away. She wanted her packed off south to Coventry, but Coventry Castle was so derelict and uninhabitable that when they arrived in the city, she had to stay in an inn. Huntingdon wondered if the tide was turning and encouraged Mary to think once more of marrying Robert Dudley. She angrily wrote to Norfolk, still hopeful that they'd marry, optimistic that Elizabeth might agree. She had little other means of escape and she was constantly ill. The Pope was shocked when he heard of the severe treatment of the northern rebels and promptly excommunicated Elizabeth, declaring Mary should be queen of England in her place. This made her even more of a threat. Any attempt to push Elizabeth off the throne had been licensed by the Pope:

> Since that guilty woman of England rules over two such noble kingdoms of Christendom and is the cause of so much injury to the Catholic faith and loss of so many million souls, there is little doubt that whosoever sends her out of the world with the pious intention of doing God's service, not only does not sin but gains merit.[8]

Any rebel, from a noble leading an army to a lone servant who managed to poison Elizabeth's soup, was thus engaged in what the Pope called 'glorious work'.

Elizabeth's ministers saw plots everywhere and her churchmen were no less frantic. The Bishop of Winchester wrote in terror of how the Pope was encouraging the 'desperate' to 'besiege the tender frame of the most noble Elizabeth with almost endless attacks and most studiously endeavour to compass her death both by poison and violence and witchcraft and treason and all other means of that kind which could ever be imagined and which it is horrible even to relate'.[9] Various Acts were passed to attempt to protect Elizabeth, including making it high treason – and thus punishable by execution – to 'compass, imagine or practice the death or bodily harm of the queen' or to practise against the Crown or publish, write or even speak that the queen was not the lawful monarch. A subject could now be executed for merely telling his neighbour in a drunken rant that the queen was a heretic. It was also punishable by death to play guessing games about how long she might live – a game that many of her subjects and nobles had previously indulged in. And, most relevant to Mary, anyone who named an heir to the queen except her 'natural issue' (who of course did not exist) was also committing a treasonous crime. One of Mary's great sources of strength had been her position as Elizabeth's heir, for it was why so many nobles had tried to support her or had refrained from castigating her. One never knew when Elizabeth might die and Mary become queen in her place.

In January 1570, Moray was walking through the streets of Edinburgh when a pistol fired through a window fatally wounded him. The assassin was never found but it was widely judged to be at the behest of the Hamilton family, keen to deprive of him of his huge influence and power. The killer appears to have been one James Hamilton of Bothwellhaugh and Woodhouselee. The Hamilton family was widely condemned and the young assassin fled to France. Moray had led the charge against Mary and repeatedly resisted her return. Mary hoped that the alliance of lords might crumble, now that Moray was no more.

Moray's wife, Agnes Keith, who had given birth to a daughter, Margaret, shortly after the assassination, threw herself into managing the family estates and attempting to get compensation. Mary wrote to Agnes in March asking for the return of her jewels that Moray and Agnes had taken when she had been thrown into prison at Lochleven. What she wanted above all was the 'great H' – the wonderful and giant diamond given to her at her marriage by the King of France. Agnes did not send them back. Huntly pressed her, Mary wrote again, and then Lennox, who had taken over as regent, demanded them for the Crown. Agnes still refused to relinquish them, requesting that the government first compensate her family for all the debts Moray had incurred as regent. As Mary saw it, 'the great H' was hers, not the Crown's. She needed the diamond, and it was a memory of her wedding day, when she considered herself the most powerful and 'happiest woman in the world'. But the jewel had been caught up in the strife of Scotland and was denied her.

Elizabeth occupied herself in trying to find a regent for Scotland who would do her bidding and returned to the old efforts to try to have young Prince James brought to England. Mary was still hopeful for her future – she was moved back to Chatsworth and there the local nobles conceived a plot for rescuing her, overseen by a member of the

Catholic Northumberland family. But Mary refused: she still hoped for Norfolk and a dignified release. If she ran, she would lose her chance to be restored to the throne by Elizabeth. After everything Elizabeth had said, Mary's belief in the importance of blood ties with her cousin was touchingly and hopelessly naive. The regency was given to men who hated Mary, such as Lennox (Darnley's father, Matthew Stewart), although he was soon after killed in a raid on Stirling. In 1571, the Earl of Mar took over, who had long been James's guardian. He, too, was no friend to the imprisoned queen. Elizabeth and Cecil had ensured regents – pro-her, anti-Mary.

Norfolk was freed from the Tower in the summer of 1570 (there had been pressure from other nobles to release him), although he was still being watched over, and almost immediately became embroiled in plots, this time helmed by Italian agent and banker Roberto Ridolfi, who was in the pay of Philip of Spain – and often dealt information to Walsingham on the side. Ridolfi had been arrested around the time of the northern uprising for funnelling money to Mary's supporters and had been taken to Walsingham's home for a period of house arrest. He was released and promptly set about plotting again to bring Catholicism to England and put Mary on the throne. Mary wrote enthusiastically of 'my constancie to you', complained 'my friends gladly hear all parts of my Enemy's against me.' She offered 'my Norfolk' everything, saying she 'in all things would follow you'.[10]

The letters flew thick and fast between the parties but then reached something of a stalemate. Philip declared he would not invade before the Catholic nobles had begun a rebellion in his favour – and the terrifying deaths of so many rebels on the gallows acted as a powerful dissuader to any further plotters. And although the question of Mary's marriage to Bothwell had now been sent to the Pope for nullifying on the basis that Bothwell and Jean Gordon had not been divorced when he married Mary (and also that Mary and Jean were related), the Pope appeared to be doing little to pursue the issue. Frederick II was still holding Bothwell in Denmark as a hostage, to win concessions from Elizabeth. Unfortunately for Mary, it was not in Frederick's interests to allow access to Bothwell for a divorce – for Cecil and the council did not want Mary to be single and thus chased after by every power-hungry aristocrat in the country. Bothwell was a useful bargaining tool and Frederick meant to keep him that way.

After an alliance was agreed between the two countries, Bothwell was, on the face of it, no longer politically useful – and yet still Frederick kept him imprisoned, in a dank and horrible castle, in case relations with Elizabeth might turn sour again. Elizabeth had actually asked that Bothwell be executed for regicide in 1570, and in the following year asked for him to be sent to England for trial. A trial in which Bothwell would be allowed to speak for himself – and would no doubt implicate as many of the other lords as possible – could have been Mary's salvation. The man who had brought Mary so low could have been the one to free her. The lords had no desire for a trial: they wanted his head chopped off and no opportunity for public discussion. It seems almost unbelievable that Elizabeth was considering putting him on trial, for any public appearance would have been a sensation and likely thrown yet more doubt on Mary's guilt. But Elizabeth was weary of Frederick using Bothwell against her as a pawn and most likely never intended to put Bothwell on trial at all, instead planning to keep him in prison in England as a way of holding Scotland to order.

Cecil visited Mary in October 1570 at Sheffield Castle and she attempted to charm him. Mary threw all her heart into it. He raised various articles and appeared to Mary and Leslie, her envoy, to be offering the possibility of Elizabeth's presence.[11] He gained a pleasant impression of her and was gratified by her willingness to listen to his advice. But he was meeting her to provide a sop to the King of France – who had written with queries about Mary's treatment – and also to extract a promise she would no longer engage in betrothals. Cecil wanted her imprisoned in England, if not executed, and if he seemed kinder, it was only momentary.

Once Mary was in England, it is difficult to know what she could have done better. She created cordial, often good relationships with her jailers, wrote to Elizabeth and was emollient and willing to listen and agree to terms when meeting any of Elizabeth's men, and she did not refuse requests unless she felt she really had to – pertaining to being tried as a subject, not a queen. So much preparation went into her meeting with Cecil – and all the Englishmen who came to visit her – the apartments spruced up, new decorations or tapestries purchased, new liveries for the servants, a new gown and endless hours perfecting her hair and cosmetics. For Mary, imprisoned and having no idea of what she might be asked to answer for, it was worrying and unsettling, as she and her secretaries ran over different scenarios and what she might say. She put weeks, months into preparations for the meetings – and nothing came of them. She should not have paid attention to plots or agreed to marry Norfolk – but if she had stayed steadfastly clear of plotting, the only likely difference would have been that she would either have wasted away in awful dank prisons, or possibly Cecil and Walsingham would have somehow found a way to try her, based on a re-examination of the casket letters. She had the chance to escape at Chatsworth, but the days when she could have galloped for miles, young and vigorous, were gone. When she had ridden through Scotland, she rode past villages and settlements who actively supported her. But in England, locals would be suspicious of such a person riding in company (even if she had disguised herself as a man), and many believed the anti-Marian propaganda that she wished to unseat and kill the queen.

Mary's life in England was small moments of light followed by long dark periods of privation and suspicion. In the spring of 1571, Charles Bailly, a young Scottish courier for John Leslie, Bishop of Ross, Mary's envoy, was arrested at Dover and found to be carrying letters from Ridolfi to Leslie that appeared to encompass a plot to seize Elizabeth's throne for Mary. Norfolk was then discovered to be in on the plans, sending word and money to those who supported Mary in Scotland. Elizabeth refused the advice of her ministers to refrain from her summer progress and set off, stately as ever, a galleon in full sail, visiting Norfolk at Audley End near Saffron Waldon and accepting his promise of allegiance. Four days later, he was arrested and sent to the Tower again.

Leslie was imprisoned and threatened with torture, and said anything that came into his head: that Mary was behind the uprising in the North of England, led by Westmorland and Northumberland, that papal funds had been used and a foreign invasion was planned, and then he finally declared that Mary had killed the dauphin and Darnley, had attempted to murder Bothwell and would dispose of Norfolk as well. Despite this, he wrote to Mary begging her to have him released.[12]

Elizabeth had lost all patience with Mary and wrote to chide her for her 'sorrowful, passionate and vindictive expressions.'[13] Cecil was sent a letter from Mary to her supporters asking, 'What works could be more acceptable to God than to succour the Catholic Church, to defend the rightful title of a prince, to deliver afflicted Christians from bondage?' Although there was no mention of war or deposition, this for Cecil was evidence of Mary's guilt and her desire to have her cousin thrust off the throne. It wasn't enough to put her on trial, so instead he used all his diplomatic powers to dissuade France from taking her side and rushed out a grimy pamphlet of Buchanan's horrible accusations, along with translations of the casket letters, titled 'A Detection of the Doings of Mary, Queen of Scots Touching the Murder of Her Husband and Her Conspiracy, Adultery and Pretended Marriage with the Earl of Bothwell'. The pamphlet was circulated privately – Elizabeth would have been furious at the leak – to all those who mattered, damning Mary again and again.

In the ensuing parliament, Cecil's clique called for Mary to be executed as a threat to the queen for she was a 'very unnatural sister' and had sought to dispossess the queen's majesty of the throne, throwing all Elizabeth's favour back in her face. Many of those present were swayed by the passion of the speakers to Cecil's view that the way to protect England was by removing Mary – as one of his circle put it, the death of Mary was 'of necessity, it may lawfully be done'. But was it really lawful? Could a queen, who was not a subject, commit treason at all? Elizabeth refused to engage with their demands. But she bowed to the protests about the behaviour of Norfolk. The Duke did his best, writing desperately to Elizabeth. His spiky hand is perfectly preserved in the British Library: bemoaning the 'lamentable complaint of my oppressed mind' and pleading with her to 'extende your most gracious mercy upon me your most desolate subject.' He vows he never desired 'any rebellion' and waxes sadly about his 'waterye chekes'. To no avail.[14] He was put on trial at Westminster Hall for treason in January 1572, and Talbot, Mary's captor, came to sit on the panel. Elizabeth signed Norfolk's death warrant in February and then took it back, only to give in and agree to it again soon after. He was executed in June. Mary was left heartbroken, weeping hopelessly and refusing to leave her room.

Chapter Thirty

'No One Can Cure This Malady as Well as the Queen of England'

The Ridolfi plot, wild and impossible as it was, changed everyone's minds about Mary. Norfolk was a sacrifice: by trying him, Cecil could ensure that the evidence of the plot and Mary's collusion was brought out into the open. There was an outcry against Mary, casting her as a serpent who wished to kill Elizabeth. More seriously, the nobles in Parliament had begun to demand her execution. Commissioners visited Mary at Sheffield Castle and attempted to extract a confession that she had participated in the Ridolfi plot and tried to seize the crown of England for herself. Mary was strong under pressure and said, as a royal, she could not be questioned or tried by them and wished to speak in front of Parliament and talk privately to Elizabeth. Parliament, too, would have wished to see her speak in front of them. But Cecil would never allow it, too afraid of what the silver-tongued queen might manage. Mary did admit to the commissioners that she had written to the kings of France and Spain to ask for help and said that she had claimed the throne of England, but only in her youth, and had not styled herself as Queen of England and Ireland since the death of her first husband, King Francis. She agreed that she had been in correspondence with Ridolfi, but only over financial matters and she said that although she had discussed marriage with Norfolk, she had thought that any marriage would be approved by England and Elizabeth.

The plot may all have been a fabrication. When Ridolfi had been put under house arrest by Walsingham after the northern rebellion, it is not impossible that Walsingham persuaded him to set up Mary, Leslie and Norfolk, in order to reveal to the country and the queen how dangerous Mary could be. Ridolfi was in France when the plot was revealed and not arrested, unlike all the others involved, which suggests that he had some favour from government. Certainly, the whole affair had played into Cecil's hands and his desire to get Mary out of the way. He also used the Ridolfi plot as an excuse to try to push Elizabeth to look once more at the question of marriage – for as long as Elizabeth remained unmarried and without an heir, so the attention of her subjects would always turn to the Queen of Scots. Various suitors were mooted and then rejected. For Cecil, the 'manifestly uncertain' state of the Crown could only be corrected by the queen's marriage. As the English ambassador told Catherine de' Medici, 'if she had a child, all these bold and troublesome titles of the Scottish queen, or of the others who make such gapings for her death would be clean choked up'.[1] Catherine was quite in accordance, believing that Elizabeth suffered challenges because she was unmarried. As she put it, 'If she marry into some good house, who shall dare attempt aught against her?' Even for the power-hungry Catherine, a woman was weak without a husband and always vulnerable to some malicious 'attempt'.[2]

The Ridolfi plot was perfect for Cecil. The inquiry into the Scottish queen's conduct had been suspended three years ago. Mary's freedom had been conditional on her being cleared and so there had been pressure from foreign powers that it should resume. There had not been enough evidence to tie her to the northern rebellion. But now, thanks to the Ridolfi plot, he could declare the inquiry no longer necessary. As Cecil could say, Mary was not captive because she may have killed Darnley. She was captive because she had tried to kill the queen.

Four years previously on 16 May, Mary had arrived in England, rowing over the Solway Firth with her sixteen attendants, hopeful of soon returning to save her throne. What had happened to her had been a swift decline, a step downhill every month or so. First of all, the guards at Carlisle Castle. Then, after only two weeks, Elizabeth's refusal to meet her until she was cleared of Darnley's murder. Then the inquiry, the constant back and forth over what was said and what would be shown, her certainty that she would be found innocent because she was, the falsified letters that proved nothing. The inquiry adjourned with no conclusion either way, no political will to start it once more and the Ridolfi plot meant it was no longer necessary. Poor Mary, only four years before, holding the diamond, convinced Elizabeth would give her an army, put her back on the throne. Then, she'd had dreams of glory. Now she just wanted to be free.

Parliament wanted Mary's blood. Elizabeth saw Mary with mercy and refused to condemn her. Still, measures were passed against her, notably that she could be tried by English peers if she were found to be plotting again. In January 1572, Elizabeth issued a proclamation about Scotland, declaring she was 'a Prince who next to quietness of her own Realme doth most earnestly of all desire to procure both onward peace amongst the subjects of the realm of Scotland.'[3] The answer was to defer to her.

In the battle for the sovereignty of England, the figure of Mary was vital. During Elizabeth's reign, parliament had encroached further on what had previously been royal prerogative – but one thing Elizabeth was resistant on was Mary. Parliament repeatedly tried to force Elizabeth to treat her as a common subject and she refused. Various examples of kings who had been killed by kings were dredged up from history to persuade Elizabeth that it would be perfectly legal. Mary was the crucible for the question of who was supreme: Parliament or the queen. For Elizabeth, to allow that Mary was a subject, liable to be judged by her peers, was to undermine her own authority. The battle over Ridolfi could be termed a draw. Elizabeth had refused to allow Mary to be put on trial. But the new measures provided that Mary, even though she was a queen appointed by God, could be tried by a set of nobles; and so ushered in the real possibility of this happening.

Elizabeth demanded that the queen be kept under closer attention. Cecil saw that if he wished to convince Elizabeth that Mary should be executed, he would have to find something indisputably terrible. He needed the queen to be part of a murder plot against Elizabeth, and for the evidence to be damning.

Although forbidden to write letters, Mary was engaging with international affairs, constantly writing to the embassies in France and Spain and demanding their protection for English Catholics who had fled after supporting her. She used secret messengers, hid letters in convoys of goods and wrote in code. Talbot was too much of a gentleman to search her chambers, restrict her secretaries or indeed stop visitors to his own house – and so Mary wrote on, against Elizabeth's rules.

A plan sprung up that Mary should marry Don John of Austria, Philip of Spain's illegitimate half-brother. The glorious marriage would be the cherry on top of a marvellous Spanish invasion and Mary and Don John would be the Catholic king and queen of both realms. But Mary was still married to Bothwell and even though there was papal enthusiasm for the invasion and Don John, her marriage had not been annulled. Mary was frustrated by the Pope's painful failure to complete the paperwork. But Rome suspected that if the Pope annulled the marriage, then Elizabeth would be instantly on alert and suspect a plot was afoot to marry Mary to a Catholic ally.

Mary was a burning problem who nobody wanted, tossed between the rulers of Europe. There were endless discussions about the problem of what to do with her. Elizabeth had her ministers suggest that Mary be sent back to Scotland for trial. The lords were equally nervous about executing a sovereign and still feared too much information might come out in a trial. When Morton became regent in 1572 after the death of the Earl of Mar (probably of natural causes but Melville declared he had been poisoned), Mary's situation looked even bleaker as he detested her obsessively. Morton told Cecil that he would agree to a trial if Elizabeth sent her troops to guard the scaffold on which Mary would die.[4] This was too much for Elizabeth, for it would look like an English execution, and the plan was dropped.

At the end of August 1572, Huguenot leaders came to Paris for the wedding of Marguerite de Valois and Henry of Navarre. On 24 August, St Bartholomew's Day, they were killed at the behest of the king. Over the following weeks, Protestants were murdered without compunction and by the autumn, 10,000 were dead. The Pope and Philip of Spain congratulated France on its work. When Elizabeth heard the news, she put the court in immediate mourning and she and the council readied for war. Towns on the coast were told to expect invasion. Cecil was convinced the Catholic powers would now move for England. More guards were sent to stop anyone getting to Mary, Queen of Scots.

Mary was hated all over again. The massacre was seen as a Guise conspiracy – and the assumption was that they would then come to rescue her and kill Elizabeth. 'Forthwith to cut off the Scottish queen's head',[5] wrote the Bishop of London. Elizabeth resented her cousin and felt besieged by the constant demands from her ministers to have her executed. Cecil told her that either Mary died, or she did. Beale, the secretary to the council and brother-in-law to Walsingham, expressed the views of many when he said that 'all wise men generally throughout Europe cannot sufficiently marvel at Her Majesty's over-mild dealing with her, in nourishing in her own bosom so pestiferous a viper'. When Elizabeth fell ill, first with stomach aches and then with a severe malady described as smallpox, her ministers panicked and prayers were given in churches for her safe recovery.

In 1573, Edinburgh Castle, so long a Marian stronghold, fell to the Protestant lords, with the assistance of the English army, and William Kirkcaldy, who had held it bravely, was executed. Maitland was imprisoned and died, possibly of illness, perhaps through suicide, and his devoted wife, Mary Fleming, wrote to Cecil begging that her husband be buried as he had died and not cut up on accusation of treason. Elizabeth wrote firmly to Morton that 'It is not our manner in this country to show cruelty on the dead bodies so unconvicted.'[6] Thanks to Mary's flight, Elizabeth had such power over Scotland that she could direct how they buried the bodies of those they considered traitors. The death of Maitland, so long loyal, was a great blow to Mary.

In France, Charles IX, already fragile, had been in a spiral of decline since St Bartholomew's Day. He chastised himself, begging for forgiveness, crying out for mercy, declaring he was lost and blamed his mother, saying 'you are the cause'. His body was engulfed in tuberculosis and on 30 May 1574, he died and his younger brother became Henry III. He had been only six when Mary married his brother, barely remembered her – and this would not help her case.

Mary was depressed and weary, unable to see an end to her torments, missing her son and watched on all sides. Her body began to express her pain, crying out the words that she wrote but to which no one would listen. Mary's superb auburn hair was growing brittle and grey, and it was cut off in an attempt to alleviate her headaches. Mary Seton dressed it as well as she could but it was thin and weak, all the glory lost. She had terrible sickness, gas and stomach pains, possibly from a gastric ulcer, suffered from fainting fits, terrible headaches and fatigue. Still only thirty, she had fallen prey to a vicious rheumatism in her legs, which were painful and swollen. In Scotland, she had been used to riding and walking for miles, but now she was still only allowed to walk on the roof or in the dining room and courtyard and her muscles were wasting away. Her legs became so sore and painful they made her cry out. She begged Talbot to allow her exercise but he refused, too afraid of Cecil to give in. Once, on an icy January day when the snow was thick on the ground, he suggested she might take some exercise, expecting she would decline, but in an instant she was in her thick winter wraps and hurrying through the snow. Such moments were few and far between. She tried to pass the time, building up something of a menagerie of pets, as she tried to keep turtle doves and barbary fowls and asked if she might have dogs: 'besides knitting and sewing, my only pleasure is in getting all the little beasts I can find'.[7]

She gained comfort from food, as well as using it to display her regal splendour, and she put on weight due to eating more than she needed and her rich diet exacerbated the stomach problems that have similarities to what we would now call stress-related irritable bowel syndrome. Mary had terrible insomnia, sometimes for weeks at a time, and complained that she threw up tough and vile phlegm. She took pills and had the constant attendance of two doctors, wore an amethyst ring 'contre la maladie', as she put it, and begged her ambassador in Paris for 'a piece of fine unicorn's horn for I am in want of it' – a prized remedy (it was in reality a walrus tusk). Nothing seemed to work. She believed her illness was all due to her broken heart. 'No one can cure this malady as well as the Queen of England', she said.[8]

Mary tried everything to win over Elizabeth. She showered her with sweets that she ordered from Paris, sugared almonds and marzipan and sweetmeats. Cecil and Walsingham fussed that they might be poisoned but Elizabeth, always fond of sweet foods, received them gratefully. Mary ordered the finest silks from Paris and embroidered a beautiful design of English flowers next to a Scottish thistle on an exquisite skirt of crimson satin. She sent it to her cousin who thought it most handsome, but it brought Mary no kindness or loosening of her bonds.

When Mary was not writing letters to her supporters or those she wished to help her, she continued to while away her time with embroidery. As Cecil's man, Nicholas White, reported her saying after his visit to Tutbury, 'all the day she wrought with her needle and that the diversity of colours made the time seem less tedious'.[9] She had been skilled with her needles ever since girlhood and she sewed for herself and to make presents for her supporters. In the flush of romance, Norfolk had received a pillow that she'd embroidered with the arms of Scotland and the motto 'VIRESCIT IN VULNERE VIRTUS', 'Courage grows strong at a wound'.[10]

Mary and Bess of Hardwick joined together in the creation of quite incredible decorative embroideries, full of Marian emblems and pictures suggestive of Mary's life, including a lioness with its cub, for Mary and James, and a representation of the endless see-sawing with Elizabeth: two women propped on the wheel of fortune, one bearing a lance and the other a cornucopia noting 'Fortinae Comites'.

When they first met, Bess was forty-one and Mary twenty-six. Bess had been Elizabeth's gentlewoman before the Katherine Grey marriage had caused her fall from favour. Mary knew that Bess would be a valuable source of information on the intimate life of the queen and used their shared endeavour of needlework to encourage her to gossip. It did not take long for Bess to talk of what she had seen while waiting on the Virgin Queen.

The tapestries are testament to Mary's skill as a needlewoman and also her brilliance in winning over her captors. She was charming with the men and made a display of attending to what they said. With the women, she listened to them, talked graciously and invited them to embroider with her. Her needle gave her heart right until the end. When she died, the inventory of her belongings included unfinished embroidery: bed hangings and chair covers.[11]

Mary was sickening every day and she begged to be allowed to take the spa waters in Buxton, and in late 1573, five years after her imprisonment began, she was allowed to visit for the first time. In summer, Buxton had a high-society feel and courtiers came from London to restore their health – including Robert Dudley, the Earl of Leicester. Mary hoped to make contacts with the great and the good and be part of proper society once more. Talbot himself owned the famous bathhouse at Buxton, where visitors relaxed and enjoyed the hot springs, as well as drinking the restorative water. Mary was generally kept in isolation and closely guarded but she did have conversations with passing courtiers and even received Leicester. It might have helped her cause if she had been able to charm Leicester. But instead she was constantly suspected of exaggerating her symptoms in order to go to Buxton and try to escape. As Talbot put it, 'I perceived her principal object was and is to have some liberty out of the gates.'[12]

By 1573, Bothwell was reported to be mad and he was moved to a yet more horrific jail, Dragsholm Castle on the north-west coast of

Right: James Hepburn, Earl of Bothwell at thirty. Three years later, Darnley would be dead and Bothwell would be prime suspect.

Below: This incredible drawing by English spies of Darnley's death on 1 February 1567 makes it clear that it was murder. Darnley and his servant are dead in the orchard with the rope, the chair, the dagger and the gown nearby. The provost's lodging is reduced to rubble. In the upper left of the picture, Prince James sits up in his cot and demands vengeance.

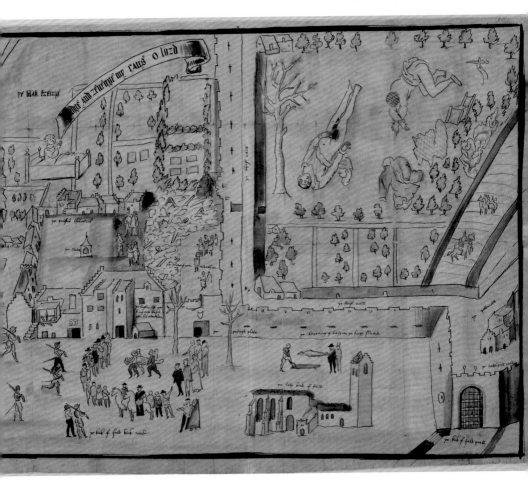

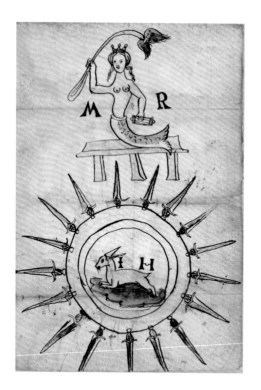

Above: This placard appeared in Edinburgh on 1 March 1567, a scandalous slur on the queen for she is depicted as a mermaid, denoting a prostitute. The sea plant she is holding represents the female genitalia, and the hare refers to Bothwell.

Right: Elizabeth's letter to Mary of 24 February 1567, horrified at Darnley's death. She tells her fellow queen to take immediate action as people were saying she was 'looking through her fingers' while the guilty escaped.

Left: Elizabeth, majestic and all-powerful, aged around forty-two. Superbly political and intelligent, skilful and diplomatic, she was a brilliant stateswoman and she feared that Mary's acts might undermine the reputation of all queens regnant.

Right: Dunbar – Mary gave this castle to Bothwell and then it became her prison.

Madame, Whiles your cause hath bene here treated vpon, we thought it not needefull
to write any thing therof vnto youe, supposing allwaie that your Commissioners, wold
therof advertise as they sawe cause.   And now sithen they haue broken this
conference, by refusing to make answer as they say by your commaundement, and for
that purpose they returne to youe; Although we thinke you shall by them perceiue
the whole proceadinge: Yet we cannot but let your vnderstand by these one bere, that
as we haue bene very sory of long tyme, for your mishappes and greate troubles, So
finde we our sorrowes now dubled in beholding such thynges as are procurd, to proue
your selfe cause of all the same.   And our grief herin is also increased, in that we
did not thinke at any tyme, to haue seen or hard suche matere of so greate apparaunce
and moment to charidge and condempne yowe. Neuertheles both in freindship, nature,
and Justice, we are moued to couer these maters, and stay our iudgement, and not to
gather any sence therof to your preiudice, Before we may heare of your direct answer
thereinto, according as your Commissioners vnderstand our meaning to be, whiche at
their request is deliuered to them in writing.   And as we truste they will advise
youe for your honor to agree to make answer, as we haue motioned them, So surely
we cannot but as one Prince and nere Cousine regarding an other, moost ernestlye,
as we may in termes of freindship require and charge yow not to forbeare from
answering.   And for our parte as we are hartely sory, and dismaide to finde suche
mater of your charidge, So shall we be as hartely gladde and well content to heare
of sufficient mater for your discharidge.   And althoughe we doubt not, but youe
are well certified of the diligence and care of your ministers hauing your Commission:
yet can we not besides an allowance generallie of them, specially note to youe, your good
choise of this bearer the Bishoppe of Rosse, who hathe not onely faithfully and wisely,
But also so carefully and dutyfully, for your honor and weale behaued himself, and that
bothe privately and publikely, as we cannot but in this sorte commende him vnto yowe,
as we wishe youe had many suche deuoted discrete seruantes.   for in our iudgement
we thinke, ye haue not any that in loyaltie, and faithfullnes can ouermatche him:
And this we are the bolder to write, considering we take it the beste triall of a good
seruante to be, in aduersitie, out of which we wishe youe to be deliuered, by the
iustification of your Innocency.   And so trusting to heare shortly from youe, we
make an ende. Geuen at Hampton Courte vnder our Signet the xxij th of December,
1568 in the Leauenthe yeare of oure Reigne :

Your good Sistar and Cousin
Elizabeth R

Vostre bien bonne soeur
MARIE R

Above: Letter from Mary to Elizabeth from her imprisonment at Sheffield Castle, October 1571, begging Elizabeth to allow her to write to her son and permit her to speak to the French ambassador. Mary sent dozens of begging letters to Elizabeth – to no avail.

Left: Thomas Howard, Duke of Norfolk. Naive Norfolk attempted to make Mary his fourth wife – and was terribly punished for doing so.

Left: The fascinating list of Mary's codes, taken from Chartley. Her son is signified by a small heart.

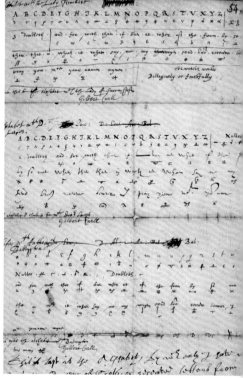

Right: The fateful letter of July 1586 from Mary to Anthony Babington, intercepted by Walsingham's man Phelippes, who then added the postscript at the bottom, asking for the identity of the other conspirators. This was the dynamite Cecil needed to put Mary on trial and deal with her once and for all.

Left: When Mary was moved to the bleak and damp Tutbury Castle in Staffordshire, there was no getting away from it – she was a prisoner.

Below: Mary's trial at Fotheringhay Castle in 1586. The throne is empty – to show that the trial is in front of the English queen, even though she was not present.

Right: Elizabeth claimed to have regretted signing the death warrant of her cousin, and punished those who carried it out with such speed. But once it had been signed, there was no going back.

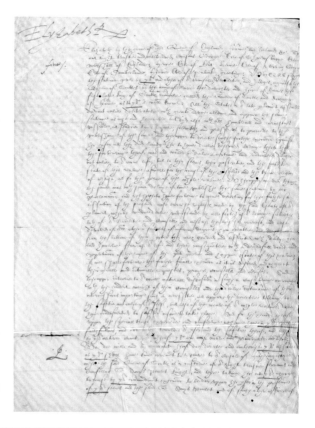

Below: Elizabeth at her most glorious in 1588, the queen who conquered the Spanish Armada and ended the Spanish threat. Rescue by Spain had been Mary's dream – but the ships came two years too late.

Denmark, denied access to anyone, seeing only those who passed his 'scurvy meat and drink' through a tiny window. There, alone and without resources, the filth in his cell never changed, he fell into a frenzy in this 'vile and loathsome prison'. Even Buchanan, his implacable enemy, noted that 'he was driven mad by the filth and other discomforts of his dungeon'. He was now no use to anyone. But Frederick II refused to release him. (Two years later, Mary tried again to have the marriage annulled and Leslie, who had been released from the Tower, was sent to Rome to enact it. And yet still nothing occurred.)[13]

At the end of 1573, Elizabeth gave Sir Francis Walsingham the position of Principal Secretary (later Secretary of State) and Cecil was Lord Treasurer. Walsingham distrusted Mary even more than Cecil had done, and moved to surround her with webs of his spectacularly efficient spies. But Mary's Guise family had one last attempt at helping her. In mid-1574, they recruited their family lawyer in Paris, Claude Nau de la Boisseliere, to be Mary's private secretary, along with Gilbert Curle, who had been with Mary since 1557, and his sister, Elizabeth Curle, as an occasional lady-in-waiting. That Elizabeth allowed Mary to employ a French secretary who was closely associated with the Guises is significant. The Guises had sent him to King Henry III of France, who had given him a passport and sent him to Elizabeth I, in a set-up in which he was essentially awarded diplomatic status. Due to his status, no doubt Elizabeth felt that turning him back would be offensive to the King of France and more trouble than it was worth. But Nau's appointment with Mary marks a sea-change: she had a man who was to a large degree a foreign agent and had networks by which to send letters to France. With him as her secretary, the danger to which she could potentially expose herself with her pen was even greater.

In December 1574, the Cardinal of Lorraine died and the great era of Guise influence was over. One of the final letters he received was from Mary, begging him to help her win over Catherine de' Medici.[14] With his death, all of Mary's hopes of Guise assistance died too. She was irrelevant to the new generation and they owed her nothing. Her health began to decline further. Her legs and heels were so swollen and inflamed that she could barely walk and burst into tears when she took a step. The jolly days of dinners and receptions were no more. Mary was only thirty-two, sick, in pain and slowly wasting away. Elizabeth cut Mary's weekly allowance from £52 to £30 and ignored

Talbot's protests. Talbot grew frustrated with his once-beautiful captive. He longed to be at court, not arguing over tiny sums and dinner menus.

It was a panoply of unhappy events. Dudley, who had been one of the few at court who supported Mary and had encouraged the Norfolk marriage, was exposed as having pursued a long affair with Douglas, Lady Sheffield, a beautiful widow and Elizabeth's gentlewoman. She had pushed for marriage but he knew Elizabeth would never allow it and their child had been born in 1574. Elizabeth was furious with him over the affair and her old favour for him was crumbling. He attempted to seize it back with a huge pageant in her honour at Kenilworth Palace, building a 600-feet bridge covered in rich fruits and an artificial floating island in the lake. When Elizabeth arrived, the great clock on the turret stopped to imply that time halted during the magical visit of the queen. There was dancing, feasting and dazzling entertainments. Unfortunately, it was all brought to an abrupt end when Elizabeth was told that Dudley had also been having an affair with one of her former gentlewomen and her cousin, the married Lettice Knollys. She left in a whirl and Dudley's chance to regain her patronage disappeared.

There was no chance that he could argue for Mary now that he had fallen in Elizabeth's estimation. Instead, Dudley moved to keenly supporting the group who feared that Elizabeth might die at any minute and stepped up the anti-Catholic enthusiasm. As he wrote, 'There is no right papist in England who wishes Queen Elizabeth to live long.'[15]

Things got worse. Mary's Master of the Household, Andrew Beaton, who had fallen in love with Mary Seton, had travelled to France to obtain permission to marry her, but he died on his return, casting poor Mary Seton into despair. In 1575, Agnes Keith was forced to give up Mary's jewels that she had been holding in Scotland (including the 'great H' diamond) to Regent Morton, after a lengthy court case in which Agnes had even appealed to Elizabeth for help. Mary would never receive them – and then two years later, the few jewels that she had left were stolen from her treasurer at Sheffield Castle.

As her little boy grew up, Mary was hopeful that he might be able to request to see her. She sent Claude Nau to take a present of golden toy guns to her eleven-year-old son in Edinburgh but Nau was forbidden to see the prince and give messages to him from his mother. Elizabeth confiscated Mary's letters and gifts to James, and so it remained impossible to get a present or even a message to her son. All the evidence suggested he was being brought up to hate her, for he was surrounded by her enemies. And yet Mary dreamed and convinced herself that he must still love her, romanticising the blood connection, believing, like so many parents, that a child owes gratitude for simply being born. When so many suitors had proved hopeless, violent, cruel and unfaithful, James became her one true love. She dreamed of taking the throne, with him at her side. She believed he must truly be a Catholic and expressed her wish he should marry a Spanish princess. She became obsessed with him, relying on the reports of supporters who sent comforting descriptions of his affection for her that betrayed more about their hopes for the future than the truth. Mary imagined herself and her son ruling together.[16]

She had no idea of his true character. A lonely child, who had been constantly watched, growing up without love or kindness, James had taken solace in a Protestantism as enthusiastic as his mother's Catholicism. And like so many children mistreated in youth, he invested all his hopes in coming of age. Then, he believed, he would have the power he deserved. Then, he would govern as a king. As he saw it, he was destined to be king and he didn't need the help of any of his manipulative advisors or ministers. He certainly did not want the help of his mother.

In summer 1578, while Elizabeth was on her summer progress, the authorities had a tip-off about witchcraft and investigators dug up a dunghill in Islington and found three wax figures, one with 'Elizabeth' scratched on its forehead and two dressed as her ministers. They had been buried so that the heat of the dunghill as it decomposed in the sweltering summer would melt the wax and so the queen would die. According to the Spanish ambassador, the queen feared it meant there was a Catholic assassination plot ranged against her. John Dee, the queen's philosopher, was sent to meet Elizabeth and cast some magic as an antidote and then promptly set off back to London, to hunt out the Islington witches. Within a fortnight, two Catholic men were being tortured on the rack at the Tower for information, and one blamed Thomas Harding, vicar of Islington, for making the figures. We might argue that the local vicar was simply the only person who the tormented souls could think of on the rack, but Harding had been arrested in the previous year for witchery. He was taken in again, tortured and sentenced to death for treason.

But, then, in the following year, a well-known conjurer, Thomas Elkes, confessed that he had made the wax figures on behalf of a rich young man who wanted a lady of his acquaintance to fall in love with him. The melting intended was not death but sexual ecstasy. The council and ministers had tortured and sentenced innocent men. One of the men originally arrested was released and the poor vicar of Islington (who had been waiting to die) was spared execution but condemned to life in the Tower.

Catholics across Europe mocked the credulous English for their panic over a few harmless dolls. But the fear of witchcraft and Catholic trickery did not dissipate, and Mary, cut off in her ivory prison, was still more detested. Elizabeth was ill with terrible pains in her face – probably as a result of gum disease – and Cecil gloomily put them down to her 'lack of marriage', a view shared by contemporary doctors. But even though Cecil optimistically declared she could still have a child and had five or so fertile years remaining, the queen was in her forty-sixth year and showing no more enthusiasm to be married than she ever had. The French Duke of Anjou was entertained but nothing was ever decided.

In 1578, Bothwell died in his horrific solitary confinement in Dragsholm Castle, after suffering terribly in his final years. Some even reported he was chained to a pillar. Of course, it was all the better for the Scottish lords' case that Bothwell had gone mad, for they could claim it was due to a mind affrighted by its terrible crimes. But his final years were so squalid that death was a release.[17] The man who had brought Mary to the brink of death and destruction was finally gone. What ruined her in the eyes of monarchs across the world was the marriage. Bothwell had forced her into submission and taken everything from her.

Mary was now finally free to marry. But Philip seemed to have lost faith in sponsoring a marriage since the failure of the Ridolfi plot, and six months after Bothwell, Don John, in whom Mary had invested so much thought, fell ill and died. It was the death of another hope.

Elizabeth, meanwhile, was trailing beauty and glory. Explorer Francis Drake was travelling the world, chasing and conquering Spanish treasure ships, and she knighted him on the *Golden Hinde* in 1581. She was the queen of a new empire: outward-looking, adventurous, her pirates spreading across the seas. Gold was pouring in. She wished to ignore her cousin. Mary was an annoying house guest, desperate and miserable, always pulling at the bottom of her gown.

Chapter Thirty-One
'That Devilish Woman'

Mary was wasting away in a gilded cage. The pains in her body grew so bad that she could barely move. She had a bad fall from her horse and her spine and legs took a permanent blow. She then fell prey to gastric flu and in 1582 the doctors thought she was dying. Much of it was due to her restrained state and her misery, the damp conditions of some of her prisons, lack of exercise and, as one observer judged, 'the painful, importunate and almost constant workings of her mind', but she probably had a genuinely debilitating condition. As historian Antonia Fraser has explored, this could very well have been a form of porphyria, suffering as Mary did with severe stomach pain, vomiting and general distress.[1] But even the strongest of constitutions would wilt under the mental misery of unending captivity.

At the end of 1580, a collection of Scottish lords, including Balfour, had moved to challenge Morton in his position as regent. His high-handed and violent behaviour had won him many enemies and the young king resented his oppressive governance. Balfour had been in exile in Denmark and had asked the king's and Morton's enemies to negotiate permission to return, offering evidence to implicate Morton in the murder of Darnley in exchange. He said he owned a copy of the by-now close to mythical Craigmillar bond agreeing the despatch of Darnley, signed by Morton.[2] On New Year's Eve, Morton was accused of the murder of Darnley and swept off to Edinburgh Castle in the presence of the king. Elizabeth panicked and sent her spies to attempt to save him – because she feared what might come out at the trial.

286

His relations and associations, including Archibald Douglas, who may have been Darnley's killer and might also have been involved in forging the casket letters, were commanded to appear. But Douglas had already fled to England and Elizabeth refused to give him up.

Morton was put on trial in June 1581 for being part of the conspiracy of Darnley's murder and although Balfour never produced the bond as evidence, Morton was found guilty and sentenced to death. He confessed that he and others had known of the murder plot in advance but did nothing because they believed the queen required it, and he also admitted to having received Archibald after the murder. The king spared him hanging and requested that he be beheaded. Young James was beginning to assert his power. It was thus near impossible for Mary to still be accused of the killing of Darnley. This would have been a moment to demand the casket letters and agree to a trial, simply to see what Elizabeth would do. But Mary had given up asking Elizabeth to clear her name. Instead, she had started to accuse the queen of attempting to undermine her from the very start. 'By the agents, spies and secret messengers sent in your name into Scotland while I was there, my subjects were corrupted and encouraged to rebel against me, and to speak, do, enterprise and execute that which has come to the said country during my troubles.'³ She was right. If Morton, the former regent, had now been found guilty of the murder, then surely Mary could be set free? As the Casket letters and the trial had come to nothing, it might seem to naturally follow that she could be released. But the Ridolfi plot had blocked all that and Cecil was looking for another charge that might get rid of her for ever. The terrible mistake of crossing the river to England rather than staying in Scotland condemned her again and again. Her only chance now lay with the new powers in her country – and whether her son James might take it upon himself to care for her.

James, now fourteen, had been deeply resentful of the close eye kept on him by the lords, most of all Buchanan, his tutor and erstwhile guard. James was infuriated, for he was supposed to be the king but was seemingly kept under restrictions not so dissimilar to those of his mother, and he was allowed no say in ruling. Later in 1581, he announced that he would rule as monarch and courtiers saw the growth of influence of Esmé Stewart, Lord Aubigny, his father's first cousin. The young king was very fond of the thirty-nine-year-old father of five and made him Duke of Lennox. There was talk they were lovers – and even more dangerously, his new friend suggested he band with Guise and they invade England from both ends, with the backing of Philip of Spain. Unfortunately for the plan, the lords hated Lennox and (probably paid for partly with English funds) lured him to a castle, where they imprisoned him and forced James to send him back to France (Lennox died not long after and left James his embalmed heart). James was also kidnapped by the lords but escaped in 1583 and again declared himself king. As he immediately began allying with France on his release, Elizabeth sprang into action, holding out the possibility that Mary could take the throne jointly with her son. Walsingham was sent to Scotland to discuss the idea, complaining as he did so. And yet, at the same time, it seemed as if Mary was still investigating and supporting plots against the queen, and when Walsingham presented this evidence to Elizabeth, her enthusiasm for a joint monarchy faded. For after all, James and Mary together would have a rock-solid claim to the English throne and Mary could stir up much resentment against Elizabeth and support from English Catholics.

Mary wished her son to demand her release as a condition for negotiating with Elizabeth, rather than Spain. Unfortunately Francis Gray, the secretary she sent to pursue it, turned to the English cause almost as soon as he left her chamber and did nothing to promote the relationship between mother and son. Perhaps he was wise. For James, newly on the throne, constantly threatened by rebel lords, his very person menaced, bringing his mother back would have been very dangerous and would have most likely undermined his position. He wrote politely to his mother talking of Elizabeth '*ma bonne soeur*' and wishing his mother 'good health and good prosperity.' He could give her nothing but fine words.[4] With the death of Maitland and the capture of Edinburgh Castle in 1573, the Marian side had been much reduced, Protestantism was established and now the teenaged king could be forgiven for thinking that the arrival of his mother might set everything on fire once more. Nothing showed his pragmatic movement towards Elizabeth better than when Archibald Douglas was captured and tried in 1586 for Darnley's murder. He was almost certainly guilty and many Scots were hoping that James would allow a trial like that of Morton's in which doubt was thrown on all the lords. But Elizabeth pressed James to make it into a whitewash, so ten jurors declined to appear and were replaced with supporters, the evidence was paltry, and Douglas was summarily cleared – and later made ambassador to England. Elizabeth and James worked together to stop the truth about how many of the lords had participated in the murder of the king. It now suited both of them that Mary be suspended in ambiguity, neither innocent nor guilty, in her gilded prisons. Mary had grown desperate. In the British Library are preserved ten beautifully handwritten pages of her pleas to Elizabeth from November 1582.

Mary complains bitterly of her treatment and how, as she writes, she has seen 'my good intentions misrepresented, the sincerity of my heart calumniated cruelly, the conduct of my affairs delayed or blocked with artifices and finally worse and more insulting treatment'. She tries to draw a parallel between the two queens saying that she wishes for the 'establishment of a good relationship between us' and arguing that her enemies with their 'coded, secret messages' tried to undermine Elizabeth in Scotland 'at the same time they were rebelling against me'. She begs for permission to send to her son so he can help with the 'overtures I have proposed to establish between the two kingdoms a good relationship and perfect intelligence in the future.' It is an impossible level of delusion. The chances of a 'perfect intelligence' between her and Elizabeth were long gone.

Mary taxes Elizabeth with her promises, declaring that when she'd fled, she sent her gentleman 'express' with the 'diamond ring that I received from you as a token that you would protect me.' Mary declares that Elizabeth promised to 'come to the border to assist me yourself' and she expected to be 'in your arms' – but was then 'arrested on my way to see you'. And now, she says, she is treated poorly with no regard for the 'diet and exercise necessary for my health'. As she complains, 'my enemies, with their long tradition of mistreating me, now feel they have the right to say how I am treated, not like a prisoner . . . but like a slave.'

None of this was likely to win over Elizabeth – least of all Mary's claim that she was the heir. 'The worst criminals in your prisons have their justifications . . . their accusers have been declared they see their accusations. Why not me, a royal sovereign, your closest relation and legitimate heir.' Mary had a point about her legal treatment but the reference to 'heir' was calculated to anger her 'sister'. Mary then declared that being the heir 'is at the bottom of what's happened to me, all their calumnies, to divide us'.

Little would annoy Elizabeth more. The letter, despite its words from 'your very sad and very closely confined and affectionate sister' was hopeless and Mary's declarations that she would die if it all continued were ignored.[5]

The matter had grown more serious, for even Elizabeth's most optimistic courtiers had accepted that she would never have a child. The marriage negotiations with the French Duke of Anjou finally collapsed in 1582 and Elizabeth turned fifty in 1583. The 'five or six' fertile years that Cecil had discussed in 1578 were lost. The question was – who would be her heir? All eyes turned to Mary, and Elizabeth, although her court was expected to keep up the vision that she would never die, preferred the focus to be on James. A great comet appeared over London in the summer and there were fears it indicated the death of a person of significance. Elizabeth's ladies tried to stop her from looking at it from her palace window in Richmond. She ignored them, looked out at its wild passage across the sky and exclaimed, '*Alea iacta est*' – the die is cast.[6]

With the possibility of a direct heir gone for ever, Elizabeth feared that the plotters were stepping up their efforts. One Catholic gentleman was even put under suspicion for popping into a new perfumery in London to buy gloves and perfume – the investigators jumped to the wild conclusion that he aimed to poison the queen with the gloves, packing them up to her as a lovely present and then rejoicing as she died in agony. At the end of 1583, young Francis Throckmorton was arrested in his house in London, caught in the act of writing a coded letter to the Queen of Scots. His house was searched for papers. The investigators found anti-Elizabeth pamphlets from the continent, a list of safe harbours where foreign forces could land, and names of Catholic nobles who would support an invasion. Walsingham had spotted him calling at the residence of Michel de Castlenau, the French ambassador, in Salisbury Court off Fleet Street, and suspected him of carrying secret letters from Mary to Castlenau. He was taken to the Tower and Cecil's spies declared he was the focus of a conspiracy between Castlenau, the Duke of Guise and the brother of the late Duke of Norfolk to restore Mary. Throckmorton denied everything and was thrown twice upon the rack before he admitted that he was carrying letters to the Spanish ambassador, Don Bernadino de Mendoza, and was part of a plot to encourage an invasion from Philip of Spain and the Duke of Guise. He was executed for treason and Mendoza was expelled.

Mary was sick and wasting but in the minds of Elizabeth's courtiers, she was an ever-growing threat. When William of Orange was shot by a Spanish Catholic in July 1584, it seemed as if Elizabeth would be next in the firing line, murdered by a Catholic plot. All the circumstances were against Mary. The Throckmorton arrest, the fact that Elizabeth was now too old to bear an heir, the behaviour of the Spanish and French ambassadors; it was all too much. Cecil and Walsingham were considering more strenuous laws to protect Elizabeth's person.

Still worse, Bess of Hardwick became jealous of Talbot's attention to Mary and his spending of her estate on Mary's entourage. He was in an impossible position, guarding a prisoner who no one wanted but who had to be kept in grandeur, without the money to do so. The happy days of conversation over embroidery over, Bess tormented Talbot with accusations. She was already resentful after Elizabeth had thrown a proverbial fit over the marriage of Bess's daughter, Elizabeth, to Darnley's brother in 1574 (it had taken place without the Queen's permission, and thus Elizabeth viewed it as a disobedient, even treasonous, act). Bess was discontented with her life and marriage, and her fury turned on Mary.

Gossip about the exact nature of Talbot's and Mary's relationship started to spread, and even Elizabeth started to discuss the scandal – and it reached courts around the world. Talbot had long been accused of being too kind to Mary, pushing for her to visit Buxton, allowing her huge retinue, subsidising her expenses and letting her socialise with local families. Now, everyone said, they knew why. Like so many men before him, he had been seduced by the Scots queen.

Mary realised that she was in serious danger once more. First, she begged for a full investigation and demanded to be allowed to clear herself. When no reply came, she lost her temper and sent Elizabeth a lengthy denunciation of Bess that was shocking in its content: Bess, who had been one of Elizabeth's Ladies of the Bedchamber before losing her position in the aftermath of the scandalous secret marriage of Katherine Grey, had been talking wildly over those embroidery sessions. She had, Mary said, accused the queen of taking Leicester as a lover, asking him to marry her and having been 'with him an infinite number of times with all the familiarity and licence as between husband

and wife'.[7] The queen had also had affairs with various other men, including favoured politician and future Lord Chancellor Sir Christopher Hatton, and kissed the French ambassador and engaged in familiarities with him, before betraying state secrets to him. She had also come close to sex with the Duke of Anjou, letting him enter her room when she was only wearing her nightdress and dressing gown. Even more hurtfully, wrote Mary, Bess had said that Elizabeth was unable to conceive and so 'would never lose your liberty to make love and always have your pleasure with new lovers'.[8] Perhaps the most damaging of all was Bess's reported claim that the courtiers competed to offer her the most excessive praise, none of which they believed.

Mary even said that when Elizabeth had been ill, Bess had prophesied a violent death and the accession of Mary. It was eye-watering stuff and written to shock Elizabeth and cause her pain. But it probably never reached her, for Cecil seized it. Cecil was stunned by the document and increasingly fretful about the growing Catholic power in Europe. Bess protested her innocence. And, fortunately for her, there was nothing in there that had not been said by other gossips or in foreign pamphlets, such as the rumour about Leicester. There was no real new information that only Bess would have been privy to. But if she were innocent, then Mary was guilty of sending evil slander. Mary had been wrong to write the letter. For although Bess was cleared, the whole affair was highly embarrassing to Talbot. He escaped criticism but he would no longer be allowed to guard Mary.

Mary was moved to the custody of Sir Ralph Sadler who, at seventy-seven, had been hoping for a quiet retirement. The passionate falling-out between Mary and Bess marked an indelible black line over her time with Talbot. Unfortunately, he felt so vulnerable to criticism after the exposure of Bess's unguarded words about the queen that he lost all sympathy for Mary. The man who had been her great friend and protector became her formidable enemy.

Sir Ralph Sadler and his son-in-law were to take Mary to Wingfield and then back to the horrors of Tutbury Castle. Sadler, who had known Mary for years, was shocked at the change in her. He found her much altered, her body wasted and 'not yet able to strain her left foot to the ground',[9] in constant pain and tearful. He felt dreadfully sorry for her and could not resist her pleas. Her rooms at Tutbury were dark and damp with no sight of the sun and she grew sicker every day. Mary begged him to let her have a little air and exercise and he agreed to take her out with his hawks along the river near the castle. He took fifty men with him to guard her and they were no more than three miles from the castle – but when Cecil heard about Mary's brief moments of liberty, he was furious. Even though she could barely walk and was still heavily guarded, she remained so dangerous, in Cecil's eyes, that she could not go out, even surrounded by fifty armed escorts.

Sadler was promptly deprived of his position and Mary was handed to Sir Amyas Paulet, who vowed from the beginning not to be swayed by Mary's pleas. His duty was to Elizabeth and, in his eyes, God, and as he put it, 'others shall excuse their foolish pity as they may'.[10] He was violently anti-Catholic, had worked against her in the French court and was a close associate of Walsingham. Her tears would have no effect on him. Up until then, the fiction had been that Mary was in protective custody. Now, she was in prison. He had been told to ensure she never left the building, even to take the air. Mary was in strict confinement and she was not allowed to correspond with associates on the outside. Paulet put all of Mary's staff in isolation, refusing to allow them to mix with the other servants, and they had to be searched leaving and entering the castle – if he allowed them to leave. Mary's servants were not even allowed to walk on the castle walls. He was particularly obsessed with Mary's three laundresses who resided outside the castle, demanding that they were strip-searched on leaving and entering. Still worse, Paulet denied Mary all of the grandeur that had supported her poor, battened-down heart. When he entered her chamber, he tore down her cloth of state, shouting that there was only one queen in the country. He burst in and searched her cabinets at random and even broke down her door. Mary had no privacy and no respect and he seized and tore open her letters and read the contents. She still had thirty-eight attendants and servants but Paulet hated them and she was not allowed to give money to the local poor in case this won them over to taking messages for her. For Paulet, Mary was a direct threat to Elizabeth and he would control, reduce and humiliate her in whatever way he could. Mary begged Elizabeth for help, complaining of his brutality. But Elizabeth replied that Mary had always said she would bow to what Elizabeth wished – and Paulet was what the queen wanted.[11]

Mary grew seriously ill under Paulet's cruel treatment. She called her new guard 'one of the most zealous and pitiless men I have ever known'.[12] Her legs were still inflamed and the slightest movement made her cry out and she could not walk without her secretaries supporting her. Her legs were covered with open wounds that had to be dressed daily in, as Paulet put it, 'gross manner' and she was constantly sick with headaches, stomach pains, fainting and insomnia. She was allowed out in a carriage only once or twice a month with armed soldiers surrounding her. Mary was frantic and desperate. Elizabeth was ignoring her and Paulet was treating her shockingly. France had given her nothing.

Mary saw no choice but to throw her lot in with Spain and beg Philip for help. And Philip himself was leaning towards war, believing that the only way to gain dominion over the Atlantic Ocean was by conquering England. Plots were beginning to spring up and Mary wrote to the Spanish ambassador for details about the activities of Catholics in England and the growing enthusiasm for invasion.

In the autumn of 1584, all London was talking about an outrageous, obscene, treasonous book that had come from Paris, brought over on the boat in secret, swapped under the tables at taverns, sold in the darkness of alleyways, taken to houses at the dead of night. The lord mayor managed to seize a copy and sent it to Walsingham. The lurid pages were all about Robert Dudley, accusing him of having and misusing his power over the queen, suggestively declaring that he had been engaged in 'diligently besieging' her and taking up 'all the ways and passages about her'.[13] He was also said to be seducing various ladies at court, naming both Lady Douglas and Lettice Knollys (who he apparently conquered with an aphrodisiac potion made of his own semen), and paying them off, and the old accusations about the mysterious death of Amy Robsart were dredged up. He was hated by Catholics on the continent for his anti-Jesuit stance and because of the gossip that he would try to put his own illegitimate children on the throne. Elizabeth announced an amnesty for the people of England to relinquish their copies of the dreadful book without punishment but few appeared. There were pages praising Mary's claim to the throne and so Dudley decided that Mary was behind the whole thing. On this occasion, the Queen of Scots was probably innocent but Dudley's attitude towards her changed for ever. He was now her implacable enemy.

In late 1584, Walsingham persuaded the queen that Mary still wished to have her killed. He pushed forth 'The Instrument of an Association for the Preservation of her Majesty's Royal Person' or the 'Bond of Association', in which signatories pledged to hunt down and kill anyone who was pursuing a plot against the queen. They vowed 'never to accept, avow, or favour any such pretended successor, by whom or for whom any such detestable act shall be committed or attempted' – Mary would be held responsible, even if she was not involved. The government directed the signatures as it was passed around the country but presented it rather as a spontaneous uprising of protectiveness.[14]

In the following Spring this became law, in an 'Act for the Queen's Safety', declaring that if she were murdered, the beneficiary (they meant Mary) and her associates were to be retrieved and killed. It essentially enabled any Englishman (or woman) to hunt down and kill anyone involved in plots 'compassed or imagined, tending to the hurt of her Majesty's royal person'. Some MPs raised objections about the possible anarchy that could ensue – what if people simply slaughtered who they felt like, killing old enemies and declaring that these men had been trying to murder the queen? If Elizabeth was killed, did this mean that both Mary and James would have to be executed? Then who would rule? Elizabeth made it clear that if Mary was executed for plotting, James should be exempt as long as he had not been involved. The Act was passed and Elizabeth decided to limit her royal progress planned for the summer and instead remain at her own residences.

The Act placed Mary and Elizabeth in direct opposition. Elizabeth then played a wily game. She turned to the young king of Scotland herself, offering the possibility of recognising him and indeed putting him in line to the English throne after her death. As she was fifty-one and suffering from illness, it would be understandable if James, a hearty teenager, decided she was almost dead anyway. The simple point for James was that Mary, imprisoned and powerless, could give him nothing.

For James, Elizabeth's recognition meant more than the words of his mother. He couldn't remember Mary and she was still a divisive figure. And he was perspicacious enough to see that being put in line as the heir to the English throne would mean more to his subjects than supporting his mother ever would. He promptly wrote to Mary saying that he would honour her with the title of 'queen mother' but she could never again be queen.[15] The poor captive fell into a frenzy of shock and vomiting when she received the letter, scribbling back in fury that he insulted her with his title and 'there is neither king nor queen in Scotland except me'. She was utterly heartbroken at what she called his 'enormous ingratitude' that she felt 'no punishment, divine or human' could ever equal. She scrawled that 'I am so grievously offended at my heart at the impiety and ingratitude that this child has been constrained to commit against me.'[16] She railed wildly that she would deprive him of the crown and give it to his greatest enemy. But her words had no effect other than making her ill. Elizabeth was delighted by her triumph and James cared only for securing his position in Scotland.

Mary had always had some hope that her son would save her. And she was growing increasingly fearful that she might be quietly poisoned, her long-term sickness used to excuse a sudden death. Now, she threw herself towards anyone who promised her rescue – entering the underworld of spies and plots. And this was just what Cecil and Walsingham wanted. For Cecil, Mary had always been a threat to Elizabeth and a talisman for English Catholics to cling to. Without her, there would be no one for them to put on the throne in place of Elizabeth – for James was occupied in Scotland, and was Protestant. Cecil had become so obsessed with Mary that he had come to believe that dispatching her would pretty much nullify the Catholic threat. As he told Leicester, 'so long as that devilish woman lives, neither her Majesty must make account to continue in quiet possession of her crown, nor her faithful servants assure themselves of safety to their lives'.[17]

Chapter Thirty-Two
'Green Ribbons'

In 1585, Mary Seton, forty-three and long suffering from illness, her heart still pained by the loss of her fiancé, decided that she must repair to a convent and fulfil her destiny as a bride of Christ. She would live in the convent of Rheims that was presided over by Mary of Guise's sister, Renée of Guise, and devote her life to God. She had served Mary faithfully for so long – essentially for all of her life. She had risked terrible punishment and death by dressing as the queen while she escaped from Lochleven and she had stayed with her in shocking prisons, been with her for her triumphant return to Scotland in 1560, her awful miscarriage and dreadful abdication in 1567. Without Mary Seton, her great link to the past and the witness to her glory, the Queen of Scots had lost a steadying influence – and started to fall down the hole of plots and schemes, a sixteenth-century Alice in Wonderland who did not see what was around her.

Tutbury was in a shocking state of repair and needed airing, so Mary and her household were shifted to Chartley Hall, also in Staffordshire, on Christmas Eve 1585 (much to the complaint of the owner, the young Earl of Essex).

Mary was hawkishly watched by Paulet but she was determined to outwit him. Her deliverance came with the arrival of the twenty-five-year-old son of a Catholic landowner, Gilbert Gifford, who popped up and offered to take Mary's letters for her. He had been engaged on and off in studying to be a Catholic priest, had a recommendation from one of her agents in Paris, and seemed an ideal saviour. Mary schemed brilliant ways to have her letters sent secretly to France and

Spain, deciding that alum, the sixteenth-century version of invisible ink, was too easily detected, and instead one could write secret messages across the agreed pages of new books, with 'green ribbons attached to the books that you've had written in this way'.[1] She and her correspondents created over sixty codes, the keys to which she kept in her papers. She also planned to hide letters in the soles of shoes that were sent to her from Paris and in the slats of the boxes used to send her clothes, even in tiny caskets floating at the top of beer casks, which were delivered every week.

Unfortunately, it was all a trap.

Cecil and Walsingham had realised that putting Mary under Paulet's strict surveillance and forbidding her correspondence had been a self-defeating project. If Mary stopped writing letters, then they would never have any evidence against her. So in a breathtakingly brilliant plan, Gifford was recruited. When living on the continent, attempting to train as a priest, he had come into contact with anti-Elizabeth groups and entered into discussions about assassinating the queen. In Paris, he met Thomas Morgan, who had been a secretary and a spy for Mary from 1569 to 1572. He had been imprisoned in the Tower for three years and then fled to France, where he busied himself creating conspiracies to put Mary onto the throne. Gifford was in conversation with Morgan and Charles Paget, exiled Catholic and son of Sir William Paget, formerly Lord Privy Seal to Mary I, who had fled to France in 1581. Morgan and Paget played a key role in Mary, Queen of Scots' life, corresponding with her secretaries, Claude Nau and Gilbert Curle, and between them they were said to have 'governed from thenceforth the queen's affairs at their pleasure'.[2] Morgan and Paget also helped the Scottish ambassador administer Mary's funds from her dower lands in France, for which they gained a pension. The Duke of Guise, Philip of Spain and powerful Catholic interests across Europe wanted Mary back on her throne.

Thus, Gifford was in conversation with the elite groups of Catholic plotters and those who were hell-bent on getting Mary into power. The problem was that Walsingham's brilliant spies were onto them – and so Paget also worked as a double agent, feeding information back to Walsingham. He probably did so only so that he could move between France and England at will and to avoid suspicion, and he spent more time enthusing to Walsingham about his devotion to

Elizabeth than he did actually passing on information. Walsingham saw through his fine words and never trusted him, writing that 'Charles Paget is a most dangerous instrument.'[3] He needed a better agent. When, in 1585, Gifford arrived in England from France, Walsingham pounced. Gifford was captured, arrested and interrogated by Walsingham, probably with the assistance of torture. He promised to be a double agent and Walsingham gave him the code name of No. 4.

When he was finally released, Gifford contacted the French embassy to note that he hoped to be transmitting letters and then headed for Chartley Hall. There, he offered himself to Mary and her secretaries, Curle and Nau, as a useful postman and they took him to their hearts. Every letter that Mary and her secretaries put in for him to transport was given to Walsingham's man to read and decipher. Nau would take down her letter, bundle it in leather and give it to the brewer to be hidden in the cork. The brewer returned to his home, extracted the letter, gave it to Gifford – who then betrayed Mary by bringing it back to Chartley, for the perusal of Paulet. She thought he was taking them straight to the French ambassador.

Mary had no idea that her superb plans for concealment were exposed, from her secret hiding places to her invented codes. She had thrown herself into the hands of Gifford, with terrible effect. As the French ambassador put it, Mary and her servants had 'placed great confidence in the said Gifford . . . and thence came the ruin'.[4] Walsingham was so sure of success that he put his crack codebreaker, Thomas Phelippes, in rooms at Chartley, so he could read and decipher letters immediately. On the occasions when Phelippes was called back to London, Paulet put the letters on fast horses to the capital. After the letter had been read, decoded and transcribed, the set of letters were sealed back into the original leather and messengers handed them to the French ambassador.

Mary's code ciphers are in the National Archives, beautifully scribed by her secretaries. Each letter has a code, and some names, titles and popular words also have codes: the Queen of England, the King of Spain, crown, ship, intelligence, secret, religion. The three names on top of the code decipherer are the Pope, the King of France and the King of Spain. Mary's code an X bearing a small dot on the right, the King of Spain and France also are Xs with dots. Even in a code guide, Mary made her alliances clear. Elizabeth is a rather odd 4 shape that looks like no one else. Poor Mary – her son was signified by a tiny heart.[5]

The usual letters in this careful code that went back and forth were not incriminating enough to have Mary put on trial. Cecil could not afford another adjournment; he liked decisive, clear outcomes. Too many of Mary's letters expressed support of the Catholic faith and of the efforts of France and Spain to pursue it, but fell short of demanding Elizabeth be deposed and executed. Although Mary was depressed, angry and resentful, she had only ever wanted her own throne back – and then to be noted as Elizabeth's successor. But after 1586, Mary was desperate. James had refused her the chance to become monarch jointly with him and he and Elizabeth seemed to be so friendly, and the old suggestion of her returning to Scotland as queen mother had faded. She was worried that she might be killed – in the words of Paulet, 'She could see plainly that her destruction was sought and that her life would be taken from her, and then it would be said that she had died of sickness.'[6] She began to entertain conspirators whom she would have always refused as foolhardy or sinful before.

It was only a matter of time before Mary fell in with another secret scheme. The ringleader was Anthony Babington, who she had known because he had served George Talbot as a page. He had secretly taken letters for her, but feared her incarceration was too strong and she was too watched after she was moved to Tutbury – he had even sent back letters conveyed to him from France in early 1586, declining to be involved. Young and idealistic, as many of the plotters tended to be, he was a Catholic and had always been sympathetic to the imprisoned queen. Through contacts in the French court, he began corresponding with Mendoza, the Spanish ambassador who had been expelled from London, who was at the Spanish embassy in Paris. Furious about being removed from England, Mendoza began to conjure wild plans: the English Catholics would form an uprising, Spain would invade, Elizabeth would be deposed and executed and Mary would be queen. John Ballard, a Jesuit priest and agent for Rome, had been in frequent contact with Catholic gentry, asking them for support in the event of a Spanish invasion. He encouraged Babington to take an active role in his plot and Babington agreed to find men to support the uprising and assassinate Elizabeth – and unfortunately for him, he invited Gifford to discuss the early plans. Babington wrote to Mary to ask if she would support them.

The letter from Babington to Mary asking whether she would agree to the assassination of her cousin and take her position as queen was sent in the tiny box suspended in the beer keg – and it was written in code. It seemed an impregnable scheme. Mary could never have guessed that Walsingham's man was reading every word, copying it out for the spymaster, and then carefully folding it back up into the box. She received the letter on 14 July 1586 – and her heart was torn. Babington had made it quite clear what would happen. As he put it, 'Myself with ten gentlemen and a hundred of your followers will undertake the delivery of your royal person from the hands of your enemies. For the dispatch of the usurper, from the obedience of whom we are by the excommunication of her made free, there will be six noble gentlemen, all my private friends, who for the zeal they bear the Catholic cause and your Majesty's service, will undertake that tragical execution.' The English queen was to suffer a 'tragical execution' at the hands of the six men. They were, he noted, not required to be obedient to Elizabeth due to her excommunication.[7]

The words 'tragical execution' were all Cecil needed.

If the plan worked, Mary would have her heart's desire. And yet, having seen so much bloodshed, she could not bear the thought of Elizabeth's death. And if the plan failed, she would be executed for treason, without a doubt. She agonised over her decision – and then made the fateful choice to throw her lot in with the plotters, for better or worse. At that point, she felt she had nothing to lose. Her secretary, Claude Nau, took down her dictation in French and then translated it to English – from which it was then written in code. Spies observing her noted she seemed in good spirits after she had sent the letter, smiling and gay. Poor Mary dreamed of gaining Elizabeth's throne in a blaze of glory.

In her letter to Babington, Mary noted his enthusiasm to stop the 'designments of our enemies for the extirpation of our religion out of this realm with ruin of us all',[8] and suggested he enter into discussion with Mendoza. 'The affairs then being thus prepared and forces in readiness both within and without the realm, then shall it be time to set the six gentlemen to work taking order, upon the accomplishment of their design, I may suddenly be transported out of this place.' She told him to burn the letter as soon as he had read it.[9]

The reference to the 'six gentlemen' was fateful proof that she knew about and assented to the plot to kill the queen. Cecil, Paulet, Walsingham and their networks were eagerly awaiting her reply.

Mary also condemned herself by her emphasis on the importance of Spanish military assistance. She did not simply ask to be freed by Babington and dash back to Scotland – which could hardly be seen as an act of treason. She wanted and needed a full Spanish invasion.

For I have long ago shown unto the foreign Catholic princes, what they have done against the King of Spain, and in the time the Catholics here remaining, exposed to all persecutions and cruelty, do daily diminish in number, forces, means and power. So if remedy be not thereunto speedily provided, I fear not a little but they shall become altogether unable for ever to rise again and receive any aid at all, whensoever it was offered . . . I shall always be ready and most willing to employ therein my life and all that I have, or may ever look for, in this world.[10]

Mary's letter was extracted from the beer keg and deciphered. Phelippes, Walsingham's genius decoder, knew he had dynamite. He sent his copy to Walsingham with a picture of the gallows on the front. Before he folded it back up into the beer keg, he added a postscript, on Walsingham's orders, trying to extract the names of the six gentlemen. 'I would be glad to know the names and quelityes of the sixe gentlemen which are to accomplish the designment', 'she' wrote, asking for further particulars and reiterating her desire for the names. It was poorly forged and sat oddly with the rest of the letter.

His task done, Gifford fled to France as he would surely be arrested as Mary's postman and scapegoated, even though he had been working for the English.

Walsingham's trap was closing in. He had the plotters surrounded on all sides. He had asked another spy, John Scudamore, to befriend Babington, and the two were dining at a local inn when a message arrived for Scudamore. Babington caught sight of it and realised it was a command to arrest him. Pretending he was going to the counter to pay, he fled the tavern, leaving his sword behind. Walsingham put a command out across the realm to find the men. John Ballard was taken on 4 August and Babington was found ten days later hiding in St John's Wood, disguised as a peasant with green slime on his face.

Walsingham's spy, Robert Poley (a man who had a gift for turning up in the midst of the action; he was later in the Widow Bull's Inn Tavern when Christopher Marlowe was killed), had also taken up Babington in an intense friendship and told all to Walsingham. Babington suspected that honeytrap Poley had betrayed him but could never admit it to himself, such was his devotion. Four days after his capture, he started to confess.

Mary continued blithely unaware of the plot closing around her, not knowing that her dear 'sister and cousin' had called her a 'wicked murderess' and that her trial had already been ordered.[11] Walsingham needed Mary out of her rooms so he could go through her papers. Her secretary, Claude Nau, had implored her to get rid of them, but she had refused, saying her dear cousin would never wish to read her private writings. This was terribly naïve. Mary was taken to the house of Sir Walter Aston near Chartley Hall. There, Paulet seemed to soften towards her and suggested they go out with a deer hunt at Sir Walter's park – she was delighted with the plan and was so keen to take some exercise that she was able to mount her horse.

On 11 August, Mary set off for the hunting trip she so desired. Beautifully gowned, for she expected to meet with the hunt, she went out accompanied by her secretaries, her page and her valet and was delighting in the fresh air and exercise. She barely noticed when Paulet and his men dropped behind her. And then, towards her came a company of men on horseback, galloping fast. For a brief moment, all was euphoria. She must have thought they had come to free her and her trials were about to be ended. But instead, they were called to a stop and the chief horsemen spoke to Paulet – and turned to her. He declared that there was a plot against Elizabeth, and Mary was to be arrested and conducted to Aston's house. 'The queen my mistress finds it very strange that you, contrary to the pact and engagement made between you, should have conspired against her and the state, a thing which she could not have believed had she not seen proofs of it with her own eyes and known it for certain.'[12] Mary was caught.

Chapter Thirty-Three
'I Am a True Queen'

Mary vehemently denied the accusations, said she had never conspired against the queen, declared herself always Elizabeth's 'good sister and friend'.[1] She begged her servants to defend her with their swords, but they were surrounded and Curle and Nau were arrested and taken away. She agreed to return with Paulet and his escort to Chartley, but then when she realised they were riding in a different direction, she pulled herself off her horse, sat on the ground and refused to move, saying piteously that she wished to die on the spot. Paulet threatened to forcibly remove her and only when her doctor came to comfort her and beg her to move did she agree to stand. He came up with the strange idea that Elizabeth was already dead and the men were simply attempting to keep her safe. Mary knew it was a lie. But she was still defiant. She knelt against a tree to pray and said she would not leave until she had finished.

While Mary was out riding, her rooms in Chartley had been searched, men ransacking her drawers and cabinets, collecting together the carefully drawn keys for codes. Four justices of the peace arrived to oversee the search and three boxes of her letters were packed up and taken post-haste to Elizabeth. Mary, meanwhile, was taken off to Aston's house, Tixall, at which there was nothing for her, not even a change of clothes. Two of her ladies and an equerry were sent to attend her in her new prison. She begged Paulet to allow her to write to Elizabeth but he refused her paper. He told her he would not speak to her either.[2]

Mary passed days of misery, afraid and terrified of when men were going to invade, seize her, accuse her. After a fortnight, she was returned to her rooms at Chartley, devastated and shocked, crying out to those who watched her go in, 'All is taken from me,' and saying she had nothing to give the beggars for she was one too. She was still defending herself, saying she had not been 'privy to anything intended against the queen'.[3] She saw how her rooms had been ransacked: her papers and drafts confiscated, the keys to her various secret codes taken. She wept bitterly and said that she still had two things that could not be taken from her: her royal blood and her religion.

Elizabeth had moved to Windsor Castle, a fortress that she disliked but which was judged her most secure of palaces. She wrote a grateful letter to Paulet, addressing him as 'my most faithful and careful servant', telling him God would reward him 'for the most troublesome charge so well discharged'.[4] But the thought of executing a queen sickened her and, as they knew, Spain might protest and use it as a ruse for invading. For if a queen could be executed, then what did it say about the special blood of monarchy?

Walsingham and Cecil were keen for a trial, her privy councillors the same. Elizabeth, with her desire to avoid upset, hoped that Mary might die of natural causes. For surely the queen's illnesses would only intensify if she was kept in confinement and her body would simply waste away. Cecil was resistant. Mary might take years to die, and in the meantime, plot against Elizabeth again. As he saw it, he had the evidence he needed and it was time to strike.

Elizabeth refused to listen to Cecil. The Scots queen was sick and ailing, looking much older than her forty-three years, and her body was nearly broken. Elizabeth sent orders to make Mary's life difficult. Her servants were taken from her and Paulet was to seize her money. When he arrived to claim it, Mary was ill in bed and refused to give him the key to her closet. She pleaded but Paulet was intransigent and ordered his burly servants to break its door. Mary gave in and asked her gentlewoman to hand him the key. Paulet's servants piled up the money under his hawkish eye and Mary dragged herself out of bed and followed him, barefoot, begging for mercy. She told him that she was keeping the money for her funeral expenses and to pay her servants their final legacies.[5] He seized it anyway.

Mary had no idea of the further humiliations to come. Babington had confessed all. Her own secretaries, under punishing interrogation, had held out bravely and denied they had ever seen the letter in which

Mary had talked of the 'six gentlemen' and given assent to Babington's plan. But when they were shown a version in which Phelippes had written Mary's letter to Babington back into code, they gave in and confessed all, for it was in the correct code, evidence that Walsingham really had seen the original. As Curle confessed, 'they showed me the two very letters written by me in cipher and received by Babington'.[6] Cecil thought them cowardly, shrugging that they would have given up all their information if they thought there was a chance of saving themselves. The confessions of the secretaries were key: since Mary had not written the letters herself she could otherwise still claim that Nau and Curle had written without her knowledge. Cecil needed them to say that they knew – and they obliged.

After a trial on 13 and 14 September, Babington and six others were hanged, drawn and quartered on 20 September. Their dispatch was so brutal and the public outcry so great that the men had been disembowelled while still sentient that the Privy Council panicked and Elizabeth sent a personal order that the next seven to be executed should be hanged but then not mutilated until they were entirely dead.

Mary was utterly friendless. The French ambassador pressed her case but Elizabeth refused to listen. Rome could not help. Her son, James, declared that Mary had gone too far and should stick to prayer. He even declared that she should be put in the Tower. Instead he occupied himself with offering marriage to Elizabeth – over thirty years his senior. The young king had not grasped the seriousness of the matter. He thought that his mother could be imprisoned for ever and had not understood that her life was under threat.

Elizabeth was accepting there must be a trial, but not in London. The sight of Mary riding through the capital's streets in disgrace might stir people to pity or even to rise up for her. Finally, Fotheringhay Castle in Northamptonshire was decided upon – far from Scotland and London, and Mary's journey there would be short, which meant that fewer people would see her. The law had been passed that Mary could be put on trial by nobles and Cecil planned that it would be heard by twenty-four nobles and privy councillors, advised by common-law judges. Careful arrangements were made for accommodating and feeding such a party. The knights and gentlemen of the county would be allowed in to watch proceedings.

On 21 September, Mary left Chartley for she knew not where, escorted by a band of Protestant gentlemen and men with guns. On a stop in Leicester, the crowd protested her incarceration and made to attack Paulet's carriage, but were driven off. She arrived after a four-day journey, in great pain due to her swollen legs. She had been much reduced but she did travel in state, with twenty baggage carts. She was still entirely unaware that all her letters had been read and intercepted – and so she believed that the evidence against her was only that which came from accusers. She naturally presumed that one of the conspirators had caved and admitted the plot, and then all the names had followed. Other men could say she knew of the plot – but how could they prove it? Her brilliant way of hiding the letters in the beer cask, put into code, meant that no one could have read her letters – and Babington had promised to burn it immediately. Even if he had not, the message had not been in her hand and was written in a code she thought no one could decipher. She was much bowed by her indignities at the hands of Paulet and the others but remained convinced that she could prove her innocence.

Mary was hopeful when she realised she was travelling south, thought she might be moved closer to London and finally receive her day in Parliament to defend herself, her journey there witnessed by all London. Instead, she was told they were not pausing at Fotheringhay but it was her new home. She was to be squirrelled away in the landlocked Midlands. Although Fotheringhay was large, Mary was lodged in a small section and at first wondered at what was now to happen. When she realised that the state rooms were empty, she guessed that she was to be put on trial. Her captors had not even told her this, so afraid were they of her creating a defence or even escaping. By moving her with short notice, not telling her where she was going and then not communicating with her when she arrived, they hoped to disorientate and reduce her completely.

On 1 October, Paulet told her that she was to be interrogated about her crimes by lords and suggested she confess all and beg for forgiveness. She said that 'as queen and sovereign, I am aware of no fault or offence for which I have to render account to anyone here below'.[7] As she could not offend anyone, she would not ask for pardon. Talbot was summoned to judge his old captive. He attempted to plead ill health but Cecil told him sharply that if he did not appear, the world would think that he had truly been Mary's lover.

The Act for the Queen's Safety was the official excuse for putting Mary on trial. But also Elizabeth had finally given in to the demands of her advisors and ministers. For so long, she had resisted the importuning of Parliament that she must try Mary for the death of Darnley, treat her as a common subject, execute her. It had been her great moment of resistance, of maintaining that an anointed queen was above all she surveyed. But now Mary was to be tried – and the very role of queen undermined. When Elizabeth had relented to the articles providing that Mary should be tried by peers if she were found plotting again, she destroyed much of Mary's position and a little of her own. For so long, she and Parliament had fought over sovereignty. She had refused what they had advised her to do. But now it was a fait accompli that she could not refuse. And if we accept that the latter part of the sixteenth century saw Parliament and the state gather more power, much of this was due to Mary and the precedent set by her trial. If a queen could be tried, then what was a queen?

On the 13th, the greatest nobles arrived at the house and others scattered themselves around dwellings nearby. A group of lords including Paulet visited Mary in her privy chamber and gave her a letter from the queen, with the formal information that she would be interrogated, since she persisted in denying the plot of which Elizabeth possessed proof. As she put it, Mary had been guilty of plotting against her in 'the most horrible and unnatural attempt on her life'.[8] Elizabeth justified it by saying that Mary was in England, so must bow to the laws of the country. They wanted to convince Mary that she must come in front of the court.

Mary refused to appear. 'I am a true queen and will do nothing that will prejudice mine own royal majesty, or other princes in my place and rank, or my son.' To her, it was a matter of principle. A queen could not be put on trial. She emphasised that she had come to England of her own volition for help and had been taken captive (this was important to stress for it made it clear that she had not been captured in battle). She told them that she had no papers or notes, did not know the laws of England and 'am alone, without counsel or anyone to speak on my behalf' and 'am destitute of all aid, taken at a disadvantage'. Her dignity and majesty were as impressive as ever. 'My mind is not dejected', she said.[9] Still, the servants took one of her crimson velvet chairs for use in the trial.

Cecil tried again, and when he led a large delegation, he found her yet more majestic. 'I am a queen and not a subject', she said. 'If I appeared, I should betray the dignity and majesty of kings and it would be tantamount to confession that I am bound to submit to the laws of England, even in matters touching religion. I am willing to answer all questions, providing I am interrogated before a free Parliament, and not before these commissioners, who doubtless have been carefully chosen, and who have probably already condemned me unheard.' Her basic point was correct: as a foreign queen, she could not be found guilty of treason. But every part of her trial was unfair: she had no lawyers to advise her before she entered, she had not been allowed to review the evidence, and the place would be packed with those who were vowed against her. 'Look to your consciences and remember that the theatre of the world is wider than the realm of England,' she said. She spoke brilliantly, but Cecil was not turning back now. He told Mary that if she did not appear, she could still be tried in her absence. And her claims of royal blood were as nothing to him. 'The queen, my mistress, knows no other queen in the realm but herself'.¹⁰

Sir Christopher Hatton, future Lord Chancellor and one of the men presiding over the trial, tried to sway Mary by telling her that the best way of proving her innocence was to appear in front of the court. Indeed, Mary herself was deeply protective of her reputation. And, fatally, she thought that the charges against her were circumstantial because she still had no idea that all her letters had been read and deciphered. She did not know that her secretaries had confessed all. Mary asked again to be tried in front of Parliament and made the condition that she should first be acknowledged as Elizabeth's kinswoman and heir to the throne. Cecil lost patience and said that the trial would continue, whether she appeared or not. Elizabeth sent a letter, accusing Mary of planning in 'divers ways and manners to take my life, and to ruin my kingdom by the shedding of blood'. She attacked Mary for ingratitude. 'I never proceeded so harshly against you; on the contrary, I have maintained you and preserved your life with the same care which I use myself.'¹¹ Elizabeth had reduced Mary's allowance, ordered her to lose the entourage, demanded close captivity and no outside access – and finally instructed Paulet to take her remaining money. But she wrote that there was still a chance: 'answer fully, and you may receive greater favour from us'.¹²

Should Mary have refused to speak at the trial? If she had, she would never have had a chance to put her case. And if she had not appeared, she would have been criticised, for it would have been said that she could have avoided a guilty verdict by defending herself. But most importantly, she did not know what evidence they had against her.

Mary agreed to appear before the court and then fainted with the strain.

Chapter Thirty-Four

'Shipwreck of My Soul'

At nine o'clock the next day, Wednesday 15 October 1586, Mary appeared at her trial, dressed in black velvet and a white cap and veil. She limped in, barely able to walk, and her steward Melville and her doctor Bourgoing had to take her arms. Her maid took her train and her surgeon, apothecary and three women came with her, including her favourite, Jane Kennedy and her secretary's sister, Elizabeth Curle. It was the most intimidating court – with a large throne at one end, symbolising Elizabeth, and rows of men watching her. Opposite the throne was Mary's own scarlet velvet chair. Thirty-six noblemen sat in judgement over her fate, including Cecil and Walsingham, as well as Talbot. As Mary moved forward, she presumed she was to sit on the large throne and when she was directed otherwise, she cried out, 'I am a queen by right of birth and my place should be there under the dais.' As she sat down, she noted how there were 'many counsellors here, but not one for me'.[1]

The Lord Chancellor laid out why the court had been convened. Mary refuted once more that the court could rule over a queen and also reminded the peers that she had entered voluntarily 'under promise of assistance and aid, against my enemies and not as a subject', which she said she could prove if she had her papers. The Lord Chancellor denied that Elizabeth had ever promised Mary anything. Strictly speaking, he was right.

Mary refuted the accusations that she had known of the plot and agreed to it, and the further accusation that she had shown the plotters 'the ways and means'. She put on a brilliantly strong defence, saying that 'I knew not Babington. I never received any letters from him, nor wrote any to him. I never plotted the destruction of the queen. If you want to prove it, then produce my letters signed with my own hand.'

When the counsel informed her that they had letters between her and Babington, Mary asked to see them and declared that they could have been forged – as had happened so often in her reign. She felt utterly sure of her position. She said that she could not be blamed for the 'criminal projects of a few desperate men without my knowledge'.

But then the counsel produced copies of the letters: Babington's letter to Mary requesting assistance and offering 'all my private friends, who for the zeal they bear the Catholic cause and your Majesty's service, will undertake that tragical execution'.[2] And then her return, her letter to Babington in which she replied to assent, expressing her concern that the Catholics in England were losing power and her desire to help them 'rise again', making it clear she wished for a Spanish invasion – including the dubiously added postscript asking for names and other information of Babington's friends, the 'six gentlemen'. Their final flourish, their *pièce de résistance*, Walsingham's master stroke: the copy of Mary's letter that the cunning Phelippes had translated back into the code. This was the shock. It showed Mary and the whole court that he and Walsingham had known all. Every time that Mary and her secretaries congratulated themselves, wrote a letter in their careful codes, folded it up in the beer keg – it had been for nothing. Walsingham's men had known every symbol of the code that Mary and her secretaries had produced with such care.

Mary's shock was terrible. Quickly, she understood that someone had betrayed her. But she still fought back and thought on her feet. For the list of ciphers had been taken from her drawers in Astley – it would be easy enough for anyone to forge a letter using one of these. She turned directly to Walsingham and accused him of forgery. He defended himself by saying, 'I have done nothing unbeseeming an honest man.'[3] Mary took it as his acknowledgement that any act of forgery was wrong (really, he was saying that he would do anything for the safety of the queen). Mary burst into tears and cried, 'I would never make shipwreck of my soul by conspiring the destruction of my dearest sister.'[4] She thought that her argument of forgery was succeeding.

The court adjourned for lunch at one, after which the most damning evidence appeared: the words of Mary's secretaries. Mary was shocked and surprised but defended herself with gusto, saying that additions to her letters could have been made – and that she should not be convicted on the words of those who worked for her. And as her secretaries had not been called as witnesses for cross-examination, how could this be fair? The letter had not been written by her hand, either in draft or in code. She suggested that Nau had sometimes added further material of his own to her letters. She generously excused them for 'I see plainly what they have said is from fear of torture and death. Under promise of their lives and in order to save themselves, they have excused themselves at my expense, fancying that I could thereby more easily save myself . . . not knowing the manner in which I am treated.' In other words, her secretaries could never have imagined she would be put on trial. Her words were clear and brilliantly convincing: 'I am not to be convicted except by mine own word or writing.'[5]

Mary's self-defence was strong, confounding at a stroke all John Knox's arguments about women's weaker understanding. She even raised the possibility that Walsingham had fabricated the entire case and intrigued with Ballard and the rest, prompting a somewhat equivocal defence from the spymaster: 'as a private person, I have done nothing unworthy of an honest man, and as a Secretary of State, nothing unbefitted of my duty'. But his audience would have known it not impossible for Walsingham to have invented the whole thing – and Mary sowed some seeds of doubt in their minds.

The queen was surrounded by hostile men on all sides but she kept her dignity, challenging them on every point. Where was their gallantry? And why be so threatened by a middle-aged lady who was in constant pain? As she pointed out, she could barely walk and 'I spend most of my time confined to bed with sickness'. She declared that her age and her poor health 'both prevent me from wishing to resume the reins of government. I have perhaps only two or three years to live in this world, and I do not aspire to any public position, especially when I consider the pain and desperance which meet those who wish to do right.'[6] Most poignantly, she said she barely knew how to be a queen, since she had not reigned for twenty years.

The counsel carried on in trying to prove that she had known and understood and agreed to the death of Elizabeth when she wrote 'then shall it be time to set the six gentlemen to work taking order, upon the accomplishment of their design, I may suddenly be transported out of this place'. The argument turned specific, with Mary claiming she did not know what 'work' the men would be embarked upon. But the very fact that she talked of 'forces in readiness, inside and outside the realm' was enough to prove that she desired an invasion, and she connected it to her freedom – and this was sufficient.[7]

Mary was accused again of having pronounced herself Queen of England, and she said once more that it was done in her youth.

The court was manifestly unfair, but what did it matter? It was sham justice – and Mary had been pitched into it by her reluctance to create the same sham justice after the death of Darnley. She demanded to speak to a full Parliament or in an interview and 'speak personally to the queen, who would, I think, show more regard of another queen'. She said God would judge her correctly.[8]

Everything turned on the evidence of the secretaries and it was clear to Cecil that, if the fig leaf of due process was to be preserved, then they would have to be questioned by the commissioners. Cecil was infuriated by Mary's spirited defence and he did not want her there when the secretaries were questioned. For, confronted by their beautiful, dignified queen to whom both were still devoted, they might very well retract their confessions or claim they had been given under torture. Claude Nau had been with Mary since 1574 and might have been swayed by his old mistress. It would appear that Nau had not only been interrogated and threatened by Walsingham, but also that he had received promises of a safe future – for he would live with Walsingham's family before returning to France. But promises were as nothing, and, with Mary face to face, Nau might have judged that the wrath of the King of France would be too great to risk and thus recant his testimony.

Mary's defence was too effective. The trial turned chaotic as various lords shouted out accusations and Cecil decided to close matters for the evening.

Mary passed a poor night, and next morning asked if she could address the lords directly. She protested how she had suffered accusations from all sides on the previous day, attacked even for claiming the throne of England when she had been a teenager. The lords had broken their agreement, for she had assented only to answer on the point that she had tried to assassinate Elizabeth. As she made clear, it was no fair trial – she had been taken by surprise, deprived of her papers and secretaries and then given no indication of the accusations that would be ranged against her. Unlike her former trial, this time she was guilty, but still she had not been properly treated. She had been attacked and importuned with little other reason than to take her by surprise and try to wrong-foot her into inconsistencies and confessions. Mary's address had an effect – and perhaps some of the gentlemen had thought better of their behaviour overnight. Cecil gave her a polite reply, and during the day's proceedings, declared that while she was being questioned on the issue of the plot to kill Elizabeth, other evidence and issues must be admitted to elucidate the matter. But otherwise, there was nothing new and the lords ran over all the accusations they had posed on the previous day.

Again and again, Mary said she knew nothing of the plots and when Cecil asked her what she would have done in the event of a Spanish invasion, she said she was not responsible for Spanish acts or motivations. 'I desired nothing but my own deliverance', she reiterated. The court tried to accuse her of the blackest crimes – and she said all she had ever wanted was to be free. It did not look good for the government, and Cecil had been right not to stage the trial in London – as public opinion could have swelled in support of the queen. Mary was not above adjusting the truth in the promotion of her own image of a victim of her people's ingratitude and England's cruelty. As she said, she had given too much tolerance to Protestants. 'It has always been the cause of my ruin for my subjects became sad and haughty, and abused my clemency.'[9] The source of her 'ruin' was not tolerating Protestants. In truth, the lords had been used to so much power before her reign that they would have continued to do as they pleased. Although Moray had framed her, she had played into his hands; the source of 'ruin' was her reluctance to publicly chase down the killers of Darnley and put Bothwell on trial. Bothwell had indeed become sad and haughty and terrifically abused her clemency.

The argument dragged on, the watching knights shuffled their heels and Cecil worried that some of the lords might be swayed by Mary. He lost his patience and told her that everything that had happened to her – her period of house arrest, her imprisonment and now her trial – were all her own fault. He even made the outrageously untruthful argument that Elizabeth had been attempting to secure her freedom in conversation with James. 'Ah, I see you are my adversary', said Mary.[10] She was coming to understand that he had been plotting against her all along.

Mary again requested that she be able to speak in front of Parliament and be allowed a private conversation with Elizabeth. She told the lords that she gave them her pardon and turned to give a few words to Walsingham, which did not please him. She faced the assembled lords once more and said that 'I place my cause in the hands of God.' She then departed the room, offering the table of lawyers her pardon as she passed.

Elizabeth had requested that the court did not pronounce before she had reviewed the evidence and Cecil suspended the commission and planned to reconvene more privately, without Mary – the fewer lords present, the less likely anyone would be to be won over by her. Mary, although sick and lame, was still a queen and an orator to rival her cousin. As Paulet complained, Mary had conjured 'long and artificial speeches'[11] in an attempt to throw blame onto the queen and council. She had succeeded in raising doubt in the minds of those around her.

Mary's speeches and conduct at the trial had been incisive and skilled and she was justly proud of herself. She had done all she could – and she was hopeful she would be invited to speak to Parliament. As Bourgoing recalled, 'I had not seen her so joyous, nor so constantly at her ease for the last seven years.'[12]

The commissioners attended the Star Chamber in Westminster on 25 October. Much of the legitimacy now depended on the secretaries, Nau and Curle, who had written the offending letter, and they were brought out in person and questioned at length. All of the nobles, save one, found Mary guilty of 'compassing and imagining since June 1st matters tending to the death and destruction of the Queen of England'.[13] Only Lord Zouche was brave enough to raise objections. Mary had not been allowed to examine the evidence against her or give a full defence against it or use her counsellors to cross-examine those who accused her or implicated her. Even Anne Boleyn, accused of adultery, had been allowed to defend herself. Ultimately, Cecil, the council and

Elizabeth had been cowardly; trying Mary and examining her witnesses when she could not be there. It was a poor reflection on the English courts. And yet, unlike the previous show trial of the casket letters, Mary was guilty.

Chapter Thirty-Five
'We Princes Are Set upon Stages'

Parliament on 29 October was passionate in its accusations against Mary. All the anti-Catholic propaganda was hauled out, along with accusations of the murder of Bothwell and scandalous adultery. But the biggest fight was between Elizabeth and Cecil. Cecil wanted Mary publicly executed, to display Elizabeth's power, discourage any further Babington-type plotters and to prevent a Spanish invasion, once and for all. Elizabeth pushed back. For her, to execute Mary as an action of Parliament was to fatally undermine the value of monarchy. It would implicitly make it possible, due to precedent, for Parliament to kill another monarch. A monarch should be above Parliament, above their sentences, and Parliament should never be allowed to commit regicide. If a king or queen had a divine right to rule – which Elizabeth strongly believed – then they could be brought to death only by God. Moreover, she was worried that if Mary were officially executed under the queen's name, then James might invade, with the help of Spain, to take revenge. The Catholic nobility in England were even more restive, after the violent deaths of young men so many of them had known, and Philip of Spain was watching England closely.[1]

There was also the problem that Mary had denied every word with strength and courage. Ideally, the court would have extracted a full confession that could be used as fit evidence against her. The Elizabethan court was enthusiastic in threatening torture to those accused, but although Mary had suffered every other possible threat and privation in England, to suggest torturing a queen was simply impossible. But Mary had not broken under the sustained attacks at Fotheringhay and there was little else they could do. The one person Mary might have been induced to give a confession to was Elizabeth herself – but the queen was adamant that she would not meet her 'dear cousin'. Still, on the order of Walsingham, Paulet did his best to make Mary's life a misery, interrupting her prayers, criticising her and refusing supplies. When Mary asked about a few lords in whom she had detected sympathy, Paulet refused to give details. 'Not one of them was favourable to your cause', he snapped and continued by declaring how 'everyone' (not that he had any idea) was surprised at how calm she was: 'No living person has ever been accused of crimes as frightful and odious as yours.' Paulet was hoping for hysteria, from which he might be able to extract an admission of guilt, but Mary was too strong to bend under his verbal assaults. 'I see no change in her, from her former quietness and serenity', he complained. He begged Walsingham to release him from his miserable task of attacking Mary for 'I do not see that any good can come of it.'[2]

In Scotland, the people were shocked to see Elizabeth and Cecil putting their queen on trial and were horrified that the English queen might execute Mary. James was reluctant to intervene and knew that Elizabeth expected his support. But his advisors warned him that he faced insurrection if he did not attempt to defend his mother. James complained to Elizabeth that he would be in danger if 'this disaster being perfected since before God I already scarce dare go abroad, for crying out of the whole people'.[3] A confession might have stayed the people's passion but Mary was refusing to relent. James issued threats and expressed panic to England but he did not perform the one act he had in his power to save his mother: threaten to break the alliance with Elizabeth. If he had switched and made a union with France, which had protested the proposed execution, it would have been deeply worrying to Elizabeth. But James did little, complained and rumbled, nothing more.

Parliament was baying for Mary's blood. Elizabeth had two refuges in times of great political import: ambiguity and refusal to decide. She deployed these cleverly in a superb speech in Parliament in which she reminded her troublesome nobles that they might demand the execution of the queen, but it was Elizabeth who would have to enact the death – and then be held responsible for it by the world. As she put it so brilliantly, 'we princes are sent as it were upon stages, in the sight and view of all the world'. Parliament had won in its desire to put Mary on trial, but the queen was fighting back. She later asked if there could not be a way in which Mary was left to live.

But Parliament was moving without Elizabeth's knowledge. Lord Buckhurst and Beale, the clerk of the council, came to Mary on 19 November and told her that she and Elizabeth could not live in the same country. They proposed she repent, and suggested the Dean of Peterborough might receive her words. If they had hoped for a confession, they would have been better offering her a Catholic clergyman clandestinely. Mary refused to speak to the Dean and presented herself as a martyr, 'the necessary instrument for the re-establishment of religion in this island'. Paulet spitefully demanded her servants tear down her cloth of state, which she was still bravely keeping up, with awful words: 'You are now only a dead woman, without the dignity or honours of a queen.'[4] Her servants stood back and Paulet's men removed it, also demanding the billiard table, for Mary surely had no time for amusing herself. Even he felt he had gone too far and offered next morning to ask the council if the cloth might be put back. Mary shook her head. She had put her crucifix in its place.

Elizabeth had given up hoping that Mary might die of natural causes and she had come to accept that Mary must be put to death. But her desire was that it would be done by one of the individuals who had signed the Bond for the Queen's Safety. She wanted Mary killed privately so it could not rebound on her and so that regicide did not become part of parliamentary precedent. Cecil said there wasn't time to add an indication of the importance of a private act of killing to the Act for the Queen's Safety (there was).[5] And it was not easy to find an individual who would agree to slaughtering Mary. English nobles were happy to sit in kangaroo courts and engage in plots and subterfuge. But all-out murder, whether they twisted the knife or hired an assassin, was shocking and it had something in it of the death of Darnley. Wisely, they refused – for if they were to kill Mary, then the responsibility would be theirs and Philip of Spain might hunt them down or Elizabeth herself might turn against them. Murder, for an English aristocrat, was simply too much. The state had put the court into motion and the state must enact its findings.

Mary, meanwhile, was still at Fotheringhay and she was better than she had been in some time. She was pleased by her spirited defence at the court and discussed it over and over again. It seemed to her as if she had won. Elizabeth would not dare execute her on such privately reviewed, shaky evidence. Paulet reported that she was contented, 'taking pleasure in trifling toys and in the whole course of her speech free from grief of mind'.[6] Her rooms at Fotheringhay were not uncomfortable and – she thought – she had escaped condemnation. Always, she invested great hope in the notion that her sister would rescue her, tempted by feminine sympathy, two women in a man's world. She must have believed that if she behaved herself from now on, she would be safe. She occupied herself with embroidery, prayer and hoping for escape. But Fotheringhay was now fortified by seventy soldiers and fifty bowmen, just in case a gallant supporter considered raising an army for her.

Finally, on 4 December, Mary was publicly declared guilty of treason against Elizabeth. But still, there was no execution. Elizabeth remained resistant and worried about inviting foreign invasion. Cecil and Walsingham began to stir up talk of an attack by Philip of Spain, declaring that another assassination plot had been discovered and that Spanish forces were nearing Wales. The 'Stafford Plot' was revealed, a conspiracy of a young gentleman, William Stafford, whose mother was Mistress of the Robes to Elizabeth. He planned to put barrels of gunpowder in his mother's room, which was under Elizabeth's, so that 'the queen could be blown up'. Stafford was put in the tower for a year and half but never tried and executed – for most likely he had been in the pay of Walsingham and the wild claims had all been set up in order to encourage Elizabeth to finally sign for Mary's death. The English queen was mired in emotion and indecision. She confessed to the French ambassador that she had never wept so much, not even for the deaths of her father, brother or sister.

In mid-December, Mary asked her jailers to give a letter to Elizabeth. In 1561, Mary had written to Elizabeth about not having safe passage, declaring if she 'be so hard-hearted as to desire my end, she may then do her pleasure and make sacrifice of me'. She had travelled regardless and Elizabeth had relented and given her a passport. All her life, Mary had talked about death and threatened to die as a strategy. Here, she did it when the stakes were highest. She raised the possibility of the practical measures for her death – in the hope that Elizabeth would be so horrified that she would take steps to help her.

Mary begged, if she were killed, for Elizabeth to allow her servants to transport her body to France, not Scotland, for she wished for a proper Catholic burial. She expressed her fear of a secret killing by those around her and pleaded to be allowed to send a final letter to James, with a jewel as a present. She wiped the sheets of paper on her face to show they were not poisoned and sealed the whole thing up with white silk. Although she had never met Elizabeth, her final sentence was perfectly judged to affect the queen. 'Do not accuse me of presumption if, on the eve of leaving this world and preparing myself for a better one, I remind you that one day you will have to answer for your charge.' She signed off, 'your sister and cousin, wrong-fully accused'.[7]

How could Elizabeth's heart not be swayed? Paulet was so afraid that the letter would push the queen to mercy that he delayed sending it. He suggested to the secretary of the council that Mary was executed forthwith and so the letter would arrive when it was too late for Elizabeth to relent. It was sent, but if Elizabeth received it, she did not reply. Mary wrote again after a miserable Christmas asking for Elizabeth to give her clarity and talked of confiding her secrets. It was a clever stroke, the best possible attempt at encouraging Elizabeth to come to visit her – the promise of a possible confession or secrets that would be most useful to know. But this time Paulet did refuse to send the letter, on the basis that he had no orders to do so. He was desperate for Mary to be executed and to be set free of his role as jailer. In late January 1587, he informed Mary that she must lose the attendance of her chaplain and Melville as her steward – she would be allowed only Bourgoing, as her doctor, from her senior attendants. There was no direction from Cecil, and Paulet had given up attempting to extract a confession. He simply hated Mary, resented her as his ball and chain and wanted her to suffer.

Elizabeth continued to fret about the horror of executing her cousin and the vengeance that might be wreaked by Catholic Europe. In late December, she had asked for the execution warrant to be drawn up for her to sign. But she did not touch it.

Further rumours spread of invasion and uprising in January, and the reports were coloured in by Walsingham and Cecil before they gave them to Elizabeth. As Walsingham put it, 'False bruits were spread abroad that the Queen of Scots was broken out of prison, that the City of London was fired, that many thousand Spaniards were landed in Wales . . . The stir and confusion was great; such as I think happened not in England these hundred years past.'[8]

It was almost beyond belief that Mary could escape her dank, heavily guarded castle. But still they feared her. Out of the two major plots in which she was involved, the Babington plot was definitely engineered by Walsingham and it was very likely that the Ridolfi one bore the marks of his hand too. She was, as Talbot's son had said, as trapped and powerless as a flea. But it was all too easy for ministers to blame the violence and unrest on Mary and believe that the only way to free the country of threat was to execute her. With the full weight of her council, ministers and many of her people ranged in support of the execution, it is astonishing that Elizabeth held out for so long.

The queen called for the execution warrant. William Davison, secretary of the council, gave it to her on 1 February along with a pile of other papers that required signature, to soften the blow. Elizabeth signed it at Greenwich, asking Davison if he was relieved to finally see her signature. She said that the execution must not be public. To see it now, in the Lambeth Palace archives where a copy is kept, is astonishing. The document so long discussed, weighed over, agonised over, is little more than a few paragraphs. The first word is 'Elizabeth', making it clear that no matter what Parliament decreed, only she could order the execution.

The warrant was written in the form of a letter to the earls of Shrewsbury, Derby, Cumberland, Kent and Pembroke. Mary was to be executed because she was a 'continuall danger' – to the realm, the church and Elizabeth. As the warrant put it:

All the Estates in the last Parliament assembled did not onlie deliberatlie with greate advice allowe and approve the same sentences as just and honourable, but did also with all humbleness and trustiness possible at sundrie times require, sollicite and press us to proceed to the publishing of the same and thereupon to direct such further execution against her person as they did adjudge her to have dulie deserved adding thereto that the forbearing thereof was and would be dailie a certaine and undoubted danger not onlie to our own life but to themselves, their posterities and the public state of this realme, as well for the cause of the gospel and the true religion of Christ, as for the peace of the whole realme.[9]

The warrant noted that there was 'some delaye of time' until the sentence was published and that 'we have hitherto forborne to give direction for the further satisfaction of the foresaid most earnest requeste made by the said Estates of our Parliament'. Elizabeth was only doing so now due to the begging of her people,

all sortes of our lovinge subjects both of our nobilitie and Counsel and also of the wisest gravest and best devoted of all other our subjects of inferior degrees, how greatlie and deeplie from the bottoms of their hartes they are grieved, afflicted with dailie and hourlie fear of our life and thereby consequentlie with a dreadful doubt and expectation of the ruine of this present godlie and happy estate of this realme if we shall forbeare the further final execution as it is desired and neglect their general and continuall requestes prayers counsels and advice. And thereupon contrarie to our natural disposition in such a Case being overcome with the evident weight of their counsels and the dailie continuance of their intercessions.[10]

Elizabeth repeated herself. She did not wish to do it. Her 'natural disposition' was to refrain. But her Parliament and all her people were constantly begging her to carry out the act. It was a letter both to her people – those who, like Cecil, believed that killing the Queen of Scots would put an end to England's problems and insecurities – and also to the world: her excuse was she could not help what she did.

Yet still, she did not wish her country to execute a queen. She begged for Mary to be quietly assassinated behind closed doors and a request was sent to Paulet. He replied swiftly from Fotheringhay on 2 February that he would never do such a thing and he even went so far as to chide Elizabeth for even asking. As he wrote:

I am so unhappy to have lived to see this unhappy day, in the which I am required, by direction from my most gracious Sovereign, to do an act which God and the law forbiddeth . . . God forbid that I should make so fowle a shipwracke of my conscience, or leave so great a blot to my posteritie, or shed blood without law or warrant . . . thus I commit you to the mercy of the Almightie.[11]

Paulet, although cruel to Mary without end, had too many scruples to commit the ultimate act. He was quite right on his own accord, for it was very possible that France and Spain could protest and Elizabeth would have him arrested and put on trial for killing Mary.

The warrant was taken to be sealed by the Lord Chancellor and then to Walsingham. He had already ordered his servant to find an executioner and Mr Bull was quickly escorted to Fotheringhay, his axe in a trunk, dressed as an ordinary servant. Sir Walter Mildmay refused to have him stay at his house and so Mr Bull and his axe were given rooms at a Fotheringhay inn.

The next morning, Elizabeth told Davison that she had suffered a terrible dream about the death of her cousin and told him to delay affixing the seal to the warrant. He told her that it had already been done and Elizabeth passed no further comment. Perhaps she thought that her councillors would come to her again before enacting a document of such vital import.

When the queen had signed the warrant for the Duke of Norfolk in 1572, she had promptly revoked it and he had remained in the Tower until she changed her mind again, five months later. This time she did not withdraw the warrant.[12]

Yet Elizabeth later said that she had signed the warrant only as a surety and had never meant it to be carried through. Certainly, everyone around her moved fast once they had her signature, because they thought there was a possibility she might rescind.

Cecil wanted the matter settled. He gathered a secret Privy Council meeting on 3 February, without the knowledge of the queen, and talked of the execution. They decided to enact it immediately without telling Elizabeth, declaring it was 'neither fit nor convenient to trouble her Majesty further'.[13] Beale, the clerk of the council, was given it and sent to Fotheringhay. The queen was to be kept in the dark and not told 'until it were done'.[14] It was, to them, essential to the safety of Elizabeth and, as Walsingham put it from his sickbed, 'the universal quietness of the realm'. Mary's old friend Talbot was to be tasked with enacting her execution, along with the Earl of Kent and Derby.

Chapter Thirty-Six
'I Am Ready'

There is no document that specifies the order of the execution, who must do it and how the hall should be arranged. Was there ever such a thing? Cecil had been obsessive about the details of the trial, who should sleep where and who should stand where in the building. Surely he couldn't have left the execution to chance? The document must have been lost or more likely destroyed; the document in which was laid out how to execute a queen.

Mary had no idea what was about to occur. But on Tuesday 7 February, news came through of arrivals at the castle, including Talbot and Kent, and the household was thrown into apprehension. Bourgoing suspected the worst.

On that Tuesday evening, Mary had eaten and was preparing for bed when Kent and Talbot arrived in her chamber, along with Robert Beale, who had been sent to find them and deliver the execution warrant. Mary asked for time to dress and received them in her room. Beale read the warrant to her and Mary spoke with dignity and clarity. 'You will do me much good in withdrawing me from this world out of which I am very glad to go.' She placed her hand on the Bible and declared herself innocent of all crimes. Kent complained that it was a Catholic Bible and Mary nimbly pointed out that her oath on a 'translation in which I do not believe' was not going to be 'more true'.[1] It was a fair point and Kent desisted from further protests.

She feared an assassination and was reassured by Drury, assistant to Paulet, who told her gently that she would be killed properly in front of noble witnesses since she was a 'Christian queen'.

Mary asked for the attendance of her chaplain to receive her confession and give her his blessing and the Last Sacrament, but she was brutally denied. Instead, they informed her she should receive, in her words, 'the consolation and instruction of their minister brought here for that purpose' – the Dean of Peterborough.[2] She was heartbroken at the blow and it must have been doubly painful to receive it from her old friend, Talbot.

She asked if she might be buried in France near her first husband or her mother. Talbot said that it would be impossible for her to be buried there, taking yet another comfort from her. She knew then that it would be unlikely she would receive a Catholic funeral. She asked for her papers and account books, to set matters in order and compose her will, but again she was refused.

Mary received her sentence with grace. She had once said that all she had was her religion and her royal blood. Now, with her death, she could die a martyr to the Catholic religion and perhaps she would be avenged in death as she had not been in life. 'In the name of God these tidings are welcome', she said. 'I bless and praise Him that the end of all my bitter sufferings is at hand. I did not think that the queen, my sister, would have ever consented to my death, but God's will be done. He is my principal witness, that I shall render up my spirit into His hands innocent of any offence against her, and with a pure heart and conscience clear before His divine majesty of the crimes whereof I am accused.'[3]

Her skill at oratory, her brilliant charm, was not undimmed. She spoke about her own claim to the throne and how her cousin had never agreed to see her. Her final thoughts were still of Elizabeth.

If her kinswoman had failed her, God was still her support. 'I am quite ready and very happy to die, and to shed my blood for Almighty God, my Saviour and my Creator, and for the Catholic Church, and to maintain its rights in this country.' She would die for the church. Elizabeth and Cecil had been right not to have Mary at the Tower and publicly executed. Such sentiments were wildly incendiary.

She asked for a little time to put her affairs in order but was told she must die and her death 'cannot be delayed'.[4] Where had this instruction come from? Elizabeth's death warrant only said that Talbot, Kent and Derby must make to Fotheringhay at their earliest convenience, with no further detail. Her death was to be at eight o'clock in the morning, and there was barely the opportunity to ready anything.

Mary's servants begged the men for mercy and to allow Mary more time. Bourgoing reminded Talbot that he had once relieved his ill health.[5] It was to no avail. They wanted Mary executed as soon as possible – presumably before Elizabeth had a chance to find out what was happening and halt proceedings.

The men departed, leaving the servants heartbroken and weeping. Mary tried to comfort them. 'Did I not tell you this would happen', she said to Jane Kennedy, 'I knew they would never allow me to live, I was too great an obstacle to their religion.'[6] She was given a little food, the servants sobbing as they brought dishes to her.

She had been denied the papers which she would need to write a full will distributing all her properties and possessions but devoted herself to doing what she could, appointing her cousin Henry, Duke of Guise as executor, and directed her debts to be paid, her servants to be rewarded and Masses to be said for her soul in France. She then looked over her wardrobes and cabinets and distributed her effects to her gentlewomen and servants. She gave Bourgoing silver boxes, two lutes, her music book and her red valances and bed curtains. The miniature gold guns she had sent her secretary to give to James were given to her surgeon and other gifts she had meant for her son to her grooms. She made bequests to the poor and divided her remaining money between her servants, asking that her coach and horses be sold for their travel expenses.

She sat down to write her final goodbye, to her brother-in-law and once childhood playmate, the little boy she had babied when she was growing up in France, Henry III. She wrote to her 'royal brother' how she wished to be remembered as a queen who died for the Catholic faith. She was desperately regretful of ever trusting Elizabeth.

Royal brother, having by God's will, for my sins I think, thrown myself into the power of the queen, my cousin, at whose hands I have suffered so much for almost twenty years, I have finally been condemned to death by her and her Estates. I have asked for my papers, which they have taken away, in order that I might make my will, but I have been unable to recover anything of use to me, or even get leave either to make my will freely or to have my body conveyed after my death, as I would wish, to your kingdom, where I had honour to be queen, your sister and old ally.[7]

If only she had remained in France, the place of her happiness, a dowager queen and a widow at court. A life of embroidering with Catherine de' Medici would have been signally without event but yet her life would have been preserved.

Tonight, after dinner, I have been advised of my sentence. I am to be executed like a criminal at eight in the morning. I have not had time to give you a full account of everything that has happened, but if you will listen to my doctor and my other unfortunate servants, you will learn the truth, and how, thanks be to God, I scorn death and vow that I meet it innocent of any crime, even if I were their subject. The Catholic faith and the assertion of my God-given right to the English throne are the two issues on which I am condemned, and yet I am not allowed to say that it is for the Catholic religion that I die, for fear of any interference with theirs.

She begged him to pay the wages of her servants that were in arrears and to commemorate her as a Catholic queen, asking him to have 'prayers offered to God for a queen who has herself been called Most Christian, and who dies a Catholic stripped of all her possessions. As for my son, I commend him to you inasmuch as he deserves it, for I cannot answer for him.'

She asked that her chaplain, de Preau, be given a small benefice in France, from where he could offer prayers for Mary's soul. She sent the king two precious stones from her collections, 'talismans against illness, trusting you will enjoy good health and a long and happy life'. It was her final farewell. She signed it 'Marie, Queen of Scotland', the last time she would ever write herself as such.[8] She did not write a final letter to Elizabeth or her son. She had now accepted that there was nothing they could do for her. As she was writing, guards lined up outside her room, marching back and forth. Paulet had doubled the men, just in case Mary managed to escape at the last moment. Downstairs, the men were hammering up the scaffold. Mr Bull arrived and sharpened his axe.

When Mary finally completed the letter, it was long past two in the morning. Her gentlewomen were busy preparing her clothing for the next day and Mary lay down and attempted to rest. She asked Jane Kennedy to read to her, asking for the life of a great sinner. Kennedy chose that of the good thief, crucified on the cross next to Jesus – who had asked Jesus to remember him in heaven. Even with Jane's soothing voice, the queen could not sleep and when the candles were lit for morning at six, it was a relief. She dressed and then asked her servants to assemble in her presence, where her will was read; she signed it and knelt to pray. Bourgoing persuaded her to take a little bread and wine. A messenger came for her, and shouted that the lords awaited her, but Mary asked for more time to pray.[9]

The prayers were scarcely completed before the sheriff of Northamptonshire and the Earl of Shrewsbury knocked violently on the door. They had come to escort her to the great hall where she had been tried. Mary met them with dignity and moved forward, holding her ivory crucifix. Her secretary reminded her to take her prayer book and she received it from him. She kissed the crucifix and moved to the men. Outside, spectators were arriving to watch the queen die.

Mary, who had worn so many magnificent gowns, had dazzled the world in white at the grand wedding to the dauphin, was now in black satin embroidered with black velvet figures, with sleeves that passed to the ground, set with buttons of jet and trimmed with pearl. Her beautiful wig, as auburn and handsome as her hair had once been, was tied into a veil of white lawn which flowed to the ground. She wore as her headdress a pomander chain and an Agnus Dei and around her neck she had a golden crucifix and a pair of beads at her girdle bearing a medal. She was every inch the queen and the Catholic martyr.

At the door, she was told that her servants could not attend her and she must die alone. Mary asked why she was not permitted attendants and she was told that Elizabeth had commanded it since her servants might scream out and cry 'and trouble you and us' or try to seize her blood 'and keep it for a relic and minister offence that way'. Mary promised that her servants would remain quiet. 'Alas, poor souls,' said Mary, 'it would do them good to bid me farewell.'[10] She recalled that other gentleladies were accompanied by their attendants and said she could not credit that Elizabeth would expect a queen to die without her ladies to assist her – for without her ladies, she would be undressed by the executioner. Kent relented, presumably because he had never been given such orders in the first place. But still, the words had been spoken and Mary went to her death not knowing if Elizabeth had decreed her immediate execution and ordered the cruel touch of forbidding her servants. Mary moved forward with Melville, Bourgoing and two other men, and Jane Kennedy and her secretary's sister, Elizabeth Curle. She had another companion too; her tiny dog had followed her down the stairs and hidden under her skirts, without anyone noticing. While the queen was preparing to die, men across England were shutting up the ports. Walsingham and Cecil wanted to prevent the news from reaching France.

As Mary entered the hall, she saw her final stage – about five feet in height and seven feet around. Three hundred spectators had crammed in to watch.

The block was in the centre, covered in black, and behind it was a small stool for Mary to sit on while she was disrobed. Mr Bull was standing upon the stage with his axe. There were stools for Talbot and Kent on either side. The sheriff and various knights were standing around the stage. Mary kept her composure and walked forward. Her ladies, Jane and Elizabeth, immediately burst into tears but Mary told them to stop since she had promised the lords they would be 'quiet and not offend them'. She gave her speech, reminding those assembled that 'all this world is but vanity and full of troubles and sorrows. Carry this message from me and tell my friends that I died a true woman to my religion, and like a true Scottish woman and a true French woman; but God forgive them that have long desired my end and thirsted for my blood.'[11]

Mary walked majestically to the block, where she heard the commission for her execution read out and then was met by Dr Fletcher, Dean of Peterborough, who told her that the 'queen his sovereign, moved with an unspeakable care of her soul, had sent him to instruct her and comfort her in the words of God'. Poor Mary, suffering attempted humiliations right until the end.[12] Her rosary was taken from her. She proudly refused to listen to the Protestant dean. 'I will have nothing to do with you or your doctrine,' she said and bowed to the block. Talbot then instructed her he would pray with her. Mary told the Protestant Dean he should 'pray secretly, by yourself, for I will not pray with you'. She kissed her two ladies, told her men to remember her to her son, promised to pray for him in heaven, and wished goodbye to her servants. The Dean was praying loudly but Mary ignored him and said her own prayers yet louder in Latin and then in English, asking blessings for the church, her son and for Elizabeth. The tears ran down her face as she prayed.

As was custom, Mr Bull and his assistants asked for Mary's forgiveness. She replied, 'I forgive you with all my heart, for I now hope you should make an end of all my troubles.'[13] Her ladies helped her to undress, with the assistance of the executioner, and removed her black dress and veil, revealing her scarlet petticoat, red sleeves and red satin bodice. She was clothed in the colours of blood and Catholic martyrdom. She had often been denied her voice – and now her clothes would speak for her. Her ladies wept to behold her. Mr Bull and his assistants asked for the queen's jewellery, which was their right.

The executioners took hold of her and Mary refused to be frightened, instead smiling out and saying, 'I never had two such grooms waiting on me before!' Jane took her handkerchief, embroidered in gold, and bound it around Mary's eyes and she and Elizabeth left their mistress, giving her a final touch in farewell. Fletcher, still determined to win, tried again, informing her she must die in the true faith of Christ. Mary was steadfast. 'I believe firmly to be saved by the passion and blood of Jesus Christ, and therein also I believe, according to the faith of the Ancient Catholic Church of Rome, and therefore I shed my blood.'[14]

Mary knelt down and spoke a psalm in Latin, then, groping for the block because she could not see it, laid her head down in position, holding her hands to her face. In Latin, she commended herself to God. One executioner reached down to hold her steady while the other brought up the axe. The executioner's hands on her were unnecessary. She did not move as the axe was brought down. Mr Bull was nervous. The first hit smite the back of the head and the queen's lips were seen to move. The second was better: he took the whole head, leaving nothing but a small sinew, which he then cut by using the axe as a saw.[15]

Some say Mr Bull held up her head by her hair, not realising it was a wig, and so the head fell to the ground. It was reported that her lips continued to move for a quarter of an hour after the execution. The Dean pronounced, 'So perish all the queen's enemies,' and Kent uttered similar words.[16] The men filed out of the hall, congratulating themselves on a job well done. Mary's poor wasted body was left on the stage, and the executioners began to strip it, as was customary. Under the petticoats, they found Mary's small dog, cowering and covered in blood, holding tight to the still-warm body of its long-tormented mistress.

The body was treated with no dignity, wrapped in the rough wool covering that had been over the queen's own billiard table and deposited in the presence chamber. Every piece of the queen's property was taken and burnt and even Mr Bull was deprived of Mary's jewels, as the officers wanted them destroyed. Mindful of Mary's declaration that she wished to be a martyr, they were ensuring that nothing remained that might be used as a relic. The queen's heart and organs were removed and the sheriff buried them deep under Fotheringhay Castle.

Chapter Thirty-Seven
'An Abundance of Tears'

The servants had been sent back to Mary's rooms to order her belongings, but some were too great to be moved. The many unfinished pieces of embroidery were taken away. The cloth of state that Mary had been so proud of was left to grow dusty and neglected in a storeroom, 'upon its front in letters of fading gold', '*En ma fin est mon commencement*': In my end is my beginning. Jane, Elizabeth, Melville, Bourgoing and the rest were imprisoned in the castle and not permitted to return home, contrary to what Mary had requested. Walsingham was too afraid of their emotive accounts reaching the outside world. In the haste to avoid anything becoming a relic, the block was burned but Mr Bull was permitted to take his axe, to be used on the next person who had fallen on the wrong side of the government.

Talbot sent his son, post-haste, to London with the death certificate. The news had a cataclysmic effect. Cecil was sent to Elizabeth and she fell into shock and 'cursed Burghley [i.e. Cecil], heaped obloquy on Davison and cried out that Marie had been executed against her will'.[1] She immediately retired to her bed, wept in 'an abundance of tears', said she would wear mourning and told Davison he had acted wrongly, that the execution decree had never meant to be enacted and she sent him to the Tower in fury. She declared she had only signed it as a back-up measure and she had given it to Davison for safekeeping only. She threatened her council that she would put them all in the Tower.

She wrote to James:

My dear Brother, I would you knew (though not felt) the extreme dolour that overwhelms my mind, for that miserable accident which (far contrary to my meaning) hath befallen . . . I beseech you that as God and many more know, how innocent I am in this case . . . I am not so base-minded that fear of any living creature or prince should make me afraid to do that were just; or done, or deny the same. I am not of so base a lineage, nor carry so vile a mind.[2]

An envoy was sent to tell James to reiterate her points of 'how innocent I am'.

Cecil told Elizabeth to mute her protests – for if there were any suggestion that Mary had been killed illegally and against the will of the queen, there could be serious consequences. France and Spain might attack. Elizabeth might have shown her sorrow by allowing Mary's body to be sent to France or even simply providing for her servants to be freed. She did not. Still, she demanded Davison pay the impossible fine of £10,000 and banished Cecil from her presence and called him 'false dissembler and wicked wretch'.[3] Cecil had to beg for mercy, offering to lie at her feet, and was not admitted back into favour until March.

In Scotland, James was publicly grieving but privately calm – he had never known his mother, after all. There were some rumours that he even happily rejoiced in being 'sole king'. But there were furious raids across the border by noblemen half mad with grief, and Elizabeth was insulted as a Jezebel, a witch and a whore on the streets of Edinburgh.

The ports were closed for nearly three weeks. The King of France received the news in early March. He was enraged, refused to see the English ambassador, arrested Elizabeth's couriers and impounded English vessels at port. A requiem Mass for the royal family was held at Notre-Dame in March and the preacher looked up at the black-draped walls and spoke with emotion. He talked of 'the axe of a low executioner spoiling the body of she who was two times a queen, the form that had graced the nuptial bed of a sovereign of France, falling dishonoured on a scaffold'. Even a year later, Walsingham said he was editing reports from France to remove the worst of the protest as he feared they would increase Elizabeth's fury with her Privy Council. Among the emotive pamphlets was one that claimed that Dudley had rushed to her in his nightgown and begged her not to execute Mary without a proper trial or 'show of justice'.

After all the claims that killing Mary was the way to make England safe, the death seemed to have done the exact opposite.

And Philip was only emboldened. He gathered his fighting men and his high-powered galleons and his stores of cannon for the blow that would destroy Protestant England for good. In late 1568, Philip's wife, Elisabeth of Valois, the old playmate of Mary in the French nursery, who had long expressed sympathy for the captive queen, died of a miscarriage. As Philip's confessor told him, he must 'avenge the wrongs done to God and to the world by that woman, above all in the execution of the Queen of Scotland'.

After death, Mary's body was put into a lead coffin and kept until the end of July, when Elizabeth ordered a burial in Peterborough Cathedral, in the same church which held Catherine of Aragon, another woman who had fallen foul of the graces of the monarch. The dreaded Dr Fletcher presided and had his revenge for Mary's refusal to listen to him on the scaffold, reminding the congregation of the adultery and murder charges and portraying the execution as having been committed by the hand of God, in order to pay Mary for killing her husband. He even declared that good weather on the execution day reflected God's approval. 'The day being fair did, as it were, show favour from Heaven and commended the justice, the eighth day of February, that judgement was repaid home to her, which . . . she measured to her husband.' Her servants were permitted out of captivity to attend the burial. The Bishop of Lincoln quoted Martin Luther, 'Many one liveth a Papist and dieth a Protestant.' It was a weak attempt at suggesting Mary converted at the last minute – which would have been the most brilliant propaganda coup for the English. Unfortunately for them, the news of Mary's grace under pressure, royal dignity and presentation of herself as a Catholic martyr was beginning to reach Europe – to cataclysmic effect. The Catholic League was emboldened and France began to look more kindly on the belligerent ambitions of Scotland.

★

Elizabeth had signed Mary's execution warrant and now she was free from the threat of Mary claiming her throne. But the execution hardened Philip's resolve to invade Britain with the Spanish Armada – the invasion that Mary had so long awaited, hoped for. Elizabeth was determined to teach Philip a lesson after what she saw as his consistent support of Mary's claim. She had backed the Dutch revolt against Spain, in which the Protestant territories of the Low Countries rebelled against Spanish rule. She had needled him by sending her privateers to chase Spanish ships as they crossed the world. She had sent Francis Drake to sack New World ports Philip claimed as his, and English ships were always disrupting Spanish trade. In the year after the death of Mary, the relationship between Philip and Elizabeth, once mooted as marriage partners, descended into bitter war. Philip intensified his desires to invade England, supported by the Pope, who decided it was a Catholic crusade. Elizabeth sent Francis Drake again to lead a pre-emptive strike and he attacked Cadiz in April 1587 and destroyed supplies and thirty ships. But Philip was determined, and on 28 May 1588, the Spanish Armada of 130 ships, 8,000 sailors and 18,000 soldiers sailed out from Lisbon. The rescuers that Mary had so long hoped for were coming, but more than a year too late. The engagement began in July, and on 8 August, Elizabeth travelled to Tilbury to speak to her forces, delivering the famed speech that declared 'I have the body of a weak and feeble woman, but I have the heart and stomach of a king'. Scholars rage over its authenticity, chiefly because it seems almost too good to be true. But current scholarship vouches for its truth.[4] In it, Elizabeth drew the brilliant comparison between the body of the queen and the body of the realm. Both were impregnable and pure.

The English forces were victorious and the Gloriana vision became all-powerful. But the brave sailors were struck down by a terrible bout of typhoid that swept the fleet after the victory, and Elizabeth, chary of spending, never actually paid those who survived and many ended up begging on the streets of port towns. However, the victory had been won and Protestant England could declare that God shone down upon her. And yet, although the Spanish could not regain control of the Channel or frighten Elizabeth off meddling in the Netherlands, they still reigned supreme on the trade routes across the Atlantic and in the Caribbean, and even Elizabeth's most intrepid pirates could gain no toehold in their Spanish Empire. Elizabeth and Philip would continue to fight, sapping resources and lives, until the queen's death.

By 1603, Elizabeth was sixty-nine and very ill, cast down by infirmity and sadness at the deaths of so many friends. When her advisor, Robert Cecil, son of William, told her she should go to bed, she replied sharply that 'Must is not a word to use for princes, little man.' But princes had to die. She took to her bed. Her coronation ring had to be cut off her badly swollen finger, which to her ministers was a gloomy omen, as if her marriage with the state was about to end. By March, she was struggling to eat or sleep, in constant pain, sitting motionless on a cushion for days. But still she would not name a successor, resistant to giving anyone the assent she had so long withheld. In the middle of the month, she refused to eat, bathe or be put to bed – for she thought if she went to bed, she would never rise again. She lay, dressed, on cushions on the floor, refusing to move. But her courtiers forced her to undress and go to her bed – even at the end, kings could not die as they wished. Robert Cecil had been negotiating secretly with James about taking the throne and he was ready to come. On 23 March, Elizabeth could no longer speak. The Privy Council came to see her and asked her outright if she agreed to James succeeding her. She lifted up her hand, which was taken as assent. They departed and left her to her ladies and ministers. In the early morning of 24 March, she breathed her last.

James VI was now king of Scotland, England and Wales. He was welcomed to London with enthusiasm. He was the beginning of a new dynasty, the Stuarts, and his son, Charles I, would lose his head to the English state, as James's mother had done before him. James, buffeted by the battles for power, pushed about as a child, even kidnapped by his nobles when he came to his majority, was now a great believer in the divine right of kings. As he said, 'Kings are justly called Gods' for they had the same power as God, of 'raising and casting down, of life and death, judge over all their subjects and in all causes and yet account-able to none but God only'.[5] Mary had believed the same, but instead of being like God, able to 'judge all and to be judged not accountable to none', she had been deprived of the royal role of dispenser of justice, instead judged by all on proofs she was not even allowed to see. It was hardly surprising, after how she had been treated, that her son clung to the dream of divine right, passing it down to subsequent Stuart kings, but the work of Elizabeth's reign had been done: in the end, with the death of Charles I, Parliament was greater than the monarch. Elizabeth had wished not to die in her bed, but was forced to do so. Although the men of state tried to deprive Mary of everything she had wished for, surprised her into execution, she still managed, with her dress and final words, to be remembered as the martyr Elizabeth's men had dreaded, and to direct her own death, which is usually forbidden to all of us, even kings.

Fotheringhay Castle was left to crumble and was sold off. Nothing remains of it now but a mound under the grass and a few pieces of stone.

'The English love queens,' said the mother of the future Queen Victoria, on Victoria's birth. But they did not love Mary, Queen of Scots. Her life was a series of failures and bloody, breathtaking betrayals. Some of them she contributed to in part, thanks to folly, passion or a fatal willingness to trust those around her too much. Everything that her cousin Elizabeth had, Mary lacked – she had ministers who might turn on her at any time, a host of lords who had been too long used to following their desires. Her nation was familiar with the vicissitudes of power and she had been brought up in France, far from Scotland. The court she knew was refined, punctilious and always deferential to royalty – unlike those around her in Edinburgh. Mary also had the bad luck to attract the two worst consorts in royal history.

In Britain, the greatest periods of progression of the state or, as we now say, constitutional monarchy, have been often under queens: Victoria, Elizabeth II. The few times that Victoria exercised a small amount of will – complaining about the change in her ladies-in-waiting after the fall of Lord Melbourne's government, for example – were met with opprobrium, despite being much less significant than William IV's meddling in the passage of the Reform Act. Victoria refused to change her attendants from supporters of Melbourne to supporters of Robert Peel, the leader of the opposition, and Peel promptly declined to form a new government. Peel was arguably looking for a reason not to rule with a wafer-thin majority and Victoria's ladies were simply an excuse. Victoria was of course the first post-Reform Act queen, but there is little doubt that male monarchs have been allowed to behave with wider licence and run over the will of the ministers. When Elizabeth II came to the throne, Winston Churchill complained she was a 'child' and she had to win his respect – which her father had never had to do. Even though a queen is a monarch, she is still a woman and it seems as if greater deference to her ministers is expected. Elizabeth I talked more of her body than any other monarch, and her body has been much discussed in scholarship. The weakness of the female sex, so often used against Mary, was something Elizabeth turned to her strength in words. But her ministers never forgot what she was.

Elizabeth herself said in the letter to Mary after Darnley's murder, 'I am sure you have no friend more true than I, and my affection may stand you in as good stead as the subtle wits of others.' Mary was betrayed by so many for their own gain – and they did benefit from her. Moray achieved power and glory, James I maintained a relationship with the Queen of England and secured his position, the various Scottish lords kept their property and despoiled Mary's belongings. Over and over, she was betrayed and exploited for power. Only Elizabeth protected her – and finally could not continue to do so. Elizabeth, by agreeing to behead a monarch, according to the point initially raised by the lords that Mary was 'unworthy' to rule, agreed to the greatest possible incursion into royal rule. If Parliament disliked a king's actions, it could now depose him and behead him. Yet although Mary met her death with little time to prepare and only the dignity she herself brought, she kept her majesty until the end.

Parliament saw Mary as a threat but she was also symbolic in the struggle between Elizabeth and the ruling class over where power was lodged, whether in the relationship between parliament and monarch or in the monarch's own person. Despite the fact that Elizabeth's body was the most discussed of any monarch in history, it was the one which suffered the greatest blows against royal power. After Elizabeth, the body of the monarch was no longer the source of government. The actions of Parliament and the signed warrant ushered in the possibility of the execution of future monarchs – Charles I and even others across Europe, Louis XVI and Marie Antoinette. In executing Mary, Elizabeth – as she knew – had executed a tiny part of herself. For if a king could be killed by his subjects, then what was special about a king?

We admire our great queens and recall their iconic imagery. We treasure the stories of their relationships with their ministers. We congratulate them on their dignified bearing and the excellence of their personal sacrifice and creation of a virtuous monarchy, whether as Virgin Queen, perfect wife or working mother. We see their reigns as more stable, less bloody, calmer than those who came before or after. But what if we look more closely at the relationships with their ministers? It has been separately argued about Elizabeth, Victoria and Elizabeth II that the state, parliament and ministers gained power in their reigns – the progress of what we now call constitutional monarchy. We may put this down to their intelligence, their sense of duty. Or we could argue that female monarchs are permitted less leeway for imposing their personality. Elizabeth II was schooled in constitutional monarchy by the provost of Eton as a young girl and her reign has exemplified political neutrality par excellence. The queen asks and comments but does not interfere. The famous instructions of what a monarch may or may not do were written by Walter Bagehot in the reign of Victoria in his book *The English Constitution* – the monarch had the right to 'be consulted, to encourage and to warn'. This was much less than her predecessors had done.

Elizabeth I's time on the throne is seen as one of brilliance, thanks to the superbly effective propaganda of Gloriana. But the queen herself was constantly battling her ministers for supremacy. Henry VIII had begun the Reformation, in seemingly the most explicit revelation of pure monarchical power possible: that he could command the religion of the country as he pleased. And yet he relied so much on Parliament both for the ensuing reforms and the dealings with Anne Boleyn. Elizabeth meant to jealously protect her prerogative and agency, to retain the rule of monarch as the ultimate source of power and all that can be decreed. But little by little, her position was depredated, and power was gained by Parliament. We see the first example of this process in her ministers' and advisors' attempts to demand she should marry (and moot that she should be told to marry an Englishman at that). Elizabeth fought hard to preserve her state but she was also fortunate that her advisors and nobles could not agree on one person – and so although they were often telling her to marry they could not decide unequivocally on a groom.

Yet throughout Elizabeth's reign, her advisors and Parliament attempted to fashion her as more figurehead than absolute monarch; signing the decrees rather than actually making them. Elizabeth herself talked a brilliant game of absolute monarchy, pronouncing that 'absolute princes ought not to be accountable for their actions to any other than God alone'. She promoted herself as a strong monarch so famously and our modern popular visions of her are of absolute power. But Henry VIII had used his advisors for his own ends, and when they failed him – as in the case of Thomas Cromwell and his counsel to marry Anne of Cleves – he had them executed. Cecil was devoted to the queen and her safety, but, whether due to his own desire for power or a belief that she did not know what was good for her, he went behind her back and acted without her decree.

The greatest battle for power was over Mary, Queen of Scots. Ultimately, Elizabeth's desire to assist Mary, to send troops to support her, to put her back on the throne and not to execute her, were thwarted. Some of what happened to undermine Mary was without Elizabeth's knowledge – such as Walsingham and Cecil using Gilbert Gifford to trap her into revealing her assent to a plot. But much was overt – Elizabeth raged but did not, could not, find her way to give the queen back her Scots crown by force, for the appetite for warmongering was not there and Parliament saw Mary as a great threat to the realm. Although Elizabeth is often seen as our most powerful queen, it was in her reign that the greatest incursion was made into royal privilege. In executing Mary, Elizabeth had cut away a part of herself. '*Je ne suis plus que je fus*', 'I am no longer who I was,' Mary wrote in her beloved Book of Hours, before her death. Mary was the queen who became a subject.

In 1612, King James I had his mother exhumed. He reburied her in Westminster Abbey, in a beautiful tomb of white marble, near Lady Lennox, once her mother-in-law, only a few feet from Elizabeth. They were closer in death than they had ever been before. 'Conquered, she was unconquerable', was inscribed on her tomb. A meeting with Elizabeth had been Mary's greatest desire for so much of her life. Finally, in Westminster Abbey, she achieved her wish.

Notes

Abbreviations

BL MSS – British Library Manuscripts
Cecil – Cecil Papers, Hatfield House
CSP, Scotland, Foreign, Venetian – Calendar of State Papers
NLR – National Library of Russia
NLS – National Library of Scotland
PRO SP – Public Record Office, State Papers

Chapter One

1 Mary Stuart to Mary of Guise, the morning of her wedding, *Foreign Correspondence with Marie de Lorraine*, ed. M. Wood (Edinburgh, 1923)
2 Brantôme, *Oeuvres Complètes*, 52
3 *Discours du grand et magnifique triumphs faict au marriage do tresnoble & magnifique Prince François de Valois Roy-Dauphin, fil aisne du tres-chrestien Roy de France Henry II. Du nome, & de treshaulte & vertueuse Princesse madam Marie d'Estuart, Roine de'Ecosse* (Paris, par Annet Brière, 1558), 325; Brantôme, 53
4 *Discours du grand et magnifique…*, 8
5 *Discours du grand et magnifique…*, 28; Brantôme, *Oeuvres Complètes*, 26
6 Labanoff, *Lettres*, II, 65
7 Labanoff, *Lettres*, II, 65
8 Fraser, 95; Estienne Perlin, 1558

Chapter Two

1 John Knox, *History of the Reformation*, I, p.37
2 Lisle to Henry, CSP Scotland. See also Foreign Correspondence (Mary of Guise) and Labanoff, *Lettres*, I. Also Henry VIII, *Letters and Papers*, 20–22 and Sadler in State Papers

3 Sadler, State Papers, I, 88
4 Sadler, State Papers, I, 107

Chapter Three

1 CSP Scottish, VII; Foreign Correspondence; State Papers; and Henry VIII, *Letters and Papers*
2 See State Papers, V; Foreign Correspondence; CSP, Foreign, VIII

Chapter Four

1 De Beaugué, *L'Histoire*, 65; Labanoff, *Lettres*, II, 33
2 Mary's Book of Hours, National Library of Russia, LAT, Qv 1, 110
3 Labanoff, *Lettres*, VII 277
4 Recueil, I, 8; Labanoff, *Lettres*, II, 65
5 Labanoff, *Lettres*, I, 29
6 Labanoff, *Lettres*, I, 34
7 CSP, Venetian, VII, 270

Chapter Five

1 CSP, Venetian, VI, ii, 1058
2 CSP, Venetian, VI, ii, 1059
3 Harrington, II, 312
4 CSP, Venetian, VI, 1060
5 CSP, Venetian, VI, 1080
6 CSP, Spanish, V, 1050
7 CSP, Venetian, VI, 288
8 CSP, Venetian, VI, 436, 446
9 CSP, Venetian, VII, 42

Chapter Six

1   Ives, *Anne Boleyn*, 248
2   See Borman, *Elizabeth's Women*, 30
3   See Whitelock, *Mary Tudor*, 25
4   CSP, Spanish, V, I, 573
5   CSP, Venetian, VI, 65; Henry VIII, *Letters and Papers*, X, 96–7
6   Weir, *Henry VIII*, 135; Henry VIII, *Letters and Papers*, X, 102
7   CSP, Venetian, VI, 85; Henry VIII, *Letters and Papers*, X, 105
8   CSP, Spanish, V, ii, 101
9   CSP, Spanish, V, ii, 105
10 Weir, *Six Wives*, 260

Chapter Seven

1 Henry VIII, *Letters and Papers*, X, 330
2 CSP, Spanish, V, ii, 125
3 Henry VIII, *Letters and Papers*, XI, 190
4 Weir, *Elizabeth*, 75
5 BL, Lansdowne MS, 1236, 35
6 Whitelock, *Elizabeth's Bedfellows*, 65

Chapter Eight

1 Borman, *Elizabeth's Women*, 123
2 For an excellent in-depth discussion of Henry VIII's will, the succession and the question of dry-stamping, see Lipscomb, *The King is Dead*, 145
3 Weir, *Six Wives*, 255. See also Skidmore, *Edward VI*; MacCulloch, *The Boy King*
4 See CSP, Spanish, VII, ii, 154
5 See also Perry, *Word of a Prince*, 85
6 CSPD, Edward VI, 92; Whitelock, *Elizabeth's Bedfellows*, 2
7 see Borman, *Elizabeth's Women*, 113; Whitelock, *Elizabeth's Bedfellows*, 4
8 Haynes, Cecil State Papers, 89–90
9 CSP, Spanish, VIII, vi, 25

Chapter Nine

1 CSP, Spanish, VIII, ii 502. For Mary and religion, see Whitelock, *Mary Tudor*
2 For more on Mary's long-ignored confidence as leader, see de Lisle, *Tudor*, 65
3 CSP, Foreign, IX, viii. For Elizabeth's impossible position, see Hilton, *Elizabeth: Renaissance Prince*; Whitelock, *Mary Tudor*; Weir, *Elizabeth*; Doran, *Elizabeth I and her Circle*
4 Mary has been too long seen as a 'failure'. For modern scholarship on her as a confident Tudor and Counter Reformation monarch, see Whitelock, *Mary Tudor*; Porter, *Mary Tudor*; and de Lisle, *Tudor* – as de Lisle points out, Mary was simply behaving as the 'ruthless Tudor monarch she was'.
5 CSP, Foreign, VIII, 85. Borman, *Elizabeth's Women*, 165
6 See Hilton, *Elizabeth: Renaissance Prince*, 105

Chapter Ten

1 Knox, *The Monstrous Regiment*, 30, 65. See also Knox, *History*, 60. See also Foreign Correspondence, I, 60; Labanoff, *Lettres*, I, 65. See also the Dubrovsky Collection in the National Library of Russia
2 CSP, Foreign, I, 347
3 CSP, Foreign, I, 348

4   CSP, Foreign, 1560–61, 291
5   CSP, Foreign, II, 347
6   CSP, Scotland, III, 85
7   Labanoff, *Lettres*, I, 70. See also Foreign Correspondence, I, 67
8   Knox, *History*, 64. See also Foreign Correspondence, I, 75
9   CSP, Foreign, I, 67; Labanoff, *Lettres*, I, 65; Foreign Correspondence, I, 77

Chapter Eleven

1   CSP, Foreign, III, 394. See also NLR, Dubrovsky, Aut 34/2, 17
2   Bothwell, 46
3   CSP, Foreign, III, 409
4   CSP, Venetian, VII, 278. See also NLR, Dubrovsky, Aut 34/2, 15
5   My translation. Also NLR Dubrovsky, Aut 34/2, 16
6   CSP, Foreign, II, 360. See also Labanoff, *Lettres*, I, 65
7   CSP, Foreign, III, 42. See also NLR Dubrovsky, Aut 34/2, 19
8   CSP, Foreign, III, 472. See also Labanoff, *Letters*, I, 78
9   CSP, Foreign, III, 423
10 CSP, Foreign, III, 565

Chapter Twelve

1   CSP, Foreign, II, 405
2   As one early biographer put it, 'Hereupon Queen Elizabeth bare secret grudge against her, which the subtill malice of men on both sides, cherished, growing betwixt them, emulation and new occasions daily arising, in such sort, that it could not be extinguished but by death.' Camden, *Historie*, 34
3   CSP, Scotland, VIII, 45. See also NLR, Dubrovsky, Aut 34/3 20
4   CSP, Foreign, Elizabeth, 1558–9, 443
5   CSP, Foreign, II, 606. BL Cotton MS Caligula, C II, 39
6   BL, Cotton MS, Caligula, C II 42
7   Sidney, *Memoir*, 154. Labanoff, *Lettres*, I, 56
8   CSP, Scotland, I, 606
9   Knox, *History*, II, 15; BL, Cotton MS, Caligula, C II, 47

Chapter Thirteen

1   CSP, Spanish, IX, 105
2   See Hilton, *Elizabeth: Renaissance Prince*, 56
3   CSP, Spanish, VIII, iv, 86. BL, Add. MS, 48027, 75
4   See Mulcaster, *The Passage of our most Drad Soveraigne Lady Quene Elyzabeth*; see also Weir, *Elizabeth*, 66

5   Neale, *Elizabeth I*, 130. See Whitelock, *Elizabeth's Bedfellows,* 85
6   Hilton, *Elizabeth: Renaissance Prince*, 134
7   Neale, *Elizabeth I*, 135
8   CSP, Spanish, VIII, 65
9   CSP, Venetian, 1558–80, 12
10 Neale, *Elizabeth I*, 160
11 See BL, Add. MS, 4847, 97–8

Chapter Fourteen

1   CSP, Spanish, VIII, 56; see also Gristwood, *Elizabeth and Leicester*; Hilton, *Elizabeth: Renaissance Prince*; Weir, *Elizabeth*
2   See Whitelock, *Elizabeth's Bedfellows*, 60
3   BL, Add. MS, 48027, 660
4   Gristwood, *Elizabeth and Leicester*, 93
5   CSP, Spanish, IX, 115
6   CSP, Spanish, IX, 164
7   CSP, Spanish, IX, 175
8   See Skidmore, *Death and the Virgin*; Gristwood, *Elizabeth and Leicester*
9   See BL, Add. MS, 48023
10 See Skidmore, *Death and the Virgin*
11 CSP, Spanish, IX, 123
12 CSP, Spanish, X, 252
13 Neale, *Elizabeth I*, 183
14 Neale, *Elizabeth I*, 183

Chapter Fifteen

1   BL, Cotton MS, Caligula C III, 65. See also NLR, Dubrovsky, Aut. 35/3, 27
2   CSP, Foreign, 78, 606
3   CSP, Foreign, VIII, 65; BL, Cotton MS, Caligula, C III, 86
4   Maitland, *Narrative*, 65, 74, 98
5   CSP, Foreign, VIII, 65
6   Maitland, 85
7   Melville, *Memoirs*, 85
8   Melville, *Memoirs*, 107
9   Teulet, *Lettres*, II, 132
10 BL, Cotton MS, Caligula, C III, 85
11 Maitland, 93. See also PRO SP, 52/12, 43
12 BL, Cotton MS, Caligula, C III, 48
13 CSP, Scotland, II, 145

Chapter Sixteen

1   CSP, Foreign, VIII, 65. See also BL, Cotton MS, Caligula, C III, 82
2   PRO SP, 52/12, 41–4
3   Melville, *Memoirs*, p123

Chapter Seventeen

1   BL, Cotton MS, Caligula, C V, 22.
2   BL, Lansdowne MS, 9; BL, Cotton MS, Caligula, B 9–10; Labanoff, *Lettres*, I, 85
3   BL, Cotton MS, Caligula, B II, 9
4   Labanoff, *Lettres*, I, 36; Nau, *Memorials*, 45
5   BL, Cotton MS, Caligula, B VIII, 25
6   BL, Cotton MS, Caligula, B III, 86

Chapter Eighteen

1   BL, Cotto.n MS, Caligula, C II, 85
2   Melville, *Memoirs*, 120
3   Labanoff, *Lettres*, I, 65
4   Melville, *Memoirs*, 130–31
5   Herries, *Memoirs*, 65
6   Nau, *Memorials*, 87
7   Keith, *History*, I, xcvi; Teulet, *Lettres*, I
8   BL, Add. MS, 48027; Keith, *History*, I; Cecil, *Papers*, 155/56
9   Keith, *History*, I, 65; Teulet, *Lettres*, I, 78
10 Tytler, *History*, II, 400
11 BL, Cotton MS, Caligula, III, 82
12 PRO SP, 52/13, 207
13 PRO SP 52/13, 210
14 See BL, Cotton MS, Caligula, C I, 34
15 BL, Cotton MS, Caligula, C I, 45
16 CSP, Foreign, VII, 85
17 PRO SP, 52/12, 130
18 Keith, *History*, II, 54
19 PRO SP, 53/2, 80
20 BL, Cotton MS, Caligula, VII, 80
21 BL, Cotton MS, Caligula, VII, 81
22 Nau, *Memorials*, 34

Chapter Nineteen

1 PRO SP, 56/13, 120
2 BL, Add. MS, 33531, 37–8
3 Labanoff, *Lettres*, 2, 83
4 CSP, Venetian, VII, 65
5 Melville, *Memoirs*, 165
6 PRO SP, 52/13, 17
7 CSP, Scotland, I, 87; PRO SP 52/14, 18
8 CSP, Spanish, II, 89
9 Keith, *History*, II, 85
10 PRO SP, 52/13, 17
11 CSP, Spanish, VIII, 65
12 PRO SP, 52/13, 101

Chapter Twenty

1 PRO SP, 59/12, 243–4
2 CSP, Scotland, VI, 85
3 PRO SP, 52/13, 98
4 CSP, Scotland, VII, 90
5 BL, Lansdowne MS, 10
6 PRO SP, 52/13, 64
7 For the Bond, see: BL, Cotton MS, Caligula, C I, 85
8 See BL, Cotton MS, Caligula, C I, 86
9 PRO SP 59/13, 37–8, 41–2
10 PRO SP, 52/13, 22–3
11 PRO SP, 52/13, 37, 40

Chapter Twenty-One

1 Melville, *Memoirs*, 35
2 Georges Vigarello, *Sexual Violence in France*, 65
3 Melville, *Memoirs*, 132
4 BL, Cotton MS, Caligula, C II, 95
5 See BL, Cotton MS, Caligula, C II, 87–115
6 Melville, *Memoirs*, 65
7 Keith, *History*, II, 85
8 BL, Cotton MS, Vespasian, III, 65
9 Labanoff, *Lettres*, II, 65
10 CSP, Foreign, II, 65

Chapter Twenty-Two

1 See PRO SP, 59/13, 91–103; CSP, Foreign, VIII, 65
2 Teulet, *Lettres*, II, 65
3 NAS GD, 1137113
4 BL, Royal MS, 18.13, 6, 242
5 BL, Cotton MS, Titus, C 12
6 BL, Cotton MS, Caligula, C 18
7 Teulet, *Lettres*, II, 82
8 Melville, *Memoirs*, 105
9 Teulet, *Lettres*, II, 85
10 Cecil, *Papers*, 155/56
11 CSP Scotland, VIII, 82
12 PRO SP, 52/12, 85
13 Maitland, *Memoirs*, 86
14 PRO SP 52/13, 64–7
15 PRO SP, 52/12, 101
16 Teulet, *Lettres*, II, 70
17 PRO SP, 59/13, 157–65; Teulet, *Lettres*, II, 85–90; PRO SP, 59/13, 189–201
18 Teulet, II, 92; PRO SP, 59/13, 101–10

Chapter Twenty-Three

1 Nau, *Memorials*, 89
2 Teulet, *Lettres*, II, 65; PRO SP, 59/13, 65
3 Hay Fleming, *Mary*, 85
4 Labanoff, *Lettres*, I, 92. And see NLR, Dubrovsky, Aut. 12, 29–30
5 PRO SP, 59/13, 118
6 PRO SP, 52/18, 116
7 PRO SP, 52/14, 1
8 CSP, Scotland, VI, 85
9 CSP, Foreign, VI, 202. See also NLR, Dubrovsky, Aut. 35/3, 68
10 PRO SP, 59/13, 165
11 CSP, Scotland, VI, 503. NLR, Dubrovsky, Aut. 35/3, 68
12 BL, Add. MS, 32091, 216
13 CSP, Rome, III, 65

Chapter Twenty-Four

1 Nau, *Memorials*, 50
2 Nau, *Memorials*, 60
3 Cecil, *Papers*, 56/75
4 CSP, Scotland, VI, 202
5 PRO SP, 59/13, 75

6　PRO SP, 59/13, 78–82
7　CSP, Scotland, VI, 82
8　BL, Cotton MS, Caligula, C I
9　Nau, *Memorials*, 65
10　CSP, Scotland, VI, 85
11　Nau, *Memorials*, 85
12　CSP, Scotland, VI, 132
13　CSP, Foreign, V, 65

Chapter Twenty-Five

1　BL, Cotton MS, Caligula, C 18
2　Nau, *Memorials*, 186
3　PRO SP, 59/13, 201
4　Labanoff, *Lettres*, II, 158
5　Labanoff, *Lettres*, II, 182
6　PRO SP, 59/14, 86
7　BL, Cotton MS, Caligula, C I
8　PRO SP, 59/14, 25

Chapter Twenty-Six

1　Nau, *Memorials*, 192
2　CSP, Scotland, VI, 85. See NLR, Dubrovsky, Aut. 12. 34
3　CSP, Scotland, VI, 85
4　BL, Cotton MS, Caligula, B 12, 85; Nau, *Memorials*, 202
5　CSP, Scotland, VI, 92
6　Nau, *Memorials*, 205
7　Herries, *Memoirs*, 82
8　SP PRO, 59/13, 122. See NLR, Dubrovsky, Aut. 90, T.1, 28
9　Styre, *Annals of the Reformation*, 580–81
10　PRO SP, 59/14, 201
11　Buchanan, *Ane detectioun of the duings of Marie Quene of Scotts*, 6
12　Buchanan, *Ane detectioun of the duings of Marie Quene of Scotts*, 30
13　PROP SP, 60/10, 22
14　BL, Cotton MS, Caligula, D 10, 85
15　My translation. BL, Cotton MS, Caligula, D 10, 90
16　CSP, Scotland, VI, 88
17　BL, Cotton MS, Caligula, B 9, 25
18　PRO SP, 53, 15
19　PRO SP, 53, 22
20　BL, Cotton MS, Caligula, C 8, 78
21　Nau, *Memorials*, 232
22　PRO SP, 53/2, 5–6

Chapter Twenty-Seven

1 PRO SP, 53/2, 14–18; BL, Cotton MS, Caligula, C 1, 301–56
2 PRO SP, 53/2, 52–8; BL, Cotton MS, Caligula, C 1, 228–350
3 BL, Cotton MS, Caligula, C 1, 261
4 PRO SP, 53/2, 14–22
5 PRO SP, 53/2, 62, 134–5
6 PRO SP, 53/2, 65, 139
7 PRO SP, 53/2, 65, 140
8 PRO SP, 53/2, 65, 142
9 PRO SP, 53/2, 62, 142
10 BL, Cotton MS, Caligula, B 9, 81
11 Cecil, *Papers*, 155/140–42
12 PRO SP, 53/2, 5–10
13 PRO SP, 53/2, 16
14 Nau, *Memorials*, 232; PRO SP, 53/2, 20

Chapter Twenty-Eight

1 Labanoff, *Lettres*, VI, 8
2 BL, Cotton MS, Caligula, C 9, 88
3 BL, Cotton MS, Caligula, C 3, 102
4 Cecil, *Papers*, 155/140–44; PRO SP, 53/2, 50–60; BL, Cotton MS, Caligula, C 1, 300–58; CSP, VIII, 65
5 Cecil, *Papers*, 155/141
6 Herries, *Memoirs*, 65
7 Herries, *Memoirs*, 66
8 PRO SP, 55
9 BL, Cotton MS, Caligula, C 1, 355–8
10 BL, Cotton MS, Caligula, C 1, 355–7
11 PRO SP, 53/2, 85; Labanoff, *Lettres*, II, 256
12 PRO SP, 53/2, 79
13 Herries, *Memoirs*, 87
14 Teulet, *Lettres*, II, 87
15 Labanoff, *Lettres*, II, 156
16 PRO SP, 52/15, 32
17 BL, Cotton MS, Caligula, B 9, 30
18 Mary's Book of Hours, National Library of Russia, Lat Qv 1, 112
19 BL, Add. MS, 48049, 150
20 PRO SP, 52/16, 85

Chapter Twenty-Nine

1   BL, Add. MS, 48049, 75
2   BL, Cotton MS, Caligula, C II, 208
3   BL, Cotton MS, Caligula, C II, 210.
4   BL, Cotton MS, Caligula, C 9, 82
5   Teulet, *Lettres*, II, 200; Labanoff, *Lettres*, VI, 50–85
6   Labanoff, *Lettres*, VII, 203
7   PRO SP, 59/13, 20; see CSP, Foreign, VIII, 65
8   PRO SP, 59/13, 85
9   PRO SP, 59/13, 82
10 BL, Cotton MS, Caligula, II, 29–30
11 BL, Add. MS, 48049, 150–60
12 Labanoff, *Lettres*, VII, 333
13 BL, Cotton MS, Caligula, II, 40
14 BL, Cotton MS, Caligula II, 73, 75

Chapter Thirty

1   Teulet, *Lettres*, II, 85
2   See NLR, Fr Q, IV, 212
3   PRO SP, 59/13, 222
4   CSP, 52/16, 51
5   CSP, 53/115, 101
6   CSP, 59/13, 202
7   Labanoff, *Lettres*, IV, 183
8   Nau, *Memorials*, 65
9   Cecil, *Papers*, 65/2, 81
10 BL, Cotton MS, Caligula, C 3, 85
11 See PRO SP, 53/18, 35–6
12 BL, Cotton MS, Caligula, C 8, 208
13 See Gore-Browne, *Lord Bothwell*, 246. See Guy, *My Heart*, 256
14 Labanoff, *Lettres*, VII, 65
15 PRO SP 59/13, 25
16 Nau, *Memorials*, 252
17 Gore-Browne, *Lord Bothwell*, 302

Chapter Thirty-One

1   Fraser, *Mary Queen of Scots*, 501
2   PRO SP, 59/13, 222
3   BL, Cotton MS, Caligula, C 9, 85
4   BL, Cotton MS, Caligula, VII, 17

5 BL, Cotton MS, Caligula, VIII, 57
6 Whitelock, *Elizabeth's Bedfellows*, 92
7 PRO SP, 58, 65/13
8 PRO SP, 58, 65/12
9 PRO SP, 59/12, 25
10 Labanoff, *Lettres*, VII, 54; Nau, *Memorials*, 335
11 Nau, *Memorials*, 336
12 BL, Cotton MS, Caligula, C 9, 85
13 See Peck (ed.), *Leicester's Commonwealth*, 5, 13, 65, 86
14 PRO SP, 12/174, 1–11
15 Labanoff, *Lettres*, VII, 202
16 Labanoff, *Lettres*, VII, 202
17 Cecil, *Papers*, 55/82, 10

Chapter Thirty-Two

1 PRO SP, 53/18, 32
2 Teulet, *Lettres*, I, 85
3 PRO SP, 53/19, 9
4 Teulet, *Lettres*, I, 89
5 PRO SP, 53/18, 25–6
6 Morris, *Paulet*, 182
7 PRO SP, 53/18, 53
8 PRO SP, 53/18, 53
9 PRO SP, 53/18, 53
10 PRO SP, 53/18, 55
11 PRO SP, 53/18, 59
12 Nau, *Memorials*, 381

Chapter Thirty-Three

1 Nau, *Memorials*, 382–3
2 Morris, *Paulet*, 225
3 Nau, *Memorials*, 88
4 Morris, *Paulet*, 277
5 Nau, *Memorials*, 390
6 Nau, *Memorials*, 392
7 Morris, *Paulet*, 330
8 BL, Cotton MS, Caligula, C 9, 460–3
9 BL, Cotton MS, Caligula, C 9, 480
10 BL, Cotton MS, Caligula, C 9, 482
11 BL, Cotton MS, Caligula, C 9, 488
12 BL, Cotton MS, Caligula, C 9, 490

Chapter Thirty-Four

1 BL, Add. MS, 48027, 492–3
2 BL, Add. MS, 48027, 492–3
3 BL, Add. MS, 48027, 510
4 BL, Cotton MS, Caligula, C 9, 471
5 BL, Cotton MS, Caligula, C 9, 480–85
6 BL, Cotton MS, Caligula, C 9, 482–9
7 BL, Add. MS, 48027, 495–500; BL, Cotton MS, Caligula, C 9, 480–95
8 BL, Add. MS, 48027, 550
9 BL, Add. MS, 48196, 540–45; BL, Cotton MS, Caligula, C 9, 480–90
10 BL, Cotton MS, Caligula, C 9, 480–95
11 Morris, *Paulet*, 85
12 Bourgoing, *Marie Stuart*, 182
13 BL, Harleian MS, 290

Chapter Thirty-Five

1 See BL, Add. MS, 48027, 651–3
2 Morris, *Paulet*, 223; BL, Cotton MS, Caligula, C 9, 85
3 BL, Cotton MS, Caligula, C 9, 366
4 BL, Cotton MS, Caligula, C 9, 387
5 See BL, Add. MS, 48027, 642–50
6 Cecil, *Papers*, 55/183
7 PRO SP, 53/18, 110
8 CSP, Foreign, 1586–8, 241
9 Lambeth Palace Archive, 4267, 19–20
10 Lambeth Palace Archive, 4267, 19–20
11 BL, Cotton MS, Caligula, C 9, 480; Morris, *Paulet*, 268
12 Beale in BL, Add. MS, 48027, 650–58
13 See Beale, BL, Add. MS, 48027, 650–58; CSP, Scotland, IV, 291–4
14 CSP, Scotland, IV, 294

Chapter Thirty-Six

1 See Beale, BL, Add. MS, 48027, 639–41
2 BL, Add. MS, 48027, 646–7; also Bourgoing, 285
3 BL, Add. MS, 48027, 648–9
4 BL, Add. MS, 48027, 649
5 Bourgoing, *Marie Stuart*, 358
6 BL, Add. MS, 48027, 647
7 NLS, Advocates MS, 54.1.1
8 NLS, Advocates MS, 54.1.1

9   BL, Add. MS, 48027, 636–40
10 BL, Add. MS, 48027, 640
11 BL, Add. MS, 48027, 642–3
12 BL, Add. MS, 48027, 649–50; Labanoff, *Lettres*, VI, 491; Morris, *Paulet*, 388
13 BL, Add. MS, 48027, 649–50
14 BL, Lansdowne MS, 51, 99–100
15 Bourgoing, *Marie Stuart*, 388; Fraser, *Mary Queen of Scots*, 662–70
16 BL, Add. MS, 48027, 649–50

Chapter Thirty-Seven

1   BL, Cotton MS, Caligula, C 10, 53–4
2   BL, Cotton MS, Caligula, C 10, 85
3   Strype, *Annales*, II, ii, 407
4   Green, 'I My Self', 421–55. The cadences fit, the army was definitely there and it does seem as if Sharpe was there as chaplain to the Earl of Leicester. On 9 August, the queen 'made an excellent Oration to her armie, which the next day after her departure, I was commanded to deliver to all the Armie together'.
5   King James I, *Works*, Chapter 20

Bibliography

It is an incredible privilege to read the original letters and documents of Mary, Queen of Scots, Elizabeth, and men and women who crafted the age. I am thus grateful to all those archives and museums which made it possible for me to turn the pages of the letters in which Mary pours out her heart – and made me so close to the words that it was almost as if I was there.

Archive Sources

Bodleian Library Manuscripts, Additional and Ashmole Manuscripts
British Library Additional Manuscripts, Egerton Manuscripts, Harleian Manuscripts and Lansdowne Manuscripts, Royal, Sloane Manuscripts. Maps. Cotton Manuscripts, particularly Caligula, Claudius, Nero and Vitellus and Vespasian Manuscripts.
British State Papers Online
Cecil Papers, Hatfield House (microfilm)
Lambeth Palace Archives
National Archives, Paris
National Archives of Scotland
National Library of Russia
Public Record Office, Kew

Primary Sources

The Accounts of the Lord High Treasurer of Scotland, Vol. XI: 1559–66, and Vol. XII: 1566–67 (ed. T. Dickson and Sir James Balfour Paul, H.M. General Register House, Edinburgh, 1877–1916)

Accounts of the Masters of Works, Vol. I, 1529–1615 (ed. H.M. Paton, HMSO, Edinburgh, 1957)

Accounts and Papers relating to Mary, Queen of Scots (ed. D.J. Crosby and John Bruce, Camden Society, 1867)

The Acts of the Parliaments of Scotland (12 vols, ed. T. Thomson and C. Innes, Edinburgh, 1814–75)

Acts of the Privy Council of England (32 vols, ed. John Roche Dasent et al. HMSO, London, 1890–1918)

Acts and Proceedings of the General Assemblies of the Kirk of Scotland (ed. T. Thomson, Bannatyne Club, 1839, Maitland Club, 1839)

Ailsa Muniments: Inventory (Historical Manuscripts Commission, Vol. III Supplement, 1431–1599)

Ancient Criminal Trials in Scotland from AD 1488 to AD 1624, embracing the entire reigns of James IV and V, Mary, Queen of Scots and James VI. Compiled from the Original Records and MSS., with Historical Notes and Illustrations (3 vols, ed. Robert Pitcairn, Bannatyne and Maitland Clubs, Edinburgh, 1833)

Anonymous: *Life of Queen Mary* (Cotton MSS. Caligula, British Library)

The Letters and the Life of Francis Bacon (7 vols, ed. J. Spedding, London, 1861–74)

Baker, Richard: *Chronicles of the Kings of England* (London, 1643)

Balcarres Paper: Foreign correspondence with Marie de Lorraine Queen of Scotland, from *Balcarres Papers* Vol. 1 1537-48, Vol. II 1548-57 (ed. Marguerite Wood, Scottish Historical Society 3rd Series. IV. Edinburgh, 1923 and 1925)

Bannatyne, George: *The Bannatyne Manuscript, written in time of Pest, 1568* (MSS. II, Bannatyne Club, Edinburgh; ed. W. Tod Ritchie, Scottish Text Society, Edinburgh and London, 1934)

Bannatyne Miscellany, containing Original Papers and Tracts, chiefly relating to the History and Literature of Scotland (Bannatyne Club, Edinburgh, 1827)

The Bardon Papers: Documents relating to the Imprisonment and Trial of Mary, Queen of Scots (ed. Conyers Read, Camden Society, 3rd Series, XVII, 1909)

Beaugué, Jean de, *L'Histoire de la Guerre d'Ecosse* (Paris, 1556)

Birch, Thomas: *An Historical View of the Negotiations Between the Courts of England, France and Brussels, from the Year 1592 to 1617* (London, 1749)

Birch, Thomas: *Memoirs of the Reign of Queen Elizabeth from 1581 till her Death* (2 vols, London, 1754)

Birrel, Robert: *The Diary of Robert Birrel, Burgess of Edinburgh, containing Divers Passages of State and Other Memorable Accidents, 1532–1605* (printed in Fragments of Scottish History, listed below)

Bittersweet within My Heart: The Collected Poems of Mary, Queen of Scots (trans. and ed. Robin Bell, London, 1992)

Blackwood, Adam: *Apologia pro Regibus* (Poitiers, 1581)

Blackwood, Adam: *History of Mary, Queen of Scots: A Fragment* (trans. anon., Maitland Club, Edinburgh/Glasgow, 1834)

Blackwood, Adam: *Martyre de la Royne d'Escosse* (Paris, 1587; Edinburgh, 1588)

Blackwood, Adam: *La Mort de la Royne d'Escosse* (Paris, 1588)

The Book of Articles (Hopetoun MSS.; ed. John Hosack in *Mary, Queen of Scots and her Accusers* – see below)

Bothwell, James Hepburn, 4th Earl of: *Les Affaires du Conte de Boduel, l'an MDLXVIII* (published 1586; ed. H. Coburn and T. Maitland, Bannatyne Club, Edinburgh, 1829)

Bouille, René de: *Histoire des Ducs de Guise* (Paris, 1850)

Bourgoing, D.: *Marie Stuart, son procès et son exécution d'après le journal de Bourgoing, son médecin* (ed. M. Regis Chantelauze, Paris, 1874)

Brantôme, Pierre de Bourdeille, Seigneur de: *Vies des Dames illustriés* (6 vols, Leyden, 1665–6; trans. Katharine Prescott Wormesley as *The Book of the Ladies: Illustrious Dames, with Elucidations of Some of those Ladies* by C.A. Sainte-Beuve, London, 1899)

Brantôme, Pierre de Bourdeille, Seigneur de: *Oeuvres complètes* (ed. Bouchon, Paris, 1823)

A Brief History of the Life of Mary, Queen of Scots, and the Occasions that brought her and Thomas, Duke of Norfolk, to their Tragical Ends (London, 1681)

Buchanan, George: *Detectio Mariae Reginae: Ane Detection of the Doings of Marie, Queen of Scots, touching the Murder of her Husband and her Conspiracy, Adultery and Pretensed Marriage with the Earl Bothwell, and a Defence of the True Lords, Maintainers of the King's Majesty's Action and Authority* (Edinburgh, 1571, 1572); published as *The Detection of the Doings of Mary, Queen of Scots* (London, 1582; trans. by 'a Person of Honour of the Kingdom of Scotland', London, 1721)

Buchanan, George: *Georgii Buchanani Opera Omnia* (ed. Thomas Ruddiman, Edinburgh, 1715, 1727)

Buchanan, George: *Indictment of Mary, Queen of Scots* (Cambridge, 1923)

Buchanan, George: *De Jure Regni apud Scotos* (Edinburgh, 1579)

Buchanan, George: *Rerum Scoticarum Historia* (Edinburgh, 1582; Frankfurt, 1584; Amsterdam, 1643; Edinburgh, 1700; ed. James Man, Aberdeen, 1762; trans. James Aikman as *The History of Scotland, Translated from the Latin of George Buchanan: with Notes and a Continuation to the Union in the Reign of Queen Anne*, 4 vols, Glasgow, 1827)

Buchanan, George: *The Tyrannous Reign of Mary Stewart* (Books XVII–XIX of *Rerum Scoticarum Historia* and *Detectio Maria Reginae Scotorum*) (trans. and ed. W.A. Gatherer, Edinburgh, 1958)

The Buik of the Kirk of the Canongait (ed. Alma B. Calderwood, Scottish Record Society, Edinburgh, 1961)

Calendar of Carew Manuscripts Preserved in the Archiepiscopal Library at Lambeth (6 vols, ed. J. S. Brewer, W. Bullen, London 1867–73)

Calendar of Letters, Despatches and State Papers relating to Negotiations between England and Spain, preserved in the Archives at Simancas and Elsewhere (17 vols, ed. G.A. Bergenroth, P. de Goyangos, Garrett Mattingly, R. Tyler et al., HMSO, London, 1862–1965)

Calendar of Letters and State Papers relating to English Affairs, in Rome, 1558–1587 (ed. J.M. Rigg, London, 1916–26, reprinted 1971)

Calendar of Letters and State Papers relating to English Affairs, preserved principally in the Archives of Simancas, Vol. I: Elizabeth, 1558–1567 (ed. Martin A.S. Hume et al., Public Record Office, 1892–9; reprinted 1971)

Calendar of the Manuscripts of the Most Honourable the Marquess of Bath (5 vols, London 1904-80)

Calendar of the Manuscripts of the Most Honourable the Marquis of Salisbury, preserved at Hatfield House (24, Historical Manuscripts Commission, London, 1883–1976)

Calendar of State Papers, Domestic Series, of the Reign of James I (ed. Mary Anne Everett Green, London, 1857)

Calendar of State Papers, Domestic Series, of the Reign of Mary I, 1553–1558 (ed. C.S. Knighton, London, 1998)

Calendar of State Papers, Foreign Series, of the Reign of Elizabeth, Vol. VIII: 1566–68, preserved in the State Paper Department of Her Majesty's Public Record Office (ed. Allan James Crosby, London, 1871)

Calendar of State Papers, Foreign Series, of the Reign of Elizabeth I, 1558–89, preserved in the State Paper Department of Her Majesty's Public Record Office (23 vols, ed. Joseph Stevenson, W.B. Turnbull et al. 1863–1950)

Calendar of State Papers, Domestic Series, of the Reigns of Edward VI, Mary and Elizabeth, 1547–1603 (12 vols, ed. Robert Lemon and Mary Anne Everett Green, 1856–72)

Calendar of State Papers and Manuscripts relating to English Affairs preserved in the Archives of Venice, Vol. VII: 1558–1580 (ed. Rawdon Brown and G. Cavendish-Bentinck, HMSO, London, 1864–98)

Calendar of State Papers relating to Scotland, 1509–1603 (ed. M.J. Thorpe, 1858)

Calendar of State Papers relating to Scotland (Edinburgh and Glasgow, 1889–1979)

Calendar of State Papers relating to Scotland and Mary, Queen of Scots, 1547–1603 Preserved in the Public Record Office, the British Museum and elsewhere in England (12 vols, ed. Joseph Bain, W.K. Boyd and M.S. Giuseppi, HM General Register House, Edinburgh, 1898–1969)

Camden, William: *Annales Rerum Anglicarum et Hibernicarum Regnante Elizabetha, or The True and Royal History of the Famous Empress Elizabeth* (London, 1594, 1615; trans. from the Latin by Abraham Darcie, London, 1625, and by R. Norton, London, 1635, and by Thomas Hearne, London, 1717)

Campbell, Hugh: *The Love Letters of Mary, Queen of Scots, with her Love Sonnets and Marriage Contracts…* (London, 1824)

Castelnau, Michel de, Seigneur de Mauvissière: *Memoires de Michel de Castlenau* (ed. Le Labourer, Paris, 1731)

Catherine de' Medici, Queen of France: *Lettres de Catherine des Medicis* (11 vols, ed. H. de la Ferrière-Percy, Paris, 1880–1919)

Caussin, N.: *L'Histoire d'incomparable Reyne Marie Stuart* (Paris, 1645)

The Cecil Papers: A Collection of State Papers relating to Affairs in the Reigns of King Henry VIII, King Edward VI, Queen Mary and Queen Elizabeth, to the Year 1596, left by William Cecil, Lord Burghley, and now remaining at Hatfield House (15 vols, ed. Samuel Haynes and William Murdin, London, 1740–59)

The Secret Correspondence of Sir Robert Cecil with James VI, King of Scotland (ed. D. Dalrymple, Edinburgh, 1766)

Chamberlain, John: Letter written by John Chamberlain during the reign of Elizabeth I (London, 1861)

Chambers, David: *Discours de la légitime succession des femmes aux possessions de leurs parents* (Paris, 1579)

A Collection and Abridgement of Celebrated Criminal Trials in Scotland (ed. Hugo Arnot, Advocate, Edinburgh, 1758)

Collections relating to the History of Mary, Queen of Scotland (4 vols, ed. James Anderson, Edinburgh, 1725–8, London, 1729)

A Complete Collection of State Trials (ed. D. Thom, William Cobbett and T.B. Rowel I, 1809–98, reprinted 1972)

Conn, G.: *Vitae Mariae Stuartae* (Rome, 1624)

Cowan, Samuel: *The Last Days of Mary Stuart and the Journal of Bourgoing, her Physician* (London, 1907)

Craig, Sir Thomas, of Riccarton: *Henrici Illustrissimi Ducis Albaniae, Comitis Rossiae etc. et Mariae Serenissimae Scotorum Reginae Epithalamium,* 1565 (trans. Wrangham in *Epithalamia Tria Mariana*, listed below)

The Private Diary of John Dee (ed. James Halliwell, London, 1842)

Lives and Letters of the Devereux, Earls of Essex, 1540–1646 (2 vols, London, 1853)

A Diurnal of Remarkable Occurrents that have passed within the Country of Scotland since the Death of King James the Fourth till the Year MDLXXV, from a Manuscript of the Sixteenth Century in the Possession of Sir John Maxwell of Pollock, Baronet (ed. T. Thomson, Bannatyne Club, XLV, Edinburgh, 1833)

Early Views and Maps of Edinburgh, 1544–1852 (Royal Scots Geographical Society, n.d.)

Edinburgh, Records of the Burgh (Scottish Burgh Records Society, Edinburgh, 1875)

Elizabeth I: The Letters of Queen Elizabeth (ed. G.B. Harrison, London, 1935, reprinted 1968)

Letters of Queen Elizabeth and James VI of Scotland (ed. J. Bruce, London, 1849)

Elizabeth I: Autograph Compositions and Foreign Language Originals (ed. J. Mueller, L.S. Marcus, Chicago, 2003)

Elizabeth I: Collected Works (ed. L.S. Marcus, J. Mueller, M.B. Rose, Chicago, 2000)

Elton, G.R. (ed.): *The Tudor Constitution: Documents and Commentary* (Cambridge, 1972)

English and Scottish Popular Ballads (ed. James Francis Child from his own collection; ed. Helen Child Sargent and George Lyman Kittredge, London, 1905)

Epithalamia Tria Mariana (ed. Revd Francis Wrangham, Chester, 1837)

d'Ewes, Sir Simonds: *The Journals of all the Parliaments during the Reign of Queen Elizabeth* (revised and published by Paul Bowes, 1682 and 1693)

Frarin, Peter: *An Oration against the Unlawful Insurrections of the Protestants of our Time under Pretence to Reform Religion* (Antwerp, 1566)

Hakluyt, Richard: *The Principal Navigations, Voyages, Traffiques and Discoveries of the English Nation* (London, 1599)

The Hamilton Papers: Letters and Papers illustrating the Political Relations of England and Scotland in the XVIth Century. Formerly in the Possession of the Dukes of Hamilton, now in the British Museum (ed. Joseph Bain, Edinburgh, 1890–92)

Harington, John: *Nugae Antiquae. Being a Miscellaneous Collection of Original Papers in Prose and Verse written during the reigns of Henry VIII, Edward VI, Queen Mary, Elizabeth and King James* (London, 1792)

Harley, T.E. (ed.): *Proceedings in the Parliaments of Elizabeth I, 1558–1581* (3 vols, London, 1981–95)

The Harliean Miscellany, Or, A Collection of Scarce, Curious and Entertaining Pamphlets and Tracts, as Well in Manuscript as in Print, Found in the Late Earl of Oxford's Library (2 vols, London, 1808)

Harrison, George: *The Elizabethan Journals. Being a Record of the Things Most Talked of during the years 1591–1603* (London, 1938)

Recueil des Lettres Missives de Henri IV (9 vols, ed. M. Berger de Xivrey, J. Gaudet, Paris, 1843–76)

Herries, John Maxwell, Lord: *Historical Memoirs of the Reign of Mary, Queen of Scots, and a Portion of the Reign of King James the Sixth* (ed. Robert Pitcairn, Abbotsford Club, Edinburgh, 1836)

Historical Records of the Family of Leslie, 1067–1869 (ed. C. Leslie, 1869)

The Historie and Life of King James the Sext (author unknown; ed. T. Thomson, Bannatyne Club, Edinburgh, 1825; ed. Malcolm Laing, Edinburgh, 1904)

Holinshed, Raphael: *The Chronicles of England, Scotland and Ireland* (London, 1587; 6 vols, ed. Sir Henry Ellis, London, 1807–8).

Illustrations of British history, biography, and manners, in the reigns of Henry VIII, Edward VI, Mary, Elizabeth, & James I: exhibited in a series of original papers, selected from the MSS. of the noble families of Howard, Talbot, and Cecil (3 vols, ed. E. Lodge, London, 1838)

Illustrations of the Reign of Queen Mary (Maitland Club, XXV, Glasgow, 1837)

Index to the Principal Papers relating to Scotland in the Historical Manuscripts Commission's Reports (ed. C.S. Terry, 1908)

Inventaires de la Royne d'Escosse, Douairière de France: Catalogues of the Jewels, Dresses, Furniture, Books and Paintings of Mary, Queen of Scots, 1556–1569 (ed. Joseph Robertson, Bannatyne Club, Edinburgh, 1863)

Letters and State Papers during the Reign of King James VI (ed. J. Maidment, Edinburgh, 1838)

James VI: *Correspondence of James VI of Scotland with Sir Robert Cecil and Others in England during the Reign of Elizabeth I* (London, 1861)

James VI: *The Workes of the Most High and Mighty Prince, James* (London, 1616)

Keith, Robert: *The History of the Affairs of Church and State in Scotland from the Beginning of the Reformation to 1585* (3 vols, ed. J.P. Lawson and J.C. Lyon, Spottiswoode Society, Edinburgh, 1844, 1845, 1850)

'Papers relating to Mary Queen of Scots, Mostly Addressed to or Written by Sir Francis Knollys', Philobiblon Society Miscellanies, 14 (1872), 14–69

Knox, John: *The History of the Reformation of Religion in Scotland* (London, 1587; Edinburgh, 1732; ed. William McGavin, Glasgow, 1831; revised and ed. Cuthbert Lennox, Edinburgh, 1905; ed. William Croft Dickinson, London, 1949)

Knox, John: *The Political Writings of John Knox* (ed. Marvin A. Breslow, The Folger Shakespeare Library, Washington, London and Toronto, 1985)

Knox, John: *The Works of John Knox* (includes *History of the Reformation in Scotland* and Knox's correspondence; 6 vols, ed. David Laing, Bannatyne Club, Edinburgh, 1846–64; reprinted New York, 1966)

Labanoff, Alexandre (ed.): *Lettres inédites de Marie Stuart 1558–87* (Paris, 1839)

Labanoff, Alexandre (ed.): *Lettres, instructions et mémoires de Marie Stuart, Reine d'Ecosse* (7 vols, Paris, 1844–5)

Laughton, John Knox (ed): *State Papers Relating to the defeat of the Spanish Armada* (2 vols, London, 1894)

The Lennox Narrative (Cambridge University Library MSS.; ed. Reginald Henry Mahon in *Mary, Queen of Scots: A Study of the Lennox Narrative in the University Library of Cambridge*, Cambridge, 1924)

Leslie, John, Bishop of Ross: *A Defence of the Honour of the right high, mighty and noble Princess Marie, Queen of Scotland* (London, 1569; revised edition under the pseudonym Philippes Morgan, Liège, 1571)

Leslie, John, Bishop of Ross: *The History of Scotland from the Death of King James I in the Year 1436 [sic] to the Year 1561* (ed. T. Thomson, Bannatyne Club, XXXIX, Edinburgh, 1829/30; 2 vols, trans. James Dalrymple and ed. E.G. Gody and William Murison, Scottish Text Society, Edinburgh, 1895)

Lettenhove, Kervyn de: *Relations Politiques des Pays-Bas et de L'Angleterre sous les Règne de Philippe II* (ed. K. de Lettenhove, 11 vols, Brussels, 1882–1900)

Letters and Papers, Foreign and Domestic, of the Reign of Henry VIII (ed. James Gairdner and R.H. Brodie, HMSO, London, 1901–2)

Letters of Royal and Illustrious Ladies (ed. Mary Anne Everett Wood, London, 1846)

Libraries of Mary, Queen of Scots and James VI (Maitland Club Miscellany, Glasgow, 1834)

Lindsay of Pittscottie, Robert: *The History and Chronicles of Scotland* (ed. J.G. Dalyell, 1824; 2 vols, ed A.J.G. Mackay, Scottish Text Society, Edinburgh, 1899–1911)

L'Isle, Lord De: *Report on the Manuscripts of Lord De L'Isle and Dudley Preserved at Penshurst Place* (6 vols, London, 1925–66)

Maisse, André de: *A Journal of all that was Accomplished by Monsieur de Maisse, Ambassador in England from King Henri IV to Elizabeth, Anno Domini 1957* (London, 1931)

Maitland, James: *A Narrative Of The Principal Acts Of The Regency, During The Minority Of Mary Queen Of Scotland* (repro, London, 2013)

Mary of Lorraine: *The Scottish Correspondence*, ed. A.I. Cameron (Edinburgh, 1927)

Mary, Queen of Scots: Letters – *see Labanoff; Teulet*

Mary, Queen of Scots: *Letters of Mary, Queen of Scots, and Documents connected with her Personal History, now first published* (ed. Agnes Strickland, 3 vols, London, 1842–3)

Mary, Queen of Scots: *Lettres inédites de Marie Stuart* (ed. Prince Alexandre Labanoff, Paris, 1839)

Mary, Queen of Scots: *Lettres, instructions et mémoires de Marie Stuart, Reine d'Ecosse* (7 vols, ed. Prince Alexandre Labanoff, London, 1844–5)

Mary, Queen of Scots: notations in the Book of Hours, National Library of Russia

Melville, Sir James of Halhill: *Memoirs of his own Life, 1549–93* (London, 1683; ed. D. Wilson, London, 1752; ed. A. Francis Steuart, London, 1929)

Miscellaneous Papers principally illustrative of Events in the Reigns of Queen Mary and James VI (Maitland Club, Glasgow, 1834)

Miscellaneous State Papers, 1501–1726 (ed. the Earl of Hardwicke, 1778)

Miscellany of the Scottish History Society, Vol. II (Scottish History Society, Edinburgh, 1904)

Mulcaster, Richard: *The Passage of our most Drad Soveraigne Lady Quene Elyzabeth through the Citie of London Westminster the daye before her coronacion* (London, 1559)

Narratives of Scottish Catholics under Mary Stuart and James VI (ed. W. Forbes-Leith, Edinburgh, 1885)

The National MSS. of Scotland (3 vols, London, 1867–73)

Nau, Claude, Sieur de Fontenage: *Memorials of Mary Stuart, or The History of Mary Stewart from the Murder of Riccio until her Flight into England, by Claude Nau, her Secretary* (BL Cotton MSS.; ed. Revd Joseph Stevenson, SJ, *with Illustrative Papers from the Secret Archives of the Vatican and other Collections in Rome*, Edinburgh, 1883)

Nichols, J.: *The Progresses and Public Processions of Queen Elizabeth*, 3 vols (London, 1788–1805)

Original Letters illustrative of English History (ed. Henry Ellis, London, 1824–46)

Papal Negotiations with Mary, Queen of Scots, during her Reign in Scotland, 1561–67, Edited from the Original Documents in the Vatican Archives and Elsewhere (ed. John Hungerford Pollen, Scottish Historical Society, XXXVII, Edinburgh, 1901)

Papers relating to the History of Mary Stuart, including 'Maitland's Narrative' of the Principal Acts of the Regency (ed. W.S. Fitch, printed for circulation, Ipswich, 1842)

Peck, D.C. (ed.): *Leicester's Commonwealth: The Copy of a Letter Written by a Master of Art of Cambridge, 1584* (Ohio, 1985)

Phillip II of Spain, *Correspondance de Philippe II sur les Affaires des Pays-Bas* (Joseph Lefevre, 2 vols, Brussels, 1940-56)

Phyllips, T.: *A Commemoration of the Right Noble and Virtuous Lady Margaret Douglas's Good Grace, Countess of Lennox* (1578)

Poulet, Amias: *The letter-books of Sir Amias Poulet, keeper of Mary Queen of Scots* (ed. John Morris, 1874)

Proceedings and Ordinances of the Privy Council of England (ed. H. Nicholas, Records Commissioners, London, 1834–7)

Proceedings in the Parliaments of Elizabeth I (3 vols, ed. T.E. Hartley, Leicester, 1981–95)

The Register of the Great Seal of Scotland, 1546–80 (ed. J.M. Thompson, Edinburgh, 1886, reprinted Edinburgh, 1984)

The Register of the Privy Council of Scotland, Vol. I: 1545–1569 (ed. John Hill Burton et al., HM General Register House, Edinburgh, 1877)

The Register of the Privy Seal of Scotland (ed. M. Livingstone et al., Edinburgh, 1908, 1957, 1963)

Registrum Honoris de Morton: A Series of Ancient Charters of the Earldom of Morton with other Original Papers (Bannatyne Club, Edinburgh, 1853)

Ronsard, Pierre de: *The Works of Ronsard* (ed. Prosper Blanchemain, Paris, 1857)

Ruthven, Patrick, Lord: Narration in R. Keith's *History of the Affairs of Church and State in Scotland down to 1567* (ed. J.P. Lawson, Spottiswoode Society, 1844)

The Manuscripts of his Grace the Duke of Rutland, Preserved at Belvoir Castle (4 vols, London, 1888–1905)

Sadler, Sir Ralph: *The State Papers and Letters of Sir Ralph Sadler, Knight-Banneret* (2 vols, ed. Arthur Clifford, Edinburgh, 1809)

Sanderson, William: *A Complete History of the Lives and Reigns of Mary, Queen of Scotland, and her Son and Successor, James the Sixth* (London, 1656)

Scottish Historical Documents (ed. Gordon Donaldson, Edinburgh and London, 1974)

Selections from Unpublished Manuscripts in the College of Arms and the British Museum, illustrating the Reign of Mary, Queen of Scotland, 1543–68 (ed. Joseph Stevenson, Maitland Club, XLI, Glasgow, 1837)

The Silver Casket, being Love Letters and Love Poems attributed to Mary Stuart, Queen of Scots, now Modernised and Translated, with an Introduction (ed. Clifford Bax, 1912, 1946)

Spottiswoode, John, Archbishop of St Andrews: *The History of the Church and State of Scotland, beginning the Year of our Lord 203, and continued to the End of the Reign of King James the VI of ever blessed Memory* (London, 1655; 3 vols, ed. M. Russell and M. Napier, Bannatyne Club and Spottiswoode Society, 1847–51)

State Papers in the Public Record Office Statutes of the Realm (11 vols, ed. A. Luder et al., Records Commissioners, London, 1810–28)

Strype, John (ed.): *Annals of the Reformation and Establishment of Religion, and Other Various Occurrences in the Church of England, During Queen Elizabeth's Happy Reign* (4 vols, 1709–31)

Teulet, Alexandre (ed.): *Lettres de Marie Stuart* (Paris, 1859)

Teulet, Alezandre (ed.): *Papiers d'Etat, pièces et documents inédits ou peu connus relatifs à l'Histoire de l'Ecosse au 16e siècle* (Paris, 1852–60; Bannatyne Club, Edinburgh, 1852–60)

Teulet, Alexandre (ed.): *Relations politiques de la France et de l'Espagne avec l'Ecosse au XVI siècle* (Paris, 1862)

Tudor Royal Proclamations (3 vols, ed. P. Hughes, J.F. Larkin, London, 1964–9)

Turnbull, W.: *Letters of Mary Stuart, Queen of Scotland* (London, 1845)

Correspondence of Sir Henry Unton, Knight, Ambassador from Queen Elizabeth to Henry IV, King of France in the Years 1591 and 1592 (London, 1847)

De Vita et Rebus Gestis Serenissimae Principis Mariae Scotorum Reginae Franciae Dotoriae (ed. Samuel Jebb, 2 vols, London, 1725)

Walsingham, Francis: 'Journal of Sir Francis Walsingham from December 1570 to April 1583', *Camden Miscellany VI* (London, 1871)

Secondary Sources

Alford, Stephen: *Burghley: William Cecil at the Court of Elizabeth I* (London, 2008)

Alford, Stephen: *The Early Elizabethan Polity: William Cecil and the British Succession Crisis, 1558–1569* (Cambridge, 1998)

Alford, Stephen: *Edward VI: The Last Boy King* (London, 2014)

Alford, Stephen: *The Watchers: A Secret History of the Reign of Elizabeth I* (London, 2012)

Allen, J.W.: *History of Political Thought in the Sixteenth Century* (1941)

Anonymous Elder of the Church of Scotland: *Mary, Queen of Scots: A Narrative and Defence* (1889)

Arbuthnot, Mrs P. Stewart-Mackenzie: *Queen Mary's Book* (London, 1907)

Archer, Jayne; Goldring, Elizabeth; and Knight, Sarah: *The Progress, Pageants and Entertainments of Queen Elizabeth I* (Oxford, 2007)

Armstrong, Robert Bruce: *The History of Liddesdale* (Edinburgh, 1883)

Armstrong Davison, M.H.: *The Casket Letters: A Solution to the Mystery of Mary, Queen of Scots and the Murder of Lord Darnley* (London and Washington, 1965)

Armstrong Davison, M.H.: 'The Maladies of Mary, Queen of Scots and her Husbands' (Scottish Society of the History of Medicine: Report of Proceedings, 1955–6)

Arnold, Janet: *Queen Elizabeth's Wardrobe Unlock'd* (Leeds, 1988)

Arnot, Hugo: *The History of Edinburgh* (London, 1788)

Ashley, Maurice: *The Stuarts in Love, with some Reflections on Love and Marriage in the Sixteenth and Seventeenth Centuries* (London, 1963)

l'Aubespine, Claude de: *Historie Particulière de la Court de Henry II* (Archives curieuses de l'histoire de France ière Serie. Vol. 3. Paris, 1834)

Balfour, Sir James: *The Scots Peerage* (Edinburgh, 1905)

Bapst, Edmond: *Les Mariages de Jacques V* (Paris, 1889)

Barwick, G.E.: 'A Sidelight on the Mystery of Mary Stuart: Pietro Bizari's Contemporary Account of the Murders of Riccio and Darnley' (Scottish Historical Review, 31, 1924)

Baschet, A: *La Diplomatie Venitiènne* (Paris, 1862)

Bates, Catherine: *The Rhetoric of Courtship in Elizabethan Language and Literature* (Cambridge, 1992)

Beaugué, Jean de: *Histoire de la Guerre en Ecosse* (London, reprint 2012)

Beckinsale, B.W.: *Elizabeth I* (London, 1963)

Beem, Charles: *The Lioness Roared: The Problems of Female Rule in English History* (New York, 2006)

Beer, Anna: *Bess, the Life of Lady Ralegh, Wife to Sir Walter* (London, 2004)

Begg, Robert Burns: *The History of Lochleven Castle* (Edinburgh, 1890)

Bellamy, John: *The Tudor Law of Treason: An Introduction* (London, 1979)

Belleval, R. de: *Les Fils de Henri II* (Paris, 1989)

Bennett, H.S.: *English Books and Readers, 1558–1603* (Cambridge, 1965)

Bentley-Cranch, Dana: 'Effigy and Portrait in Sixteenth Century Scotland' (Review of Scottish Culture, 4, 1988)

Berry, Philippa: *Of Chastity and Power: Elizabethan Literature and the Unmarried Queen* (London, 1989)

Bertelli, Sergio: *The King's Body: Sacred Rituals of Power in Mediaeval and Early Modern Europe* (trans. R. Burr Litchfield, Pennsylvania, 2001)

Bertière, Simone: *Les Reines de France au temps les Valois* (Paris, 1994)

Bingham, Caroline: *Darnley: A Life of Henry Stuart, Lord Darnley, Consort of Mary, Queen of Scots* (London, 1995)

Bingham, Caroline: *James VI of Scotland* (London, 1979)

Bingham, Caroline: *The Kings and Queens of Scotland* (London, 1976)

Bingham, Caroline: *The Making of a King: The Early Years of James VI and I* (London, 1968)

Bingham, Caroline: *The Poems of Mary, Queen of Scots* (Royal Stuart Papers, X, The Royal Stuart Society, 1976)

Bingham, Madeleine: *Mary, Queen of Scots* (London, 1969)

Bingham, Madeleine: *Scotland under Mary Stuart: An Account of Everyday Life* (London, 1971)

Black, J.B.: *Andrew Lang and the Casket Letter Controversy* (Edinburgh, 1951)

Black, J.B.: *The Reign of Elizabeth, 1558–1603* (Oxford, 1959)

Blake, William: *William Maitland of Lethington, 1528–1573* (Studies in British History, XIX, Lampeter, 1990)

Borman, Tracy: *Elizabeth's Women: The Hidden Story of the Virgin Queen* (London, 2009)

Borman, Tracy: *The Private Lives of the Tudors: Uncovering the Secrets of Britain's Greatest Dynasty* (London, 2016)

Borman, Tracy: *Thomas Cromwell, the untold story of Henry VIII's most faithful servant* (London, 2014)

Bossy, John: 'Rome and the Elizabethan Catholics: A Question of Geography' (Historical Journal, 7, 1964, 135–49)

Bourciez, Edouard: *Littérature de cour sous Henri II* (Librairie Hachette, Paris, 1886)

Bowen, Marjorie: *Mary, Queen of Scots, the Daughter of Debate* (London, 1934; reprinted London, 1971)

Breeze, David J., and Donaldson, Gordon: *A Queen's Progress. An Introduction to the Buildings associated with Mary, Queen of Scots, in the Care of the Secretary of State for Scotland* (HMSO, Edinburgh, 1987)

Brigden, Susan: *London and the Reformation* (London, 1989)

Brigden, Susan: *New Worlds, Lost Worlds: The Rule of The Tudors, 1485–1603* (London, 2000)

Bridgen, Susan: *Thomas Wyatt: the Heart's Forest* (London, 2012)

Brown, P. Hume: *History of Scotland* (3 vols, Cambridge, 1908–12)

Brown, P. Hume: *John Knox: A Biography* (2 vols, London, 1895)

Brown, P. Hume: *Scotland in the Time of Queen Mary* (London, 1904)

Bryce, W.M: *The Voyage of Mary Queen of Scots in 1548* (English Historical Review Vol. XXII. 1907)

Buchanan, Katherine and Lucinda Dean (eds), *Medieval and Early Modern Representations of Authority in Scotland and Great Britain* (London: Routledge, 2016)

Burns, E.: *Scottish Coins* (London, 1887)

Burton, J. Hill: *The History of Scotland* (8 vols, Edinburgh, 1873–4)

Calderwood, David: *The True History of the Church of Scotland from the Beginning of the Reformation unto the End of the Reign of King James VI* (Rotterdam, 1678; ed. T. Thomson and D. Laing, 8 vols, Wodrow Society, Edinburgh, 1842–9)

Canny, Nicholas: *The Elizabethan Conquest of Ireland: A Pattern Established* (Hansocks, 1976)

Carpenter, Sarah: 'Masking and Politics: The Alison Craik Incident, Edinburgh 1561', Journal of the Society for Renaissance Studies (21), 2007, 625–636

Carpenter, Sarah: '"Gely wyth tharmys of Scotland England": Word, Image and Performance at the marriage of James IV and Margaret Tudor' in eds. Janet Hadley Williams and J. Derek McClure, *Studies in the Culture of Medieval and Early Modern Scotland* (Newcastle: Scholars Press, 2013), 165–177.

Carroll, Stuart: *Martyrs and Murderers: The Guise Family and the Making of Europe* (Oxford, 2009)

Carruth, Revd. J.A.: *Mary, Queen of Scots* (Norwich, 1988)

Castor, Helen: *Blood and Roses: The Paston Family in the Fifteenth Century* (London, 2004)

Castor, Helen: *Elizabeth I: A Study in Insecurity* (London, 2018)

Castor, Helen: *Joan of Arc: A History* (London, 2015)

Castor, Helen: *She Wolves: The Women who Ruled England before Elizabeth* (London, 2010)

Cavanagh, Sheila: *Wanton Eyes and Chaste Desires: Female Sexuality in 'The Fairie Queene'* (Bloomington, 1994)

Chalmers, George: *A Detection of the Love Letters Lately Attributed to Mary* (London, 1825)

Chalmers, George: *Life of James I* (Edinburgh, 1830)

Chalmers, George: *Life of Mary, Queen of Scots* (2 vols, London, 1818)

Chamberlain, Frederick: *The Private Character of Queen Elizabeth* (New York, 1922)

Chambers Biographical Dictionary (ed. Magnus Magnusson, Edinburgh, 1990)

Chauviré, Mons. Roger: *Le Secret de Marie Stuart* (Paris, 1937)

Cheetham, J. Keith: *On the Trail of Mary, Queen of Scots* (Edinburgh, 1999)

Cherry, Alastair: *Princes, Poets and Patrons: The Stuarts and Scotland* (Edinburgh, 1987)

Childs, Jessie: *God's Traitors: Terror and Faith in Elizabethan England* (London, 2014)

Childs, Jessie: *Henry VIII's Last Victim: The Life and Times of Henry Howard, Earl of Surrey* (London, 2006)

Christy, Miller: 'Queen Elizabeth's Visit to Tilbury in 1588', English Historical Review, 34 (1919), 43–61

Clarke, Andrea: *Tudor Monarchs: Lives in Letters* (London, 2017)

Clegg, Melanie: *Scourge of Henry VIII: the Life of Marie de Guise* (London, 2016)

Cochran-Patrick, R.W.: *Catalogue of the Medals of Scotland: From the Earliest Period to the Present Time* (Edinburgh, 1884)

Collinson, Patrick: 'The Elizabethan Exclusion Crisis and the Elizabethan Polity', Proceedings of the British Academy, 84, 1994, 51–92.

Collinson, Patrick: *The English Captivity of Mary, Queen of Scots* (Sheffield, 1987)

Cooper, John: *The Queen's Agent: Francis Walsingham at the Court of Elizabeth I* (London, 2011)

Cowan, Ian B.: *The Enigma of Mary Stuart* (London, 1971)

Cowan, Ian B.: *Mary, Queen of Scots* (Edinburgh, 1987)

Cowan, Ian B.: *The Scottish Reformation: Church and Society in Sixteenth Century Scotland* (London, 1982)

Cowan, Ian B., and Shaw, Duncan: *The Renaissance and Reformation in Scotland* (Edinburgh, 1983)

Cowan, Samuel: *Mary, Queen of Scots, and Who Wrote the Casket Letters* (2 vols, London, 1901)

Crawford, Katherine: 'Cathérine de' Medici and the Performance of Political Motherhood', Sixteenth-Century Journal, 31:3 (2000), 643–73

Crawford, Thomas: *The History of Mary, Queen of Scots* (Edinburgh, 1793)

Crawford, P. and Gowing, L.: *Women's Worlds in Seventeenth-Century England* (London, 2000)

Creighton, Mandell: *Queen Elizabeth* (London, 1899)

Cunningham, C.W. & P: *Handbook of English Costume in the 16th Century* (1959)

Cust, Lady Elizabeth: *Some Account of the Stuarts of Aubigny in France, 1422–1672* (privately printed, London, 1891)

Cust, Lionel: *Notes on the Authentic Portraits of Mary, Queen of Scots* (London, 1903)

Dalrymple, Sir David, Lord Hailes: *Annals of Scotland* (3 vols, London, 1797)

Dalrymple, Sir David, Lord Hailes: *Miscellaneous Remarks on 'The Enquiry into the Evidence against Mary, Queen of Scots'* (London, 1784)

Dawson, Jane E.A.: 'Mary, Queen of Scots, Lord Darnley and Anglo-Scottish Relations in 1565' (International History Review, 8, 1986)

De Lisle, Leanda: *After Elizabeth: How James King of Scots Won the Crown of England in 1603* (London, 2005)

De Lisle, Leanda: *The Sisters who would be Queen: The Tragedy of Mary, Katherine and Lady Jane Grey* (London, 2009)

De Lisle, Leanda: *Tudor: The Family Story* (London, 2013)

Dickinson, W. Croft: *A New History of Scotland*, Vol. I (London, 1961)

Dickinson, W. Croft, Donaldson, Gordon, and Milne, Isobel: *A Source Book of Scottish History*, Vol. II (Edinburgh, 1958)

Diefendorf, Barbara: *Beneath the Cross: Catholics and Huguenots in Sixteenth-Century Paris* (Oxford, 1991)

Dillon, Anne: *The Construction of Martyrdom in the English Catholic Community 1535–1603* (Aldershot, 2002)

Donaldson, Gordon: *All the Queen's Men: Power and Politics in Mary Stewart's Scotland* (London, 1983)

Donaldson, Gordon: *The First Trial of Mary, Queen of Scots* (London, 1969)

Donaldson, Gordon: *Mary, Queen of Scots* (London, 1974)

Donaldson, Gordon: *Scotland: Church and Nation through Sixteen Centuries* (Edinburgh and London, 1972)

Donaldson, Gordon: *Scotland: James V to James VII* (Edinburgh and London, 1965)

Donaldson, Gordon: *Scottish Kings* (London, 1967)

Donaldson, Gordon: *The Scottish Reformation* (Cambridge, 1960)

Donaldson, Gordon, and Morpeth, Robert S.: *Who's Who in Scottish History* (Oxford, 1973)

Doran, Susan: *Monarchy and Matrimony: The Courtships of Elizabeth I* (London, 1996)

Doran, Susan: *Elizabeth I and Her Circle* (Oxford, 2015)

Doran, Susan: *Elizabeth I and Foreign Policy* (Lancaster, 1993)

Doran, Susan: *Elizabeth I and Religion* (Lancaster, 1993)

Doran, Susan and Starkey, David (eds): *Henry VIII: Man and Monarch* (London, 2009)

Doran, Susan and Durston, Christopher: *Princes, Pastors and People: the Church and Religion in Scotland, 1500–1700* (London, 2002)

Doran, Susan and Starkey, David (ed.): *Elizabeth: The Exhibition at the National Maritime Museum* (London, 2003)

Douglas-Irvine, Helen: *Royal Palaces of Scotland* (London, 1911)

Drummond, Humphrey: *Our Man in Scotland: Sir Ralph Sadler, 1507–1587* (London, 1969)

Drummond, Humphrey: *The Queen's Man: James Hepburn, Earl of Bothwell and Duke of Orkney 1536–1578* (London, 1975)

Duffy, Eamon: *Fires of Faith: Catholic England under Mary Tudor* (London, 2009)

Duffy, Eamon: *Saints, Sacrilege and Sedition: Religious Conflict in the Tudor Reformation* (London, 2012)

Duffy, Eamon: *Saints and Sinners: A History of the Popes* (London, 2001)

Duffy, Eamon: *The Stripping of the Altars: Traditional Religion in England, 1400–1580* (London, 2005)

Duffy, Eamon: *Voices of Morebath: Reformation and Rebellion in an English Village* (London, 2003)

Duffy, Eamon and David Loades: *The Church of Mary Tudor, 1300–1600* (Basingstoke, 2006)

Dunbar, John G.: 'The Palace of Holyroodhouse during the First Half of the Sixteenth Century' (Archaeological Journal, 120, 1964)

Dunbar, John G.: *Scottish Royal Palaces: The Architecture of the Royal Residences during the Late Mediaeval and Early Renaissance Periods* (East Linton, 1999)

Duncan, Thomas: 'Mary Stuart and the House of Huntly' (Scottish Historical Review, 4, 1906/7)

Duncan, Thomas: 'The Queen's Maries' (Scottish Historical Review, 2, 1905)

Duncan, Thomas: 'The Relations of the Earl of Murray with Mary Stuart' (Scottish Historical Review, 6, 1909)

Dunlop, Ian: *Palaces and Progresses of Elizabeth I* (New Haven, 1993)

Dunn, Jane: *Elizabeth and Mary: Cousins, Rivals, Queens* (New York, 2004)

L'Ecole de Fontainebleau (Exhibition Catalogue, Grand Palais, Paris, 1972)

Edwards, Francis: *The Dangerous Queen* (London, 1964)

Edwards, Francis: *The Marvellous Chance* (London, 1968)

Edwards, John: *Mary I: England's Catholic Queen* (London, 2011)

Elton, G.R.: *England under the Tudors* (London, 1965)

Elton, G.R.: *The Parliament of the Tudors, 1559–1581* (Cambridge, 1986)

Elton, G.R.: *Reform and Reformation, 1509–1558* (London, 1977)

Elton, G.R.: *The Tudor Revolution in Government: Administrative Changes in the Reign of Henry VIII* (Cambridge, 1953)

Erickson, Carolly: *The First Elizabeth* (New York, 1983; London, 1999)

Evans, Joan: *A History of Jewellery, 1100–1870* (London, 1953)

Evans, Victoria Sylvia: *Ladies in Waiting: Women who Served at the Tudor Court* (London, 2014)

Exchequer Rolls, Vol. 19 (ed. G.P. McNeill, Edinburgh, 1989)

Eyre-Todd, George: *The History of Glasgow*, Vol. II (Glasgow, 1931)

Falkland Palace and Royal Burgh (The National Trust for Scotland, Edinburgh, 1995)

Fawcett, Richard: *The Palace of Holyroodhouse* (Royal Collection, London, 1992)

Fawcett, Richard: *Stirling Castle* (Edinburgh, 1983)

Fergusson, Sir James: *Lowland Lairds* (London, 1949)

Fergusson, Sir James: *The Sixteen Peers of Scotland* (London, 1960)

Fleming, David Hay: *Mary, Queen of Scots: From her Birth to her Flight into England: A Brief Biography with Critical Notes, and a Few Documents, hitherto Unpublished, and an Itinerary* (London, 1897)

Forneron, Henri: *Les Ducs de Guise et leur Epoque* (Paris, 1877)

Fox, Julia: *Jane Boleyn: The True Story of the Infamous Lady Rochford* (London, 2007)

Fox, Julia: *Sister Queens: Katherine of Aragon and Juana of Castile* (London, 2011)

Francis, Grant R.: *Scotland's Royal Line: The Tragic House of Stuart* (New York, 1929)

Fraprie, Frank: *The Castles and Keeps of Scotland* (London, 1908)

Fraser, Lady Antonia: *King James VI and I* (London, 1974)

Fraser, Lady Antonia: *Mary, Queen of Scots* (London, 1969)

Fraser, Lady Antonia: *Mary, Queen of Scots and the Historians* (Royal Stuart Papers, VII, the Royal Stuart Society, 1974)

Fraser, Lady Antonia: *The Gunpowder Plot: Terror and Faith in 1605* (London, 1998)

Fraser, Lady Antonia (ed.): *The Lives of the Kings and Queens of England* (London, 1975)

Fraser, Lady Antonia: *The Six Wives of Henry VIII* (London, 1992)

Fraser, Lady Antonia: *The Weaker Vessel: Women's Lot in Seventeenth Century England* (London, 1984)

Fraser, William: *The Book of Douglas* (4 vols, Edinburgh, 1884/5)

Fraser, William: *The Lennox* (2 vols, Edinburgh, 1874/6)

Freebairn, James: *Life of Mary Stewart* (Edinburgh, 1725)

Freeman, Arthur: *Elizabeth's Misfits: Brief Lives of English Eccentrics, Exploiters, Rogues and Failures, 1580–1660* (London, 1978)

Frieda, Leonie: *Catherine de Medici* (London, 2004)

Frieda, Leonie: *Francis I: the Maker of Modern France* (London, 2018)

Froude, James Anthony: *The History of England from the Fall of Residences during the Late Mediaeval and Early Renaissance Periods* (East Linton, 1999)

Frye, Susan: *Elizabeth I: The Competition for Representation* (Oxford, 1993)

Fuller, Thomas: *The Church History of Britain* (1655; ed. John Gough Nichols, 1868)

Gauthier, Jules: *Histoire de Marie Stuart* (2 vols, Paris, 1875)

Girouard, Mark: *Life in the French Country House* (London, 2000)

Glasford Bell, Henry: *Life of Mary, Queen of Scots* (2 vols, Edinburgh, 1828, 1831)

Goldstone, Nancy: *Daughters of the Winter Queen: Four Remarkable Sisters, the Crown of Bohemia and the Legacy of Mary, Queen of Scots* (London, 2018)

Goldstone, Nancy: *Rival Queens: Catherine de Medici, her daughter Margaret de Valois and the Betrayal that Ignited a Kingdom* (London, 2015)

Goodall, Walter: *An Examination of the Letters Said to be Written by Mary, Queen of Scots, to James, Earl of Bothwell; shewing by Intrinsic and Extrinsic Evidence that they are Forgeries; also, an Enquiry into the Murder of King Henry* (2 vols, Edinburgh and London, 1754)

Gore-Browne, Robert: *Lord Bothwell: A Study of the Life, Character and Times of James Hepburn, 4th Earl of Bothwell* (London, 1937)

Gow, Ian: *The Palace of Holyroodhouse* (Royal Collection, London, 1995)

Grant, I.F.: *The Social and Economic Development of Scotland* (Edinburgh, 1930)

Green, Janet: 'I My Self: Queen Elizabeth's Oration at Tilbury Camp', Sixteenth-Century Journal, 28 (1997) 421–5.

Grierson, Elizabeth Wilson: *Edinburgh Castle, Holyrood and St Giles' Cathedral* (London, 1908)

Gristwood, Sarah: *Arbella, England's Lost Queen* (London, 2002)

Gristwood, Sarah: *Elizabeth and Leicester: Power, Passion, Politics* (London, 2007)

Gristwood, Sarah: *Game of Queens: The Women who made Sixteenth-Century Europe* (London, 2016)

Guy, John: *The Children of Henry VIII* (Oxford, 2013)

Guy, John: *Elizabeth: The Forgotten Years* (London, 2016)

Guy, John: *My Heart is My Own: The Life of Mary, Queen of Scots* (London, 2003)

Guy, John: *Thomas More: A Very Brief History* (London, 2017)

Guy, John: *Tudor England* (Oxford, 1988)

Guy, John (ed.): *The Reign of Elizabeth I: Court and Culture in the Last Decade* (Cambridge, 1995)

Hackett, Helen: *Virgin Mother, Maiden Queen: Elizabeth I and the Cult of the Virgin Queen* (London, 1995)

Hadfield, Andrew (ed.): *Literature and Censorship in Renaissance England* (London, 2001)

Haigh, Christopher: *Elizabeth I* (Harlow, 2001)

Haigh, Christopher: *Elizabeth I: Profile in Power* (London, 1988)

Haigh, Christopher: *The Reign of Elizabeth I* (London, 1984)

Hamilton, Angus, Duke of: *Maria R.: Mary, Queen of Scots, the Crucial Years* (Edinburgh and London, 1991)

Hannan, Thomas: *Famous Scottish Houses: The Lowlands* (London, 1928)

Hannay, R.K.: 'The Earl of Arran and Queen Mary' (Scottish Historical Review, 18, 1920)

Harkness, Deborah: *The Jewel House: Elizabethan London and the Scientific Revolution* (New Haven, 2007)

Harris, Stuart: *Mary, Queen of Scots, and Sir Simon Preston's House, Edinburgh* (Edinburgh, 1983)

Harrison, John: *The History of the Monastery of the Holy Rude and of the Palace of Holyroodhouse* (Edinburgh, 1919)

Haugaard, William: 'Elizabeth Tudor's Book of Devotions; A Neglected Clue to the Queen's Life and Character', Sixteenth-Century Journal, 12:2 (1981), 79–106

Hay Fleming, David: *Mary Queen of Scots from her Birth to her Flight into England* (London, 1897)

Hearn, Karen (ed.): *Dynasties: Paintings in Tudor and Jacobean England, 1530–1630* (London, 1995)

Henderson, Thomas Finlayson: *The Casket Letters and Mary, Queen of Scots* (Edinburgh, 1889; Edinburgh and London, 1890)

Henderson, Thomas Finlayson: *Mary, Queen of Scots: Her Environment and Tragedy* (2 vols, London, 1905)

Henderson, Thomas Finlayson: *The Royal Stewarts* (Edinburgh and London, 1914)

Heritier, Jean: *Marie Stuart et le meurtre de Darnley* (Paris, 1934)

Hibbert, Christopher: *The Virgin Queen: The Personal History of Elizabeth I* (1992 edition)

Hilton, Lisa: *Elizabeth: Renaissance Prince* (London, 2014)

Hilton, Lisa: *Queens Consort: England's Medieval Queens* (London, 2008)

Hind, A.M.: *Engraving in England in the 16th and 17th Centuries* (2 vols, Cambridge, 1952, 1955)

Holmes, Peter: 'The Authorship and Early Reception of *A Conference about the Next Succession to the Crown of England*', Historical Journal, 23 (1980), 415–29

Hosack, John: *Mary, Queen of Scots, and her Accusers* (2 vols, Edinburgh and London, 1870, 1874; Edinburgh, 1969)

Howard, Maurice: *The Early Tudor Country House: Architecture and Politics, 1490–1550* (London, 1987)

Hume, David: *History of England under the House of Tudor* (2 vols, London, 1759; with a continuation by Tobias Smollett, 3 vols, London, 1824)

Hume, David: *The History of the House and Race of Douglas and Angus*, Vol. II (Edinburgh, 1748)

Hume, Martin A.S.: *The Courtships of Queen Elizabeth* (London, 1904)

Hume, Martin A.S.: *The Love Affairs of Mary, Queen of Scots: A Political History* (London, 1903)

Hume Brown, P.: *Early Travellers in Scotland* (Edinburgh, 1891)

Hume Brown, P.: *George Buchanan, Humanist and Reformer* (Edinburgh, 1890)

Hume Brown, P.: *Scotland in the Time of Queen Mary* (Edinburgh, 1904)

Hunt, Alice: *The Drama of Coronation: Medieval Ceremony in Early Modern England* (Cambridge, 2008)

Hunt, Lynn (ed.): *The Invention of Pornography: Obscenity and the Origins of Modernity, 1500–1800* (New York, 1993)

Hunter, John: *Mary Stuart* (Edinburgh, 1996)

Hurstfield, Joel: *Elizabeth I and the Unity of England* (London, 1960)

Hutchinson, Robert: *England's Spy Master: Francis Walsingham and the Secret War that Saved England* (New York, 2007)

Ireland, William: *Effusions of Love from Chastelar to Mary, Queen of Scots* (London, 1805)

Ives, Eric: *The Common Lawyers of Pre-Reformation England* (London, 1983)

Ives, Eric: *Lady Jane Grey: A Tudor Mystery* (Oxford, 2009)

Ives, Eric: *The Life and Death of Anne Boleyn* (Oxford, 2004)

Ives, Eric: *The Reformation Experience: Living through the Turbulent Sixteenth Century* (London, 2012)

Jauncey, James: *Blair Castle* (London, 1999)

Jenkins, Elizabeth: *Elizabeth the Great* (London, 1958)

Jensen, De Lamar: 'The Spanish Armada: The Worst-kept Secret in Europe', Sixteenth-Century Journal, 19 (1988), 621–41

Johnson, Paul: *Elizabeth I: A Study in Power and Intellect* (London, 1974)

Jones, Norman: *The Birth of the Elizabethan Age: England in the 1560s* (Oxford, 1993)

Jones, Norman: *Faith by Statute: Parliament and the Settlement of Religion, 1559* (London, 1982)

Jordan, Constance: 'Women's Rule in Sixteenth-Century British Political Thought', Renaissance Quarterly, 40 (1987), 421–51

Kendall, Alan: *Robert Dudley, Earl of Leicester* (London, 1980)

King, John: 'Queen Elizabeth I: Representations of the Virgin Queen', Renaissance Quarterly, 43 (1990), 41–84

King, John: *Tudor Royal Iconography: Literature and Art in an Age of Religious Crisis* (Princeton, 1989)

Knecht, Robert: *Catherine de' Medici* (London, 1998)

Laing, Malcolm: *The History of Scotland from the Union of the Crowns on the Accession of James VI to the Throne of England, to the Union of the Kingdoms in the Reign of Queen Anne. With a Preliminary Dissertation on the Participation of Mary, Queen of Scots, in the Murder of Lord Darnley* (4 vols, London, 1819)

Lamartine, Alphonse de: *Mary Stuart* (Edinburgh, 1859)

Lamont-Brown, Raymond: *Royal Murder Mysteries* (London, 1990)

Lang, Andrew: 'The Casket Letters' (Scottish Historical Review, 5, 1904)

Lang, Andrew: *History of Scotland* (4 vols, London, 1900–7)

Lang, Andrew: *The Mystery of Mary Stuart* (London, 1901; revised editions 1904 and 1912)

Lang, Andrew: *Portraits and Jewels of Mary Stuart* (Glasgow, 1906)

Leader, J.D.: *Mary, Queen of Scots, in Captivity, 1569–1584* (London, 1880)

Lee, David John: *The Secrets of Niddrie Castle* (Thornhill, 1984)

Lee, Maurice: *James Stewart, Earl of Moray: A Political Study of the Reformation in Scotland* (New York, 1953)

Lehmberg, S.E.: *Sir Walter Mildmay and Tudor Government* (Austin, Texas, 1964)

Levin, Carole: *'The Heart and Stomach of a King': Elizabeth I and the Politics of Sex and Power* (Pennsylvania, 1994)

Levine, Mortimer: *The Early Elizabethan Succession Question, 1558–68* (Stanford, California, 1966)

Lindsay, Ian G.: *Old Edinburgh* (Edinburgh, 1944)

Linklater, Eric: *Mary, Queen of Scots* (Edinburgh, 1933)

Lipscomb, Suzannah: *1536: The Year that Changed Henry VIII* (London, 2009)

Lipscomb, Suzannah: *The King is Dead; The Last Will and Testament of Henry VIII* (London, 2016)

Lipscomb, Suzannah: *A Visitor's Companion to Tudor England* (London, 2012)

Loades, David: *The Cecils: Privilege and Power behind the Throne* (London, 2009)

Loades, David: *Elizabeth I* (London, 2001)

Loades, David: *Mary Tudor* (London, 1992)

Loades, David: *The Tudors: History of a Dynasty* (London, 2012)

Lockie, D.M.: 'The Political Career of the Bishop of Ross, 1568–90' (University of Birmingham Historical Journal, 1953)

Loomis, Catherine: *The Death of Elizabeth I: Remembering and Reconstructing the Virgin Queen* (Basingstoke, 2010)

Lovell, Mary: *Bess of Hardwick: First Lady of Chatsworth* (London, 2005)

Lynch, Michael: *Edinburgh and the Reformation* (Edinburgh, 1981)

Lynch, Michael (ed.): *Mary Stewart: Queen in Three Kingdoms* (London, 1988)

Lynch, Michael: 'Queen Mary's Triumph: The Baptismal Celebrations at Stirling in December, 1566' (Scottish Historical Review, 69, no. 187, April, 1990)

Lynch, Michael: *Scotland: A New History* (London, 1991)

MacCulloch, Diarmaid: *All things Made New: The Reformation and Its Legacy* (London, 2016)

MacCulloch, Diarmaid: *The Boy King: Edward VI and the Protestant Reformation* (London, 2001)

MacCulloch, Diarmaid: *Henry VIII: Politics, Policy and Piety* (London, 1995)

MacCulloch, Diarmaid: *A History of Christianity* (London, 2009)

MacCulloch, Diarmaid: *The Later Reformation in England* (London, 1990)

MacCulloch, Diarmaid: *The Reformation: A History* (London, 2005)

MacCulloch, Diarmaid: *Suffolk and the Tudors: Politics and Religion in an English County 1500–1600* (Oxford, 1986)

MacCulloch, Diarmaid: *Thomas Cranmer: A Life* (London, 1996)

MacCulloch, Diarmaid: *Tudor Church Militant: Edward VI and the Protestant Reformation* (London, 1999)

MacCunn, Florence A.: *A Life of John Knox* (London, 1895)

MacCunn, Florence A.: *Mary Stuart* (London, 1905)

MacDonald, Alasdair A.: 'The Bannatyne Manuscript – a Marian Anthology' (Innes Review, 37, no. 1, Spring 1986)

Mackay, James: *In my End is my Beginning: A Life of Mary, Queen of Scots* (Edinburgh, 1999)

MacKay, Lauren: *Inside the Tudor Court: Henry VIII and his Six Wives through the Writings of his Spanish Ambassador* (London, 2014)

Mackie, J.D.: 'The Will of Mary Stuart' (Scottish Historical Review, 11, 1987)

Mahon, Reginald Henry: *The Indictment of Mary, Queen of Scots as derived from a Manuscript in the University Library at Cambridge, hitherto unpublished* (Cambridge, 1923)

Mahon, Reginald Henry: *Mary, Queen of Scots: A Study of the Lennox Narrative in the University Library of Cambridge* (Cambridge, 1924)

Mahon, Reginald Henry: *The Tragedy of Kirk o'Field* (Cambridge, 1930)

Marshall, Rosalind K.: *Elizabeth I* (HMSO, London, 1991)

Marshall, Rosalind K.: *Mary of Guise* (London, 1977)

Marshall, Rosalind K.: *Queen of Scots* (HMSO, Edinburgh, 1986)

Marshall, Rosalind K.: *Virgins and Viragos: A History of Women in Scotland from 1080 to 1980* (London, 1983)

Mary, Queen of Scots: The Scottish Setting (National Galleries of Scotland, Edinburgh, undated – 1980s–90s)

Matheson, C.: *Catalogue of the Publications of Scottish Historical Clubs and Societies and of the volumes relative to Scotland published by the Stationery Office &c.* (1928)

Mathieson, W.L.: *Politics and Religion: A Study in Scottish History from the Reformation to the Revolution, 1550–1695* (2 vols, Glasgow, 1902)

Maxwell, Sir Herbert: *A History of the House of Douglas, from the Earliest Times down to the Legislative Union of England and Scotland* (1902)

McKechnie, W.: *Mary, Queen of Scots in Jedburgh, 1566* (Selkirk, 1978)

McKenzie, Dan: 'The Obstetrical History of Mary, Queen of Scots' (Caledonian Medical Journal, 15, 1921)

McLaren, Anne: *Political Culture in the Reign of Elizabeth I: Queen and Commonwealth, 1558–1585* (Cambridge, 1999)

Michael of Albany, HRH Prince: *The Forgotten Monarchy of Scotland* (Shaftesbury, 1998)

Michel, Francisque: *Les Ecossais en France* (Paris, 1862)

Mignet, Francis A.: *Histoire de Marie Stuart* (2 vols, Paris, 1851; published as *The History of Mary, Queen of Scots*, 2 vols, London, 1851)

Millar, A.H.: *Mary, Queen of Scots: Her Life Story* (Edinburgh, 1905)

Millar, A.H.: *Traditions and Stories of Scottish Castles* (Edinburgh and London, 1947)

Millar, Oliver: *The Tudor and Stuart and Early Georgian Pictures in the Collection of Her Majesty the Queen* (London, 1963)

Miller, Joyce: *Mary, Queen of Scots* (Edinburgh, 1996)

Mitchell, C. Ainsworth: *The Evidence of the Casket Letters* (Historical Association Pamphlet, London, 1927)

Mitchison, Rosalind: *A History of Scotland* (London, 1970)

Morris, Christopher: *The Tudors* (London, 1955)

Mulvey, Kate: *Mary, Queen of Scots: An Illustrated Historical Guide* (Norwich, 2001)

Mumby, Frank Arthur: *The Fall of Mary Stuart: A Narrative in Contemporary Letters* (London, 1921)

Mumby, Frank Arthur: *Mary, Queen of Scots and Queen Elizabeth: The Beginning of the Feud* (Boston, 1914)

Mure Mackenzie, Agnes: *The Scotland of Queen Mary and the Religious Wars* (London, 1936)

Neale, John Ernest: *Elizabeth I and her Parliaments* (2 vols, London, 1953 and 1957)

Neale, John Ernest: *Queen Elizabeth* (London, 1934)

Norris, Herbert: *Tudor Costume and Fashion* (London, 1938; reprinted New York, 1997)

Norton, Elizabeth: *The Boleyn Women* (London, 2013)

Norton, Elizabeth: *The Lives of Tudor Women* (London, 2016)

Oakley-Brown, Liz and Wilkinson, Louise (eds): *The Rituals and Rhetoric of Queenship: Mediaeval to Early Modern* (Dublin, 2009)

Paranque, Estelle: 'Queen Elizabeth I and the Elizabethan Court in the French Ambassador's Eyes' in Anya Riehl-Bertolet (ed.), *Queens Matter in Early Modern Studies: Essays in Honor of Professor Carole Levin* (New York, 2017)

Paranque, Estelle: 'The Representations and Ambiguities of the Warlike Female Kingship of Elizabeth I of England' in Katherine Buchanan and Lucinda Dean (eds): *Medieval and Early Modern Representations of Authority in Scotland and Great Britain* (London, 2016)

Paranque, Estelle: 'Catherine of Medici: Henry III's inspiration to be a Father to his People' in Elena Woodacre and Carey Fleiner (eds): *Royal Mothers and their Ruling Children: Wielding Political Authority from Antiquity to the Early Modern Era* (New York, 2015)

Parker, Geoffrey: *The Grand Strategy of Phillip II* (New Haven and London, 1998)

Parry, His Honour Sir Edward: *The Persecution of Mary Stewart: The Queen's Cause: A Study in Criminology* (London, 1931)

Parry, Glyn: *The Arch-Conjurer of England, John Dee* (London, 2011)

Perry, Maria: *Elizabeth I: The Word of a Prince* (London, 1990)

Perry, Maria: *Sisters to the King* (London, 1998)

Petit, J.A.: *History of Mary Stuart, Queen of Scots* (trans. Charles de Flandre, 2 vols, Edinburgh, 1873)

Philippson, Martin: *Histoire du regne de Marie Stuart* (3 vols, Paris, 1891–2)

Phillips, James Emerson: *Images of a Queen: Mary Stuart in Sixteenth Century Literature* (Berkeley and Los Angeles, 1964)

Plowden, Alison: *Danger to Elizabeth: The Catholics under Elizabeth I* (London, 1973)

Plowden, Alison: *Marriage With My Kingdom: The Courtships of Elizabeth I* (London, 1977)

Plumb, J.H.: *Royal Heritage* (London, 1977)

Plumptre, James: *Observations on 'Hamlet' and on the motives which most probably induced Shakespeare to fix upon the story of Amleth, from the Danish chronicle of Saxo Grammaticus, for the plot of that tragedy: being an attempt to prove that he designed it as an Indirect Censure on Mary, Queen of Scots* (1796)

Pollen, J.H.: 'The Dispensation for the Marriage of Mary Stuart with Darnley and its Date' (Scottish Historical Review, 4, 1907)

Pollen, J.H.: *Mary, Queen of Scots and the Babington Plot* (Scottish History Society, 1922)

Porter, Linda: *Crown of Thistles: The Fatal Inheritance of Mary, Queen of Scots* (London, 2013)

Porter, Linda: *Katherine the Queen: the Remarkable Life of Katherine Parr* (London, 2010)

Porter, Linda: *Mary Tudor: The First Queen* (London, 2007)

Pringle, Denys: *Craigmillar Castle* (Historic Scotland, Hawick, 1996)

Puttfarken, Thomas; Hartley, Christopher; Grant, Robert; and Robson, Eric: *Falkland Palace and Royal Burgh* (National Trust for Scotland, 1995)

Rait, Sir Robert Sangster: *Mary, Queen of Scots, 1542–1587: Her Life and Reign* (London, 1899)

Raumer, F. von: *Elizabeth and Mary Stuart* (London, 1836)

Read, Conyers: *Lord Burghley and Queen Elizabeth* (London, 1960)

Read, Conyers: *Mr Secretary Cecil and Queen Elizabeth* (London, 1955)

Read, Conyers: *Mr Secretary Walsingham and the Policy of Queen Elizabeth* (3 vols, Oxford, 1925)

Rich, D.C.: *European Paintings in the Collection of Worcester Art Museum* (1974)

Richardson, Ruth Elizabeth: *Mistress Blanche: Queen Elizabeth I's Confidante* (Glasgow, 2007)

Ridley, Jasper: *John Knox* (Oxford, 1968)

Riehl, Anna: *The Face of Queenship: Early Modern Representations of Elizabeth I* (New York, 2010)

Ritchie, Pamela: *Mary of Guise in Scotland, 1548–1560: A Political Career* (East Lothian, 2002)

Robertson, Thomas: *The History of Mary, Queen of Scots* (Edinburgh, 1793)

Robertson, William: *The History of Scotland during the Reigns of Queen Mary and of King James VI till his Accession to the Crown of England, with a Review of Scottish History previous to that Period, and an Appendix containing Original Papers* (3 vols, London, 1759)

Rogers, Charles: *History of the Chapel Royal in Scotland* (Grampian Club, 1882)

Ross, Josephine: *Suitors to the Queen: the Men in the Life of Elizabeth I of England* (London, 1975)

Ross, Josephine: *The Tudors* (London, 1979)

Rossaro, Massimo: *The Life and Times of Elizabeth I* (Verona, 1966)

Roulstone, Michael: *The Royal House of Tudor* (St Ives, 1974)

Royston, Angela: *Mary, Queen of Scots* (Andover, 2000)

Russell, E.: *Maitland of Lethington, the Minister of Mary Stuart* (London, 1912)

St John Brooks, Eric: *Sir Christopher Hatton: Queen Elizabeth's Favourite* (London, 1946)

Sanderson, Margaret: *Mary Stewart's People* (Edinburgh, 1987)

Scarisbrick, Diana: *Tudor and Jacobean Jewellery* (London, 1995)

Schiern, Frederik: *The Life of James Hepburn, Earl of Bothwell* (trans. from the Danish by Revd. David Berry, Edinburgh, 1880)

Schulte, Regina (ed.): *The Body of the Queen: Gender and Rule in the Courtly World* (New York, 2006)

Schutte, Kimberley: *A Biography of Margaret Douglas, Countess of Lennox (1515–1578), Niece of Henry VIII and Mother-in-Law of Mary, Queen of Scots* (Lewiston, 2002)

Scott, J.: *Bibliography of Works relating to Mary, Queen of Scots, 1544–1700* (Edinburgh Bibliographical Society, II, 1896)

Scott, Mrs Maxwell: *The Tragedy of Fotheringhay* (London, 1895/1905)

Scott-Moncrieff, George: *Edinburgh* (Edinburgh, 1965)

The Scots Peerage (9 vols, ed. J. Balfour Paul, London, 1904)

The Secret History of Mary Stuart (trans. from the French by Eliza Haywood; Edinburgh, 1725)

Semple, David: *The Tree of Crocston: Being a Refutation of the Fables of the Courtship of Queen Marie and Lord Darnley at Crocston Castle under the Yew Tree* (Paisley, 1876)

Sepp, B.: *Maria Stuart und ihre Anklager zu York, Westminster und Hampton Court (1568–9)* (Munich, 1884)

Sepp, B.: *Tagebuch der unglücklichen Schottischen-Königen zu Glasgow* (Munich, 1882)

Seton, G.: *History of the Family of Seton* (London, 1896)

Shapiro, James: *1599: A Year in the Life of William Shakespeare* (London, 2005)

Sharpe, Kevin: *Selling the Tudor Monarchy* (London, 2009)

Shephard, Amanda: *Gender and Authority in Sixteenth-Century England* (Keele, 1994)

Shire, Helena M.: *Song, Dance and Poetry of the Court of Scotland under James VI* (Cambridge, 1969)

Simmonds, Edward: *The Genuine Letters of Mary, Queen of Scots, to James, Earl of Bothwell* (Westminster, 1726)

Sitwell, Edith: *The Queens and the Hive* (London, 1962)

Skelton, Sir John: *The Impeachment of Mary Stuart* (Edinburgh, 1876)

Skelton, Sir John: *Maitland of Lethington and the Scotland of Mary Stuart* (2 vols, Edinburgh, 1887–8)

Skelton, Sir John: *Mary Stuart* (London, 1893)

Skidmore, Chris: *Bosworth: The Birth of the Tudors* (London, 2013)

Skidmore, Chris: *Death and the Virgin: Elizabeth, Dudley and the Mysterious Fate of Amy Robsart* (London, 2012)

Skidmore, Chris: *Edward VI: The Lost King of England* (London, 2011)

Smailes, Helen, and Thomson, Duncan: *The Queen's Image: A Celebration of Mary, Queen of Scots* (Edinburgh, 1987)

Smith, Lacey Baldwin: *The Elizabethan Epic* (1966)

Somerset, Anne: *Elizabeth I* (New York, 1991)

Somerset, Anne: *Ladies in Waiting from the Tudors to the Present Day* (London, 1984)

Speedy, Tom: *Craigmillar and its Environs* (Selkirk, 1892)

Starkey, David: *Elizabeth: Apprenticeship* (London, 2000)

Starkey, David: *Henry: Virtuous Prince* (London, 2008)

Steuart, A. Francis: *Seigneur Davie: A Short Life of David Riccio* (London and Edinburgh, 1922)

Stevenson, Joseph: *Mary Stuart* (Edinburgh, 1886)

Stewart, A.F.: *The Trial of Mary, Queen of Scots* (Edinburgh, 1923)

Stewart, I.M.: *Scottish Coinage* (London, 1955)

Stone, Lawrence: *An Elizabethan: Sir Horatioa Palavicino* (Oxford, 1956)

Stone, Lawrence: *The Family, Sex and Marriage in England 1500–1800* (New York, 1979)

Strachey, Lytton: *Elizabeth and Essex: A Tragic History* (London, 1928)

Stranguage [Udall], William: *The History of the Life and Death of Mary Stuart, Queen of Scotland* (London, 1625)

Strickland, Agnes: *The Life of Mary, Queen of Scots* (2 vols, London, 1888)

Strickland, Agnes: *Lives of the Queens of England* (London, 8 vols, 1854)

Strickland, Agnes: *Lives of the Queens of Scotland and English Princesses connected with the Regal Succession of Great Britain* (8 vols, Edinburgh and London, 1850–9)

Strickland, Agnes: *Lives of the Tudor Princesses* (London, 1868)

Strong, Roy: *Artists of the Tudor Court: The Portrait Miniature Rediscovered 1520–1620* (London, 1983)

Strong, Roy: *The Cult of Elizabeth: Elizabethan Portraiture and Pageantry* (Berkeley, 1977)

Strong, Roy: *The English Icon: Elizabethan and Jacobean Portraiture* (London, 1969)

Strong, Roy: *Gloriana: The Portraits of Queen Elizabeth* (London, 1987)

Strong, Roy: *Hans Eworth: A Tudor Artist and his Circle* (Leicester Museums and Art Gallery, 1965)

Strong, Roy: *Portraits of Queen Elizabeth I* (Oxford, 1964)

Strong, Roy: *Tudor and Jacobean Portraits* (2 vols, London, 1969)

Strong, Roy, and Oman, Julia Trevelyan: *Mary, Queen of Scots* (London, 1972)

Stuart, Gilbert: *History of Scotland* (London, 1782)

Stuart, John: *A Lost Chapter in the History of Mary, Queen of Scots Recovered: Notices of James, Earl of Bothwell and Lady Jane Gordon and of the Dispensation for their Marriage; Remarks on the Law and Practice of Scotland relative to Marriage Dispensations; and an Appendix of Documents* (Edinburgh, 1874)

Sutherland, Nicola: *The Massacre of St. Bartholomew and the European Conflict, 1559–72* (London, 1973)

Tabraham, Chris: *Edinburgh Castle* (Historic Scotland, 1995)

Tabraham, Chris: *Stirling Castle* (Historic Scotland, 1999)

Tallis, Nicola: *Crown of Blood:The Deadly Inheritance of Jane Grey* (London, 2016)

Tallis, Nicola: *Elizabeth's Rival: The Tumultuous life of the Countess of Leicester* (London, 2018)

Tait, Hugh: 'Historiated Tudor Jewellery' (The Antiquaries' Journal, 42, 1962)

Tannenbaum, S.A. and D.R.: *Marie Stuart: Bibliography* (3 vols, New York, 1944–6)

Terry, Charles S.: *A History of Scotland* (Cambridge, 1920)

Thomas, Keith: *Religion and the Decline of Magic: Studies in Popular Beliefs of Sixteenth and Seventeenth-Century England* (London, 1971)

Thomson, Duncan; Marshall, Rosalind K.; Caldwell, David H.; Cheape, Hugh; and Dalgleish, George: *Dynasty: The Royal House of Stewart* (Edinburgh, 1990)

Thomson, George Malcolm: *The Crime of Mary Stuart* (London, 1967)

Thurley, Simon: *Hampton Court:A Social and Architectural History* (London, 2003)

Thurley, Simon: *The Royal Palaces of Tudor England* (London, 1993)

Thurley, Simon: *Whitehall Palace: An Architectural History of the Royal Apartments, 1240–1690* (London, 1999)

Tranter, Nigel: *The Fortalices and Early Mansions of Southern Scotland, 1400–1650* (Edinburgh and London, 1935)

Trinquet, Roger: 'L'Allegorie politique au XVI siècle dans le peinture française – ses Dames au Bain' (Bulletin de la Société de l'histoire de l'art française, 1967)

Turner, Sir George: *Mary Stuart: Forgotten Forgeries* (London, 1933)

Tytler, Patrick Fraser: *An Account of the Life and Writings of Sir Thomas Craig of Riccarton* (Edinburgh, 1823)

Tytler, Patrick Fraser: *The History of Scotland* (8 vols, Edinburgh, 1841–5)

Tytler, William: *An Inquiry, Historical and Critical, into the Evidence against Mary, Queen of Scots* (2 vols, Edinburgh, 1760)

Vigarello, Georges: *History of Rape: Sexual Violence in France from the 16th to the 20th Century* (Cambridge, 2001)

Villius, H.: 'The Casket Letters: A Famous Case Reopened' (Historical Journal, 28, 1985)

Watkins, Joan: *Representing Elizabeth in Stuart England: Literature, History and Sovereignty* (Cambridge, 2002)

Watkins, Susan: *Mary, Queen of Scots* (London, 2001)

Weir, Alison: *Britain's Royal Families* (London, 1989)

Weir, Alison: *Children of England: the Heirs of King Henry VIII, 1547–1558* (London, 2007)

Weir, Alison: *Elizabeth the Queen* (London, 1998)

Weir, Alison: *Henry VIII: The King and his Court* (London, 2001)

Weir, Alison: *The Lady in the Tower: The Fall of Anne Boleyn* (London, 2009)

Weir, Alison: *The Lost Tudor Princess: A Life of Margaret Douglas, Countess of Lennox* (London, 2015)

Weir, Alison: *Mary Boleyn: The Mistress of Kings* (London, 2011)

Weir, Alison: *Mary, Queen of Scots and the Murder of Lord Darnley* (London, 2003)

Weir, Alison: *Queens of the Conquest, England's Medieval Queens* (London, 2017)

Weir, Alison: *The Six Wives of Henry VIII* (London, 1993)

Wernham, Richard Bruce: *After the Armada: Elizabethan England and the Struggle for Western Europe, 1588–1595* (Oxford, 1984)

Wernham, Richard Bruce: *Before the Armada: The Growth of English Foreign Policy, 1485–1588* (London, 1966)

Wernham, Richard Bruce: *The Making of Elizabethan Foreign Policy, 1558–1603* (Berkeley, 1980)

Whitaker, John: *Mary, Queen of Scots, Vindicated* (3 vols, Edinburgh, 1787/1793)

Whitelock, Anna: *Elizabeth's Bedfellows: An Intimate History of the Queen's Court* (London, 2013)

Whitelock, Anna: *Mary Tudor: England's First Queen* (London, 2009)

Whitelock, Anna and Hunt, Alice (eds): *Tudor Queenship: The reigns of Mary and Elizabeth* (Basingstoke, 2010)

Wiesener, Louis: *The Youth of Queen Elizabeth, 1533–1558* (2 vols, London, 1879)

Wilkinson, Alexander: *Mary Queen of Scots and French Public Opinion, 1542–1600* (Basingstoke, 2004)

Williams, Neville: *Elizabeth I, Queen of England* (London, 1967)

Williams, Neville: *The Life and Times of Elizabeth I* (London, 1972)

Wilson, David Harris: *King James VI and I* (London, 1956)

Wilson, Derek: *Sweet Robin: A Biography of Robert Dudley, Earl of Leicester, 1533–1588* (London, 1981)

Wilson, Jean: *Entertainments for Queen Elizabeth I* (Woodbridge, 1980)

Woolley, Benjamin: *The Queen's Conjuror: The Science and Magic of Dr Dee* (London, 2001)

Wormald, Jenny: *Court, Kirk and Community: Scotland 1470–1625* (London, 1981)

Wormald, Jenny: *Lords and Men in Scotland: Bonds of Manrent, 1442–1603* (Edinburgh, 1985)

Wormald, Jenny: *Mary, Queen of Scots: A Study in Failure* (London, 1988; reprinted as *Mary, Queen of Scots: Politics, Passion and a Kingdom Lost*, London, 2001)

Wright, T.: *Queen Elizabeth and her Times* (London, 1838)

Youngs, Frederick: *The Proclamations of the Tudor Queens* (Cambridge, 1976)

Zweig, Stefan: *The Queen of Scots* (London, 1935)

Index

Acknowledgements

It has been an incredible journey into the world of Mary and Elizabeth and the sixteenth century. I have often been told while writing this book that one is either Elizabeth or Mary – you can't be both. You have to pick a side. I hope I have proved that you don't!

I always wanted a time machine. As a child, I made one myself out of a large cardboard box and put my brother into it and took him travelling across time. I got in myself but I could never get it to work for me. And now, I have one in the form of the letters that I read. It is so exciting to read one of Mary's original letters in the archives, touching the page where she once did. And it is wonderfully satisfying when, after an hour of trying to make it out, you finally realise what a particularly faded or scribbled sentence says. It feels like a key when you are truly unlocking the secrets. I am very grateful to the staff of all the archives who were very generous with their time, particularly at the British Library, where I spend so much happy time, and the Manuscripts Staff and the staff of the Public Record Office, Bodleian Library, and Lambeth Palace Archives, as well as the overseas archives I have visited in France and Russia. We are so fortunate that with their hard work, and that of their predecessors, these letters and archives are preserved for us to read.

I couldn't have written this book – or any of my books – without the support of fellow historians, their friendship and scholarship. For the help, support and discussions about Mary, Elizabeth and the sixteenth century, I am grateful to the distinguished and brilliant historians and friends Tracy Borman, Helen Castor, Jessie Childs, Lisa Hilton, Dan Jones, Suzannah Lipscomb, Sarah Gristwood, Charles Spencer, Nicola

Tallis, Melita Thomas and Alison Weir, all of whom kindly shared scholarship, points of view, very generously sent me notes and transcripts from their research, and saved me from many errors! I am so very fortunate that the superb historians Charles Spencer, Lisa Hilton, Nicola Tallis, Sarah Gristwood and my old tutorial partner Sarah Baker read the manuscript in its entirety and noted many points – and so I no longer call Mary a 'hot potato'! I also learned that as well as being a Stuart himself, one of Charles Spencer's relatives was actually at Mary's execution – which is so fascinating to think – thank you to him for reading it. My father, Gwyn, read it through with legal precision and picked up many anachronisms and dubious word uses.

I am very grateful to Antonia Fraser, the queen and trailblazer of us all, for always being so kind. Alison Weir was one of the first historians I ever met, gives so much great advice and she has been the most supportive friend. Lisa Hilton gave me so much of her generous time in long conversations in Venice and deftly unknotted a particularly problematic Gordian narrative knot, has shared so much of her excellent scholarship and is always there for me.

I am grateful to all the scholars who have written on Mary, Queen of Scots and Elizabeth over time. The scholarship is dazzling and I have been in awe of it. Antonia Fraser, John Guy, Linda Porter, Leanda de Lisle and Alison Weir in particular have all written magnificent books about the period and its legacy.

Hutchinson published my first book and turned me into an author and I am so grateful to be with them. Hutchinson have gone beyond the call of duty in their patience, kindness and time given to me – thank you to Jocasta Hamilton, Sarah Rigby, Isabelle Everington and Grace Long for their utter brilliance, editorial genius and enthusiasm for the book. Many thanks to the eagle-eyed copyeditors and proof readers. Thank you to Susan Sandon and all the team at Cornerstone for their support and friendship and for making the world of books such great fun. I am grateful to my agents, Robert Kirby and Ariella Feiner, who are always there for me with patience and friendship and kindness; and to my television agents, Sue, Sue, Helen and all at Knight Ayton for always cheering on my endeavours. Thank you also to my students who have engaged in such detail in the question of sixteenth-century queens while studying 'History of Women' with me. Thank to the staff at University of Reading for their friendship.

ACKNOWLEDGEMENTS

Marcus Gipps has read this book more times than he can count, kept track of the different versions and pages, made brilliant points and even scanned quite a lot of it page by page when things got close to the deadline – thank you and I am so grateful!

I am most grateful to the readers – without you, we authors wouldn't exist! Thanks to all of you who read my books, come to my events, review my work and contact me on social media. To use an un-Elizabethan term, you rock.